Baedeker

Scotland

Hints for using the Guide

Following the tradition established by Karl Baedeker in 1844, buildings and works of art, places of natural beauty and sights of particular interest, as well as hotels and restaurants of especially high quality, are distinguished by one ★ or two ★★ .

To make it easier to locate the various places listed in the "A to Z" section of the Guide, their co-ordinates are shown in red at the head of each entry: e.g., Edinburgh K 6 .

Coloured lines down the right-hand side of the page are an aid to finding the main heading in the Guide: blue stands for the Introduction (Nature, Culture, History, etc.), red for the "A to Z" section, and yellow indicates Practical Information.

Only a selection of hotels, restaurants and shops can be given; no reflection is implied therefore on establishments not included.

In a time of rapid change it is difficult to ensure that all the information given is entirely accurate and up-to-date, and the possibility of error can never be entirely eliminated.

Although the publishers can accept no responsibility for inaccuracies and omissions, they are constantly endeavouring to improve the quality of their Guides and are therefore always grateful for criticisms, corrections and suggestions for improvement.

Preface

This guide to Scotland is one of the new generation of Baedeker guides.

Illustrated throughout in colour in a handy format, they are designed to meet the needs of the modern traveller. They are quick and easy to consult, with the principal places of interest described in alphabetical order, and the information is presented in a way that is both attractive and easy to follow.

The subject of this guide is Scotland. The home of the kilt, bagpipes, golf and malt whisky is renowned for its wild romantic Highlands, its breathtaking rocky coasts, its countless fortified castles and magnificent stately homes and its melancholy abbey ruins and unique prehistoric sites.

The guide is in three parts. The first part gives a general account of the country, its landscape, climate, flora and fauna, political structure and population, economy, history, famous people, art and culture, language and literature, Highland Games, festivals and folk music. A selection of quotations and a number of suggested itineraries provide

a transition to the second part, in which the country's places and features of tourist interest – towns, provinces, regions, rivers – are described. The third part contains a variety of practical information which the visitor will find of great help. Both the sights and the practical information are listed in alphabetical order.

Fine example of Scottish Baronial architecture: Blair Castle, historic seat of the Dukes of Atholl

The new Baedeker guides are noted for their concentration on essentials and their convenience of use. They contain numerous specially drawn plans and colour illustrations; and at the end of the book is a large map making it easy to locate the various places described in the "A to Z" section of the guide with the help of the co-ordinates given at the head of each entry.

Contents

Nature, Culture, History
Pages 10–81

Sights from A to Z
Pages 84–313

Practical Information from A to Z
Pages 316–371

Baedeker Special

Welcome to

"So you're off to Scotland!" Like Theodor Fontane the German writer – who in his travel notes written in about 1860 enthused about the country "beyond the Tweed" – today's visitors to this most northerly part of the British Isles usually have definite expectations as to what they will find. Mention of Scotland conjures up images of kilted Highlanders, skirling bagpipes, the cult of clan and tartan, the Loch Ness Monster, lonely castles, woollens, whisky, golf, and tossing the caber at spectacular Highland gatherings, not to mention magnificent scenery, sheep grazing amid heather and gorse, shaggy Highland cattle like overgrown cuddly toys, and seemingly endless drizzle. And of course all this is indeed part of the Scottish scene. There is though a great deal more besides, and the weather is seldom as bad as its reputation.

Melrose
Medieval Border abbey

Scotland lends itself to exploration in countless different ways, each a unique journey of discovery rich in unforgettable experiences. You can tour the many castles and fabled battlefields where clans fought fiercely, so bringing to life the country's eventful history; you can trace the footsteps of Mary Stuart, the queen who was a legend in her own lifetime, or follow a literary trail through the land of Robert Burns and Sir Walter Scott. You can take the Woollen Route through the Scottish Borders and admire the kiltmaker's art, visit Harris, famous for its tweeds, or the Shetlands, equally famous for their knitwear. Then there are the myriad distilleries where you can learn the secret of fine malt whisky and sample what George Bernard Shaw aptly called Scotland's "bottled sunshine".

One of Scotland's special charms is its delightful mixture of richly contrasting heritages including Norse, Celtic, Anglo-Saxon and Norman, from Maes Howe

Glencoe
Scenic grandeur in the "Valley of the Dogs"

Edinburgh
Regimental Pipes and Drums rehearse for the annual Edinburgh Tattoo

Scotland . . .

in the Orkneys – the best preserved prehistoric chamber tomb in Europe – to medieval fortified castles, splendid baronial mansions, turf-roofed crofts and the much-imitated Art Nouveau architecture of Charles Rennie Mackintosh. Another of Scotland's great attractions is its solitude. Even today there are remote stretches of heather-covered moorland where it is possible to wander for days without meeting another soul. Complementing the wild romantic beauty of the lonely Scottish mountains with their deep glens and lochs teeming with fish, are breathtaking rocky coasts, gently undulating hills, mile upon mile of white sandy beaches, lush parks and enchanting gardens.

Although since 1707 Scotland has been part, the most northerly part, of Great Britain, this has done little to diminish the contrast between the Scottish and English identities. North of the border the country has its own face, at once familiar yet also fascinatingly different. Scottish cooking, for example, at its best approaches the excellence of French cuisine, from which, thanks to the "Auld Alliance", it has borrowed much. And where but in Scotland could persistent drizzle be so easily forgiven – what ghost, after all, would haunt a castle perennially bathed in sunshine! Last but by no means least there is the extraordinary hospitality of the people. No other quality of the gregarious Scots more belies their reputation for meanness, a myth originating in the Scottish habit of countering hardship with humour. That their own jokes so often allude to miserliness shows just how much the Scots enjoy laughing at themselves. Discover Scotland in all its intriguing variety and you may come to look on this as one of the most delightful journeys of your life.

Bute

Sheltered moorings in Rothesay marina

Highland Cattle

Outsize cuddly toys

Highland Games

Throwing the Hammer

7

Nature, Culture
History

Facts and Figures

General

Position
and size

England, Wales, Scotland and Northern Ireland together form the United Kingdom of Great Britain and Northern Ireland. Of the kingdom's total area, Scotland represents roughly a quarter, comprising the northern part of the UK mainland and four groups of islands, the Orkneys and Shetlands in the North Sea and the Inner and Outer Hebrides in the Atlantic. The border with England to the south runs from the Solway Firth on the Irish Sea, through the Cheviot Hills, to the mouth of the Tweed on the North Sea coast. South-west Scotland is separated from Ireland by the North Channel, gateway from the north Irish Sea to the Atlantic. From Cape Wrath in the far north of mainland Scotland to the Mull of Galloway in the south (i.e. excluding the islands), the distance is some 274 miles/441km; at its widest point – from Applecross on the coast of the North-west Highlands opposite the Isle of Skye, to Buchan Ness on the North Sea coast – the Scottish mainland is barely 154 miles/248km across, shrinking at its narrowest point – between the Firth of Clyde and Firth of Forth in the Central Lowlands – to a mere 30 miles/48km. Because of the heavily indented coastline, one of the country's major attractions, there is hardly a town or village not within 37 to 44 miles/60 to 70km of the sea.

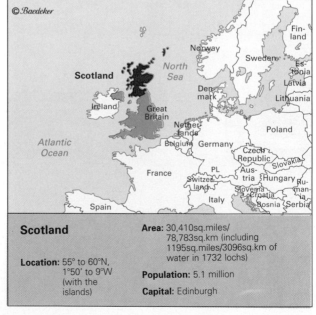

Scotland

Location: 55° to 60°N, 1°50' to 9°W (with the islands)

Area: 30,410sq.miles/ 78,783sq.km (including 1195sq.miles/3096sq.km of water in 1732 lochs)

Population: 5.1 million

Capital: Edinburgh

◀ *Edinburgh – historic and cultured capital Scotland*

Geography

Geographically Scotland divides into three distinct areas. To the south are the hilly Southern Uplands, to the north the much more mountainous Highlands to which, in geographical terms, the islands also belong. Between them lie the Central Lowlands, a narrow tract of sometimes flat, sometimes undulating country, open to the sea through the estuaries (Firths) of the rivers Clyde and Forth which cut deep inland, and forming the most important region of Scotland from an economic point of view. The upland areas, both north and south, consist predominantly of Palaeozoic metamorphic and igneous rock. Dating from the era of the Caledonian fold and aligned roughly southwest to north-east, they are an extension of the Scandinavian mountain system. They in turn are continued south-westward in the mountainous regions of Ireland, Cumbria (Lake District) and North Wales.

Geographical
divisions

See map on p. 15

At first sight the green hills of the Southern Uplands seem one very much like another, waves on a green ocean advancing towards the bastions of the English border. Closer observation however soon reveals the geological diversity of the various hill ranges, low mountains and numerous valleys which divide this area of Palaeozoic slates, greywacke, green and red sandstone and coal-bearing carboniferous shale. Granite and igneous rock (basalt), formed during the Tertiary, are also found in places. Particularly in the west there are glacial valleys and moraines, legacy of a local centre of glaciation which developed during the last Ice Age in what is now the headwater region of the Tweed, Yarrow and Ettrick in the Tweedsmuir Hills (2600ft/800m plus). Other well known upland ranges are the Cheviots on the English border, the Merrick Hills, the Moorfoot Hills and the Lammermuirs, reaching heights, including the summits of Merrick (2767ft/843m) and Broad Law (2757ft/840m), of about 2750ft/840m. The entire area is criss-crossed by rivers and streams which, due to the proximity of the coast, flow for only a relatively short distance before disgorging into the North Sea, Irish Sea or North Channel. The most important rivers are the Tweed, Clyde, Tyne, Annan, Cree, Nith and Ayr, each an anglers' paradise. Many have been dammed for hydro-electric generation or to create drinking water reservoirs.

Southern
Uplands

On their northern edge a well-defined fault line, the Southern Uplands Fault, marks the boundary between the Uplands and the Central Lowlands, a tectonic depression zone where minerals (carboniferous limestone with coal seams, iron ore and oil shale, sandstone and granite) have been mined and quarried for centuries, thus creating a landscape fashioned extensively by human hands. Formed largely from upper Palaeozoic rocks (including carboniferous limestones), these central lowlands – Scotland's heartland in population terms as well as economically – constitute anything but a monotonous countryside, being articulated by little plains, hills and low mountains of volcanic origin. The funnel-shaped estuaries (Firths) of the Clyde in the west and Forth and Tay in the east inject a maritime influence deep inland. The soils – mainly boulder clays and glacial ground moraine – are relatively favourable to agriculture.

Central
Lowlands

The northern extremity of the Central Lowlands is marked by a second tectonic fault, the Highland Boundary Fault, cutting diagonally across Scotland from the Firth of Clyde in the south-west to Stonehaven in the north-east. Beyond lie the Highlands, encompassing the northern two-thirds of the country, bisected in turn by the 60 mile/95km Glen More (Great Glen) Fault. The elongated valley of the Great Glen, considerably deepened by glacial action during the last Ice Age, contains three lakes – or "lochs" as they are called in Scotland – reaching depths

Highlands

of up to 755ft/230m, of which Loch Ness is the best known. In the first half of the 19th c. these lochs were linked by artificial waterways to form the Caledonian Canal, running from the Firth of Lorne in the south-west to the Moray Firth in the north-east. The canal has long since lost its significance as a commercial waterway, but the main east–west trunk road through the Scottish Highlands, which runs parallel to it, is now the major axis for the development of industry and commerce in this region of generally poor infrastructure.

Grampian Mountains

The highest mountains in the Highlands, the Grampians, are found south-east of the Great Glen, aligned in a south-west to north-east direction. Ben Nevis (4407ft/1343m), and Ben Mcdhui (4296ft/1309m) in the Cairngorms, are not only the highest peaks in Scotland but in the whole of Great Britain. The Grampians are a residual Palaeozoic mountain range of Devonian (Old Red) sandstone and pre-Cambrian igneous rock. Some of the summits, e.g. those of the red granite Cairngorms, are gently rounded; others have been carved by glacial erosion into something approaching high alpine forms. The innumerable corries, usually containing lochs, the U-shaped valleys and the undulating plateaux covered with gravels from moraines formed by glacial abrasion, are other tell-tale signs of Ice Age glaciation. North-eastwards the Grampians give way to a coastal lowland with flat-topped hills and characteristic covering of boulder clays and Ice Age gravel beds (on top of Palaeozoic sandstone). The north-east coast has virtually no bays or islands.

North-west Highlands

The northern side of the Great Glen marks the beginning of the North-west Highlands. The mountains here, composed principally of granites, gneisses and Devonian sandstones, typically reach heights of between 2950 and 3300ft/900 and 1000m (Carn Eighe 3879ft/1182m). Due to higher levels of precipitation, glaciation during the Pleistocene was markedly more pronounced in this area than further south in the vicinity of the Grampians. In addition to elongated inland lochs and the glacially reshaped firths and sea lochs, some carved out to great depth by the ice, the most obvious legacy of the Ice Age are the numerous corries. In contrast to the generally flat coastal plains bordering the North Sea, the coasts of the North-west Highlands are heavily indented by sea lochs and bays, with high cliffs. A hostile climate together with lack of topsoil resulting from Ice Age glaciation means that agriculture is virtually non-existent in this part of the Highlands.

Hebrides

The indented structure characteristic of the North-west Highlands is a feature also of the Inner Hebrides. Together with granite and gabbro the isles are composed of basalt resulting from volcanic activity during the Tertiary, later broken up into separate blocks by tectonic movement. Although of modest altitude (due to the severity of glaciation), some of the islands are distinctly alpine in character with corries and sharp ridges, as, for example, in the Cuillins of Skye (2950ft/900m plus). The Outer Hebrides, formed from pre-Cambrian granites and gneisses, are much lower, the hills having been flattened by glacial erosion, and largely peat covered; their coasts are almost without exception rocky. The countless small basins filled with tiny lakes called "lochans", of which there are more than 100 in the Outer Hebrides alone, are another relic of Ice Age erosion.

Orkney and Shetland Islands

The Orkneys, a group of 67 islands of which eighteen are inhabited, lie just off the north-east tip of the Scottish mainland. Formed from pre-Cambrian sandstone they are predominantly flat, such hills as there are being no more than 1558ft/475m in height. The islands boast picturesque stretches of rocky coastline with numerous bays. The same is true of the Shetlands, situated further to the north, comprising about 100 islands of which only thirteen are inhabited. The Shetlands are distinguished by their steep cliffs, majestic sea lochs and deeply indented bays. The highest point is Ronas Hill (1477ft/450m).

Loch Assynt in the North-west Highlands

Sumburgh Head in the Shetlands

Distinctive twin peaks of the Paps of Jura

Climate

The Scottish climate exhibits all the features typical of the climate of Great Britain as a whole, only even more so. Maritime influences, intensified by the effects of the Gulf Stream, produce a cool, moderate oceanic regime considerably milder and more equable than the norm for similar latitudes. Winters are mild, summers rather cool; both are relatively wet. The combination of a maritime situation, proximity of all points to the sea and high latitudes with prevailing westerly winds and rapidly changing cyclonic weather patterns (areas of low pressure moving swiftly west to east), is reflected particularly in:

- relatively small fluctuations in temperature between day and night and between summer and winter;

- high precipitation in all seasons of the year, particularly at higher altitudes and on the windward (west) side of mountains.

- frequent strong to storm force winds, again especially in the west, i.e. in those areas facing the Atlantic.

North-west Highlands and Islands

These climatic features are most pronounced in the North-west Highlands and Islands, directly exposed to the Atlantic. Here annual precipation ranges from 55in./1400mm in sheltered coastal locations to more than 118in./3000mm over the higher mountains of the West Coast (157in./4000mm on Ben Nevis). The wettest periods occur in the autumn and during the winter months. On the coast monthly mean temperatures fluctuate little throughout the year, ranging from 39–45°F/4–7°C in January (e.g. 40.5°F/4.7°C at Stornoway on Lewis in the Outer Hebrides) to 53–57°F/12–14°C in July (Stornaway 55.7°F/13.2°C). Frost and snow are a rarity in these coastal areas, as also is fog (due to the almost constant wind and lack of air pollution). Temperatures are naturally lower in the mountains, and at higher levels, above 1650ft/500m, precipitation falls as snow from October to April. Ben Nevis, Glen Coe and the Cairngorms in particular are well-established winter sports areas. The high rainfall produces an abundance of water in the islands and throughout North-west Scotland. The short, fast-flowing rivers and streams, carrying huge quantities of water, have fashioned lovely waterfalls in many places; large tracts of bog and moorland typify the landscape (see Flora and Fauna).

Grampian Mountains and Lowlands

Southwards and eastwards and as altitudes drop, i.e. in the eastern Grampians, on the east coast of the Highlands and in the Lowlands, direct oceanic influences are felt less strongly. Annual precipitation is lower and the summers are warmer. Variations in mean temperature between summer and winter, less than 14–16°F/8–9°C in the Western Isles, widen to 20–22°F/11–12°C on the East Coast plain. The data for Edinburgh, where the mean temperature in the coldest month (January) is 38.6°F/3.7°C and in the warmest month (July) 58.5°F/14.7°C, and where annual precipitation is 27½in./700mm, reflect this transition to a somewhat less maritime climate. Though considerably drier and milder than the Highlands (especially the Western Highlands), the climate of the Lowlands is still cooler than that of e.g. southern England. The south-eastwards amelioration in temperature and precipitation is naturally marked also by a corresponding increase in the number of hours of sunshine per annum, fewer days with strong winds or storms, and an increase in the number of foggy days.

Southern Uplands

The upland region of southern Scotland occupies an intermediate position from a climatic point of view. Here too rainfall decreases from west to east (about 47in./1200mm in the Cheviot Hills), while the Janu-

Scotland
Climate and principal topographical features

········ Great Glen Fault/Glen More
········ Highland Boundary Fault
········ Southern Uplands Fault

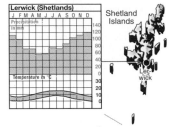

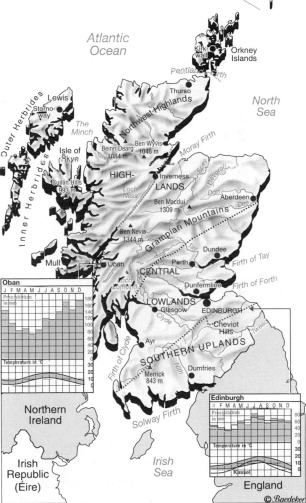

15

ary and July temperatures are comparable to those found at similar altitudes in the eastern Grampians. As also in the Grampians, winter high pressure brings icy winds and dry continental air, resulting in extended cold spells. In summer on the other hand, continental-style anticyclones produce unusually long periods of fine weather from time to time.

Flora and Fauna

Flora

Indigenous
vegetation

The vegetation in Scotland is greatly influenced by the different types and amounts of precipitation, the degree of exposure to wind, and the pattern of land use. In the mountains, distinct vegetation zones occur, reflecting changes in temperature and ground conditions. In their natural state the low-lying areas of southern and eastern Scotland were originally forest covered, ash forest in the Lowlands giving way to durmast oak forests at low altitudes in the Southern Uplands and eastern Highlands, and to woodlands of birch and pine on the east slopes of the Grampians. The tree-line, governed by climate, was between 1650 and 1970ft/500 and 600m. Most of these once extensive forests were cut down in medieval and early modern times or during industrialisation in the 19th c., for settlements, for timber, or to free land for arable farming and grazing. As a result the ancient forests survive only in pockets, e.g. in Glen More and on the coastal lowlands of Caithness in the far north-east. The Outer Hebrides, the Orkneys and Shetlands and the exposed windward slopes of the North-west Highlands were presumably never forested, the stormy weather impeding or completely inhibiting the growth of large trees.

Rhododendrons and . . .   *. . . flowering gorse in the Highlands*

Following the Second World War large-scale re-afforestation programmes were undertaken, initially by the state Forestry Commission
but later by private landowners and commercial investors as well. The
principal aims were to protect the land from erosion and to create jobs
in forestry and the timber trade, the emphasis being on the monoculture of fast-growing conifers for intensive timber production. For
ecological reasons this continuing process of re-afforestation has
come to be regarded in an increasingly critical light, especially since it
is feared that tourism could suffer if too many Highland glens lose their
distinctive character as a result of monoculture.

Today some 1000sq.miles/2600sq.km in the Highlands have been
re-afforested – 250sq.miles/650sq.km since 1980 – and similar
schemes are in operation in the Southern Uplands. Consequently,
while Scotland represents about a third of the land area of Great
Britain, it possesses 40% of the nation's forests. These young forests
are made up predominantly of sitka and Norwegian spruce, Scotch
pine and larch. The largest forested areas in Scotland are in the Southern Uplands – the Galloway Forest Park in the far west and the Border
Forest Park in the Cheviot Hills straddling the border with England.
Extensive woods and forests are also found in the south-west Grampians around Loch Lomond, on the Mull of Kintyre, and in sheltered
valley locations in the north-west Grampians, the Cairngorms (on the
upper reaches of the River Spey) and the north-west Highlands. The
tree-line in the Central Highlands is between 1800 and 1970ft/550 and
000m, dropping almost to sea level in the cool, damp West, exposed to
Atlantic winds.

The vegetation of Scotland today, forestry plantations apart, is best
described zone by zone. Note however that zones can vary considerably depending on the degree of oceanity, i.e. the extent to which
any particular area is subject to Atlantic influences. Five different zones
are, generally speaking, identifiable:

1. The oak forest zone: extending to altitudes of approx. 650–820ft/
200–250m in the Central Lowlands and coastal plains of the Southern
Uplands and eastern Highlands. Apart from extensive re-afforestation
schemes and small pockets of surviving ancient woodland, this zone is
predominantly agricultural – intensive arable farming on the North Sea
coastal plains and, in the Southern Uplands and eastern Grampians,
grassland supporting sheep and dairy cattle.

2. The spruce and birch forest zone: found mainly at intermediate
altitudes in the Grampians (i.e. between 650–820ft/200–250m and
1300ft/400m, though reaching 1950ft/600m in places depending on the
degree of exposure). Primarily an area of extensive rough pasture
given over to sheep-rearing. The native forest, now reduced to a few
sparse fragments, has been replaced by dwarf shrub moorland. Grazing consists primarily of fescue and marram grasses interspersed,
depending on the underlying strata and moisture levels, with heathers
(varieties of calluna and erica), gorse, bilberries, whortleberries and
ferns; bracken in particular often covers large areas. The moorland
vegetation is very distinctive – oceanic in type with heather predomin-
ating alongside wetland plants on acid peat soil. Moors of this kind
cover more than 3000sq.miles/8000sq.km in the Grampians alone.

3. The dwarf shrub moorland and raised bog zone: between approx.
1000ft/300m and 2100ft/650m, though considerably lower in the west,
sometimes even down to sea level. The original localised spruce and
birch forest has today been replaced by wet heath and raised bogs,
often in the form of extensive blanket bogs completely covering large
tracts apart from hill slopes. Typical plants include sedges, rushes,
cotton grass, pondweed and varieties of spagnum. Whereas the more

usual sort of bog forms in a depression in the surface as a result of high ground water levels, raised bogs develop above ground water level as a consequence of high rainfall. Colonised by plants tolerant of such conditions which, on dying, produce a thin layer of peat, the bog acquires a convex, lens-shaped section due to more vigorous growth occurring at the centre. The commonest plant found in raised bogs is peat moss. Bogs of this type are found extensively on the Hebridean islands as well as in mountain areas.

4. The arctic-alpine grassland zone: at altitudes up to 2950ft/900m in the Grampians and North-west Highlands. Corresponds roughly to the Alpine pasture zone but with grazing too poor to sustain cattle. Typical plant species include sedges, rushes and cushion-plants such as cinquefoil.

5. The upper arctic-alpine zone: above 2950ft/900m (1800ft/550m in the Hebrides). Corresponds to the cushion-plant zone in the Alps, with moss and lichens widespread on rock debris covering the plateaux and summits; often referred to as the fjeld zone, the vegetation being more akin to that of the high, damp plateaux of Scandinavia than to high altitude alpine farmland.

Fauna

Mammals

Scotland is relatively rich in animal species. Among the more noteworthy wild mammals are red and fallow deer, foxes, badgers, hares, rabbits, pine-martens and wild cats. Sheep and cows are the most common domestic animals. In some parts stock are left to graze in the open almost throughout the year, living virtually wild on the rough mountain pastures. Upland breeds such as the Galloways, and the shaggy Highland cattle, are well adapted to the climate.

Brown Highland cow . . .   *. . . Blackface sheep*

Song-birds apart, Scotland's most characteristic species are birds of
prey, game birds and the myriad sea-birds for which many stretches of
coast on both the mainland and the islands are famous. Birds of prey
include buzzards, kestrels, peregrine falcons, kites, ravens and golden
eagles; traditional game-birds among the gallinacea are black and red
grouse, ptarmigan and the recently re-introduced capercaillie. Only the
principal species of sea-birds populating the coasts and offshore
islands of the west and north can be mentioned here. Some come to
Scotland to breed, others (from Scandinavia) to overwinter; they include herring gulls, kittiwakes, skuas, sandwich, common, coastal and
little terns, widgeon, pintail and teal, several kinds of wild geese,
shearwaters, guillemots, gannets, razorbills, fulmars, puffins, sand-
pipers and cormorants. Many islands, in the Hebrides, the Orkneys and
the Shetlands, have been designated bird sanctuaries and offer excellent bird-watching. The largest colonies of several sea-bird species are
found on islands of the inaccessible and rocky St Kilda group, situated
in the Atlantic 43 miles/70km west of the Outer Hebridean island of
North Uist.

The rivers and lochs of the Southern Uplands and Highlands are   Fish and
famous for their trout and salmon. The coastal waters, especially those   marine animals
around the islands, are frequented by salmon, herring, plaice, sea-
trout, dolphins and small species of whale; several different kinds of
seal are also found in large numbers. Many fish farms producing
salmon, lobster and shellfish (oysters, mussels, etc.) have been established in sheltered bays around the Scottish coast, mainly on the west
coast and in the Hebrides.

In Scotland, as throughout Great Britain, rare plants and animals and   Nature
areas of special scenic beauty are protected. At the same time recre-   conservation
ational access to the countryside and the requirements of tourism are
safeguarded by rights of way and an environmentally friendly tourist
infrastructure. While Scotland lacks the National Parks which are such
a feature of England, it does have several Forest Parks and other
extensive areas of countryside under conservation fulfilling a similar
function. These include the Cairngorms, Ben Nevis, Loch Maree (in the
far north-west), Loch Lomond (Queen Elizabeth Forest Park) and the
Galloway Forest Park in the Southern Uplands. There are also desig
nated areas of Outstanding Natural Beauty, Sites of Special Scientific
Interest and National Scenic Areas, all well worth visiting. The National
Trust for Scotland plays an equally important role, owning and maintaining not only castles and pre-historic monuments but areas of special natural significance as well – moorland, mountain summits,
stretches of coast, etc.

Political structure and Population

Administratively Scotland is divided into nine regions and three island   Administrative
areas, the former subdivided into 53 districts (see map p. 20). These   divisions
arrangements were introduced in 1975, replacing the old system of
counties.
   Once the seat of the Scottish kings and today Scotland's capital,
Edinburgh has been the cultural centre of Scotland for more than five
centuries. It is also the United Kingdom's second city after London for
financial services and similar industries.

Despite the many differences between it and other parts of Great   Special status
Britain (including having its own legal system, Church, education system and party political structure), unlike in a federal arrangement such

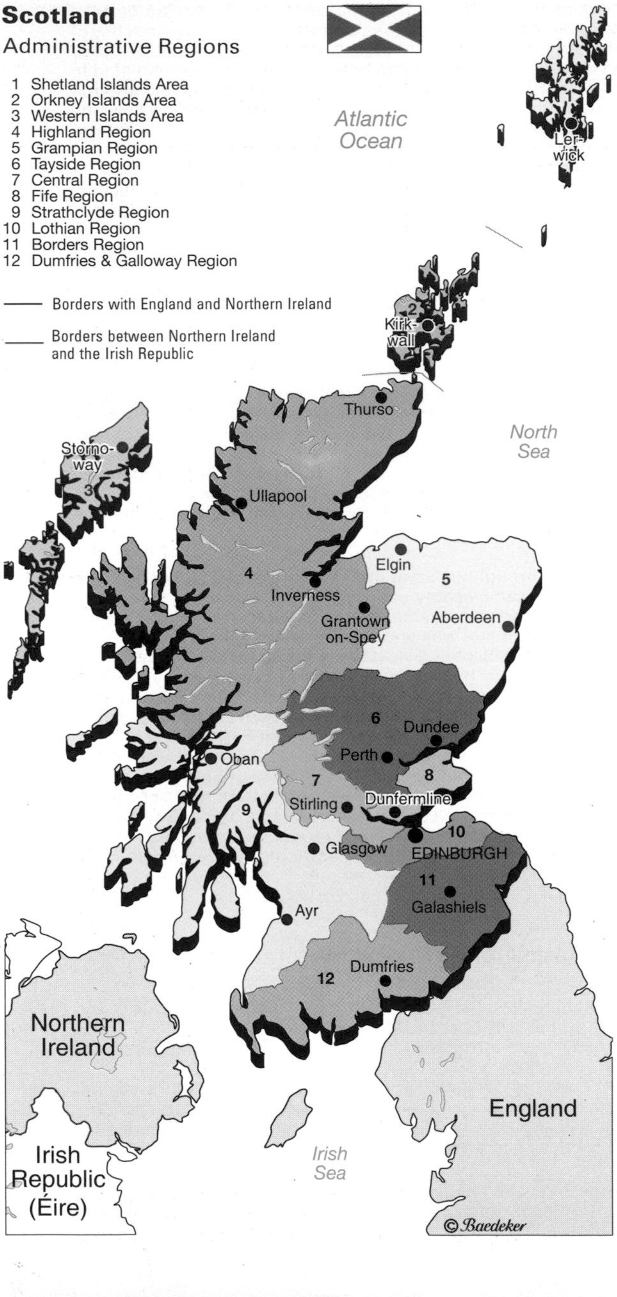

Scotland

Administrative Regions

1 Shetland Islands Area
2 Orkney Islands Area
3 Western Islands Area
4 Highland Region
5 Grampian Region
6 Tayside Region
7 Central Region
8 Fife Region
9 Strathclyde Region
10 Lothian Region
11 Borders Region
12 Dumfries & Galloway Region

—— Borders with England and Northern Ireland

—— Borders between Northern Ireland and the Irish Republic

Atlantic
Ocean

Ler-
wick

Kirk-
wall

Thurso

North
Sea

Storno-
way

3

Ullapool

4

Elgin

5

Inverness

Aberdeen

Grantown
on-Spey

6

Dundee

Perth

8

Oban

7

Stirling

Dunfermline

10

9

Glasgow

EDINBURGH

11

Ayr

Galashiels

12

Dumfries

Northern
Ireland

England

Irish
Sea

Irish
Republic
(Éire)

© Baedeker

Region or administrative area	Administrative centre	Area (sq.km) 1995	Population (1000s) (per sq.km) 1995	Population density (per sq km) 1993
Administrative divisions: size and population				
Borders Region	Newton Saint Boswells	4,698	102.5	22
Central Region	Stirling	2,631	267.9	102
Dumfries and Galloway Region	Dumfries	6,425	147.3	23
Fife Region	Cupar	1,319	338.5	257
Grampian Region	Aberdeen	8,752	491.0	56
Highland Region	Inverness	26,137	209.6	8
Lothian Region	Edinburgh	1,770	723.5	409
Strathclyde Region	Glasgow	13,773	2216.5	161
Tayside Region	Dundee	7,643	382.3	50
Orkney Islands Area	Kirkwall	976	19.2	20
Shetland Islands Area	Lerwick	1,432	22.3	16
Western Isles Islands Area	Stornoway	2,898	30.9	11
Scotland	Edinburgh	78,783	5,100	63

*This total includes areas of water not part of any administrative division

as Germany's, Scotland does not enjoy the autonomy of a state within the United Kingdom. Ten years later plans for the establishment of a Scottish parliament as part of the constitutional reform of Great Britain as a whole, drafted by a broadly based Scottish Constitutional Convention, met with no greater success following the surprise Conservative victory in 1992. Following the Labour party's victory in the General Election in Spring 1997 a referendum was held which voted overwhelmingly in favour of Devolution and plans for a Scottish Assembly are in hand.

Scotland does however have a special status from a governmental point of view, with its own minister, the Secretary of State for Scotland, responsible for Scottish affairs in the fields of education, health, agriculture and fisheries, trade and industry and regional development. He is advised by a parliamentary committee composed of Scottish members. With 72 parliamentary constituencies Scotland is represented at Westminster by 72 MPs in the House of Commons (out of a total of 651) as well as by Scottish peers sitting in the House of Lords. In addition to the major British political parties, all of which have their Scottish branches, there is also the Scottish Nationalist Party (SNP), committed to an independent Scotland but supported by only a minority of the population and at present with only three seats in Parliament. The Labour Party is the dominant political force in Scotland, regularly holding the majority of the 72 parliamentary seats as well as controlling local government in most of the Scottish regions and districts. Education, health, social services, transport and the police are administered regionally, the districts being responsible for housing, culture and the arts, sport and recreation. These regional and district services are financed partly by grants from central government and partly by local taxes.

The Scottish legal and judicial system are distinctive, grounded in a common law which, in contrast to that of England and Wales, evolved strongly influenced by Roman law. Today the English and Scottish systems are tending more and more to converge, the result of progressive modification by act of Parliament (Statute Law). The Scottish High Court sits in Edinburgh.

Flag

Scotland's national flag is a white St Andrew's cross on a blue background (see p. 20). St Andrew, a brother of St Peter, preached Christianity in Asia Minor; according to legend he was crucified on an X-shaped cross on the island of Patras sometime after A.D. 69. It is said that God instructed St Regulus to bring the apostle's bones to Scotland for burial. As early as the 11th c. St Andrew was already recognised as the country's sole patron saint and from the 14th c. onwards Scottish armies always carried a white cross of St Andrew on a dark cloth (today's familiar blue dating only from the 17th c.).

Coat of arms

Since 1910 the royal coat of arms of Scotland has differed in certain respects from the arms of the United Kingdom as a whole. In the

arms of Great Britain and Northern Ireland the first and fourth quarters of the field bear the three leopards of England, the second the Scottish lion and the third the Irish harp. In the arms of Scotland on the other hand, the Scottish lion appears in the first and fourth quarters, the second being reserved for England. The bearers are the Scottish unicorn and English lion surmounted by the Scottish royal crown and the motto "In Defens", with the crest of the Scottish Order of the Thistle below the shield.

The ancient arms of Scotland (13th c. onwards) have a golden shield bordered by a double band of lilies in red encircling a red lion (probably after William the Lion). It usually has a pair of unicorns as bearers and the Scottish royal crown above.

Population

Demographic structure

The population of Scotland is just over 5 million and the population density 163 per sq.mile/63 per sq.km (compared with 616 per sq.mile/238 per sq.km in Britain as a whole). The distribution however is very uneven. Seventy-five per cent of Scots live in the Central Lowlands, a large proportion in the major conurbations of Glasgow and Edinburgh. Of the two cities the capital Edinburgh is actually the smaller, with 435,000 inhabitants to Glasgow's 689,000. The upland regions, the Highlands and Islands in particular, are very sparsely populated; densities vary between 39 and 65 per sq.mile/15 and 25 per sq.km, falling as low as 20 per sq.mile/8 per sq.km in the Highland region. Even then the population of these areas, both north and south, is concentrated mainly in communities on the coast, leaving extensive tracts of the Central Highlands and Southern Uplands virtually uninhabited. Lowland districts in contrast have densities of between 650 and 1300 per sq.mile/250 and 500 per sq.km, comparable to those of Southern England or Central Europe.

Demographic history

While largely governed by topography, the uneven distribution of Scotland's population also reflects the country's social and economic history. During the centuries of Scottish independence, prior to the union with England and Wales (see History), the old feudal agrarian system survived much longer in Scotland than elsewhere in western Europe. A decisive factor was the continuing dominance of the clan system, a survival of the old Celtic tribal structure. Clan members took the name of their common ancestor prefixed by the Gaelic "Mac" or "Mc" meaning "son of". In the High Middle Ages, Norman feudalism

Clans

Clans of the Scottish Highlands and Lowlands

MacLeod

Mackay
Gunn
Keith
Sinclair
© Baedeker
MacLeod
Ross
Munro
Sutherland
Mackenzie
Ross
Munro

Macdonell

Macdonald
MacLeod
Macdonell
Mackenzie
Mackinnon
Macdonald
Macdonald
Matheson
Macrae
MacLeod
Macdonald
Macdonald
Macdonell
Mackenzie
Chisholm
Fraser
Chisholm
Urquhart
Rose
Campbell
Brodie
Stuart
Dunbar
Cumming
Macduff
Gordon
Innes
Ogilvy
Innes
Urquhart
Keith
Forbes
Fraser
Hay
M a c k e n z i e
Grant
MacBean
Shaw
Mackintosh
MacGillvray
Grant
Cumming
Cumming
K e i t h
Gordon
Hay
Grant
Gordon
Forbes
Leslie
Seton
Forbes
Johnston
Keith
Menzies
Gordon
Skene
Seton
Forbes
Erskine
Forbes
Macdonald
Cameron
Macdonell
Macpherson
Clan Grant
Gordon
Murray
Stewart
Flarquharson
Ogilvy
Gordon
Keith
Lindsay
Menzies
Fraser
Hay
Douglas
Keith
Maclean
Macdonald
Maclean
Maclean
Stewart
Macdonald
Menzies
Clan Chattan
MacThomas
Robertson
Ogilvy
Lyon
Lindsay
Carnegie
Carnegie
Graham
Macquarrie
Maclaine
Macfie
Macdonell
MacDougall
Campbell
Campbell
MacGregor
MacNab
MacLaren
Stewart
Menzies
Murray
Robertson
Ruthven
Hay
Hay
Senry
geour
Graham
Hay
Hay
Leslie
Lindsay
Campbell
MacNaughten
Campbell
MacGregor
Mac
Laughten
Macaulay
Colquhoun
Murray
Stuart
Drummond
Murray
Douglas
Graham
Leslie
Maclachlan
Lamont
Graham
Buchanan
Erskine
Bruce
Stuart
Stewart
Cunningham
Graham
Hamilton
Dundas
Seton
Ruthven
Home
Douglas
Home
Macneill
Macmillan
Campbell
MacAlister
Lamont
Stewart
Cunningham
Hamilton
Stewart
Hamilton
Montgomerie
Maxwell
Montgomerie
Douglas
Dalzell
Hamilton
Ruthven
Ramsay
Dundas
Hay
Douglas
Murray
Gordon
Home
Kerr
Kerr
Hamilton
Macdonell
Wallace
Campbell
Hamilton
Hamilton
Douglas
Hay
Johnstone
Murray
Scott
Kerr
Elliot
Fergusson
Dunbar
Cunningham
Fergusson
Hay
Douglas
Johnstone
Armstrong
Kennedy
Gordon
Stewart
Dunbar
Hannay
Maxwell
Murray
Maxwell
Johnstone
Hay
Hay
Scott
Douglas

Tartan, Plaid and Kilt

Of all the images conjured up by Scotland, the most vivid is surely that of the kilt (or perhaps more accurately, the kilt and bagpipes). Even if kilts themselves have become an increasingly rare sight on the streets of Edinburgh or Glasgow, tartan in various guises is still very much in evidence everywhere.

To describe tartan – the word probably derives from the French "tartaine" – as "Scottish check", fails utterly to do it justice. In the 15th and 16th c. the term was used to refer to a woollen shawl worn by Highlanders. Today it designates a woollen cloth with a unique pattern formed from a strictly laid down sequence of colours in the weft and warp. Experts, it is said, can tell from the breadth and spacing of the stripes and the particular range of colours, from whence the wearer comes, to which clan he belongs, and sometimes even his status. Nowadays such associations are not to be relied upon, traditions having weak-

The well-dressed Highlander c. 1860
Chisholm and Clan Cameron

ened and become blurred with time. Originally tartans were woven utilising only the natural colours of the wool; later plant dyes were used for colouring. Weavers would carve the all important sequence of colours into a block of wood, so preserving the pattern for the next generation.

The forerunner of today's kilt was a garment made from lengths of tartan about 16ft/5m long and a little over 2ft/70cm wide, wound around the waist and fastened with a belt. The remainder was then passed across the chest and thrown over the shoulder, thus completing the plaid or "féidleadh-bhreacain" which, roughly translated from the Gaelic, means "large fold". Echoes of these original plaids can still be seen today in the magnificent uniforms worn by members of a pipe band. Around the beginning of the 18th c. the "féidleadh-bheag" (filibeg or "small fold"), the now familiar kilt, made its appearance, probably because of the cumbersome nature of the plaid and the introduction of more convenient modern garments such as jackets and coats. A leather pouch known as a "sporran" was worn on the front of the kilt, suspended from the hips; in the course of time sporrans, still worn with the kilt today, have become more and more decorative and splendid. Stockings used to be in matching tartan but are now generally of one colour. A thin dagger known as a "dirk" is still occasionally seen protruding from the top of the stocking on the outside of the calf. "Trews" on the other hand – tartan trousers, narrow-cut for warmth – have nowadays all but disappeared.

Whereas today the wearing of tartan is largely a matter of fashion, at one time it was fundamental to the Highlander's or Lowlander's idea of his own identity. Far from its principal role being, as is often said, to allow clansmen to recognise one another, it served rather to express its wearer's deep-rooted sense of belonging to his native locality and clan. When in 1746 the Scottish pretender to the throne, Bonnie Prince Charlie, was defeated at the Battle of Culloden, the power of the clans, which had dominated Scottish society for centuries, was finally broken. Afterwards, as well as the carrying of weapons, the wearing of tartan was proscribed, a measure which more than any other offended against Scottish pride.

During the 35 years in which the ban was rigidly enforced, much of a traditional way of life was also lost. It was not until 1782 that the Marquis of Graham felt able to petition Parliament for a lifting of the ban. News of his success was greeted with jubilation. The real renaissance however came in 1822 after George IV, making the first visit to Edinburgh by a reigning monarch since Charles II, elected to appear in the Royal Stewart tartan. Among other prominent figures who helped sow the seeds of revival was Sir Walter Scott, whose writings did much to establish the legend of the kilted Highlander. When Queen Victoria, having acquired Balmoral Castle, chose to have even the curtains made from tartan, she initiated something of a craze, greatly to the benefit of Scottish weavers. Entire regiments were kitted out with kilts and tartan trews irrespective of any tradition of wearing them. (The Queen's Own Cameron Highlanders finally discarded the kilt in 1940, the last front line regiment to do so.)

Soon it was *de rigueur* among upper-class families to possess a "Scottish wardrobe", though few could vouch for the authenticity of their tartans. The services of "authorities" on tartan, who researched the history and traditions of the clans, came much into demand. One, an Aberdonian called James Logan, travelling the length and breadth of the Highlands, brought out between 1842 and 1845 a kind of standard reference work, "The Clans of the Scottish Highlands", still considered reasonably reliable. But many of these "experts" were little more than charlatans. Among them were the brothers John and Charles Sobieski Stuart who claimed to be grandsons of Bonnie Prince Charlie. They published a splendidly colourful book, "The Costume of the Clans", purportedly based on a 16th c. manuscript uncovered in France – but on which no one else ever set eyes.

Today the guardians of tradition are the Scottish Tartans Society, without whose approval no tartan can be declared genuine. There are now more than 1800 different tartans, some of them the old clan patterns, others completely new. A handmade kilt for everyday wear costs about £200 plus another £300 for the rest of the trappings – jacket, shoes, stockings, sporran, etc. Several kiltmakers of repute have premises on Edinburgh's Royal Mile and in Huntly Street, Inverness. (Note that the description "old" does not necessarily mean that a tartan is traditional, only that the colours reproduce as nearly as possible those of the old plant dyes. "Modern" or "ordinary" indicate newer, more recently introduced, shades.)

Buchanan

MacDonald of the Isles

Royal Stewart

became superimposed on this ancient Celtic-Scottish social order. Each clan was headed by a chief, overlord of a lesser nobility by whom he was owed allegiance military and otherwise. Further down the hierarchy were the clansmen who, in groups or with kinsmen, farmed fiefs known as crofts while also rendering services to the chief. Land belonged not to the chief but the clan, membership of which brought rights as well as duties. In the Highlands where the system was most deeply entrenched, there were some 180 clans (see map p. 23), mostly living in relative isolation from one another in their separate Highland glens. They grew barley, oats and later also potatoes for their own use, and raised cattle. Although officially abolished following union with England in 1707, the clan system effectively survived for several decades thereafter. The majority of Highland clans opposed the Union and supported the Young Pretender, Bonnie Prince Charlie. After his defeat at Culloden in 1746, the clan system was vigorously suppressed; rebel clans had their land confiscated and the whole area was placed under English administration. Towards the end of the 18th c. clan chiefs who had remained loyal to the Crown were able in many cases to re-acquire the land, this time in the form of estates of which they as "lairds" were the sole proprietors.

Highland
Clearances

The suppression of the clans and transfer of their lands into private ownership were, together with the growing industrialisation of the Lowlands, crucial factors leading to the radical redistribution of population known as the Highland Clearances. The new Highland landowners were quick to recognise the benefits of a switch from the traditional labour-intensive system of agriculture – aimed at self-sufficiency but resulting all too often in poverty – to large-scale sheep rearing catering for the growing demand for wool in the British textile industry. This led, in the first half of the 19th c., to more than 60% of Highlanders dependent on the land being driven from their holdings and forceably resettled on the coast. The Clearances resulted in the almost total depopulation of the highland areas, entire estates being turned over to grazing or set aside in part as deer forest and grouse moor. Those who remained became tenant farmers on small crofts, as did those resettled on the coast; but plots were generally too small to guarantee a livelihood and most crofters were forced to seek other sources of income, either from a trade, fishing or forestry. Many crofting families moved away to the newly industrialised Lowlands (mainly Glasgow), to industrial cities in England, or overseas; between 1840 and 1860 more than 100,000 Scots left their homes.

Contemporary
trends

The population of the Highlands peaked at about 400,000 as recorded by the 1841 census. Since then, despite very high birth-rates from time to time, resettlement and voluntary migration have reduced it to approximately 280,000, of whom almost 90% live on or near the coast. The exodus from inland areas continues even today, only a few tourist centres defying the trend. At the same time, limited economic opportunities and consequent low incomes still force many among the 60,000 or so crofters (small farmers, often with secondary occupations) remaining in the Hebrides and coastal areas of the Highlands to give up their land.

The demand for labour in the North Sea oil industry (see Economy, Industry) has further intensified migration from rural areas to coastal towns, particularly the East Coast towns. In fact the population of Scotland as a whole is becoming increasingly urbanised. Abandoned homes, clachans (small hamlets), and even sometimes villages, are a not uncommon sight throughout the Highlands and Islands. Meanwhile it becomes ever more difficult to justify meeting the spiralling cost of services to those who remain. In the Hebrides, the Orkneys and the Shetlands more and more of the smaller islands are becoming uninhabited. Whereas in 1850 some 34 of the Shetland Isles were

occupied, today the number is down to thirteen; and the trend continues. The fall in population in rural areas and increasing concentration
in the cities is exacerbated by the low birth-rate among the ageing
communities of the Highlands, Uplands and Islands. In 1993 the annual
birth and death rates in Scotland as a whole were 12.8 and 12.2 per
1000 respectively. That births exceed deaths by even this small margin
(0.6 per 1000) is due entirely to the existence of urban centres with
comparatively young demographic profiles.

Migration and immigration throughout its history have left Scotland
with a relatively heterogenous ethnic mix. Mainly for economic reasons, immigration since the Second World War has been much lower
in Scotland than in e.g. southern England. Only Glasgow, Edinburgh
and the East Coast industrial cities and ports have sizeable minorities
from Commonwealth countries, mainly Pakistani and West Indian.

Ethnic mix

Most Scots are of a religion different from that of other Britons. In 1560
John Knox carried through the Scottish Reformation (see History,
Confessio Scotica) inspired by the teachings of Calvin in Geneva. He
founded a reformed Church with a synodal-presbyterial structure, to
which some 50% of Scots still belong. This constitutionally established
Church of Scotland is made up of largely autonomous parishes united
under a synod and a General Assembly meeting annually in Edinburgh. Scotland also has an Episcopalian (Anglican) Church. The
Roman Catholic Church has two Scottish archdioceses and six dio-
ceses; there are also Methodist, Baptist, Congregationalist and other
religious communities.

Religions

Economy

The Scottish economy and its structural problems today reflect:

Economic
profile

- firstly the country's geography – especially its peripheral location
  (not just within Great Britain but within the EU and European economic sphere as a whole), and its climate and topography neither of
  which are favourable to agriculture;

- secondly its history, three important historico-economic developments in particular – the destruction of traditional agriculture following the Highland Clearances in the 18th and 19th c., with consequent
  profound economic and demographic effects; the industrialisation
  of the Lowlands in the 19th c., and the demise of Scotland's heavy
  industry following the Second World War; and, since the 1970s, the
  discovery and exploitation of North Sea oil and gas reserves.

Overall, the most striking feature of Scotland's economy today is the
disparity between areas of great economic vitality on the one hand and
stagnating regions with falling output and obsolete economic structures on the other. The parts of the country which represent problems
not just for Scotland but Great Britain as a whole, are those which have
failed to profit directly from North Sea oil and other new, high-tech
industries. In recent years the monthly Scottish unemployment figures
have been between 8.5 and 10.0%, roughly in line with the UK national
average. In some regions however, especially in the North-west Highlands and Islands, the figures are consistently higher, between 12 and
15%.

At the end of the Second World War some 90,000 Scots were employed
full-time on the land; by the early 1990s the figure had fallen to 26,000.
Four types of agricultural production are identifiable, reflecting differences in geography:

Farming

Peat cuttings on Islay, Inner Hebrides

- in the Highlands and at higher altitudes in the Southern Uplands, labour-intensive cattle and sheep farming, mainly producing meat and wool;
- in less cool and damp locations at intermediate altitudes in the south-west Uplands (Dumfries and Galloway) and hillier parts of the Lowlands, intensive milk production;
- at lower levels in the glens and coastal areas of the Highlands and Islands, small-scale crofting producing cereals, root crops, oil seed and fodder crops (barley, oats, wheat, rape, potatoes, hay, etc.), often as a secondary occupation and in conjunction with cattle, sheep and pig rearing.
- in the Central Lowlands, especially in the vicinity of cities and larger towns, intensive arable and livestock farming (wheat, cattle), market gardening and fruit-growing.

Fishing

Fishing in Scotland takes two forms, coastal and deep sea. The first is often a subsidiary activity (e.g. in the Islands, where it supplements farming), the second industrial in scale supplying fish to processing plants at the home port (e.g. Wick, Helmsdale, Lybster, Dunbeath and Peterhead on the north-east coast, Kinlochbervie, Lochinver, Ullapool, Mallaig and Oban in the North-west Highlands, Stornaway on Lewis, Stromness in the Orkneys or Lerwick in the Shetlands). More than two thirds of the entire UK catch is landed in Scotland, mainly herring, cod, plaice, mackerel, salmon and shellfish (mussels, prawns, lobsters, etc.). Although the majority of modern trawlers head for fishing grounds in the Atlantic, a considerable proportion of the UK catch comes from the shallow waters around Scotland. An important development in recent years has been the widespread introduction of fish farming, chiefly in sheltered bays on the West Coast and in the Hebrides where there are now over 200 salmon, oyster, lobster and mussel farms.

Scottish industry has undergone particularly radical change. In its industrial heydey in the mid 19th c., the country's prosperity was rooted in heavy industry centred on the western Lowlands (the Glasgow conurbation) and some East Coast towns – coal mining, iron and steel, engineering and shipbuilding, the latter chiefly on the Clyde estuary. In addition there were thriving textile industries in the Border region, on the East Coast (Aberdeen, Dundee), and in the Highlands and Hebrides (Harris Tweed). Even before the Second World War all these industries, textiles especially, had begun to feel the effects of competition; the post war years brought an influx of cheaper foreign products and a corresponding fall in demand. Greater Glasgow in particular suffered from widespread factory closures and the consequent loss of jobs. Each time a shipyard, steelworks or coal mine shut down, large numbers of employees were laid off. The population of Glasgow, still over a million in the 1960s, fell to 689,000 by 1993, partly as a result of migration to other industrial areas and partly due to rehousing programmes in the course of which the over-crowded, often slum-like, working class residential districts were greened or redeveloped for other purposes.

With the aid of regional development programmes funded by central government, the EC and the EU, job losses in traditional industries and mining have been partially offset by the emergence of new industries, many of them high-tech (electrical and electronic engineering, office machinery, computer and robot manufacture, light engineering, petro chemicals and manufacture of oil and gas extraction equipment ranging from drilling platforms to pipelines and refinery installations). The regions to benefit most from these new growth industries have been Fife, Lothian and Strathclyde. Taking advantage of government funded "start-up" schemes, many foreign and in particular American companies have invested heavily in modern industrial estates such as the new high-tech park in Dundee.

Among the more traditional industries to survive are printing (Edinburgh and Glasgow), timber and paper (in the Highlands), brewing (chiefly in Glasgow), whisky distilling (centred on Speyside), and weaving (Scottish woollen cloth produced principally for export in the Highlands, Border region and Hebrides).

The oil industry fulfils a unique role with profoundly important consequences. Extraction began in the early 1970s with the Montrose and Forties oilfields off Scotland's East Coast. Since then fields have been developed to the south (e.g the Auk and Argyll fields) and further north (e.g. the Ninian, Brent, Magnus and other fields north-east of the Shetlands). As many as 50 different fields are now in production. Most of the oil and natural gas is brought ashore by submarine pipeline to terminals at Peterhead, Flotta (Orkneys) and Sullom Voe (Shetlands), where it is either refined or loaded aboard tankers for export. Total oil production in 1993 was 95 million tons. From the beginning the principal port serving the oil industry has been Aberdeen, much the most favourable in terms of location, infrastructure, availability of labour, and transport links. The arrival of the big international oil companies brought a huge increase in the demand for services in the Aberdeen area, as a result of which supply companies mushroomed in many East Coast towns. By 1995 more than 147,000 new jobs had been created in and around Aberdeen, a rise of nearly 50%. Of these a third are in the oil industry, 20,000 offshore. Because oil is now being extracted from fields much further north, new supply bases have been established at Peterhead and on the Cromarty Firth. Today more than 75,000 jobs throughout Scotland are either directly or indirectly dependent on the oil and natural gas industries.

The discovery of oil and natural gas had a dramatic effect on the pattern of energy supply in Scotland and England, leading to a rapid

North Sea oil installations at Peterhead

switch away from coal as the principal fuel for heating and power generation. The use of peat, hitherto the main source of domestic heating in the Highlands, declined even more than that of coal. Electricity produced in Scotland by the two generating companies privatised in 1991, is derived from three primary energy sources: nuclear power from several stations, including older ones at Chapel Cross on the Solway Firth and Dounreay on the north-east coast as well as the newer one at Torness east of Edinburgh; thermal power from stations burning coal, oil and gas; and hydro-electricity from numerous schemes in the Southern Uplands and Highlands, many of them large stations of the pumped storage type. In late 1995 the world's first commercial wave-powered generating station was brought into operation close offshore abreast the Dounreay nuclear complex.

Environmental problems

The rundown of the coal and steel industries in the Central Lowlands represents a definite gain from an environmental point of view. But in the urban agglomeration around Glasgow and along the banks of the Clyde, old waste tips, contaminated ground and other environmental hazards are the all too common legacy of abandoned pits and derelict industrial sites, often impeding urgently needed redevelopment. And while the substitution of oil and gas for peat and coal as heating fuels has improved air quality immeasurably in towns and cities, this too has its debit side. Oil, whether escaping during extraction, loading or transportation, dumped by tankers or spilled in marine accidents such as befell the "Braer", driven aground in the Shetlands in 1993, has become a dangerous threat to marine life throughout the region.

Service sector

The trend in recent years towards modern industries including services, banking and insurance, has considerably increased employment in what was historically a relatively minor component of the Scottish economy. Edinburgh is the tertiary sector's principal centre today. The capital enjoys a leading position not only in Scotland but the UK as a whole, being second only to London for banking, insurance, business advisory services, wholesaling, etc. Other service sector centres include Glasgow, Aberdeen and Dundee. Scottish universities also contribute significantly to research and development. While the four ancient universities of Edinburgh, Glasgow, St Andrews and Aberdeen tend to be more academically orientated, the four "new" ones founded since the Second World War, Dundee, Stirling, Glasgow-Strathclyde and Edinburgh Technical University, play a leading role in technology transfer.

Since the Second World War, and especially since the 1980s, one particular service industry, tourism, has experienced continuous growth. In addition to the many visitors from England there has been a substantial increase in the number of foreign tourists. Attracted initially to the Highlands by the lure of magnificent scenery, once arrived in Scotland most visit the famous castles, the capital Edinburgh, and other historic towns; some venture further afield, crossing to the Islands for example. Because of its many socio-economic benefits – not least of which is helping to stem the exodus from rural areas by providing additional sources of income e.g. from the Bed and Breakfast trade – tourism receives substantial state support channelled through the Highlands and Islands Development Board. One of the aims is to extend the relatively short summer tourist season into spring and autumn, thus making better use of existing facilities.

Tourism

Transport

Scotland's often mountainous terrain is not conducive to an efficient transport system. Even so, for a country of its size and population, transport links are good, including those with the rest of the UK. Especially in the more sparsely populated areas, the principal mode of transport is the private car. As car ownership increases, fewer journeys are made by bus, leading to the withdrawal of many bus services. Even in the Highlands and Uplands the road network is comparatively dense, though many minor roads are single lane with passing places. Several major road improvement schemes have recently been undertaken with assistance from the EC and EU. By upgrading existing trunk roads to motorways and building new bridges over firths extending far inland (e.g. Cromarty Firth, Firth of Tay), journey times have been considerably shortened.

Roads

Line closures have reduced the rail network from some 2800 miles/4500km in 1948 to about 1740 miles/2800km today. Indeed a network in the true sense exists only in the Lowland conurbation; in the Highlands and Uplands no more than a handful of lines survive. The main East Coast line from Edinburgh to London and the South has recently been electrified and journey times cut.

Railways

Scotland's major ports are Glasgow (for general cargo), Sullom Voe in the Shetlands and Flotta in the Orkneys (oil terminals), and Greenock and Grangemouth (recently expanded for container traffic). Unable to compete with road haulage, the once thriving coastal trade with English seaports has dwindled almost to nothing. The ferries serving the Islands, on the other hand, retain their importance. Inland waterways have never played more than a minor role, not even the Caledonian Canal at the beginning of the 19th c.

Ports

Arran car ferry across Kilbrannan Sound to Kintyre

Air traffic

Air traffic has increased substantially, as it has throughout Europe. This is true of both international and inland flights, including to the Islands where ferry services have suffered as a result. The principal airports in Scotland are Glasgow, Edinburgh, Prestwick (south-west of Glasgow, now mainly used for transatlantic flights) and Aberdeen. There are also small airfields on the larger islands. Journeys to and from the oil rigs – other than by boat – are made by helicopter.

History

From initial settlement to Roman times

In the 5th and 4th millennia B.C. the first settlers arrive in Scotland from Ireland and continental Europe via England. Stone Age remains include the village of Skara Brae in the Orkneys, engulfed by a storm in about 2100 B.C.

Pre- and early history

Bronze Age beaker people penetrate into Scotland prospecting for copper. Chambered cairns found especially in the Orkneys (Maes Howe, c. 2000 B.C.) and Western Isles, and stone circles in the Northern Isles and Hebrides (Callanish on Lewis, c. 1800 B.C.) are among the earliest signs of prehistoric settlement.

2nd m. B.C.

Chariot and other remains testify to the presence of Iron Age Celts, migrants from the continent. Iron Age settlers from Ireland leave behind more than 500 duns or brochs (fort-like stone towers) in Northern Scotland and the Hebrides.

2nd–3rd c. B.C.

In A.D. 43 the Romans land in England for a second time and embark on their subjugation of the province they call Britannia. In 77 Agricola erects forts between the Clyde and Forth in an attempt to secure the northern frontier. Tacitus, Agricola's son-in-law, names this northern part of the land of the Britons "Caledonia".

The Romans in Scotland

The Romans abandon plans to conquer Scotland and content themselves with safeguarding their northern frontier. In 122 the Emperor Hadrian orders construction of a fortified wall between the Solway and the Tyne – Hadrian's Wall. In about 142, legionaries erect a second wall, the Antonine Wall, further north, between the Firths of Clyde and Forth; it survives only 35 years.

2nd c.

Under attack in the north and west by the Picts and Scots and in the south by the Saxons, the Roman grip on Britain loosens. Withdrawal begins in about 383.

3rd–4th c.

Early history of the Scottish kingdom

Despite political, economic and cultural ties, the non-Germanic, predominantly Celtic, peoples of Scotland (Picts, Scots, Angles and Vikings) remain divided. Scotland lies at the northern end of an arc of Celtic territory which includes Ireland, parts of former Roman Britain, and Brittany. From the 5th to the 7th c., Celtic-Christian rulers hold sway from Dumbarton, south through Cumberland, Lancashire, Wales, Devon and Cornwall, to Brittany. Reaching the Irish Sea by the end of the 7th c., the advancing Anglo-Saxons cut a swathe through Celtic Britain, consolidating their hold by the 10th c.

5th–7th c.

After an initial attempt by St Ninian in 397, the first major step in the conversion of Scotland to Christianity is taken in 563 by the Irish missionary St Columba. He founds a monastery on Iona, for centuries the centre of Irish-Anglo-Saxon monastic culture.

The spread of Christianity

The primacy of the Irish-Celtic Church is finally ended by the Whitby Synod.

663–664

The kingdom of Scotland evolves from the merging of four peoples:

8th–11th c.

- The **Picts** (Latin "Picti" = painted men, originally the Roman name for all "barbarian" tribes in Britain), first mentioned in a document of 297. In the early Middle Ages they establish a powerful kingdom north of the Firth of Forth. Pictish influence reaches a peak under Oengus (Angus) I (729–761).
- The **Scots**, Irish Celts known to the Romans as the Scotti. Around 500 they mount attacks along the west coast of Roman Britain, establishing a

kingdom called Dalriada in Argyll and the Western Isles and building a fortress on a rocky hilltop at Dunadd.

843–858   The Scottish chieftain Kenneth MacAlpin becomes king (Kenneth I) of the Picts as well as the Scots. He transfers his seat to Scone. At first the new kingdom is called Alba, a name originally referring to the whole of Britain but, from the 9th c., used only of Scotland. From the 10th c. onwards it becomes the kingdom of Scotia or Scotti.

- The **Britons**, occupying the area of the Lowlands today. Allies-by-conquest of Rome, they belong to Roman-Celtic Britain. Following the Roman withdrawal, small kingdoms arise. When one of these, Bernicia, is threatened by the Vikings, the Scottish king Constantine II (900–943) comes to its aid, halting the invaders on the banks of the Tyne (918). Scotland begins to extend its frontier southward.
- The **Angles** who, around 600, push northwards as far as Lothian, establishing the kingdom of Deira in Northumbria. In the 8th c., Viking incursions in the far north and west lead to closer Scottish ties with these southern neighbours.

c. 1018   The process of integration is finally completed during the reign of Malcolm II (1005–34). Scotland's borders are roughly those of today.

8/9th c.   The Orkneys, and at much the same time the Shetlands, are settled by the Norsemen and so come, albeit distantly, under Norwegian rule. Following the sacking of the island monastery of Lindisfarne off the Northumbrian coast in 793, Viking incursions become more and more frequent. In the 9th c. the Vikings occupy and settle the Hebrides, Galloway, the Isle of Man, the east coast of Ireland and the west coast of Wales. The jarls (rulers) of Orkney control Caithness, Sutherland and parts of Ross. These areas of the Scottish mainland continue in Norwegian hands until 1266.

Middle Ages

1058–93   Under Malcolm III, brought up in England, the anglicisation of Scotland gathers pace. In 1068 he marries Margaret, the sister of Edgar, claimant to the Anglo-Saxon throne. The Scottish Church is increasingly Romanised.

12th c.   With the introduction of the feudal system, the Celtic kingdom of Scotland becomes a feudal monarchy on the Anglo-Norman model. Although during the course of the Middle Ages, the power of the monarchy is strengthened, the country itself remains divided into an English-style feudal south-east and a constantly rebellious Gaelic north-west. Under Malcolm III's sons Edgar, Alexander I and David I, all of whom pay homage to the English king, Scottish and English fortunes become further intertwined.

1138   David I attempts the seizure of Cumberland, Westmorland and Northumberland but is killed at the Battle of the Standards.

1174   Under the Treaty of Falaise, William I the Lion swears an oath of fealty to the English king.

1192   The autonomy of the Scottish Church (as "filia specialis" = special daughter) is affirmed by papal bull, giving a powerful boost to Scottish independence.

13th c.   A centralised administration on the English model is introduced. The burghs (towns), growing in importance, develop into an influential Third Estate. Many office holders in both Church and State are of English descent.

1237   Under the Treaty of York Alexander II gives up any claim to the northern counties of England; Scotland's border with England is redrawn along a line from the Tweed to the Solway.

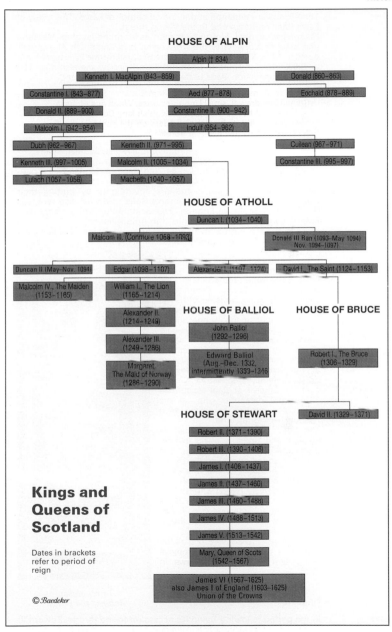

HOUSE OF ALPIN

Alpin († 834)

Kenneth I. MacAlpin (843–859) — Donald (860–863)

Constantine I. (843–877) — Aed (877–878) — Eochaid (878–889)

Donald II. (889–900) — Constantine II. (900–942)

Malcolm I. (942–954) — Indulf (954–962)

Dubh (962–967) — Kenneth II. (971–995) — Cuilean (967–971)

Kenneth III. (997–1005) — Malcolm II. (1005–1034) — Constantine III. (995–997)

Lulach (1057–1058) — Macbeth (1040–1057)

HOUSE OF ATHOLL

Duncan I. (1034–1040)

Malcolm III. (Conmore 1058–1093) — Donald III Ban (1093–May 1094, Nov. 1094–1097)

Duncan II (May–Nov. 1094) — Edgar (1098–1107) — Alexander I. (1107–1124) — David I., The Saint (1124–1153)

Malcolm IV., The Maiden (1153–1165) — William I., The Lion (1165–1214)

Alexander II. (1214–1249)

Alexander III. (1249–1286)

Margaret, The Maid of Norway (1286–1290)

HOUSE OF BALLIOL

John Balliol (1292–1296)

Edward Balliol (Aug.–Dec. 1332, intermittently 1333–1346)

HOUSE OF BRUCE

Robert I., The Bruce (1306–1329)

HOUSE OF STEWART

David II. (1329–1371)

Robert II. (1371–1390)

Robert III. (1390–1406)

James I. (1406–1437)

James II. (1437–1460)

James III. (1460–1488)

James IV. (1488–1513)

James V. (1513–1542)

Mary, Queen of Scots (1542–1567)

James VI (1567–1625) also James I of England (1603–1625) Union of the Crowns

Kings and Queens of Scotland

Dates in brackets refer to period of reign

© Baedeker

35

| 1263/66 | The Vikings are defeated at the "naval battle" of Largs. The Treaty of Perth finally puts an end to the Viking threat. |
| 1281–90 | His son having died, Alexander III marries his granddaughter Margaret (the Maid of Norway) to the Norwegian king Eric II. On Alexander's death in 1286, Margaret's claim to the Scottish throne is accepted; but in 1290, while en route to Scotland from Norway, she also dies. The disputed succession leads to decades of wars with England. |

The Wars of Independence

1290–1306	Following Margaret's death there are thirteen claimants to the Scottish throne. Edward I of England is invited to adjudicate between them.
1291	John Balliol is made king and swears an oath of fealty to Edward. The latter appoints his own representative to oversee Scottish affairs.
1296	John Balliol abdicates. Edward himself assumes the mantle of ruler. In a 21-week campaign (known as "the Rape of Scotland") he rampages through the country as far north as Elgin. The Scottish nobility are forced to acknowledge his sovereignty by putting their signature to the so-called "Ragman's Rolls". Edward also removes the Stone of Scone to London. The Scots enter into a treaty with France, so forging the first link in "the Auld Alliance".
1297	William Wallace leads a revolt against England. Defeated at Falkirk in 1298 he is brutally executed in London in 1305.

1306–29 **Robert I** **the Bruce**	From 1304 continuing resistance to English rule finds new leaders in John Comyn and Robert the Bruce. In 1306 Bruce murders Comyn. Excommunicated by the pope, he is nevertheless crowned king. In 1309 France recognises his right to the throne; in the same year the first parliament is convened. Bruce embarks upon a series of military campaigns against the English under Edward II, recovering all the Scottish possessions lost to
1314 Bannockburn	Edward's father. His historic victory over the English at Bannockburn in 1314 consolidates his grip on the crown and secures his place as a national hero for all time.
1320 Declaration of Arbroath	The pope intervenes on behalf of England and Bruce is again excommunicated. The Scottish clergy and nobility respond by issuing the Declaration of Arbroath, one of the most inspiring documents in Scottish history. It decisively rejects English and papal interference and asserts Scotland's right to independence – also the right of individual Scots to live in freedom under their king.
1324	The pope acknowledges Bruce as the legitimate ruler of Scotland; official recognition by England follows in 1328.
1329	In 1329 Robert the Bruce dies. He leaves behind a stable Scottish kingdom.

Tomb brass:
Robert I the Bruce

| **1329–71** | In the period following David II's accession to the throne, Edward III seeks to re-establish English influence, supporting a rebellion by dis- |

affected nobles dispossessed by Robert the Bruce. In 1332 Edward Balliol's counter claim to the throne is accepted; he weakly subordinates himself to the English king.

David II is an exile in France.

Five years after returning to Scotland, with his country allied to France in the Hundred Years' War, David invades northern England. He is taken prisoner at Neville's Cross and held captive for eleven years.

The plague spreads to Scotland.

David II is freed for a ransom of 100,000 marks sterling. His death in 1371 restores a settled line of succession to the Scottish throne.

The Wars of Independence against England foster a strong sense of nationalism with many from the "Celtic" highland clans fighting in the victorious Scottish army at Bannockburn. Even so, 14th c. Scotland remains divided, effectively into three: (1) an area incorporating the Royal Burghs of Aberdeen, Dundee, Perth, Stirling, Edinburgh and Berwick, relatively rich and loyal to the crown; (2) the great earldoms, stretching from Galloway, north through the Central Highlands and Moray, to Sutherland and Caithness, Celtic in tradition and given to rebellion against any centralised authority; (3) the western Highlands and Hebrides, heartland of the clans which, while paying lip service to the monarchy, jealously guard their independence. Throughout the Middle Ages the Scottish kings must defend the country against encroaching English hegemony while simultaneously seeking to assert the authority of the Crown over a stubbornly dissident nobility.

The Crown and the nobility

Under the early Stewart kings royal power declines as the nobility strive increasingly to assert their independence. Creation of the first Scottish dukedoms in 1398 serves to strengthen the nobility, particularly the Black Douglases in the south. In 1406 James, heir to the throne, is taken prisoner by the English. During the regency of the Dukes of Albany the power of the Crown is further diminished.

In 1423 James I is freed on payment of a large ransom. He determinedly re-asserts the authority of the Crown and stems the growing anarchy in the Highlands, so earning the hatred of the nobility. In 1437 he is murdered.

In the next 200 years every Scottish monarch acceding to the throne is a minor. This means a series of regencies and continual scheming among the nobility. Even so the 15th c. is for the most part a period of political and cultural advancement.

The struggle between Crown and nobility continues under James II and his successor James III. After 1440 the power of the Douglases weakens; in 1454 the Earl of Douglas is murdered and his estate confiscated. From 1450 new small burghs known as Burghs of Barony are founded. Even so the great aristocratic families – the Hamiltons, Humes, Hepburns, Kennedys and Gordons – retain their influence. Inclusion of the minor nobility increases the authority of the parliament; from 1466 onwards regular parliamentary records are kept. Towns in the east of Scotland prosper as a result of a thriving trade with the Baltic.

James III, having antagonised most of his barons, is killed at the Battle of Sauchieburn.

Renaissance and the "new" monarchy

James IV, a Renaissance-style monarch and man of many parts, further enhances the position of the Crown. Between 1493 and 1499 he

Margin notes:

1332

1334–41
1346

1350
1357

Rise of national feeling

1371–1406

1406

1423–37

1437–88

1454

1488

1488–1513

1494	embarks on half a dozen campaigns in the Highlands, pacifying the clans whom he skilfully plays off one against another. In 1494 he concludes the "Eternal Peace" with Henry VII of England and in 1503 marries Margaret Tudor. A cultural heyday begins. In 1507 printing is introduced.
1509	With the accession of Henry VIII to the English throne, Anglo-Scottish relations deteriorate sharply. The formation in 1511 of the Holy Alliance (England, the Papacy, Spain and Venice) against France, forces Scotland to choose between the Auld Alliance and the Anglo-Scottish pact. James, loyal to France, dispatches a fleet and marches against England.
1513	On September 9th 1513 the Scots suffer a disasterous defeat at Flodden Field. 12,000 are slain.
1513–42	The power of the monarchy is again strengthened under James V, aided by his staunch support of the Scottish Church. In 1529–30 he undertakes a punitive campaign in the Borders followed, in 1540, by ruthless action against the clans in the Highlands and Western Isles. The gulf between the civilised Scots in the south and the "wild" Gaelic Scots in the north widens.
1537–38	In 1537 James V marries Marie de Bourbon, thus electing for France and Rome against England and the new Protestantism. His marriage the following year to Mary of Guise further reinforces the Auld Alliance.
1542	At war with Henry VIII, the Scots are at first victorious at Hadden Rig before being defeated at Solway Moss. In December James V dies. The Scottish throne passes to the one-week old Mary Stuart, a great-niece of Henry VIII. Henry himself has a young male heir for whom a marriage is still to be arranged.

Reformation and Counter-Reformation

	The Reformation in Scotland takes place against a background of political rivalries – between England and France over Scotland and between Scottish Crown and nobility, the latter divided in their support for Protestantism or Catholicism, the English or the French.
1542–67	Between 1542 and 1561 the Earl of Arran and (from 1554) Mary of Guise act as regents for the young Mary Stuart. In 1543 Mary's eventual marriage to Edward, Prince of Wales, is agreed under the Treaty of Greenwich. The Scottish parliament refuses to endorse the Treaty however.
1544–47	The English under Somerset lay waste to southern Scotland. After defeating a Scottish army at Pinkie in 1547, the English establish military garrisons in Scotland.
1548	The Scottish parliament negotiates Mary's engagement to the French Dauphin whom she marries in 1558.
1549–60	Despite a parliamentary ban imposed in 1525 on books favourable to the Reformation, from 1549 the movement gathers pace in Scotland under the leadership of John Knox (1512–72), deeply influenced by events both in England and on the continent, especially Calvinist Geneva. Political support comes from the burghs and those among the nobility who are opposed to France. In 1557 the first Covenant is signed, subsequently serving to unite Scottish Protestants as the "Congregation of Christ" against the "Congregation of Satan". At the same time an alliance is forged with those nobles resentful of the power of the Crown (which still supports the old Catholic order).
1559	Knox's return from Geneva sparks an outbreak of iconoclastic violence during which monasteries in Perth are destroyed. Reformation literature, catechisms and psalms are translated into Scottish. French forces land at Leith but are driven off with the aid of an English fleet sent in

response to a request by Protestant sympathisers among the nobility. The Treaties of Berwick and Leith, signed in 1560, put an end to French intervention. The Reformation Parliament adopts the "Confessio Scottica", the first time an entire country has committed itself to Calvinism. Henceforth God's word alone will resolve all matters public and private. Though never officially adopted, the "Book of Discipline" enunciates all the principles necessary for establishing a kingdom of God on earth under the guidance of the Church. The uncompromising strictness of the Scottish Reformation is in stark contrast to the pragmatic syncretism of the largely politically-motivated Reformation in England. Whereas the English Act of Supremacy of 1559 transfers the powers of the papacy to the monarch, the Scottish Reformation insists as a matter of doctrine on the total separation of the "Two Realms".

1560
Confessio Scottica

Following the death of the French king, Mary returns to Scotland where she refuses to endorse the events of the previous year. In 1565 she marries Lord Darnley and, after Darnley's murder, in 1567, the Earl of Bothwell. She is forced by her nobles to abdicate in favour of her year-old son. Defeated by the Regent Moray at the Battle of Langside, she flees to England to seek the assistance of Elizabeth I. This is refused and in 1587, on Elizabeth's orders, she is executed.

1561

James VI, king of Scotland since 1567, mounts a challenge to the doctrine of the "Two Realms" and seeks to re-establish the episcopacy. Politically he moves closer to England so as not to endanger his claim to the English throne. Thus it is that on the death of Elizabeth I of England, Mary Stuart's son, James VI of Scotland, becomes the first monarch to rule over the United Kingdom.

Union of the Crowns
1603

Much of what is distinctive about Scotland within the United Kingdom can be traced to the special character of the Scottish Reformation, that expression of patriotic feeling against an absent papist queen which ended with Calvinist principles admitted to every sphere of life. The hallmarks of Calvinism – high moral values, a regard for personal integrity, a spirit of independence and a deep mistrust of state authority – characterise Scottish society to this day. The special importance attached by Calvinism to education and learning does much to explain the disproportionately large contribution of the United Kingdom to scientific and intellectual advancement in the intervening centuries. Scottish technological inventiveness, especially in the 19th c., confirms Max Weber's thesis of a link between the Calvinist ethic and capitalism. Even today the General Assembly of the Church of Scotland remains an important forum for debate on Scottish affairs in general, with an influence extending far beyond the confines of the "kirk".

Scottish identity

17th century

James VI's treatise "The Trew Law of Free Monarchies" attempts to reconcile the doctrine of absolute monarchy with Calvinism. In 1606 the episcopacy is reintroduced. From 1610 James works towards a more effective centralisation of power in Scotland such as already exists in England. In 1617 he comes in person to Scotland and ruthlessly suppresses lawlessness in the Highlands, Islands and Borders, taking particularly fierce action against the MacGregors who are barred from using their name.

1567–1625

1617

At the Scottish court the Anglican form of worship is adopted, a step which flouts the authority of the General Assembly.

Charles I continues to rule in absolutist fashion, divesting parliament and the General Assembly of their power. In 1634 he issues the "Book of the Canons" and appoints himself head of the Scottish Church. His

1625–49
1634

opponents unite behind a National Covenant demanding a free parliament and a free Assembly. The conflict gives rise to the Bishops' Wars, ending in 1639 when, with the two armies facing each other at Duns Law, Charles accedes to the Covenanters' demands.

Scotland is drawn increasingly into the disputes between the king and the English Parliamentarians; in 1642 both sides seek Scottish support. In 1643 the three Scottish Estates and the General Assembly join the Parliamentarians in a "Solemn League and Covenant" against the king. The English Civil War which in 1649 with the execution of Charles I.

1643

1649

1649–85

1651

In Scotland Charles II is proclaimed king and in 1650 signs the Covenant in Breda. Cromwell now launches a military campaign against the Scots, winning victories at Dunbar and, in 1651, the year of Charles's coronation at Scone, at Worcester. The "Lord Protector" treats Scotland like a conquered land. Charles escapes into exile. In 1660 he is invited back and the united monarchy is restored. Charles insists on acceptance of his absolute rule as a Catholic monarch, to which Parliament accedes in 1661. Bishops are reintroduced in the Scottish Church and opposition among the clergy mercilessly quashed by methods reminiscent of a police state.

1679

The Covenanters are defeated by forces of the Crown at Bothwell Bridge. In 1681 the government of Scotland is entrusted to James, Duke of York. The resistance of the Covenanters, especially the "Cameronians" or "Society People", grow. On his death in 1685, Charles leaves Scotland under uncompromisingly authoritarian rule.

1685

1688–1702

Following the Glorious Revolution in England, James VII flees into exile in France. In 1689 the Three Estates offer the Scottish Crown to William of Orange. The "Claim of Right" repudiates the absolute monarchy re-established under Charles II, together with all its laws and institutions. William takes the Scottish coronation oath. The Settlement is opposed by the bishops (who are against the reintroduction of Presbyterianism), by the Covenanters (who consider themselves unfairly treated), and by royalist Jacobites. In 1689 Jacobite clans from the Scottish west rout a loyalist force at the Battle of Killiecrankie but are themselves defeated soon afterwards. In 1691 a pardon is offered to all on the Jacobite side who, before January 1st 1692, swear an oath of loyalty to King William.

1689

1692
Glencoe

The MacDonalds of Glencoe, delayed by winter weather, fail to meet the deadline. The Campbells are sent to butcher them, which they do while accepting the MacDonalds' hospitality. The iniquity of the Massacre of Glencoe is for ever etched on the Scottish conscience.

Union with England (Union of the Parliaments)

Various Royal Commissions set up by the two parliaments explore the feasibility of union, a step proposed by William shortly before his death. Scotland hopes for free trade, England for an end to enmities between the two, leaving it free to pursue its disagreements with France.

Union of the
Parliaments
May 1st 1707

The Act of Union comes into force, with a single parliament, common flag and common currency. Scotland retains, among other things, its old legal system and its Presbyterian church. Problems are experienced on three counts: the single parliament neglects Scottish economic interests; Scotland is not fairly represented either in parliament or government; the Toleration Act of 1712 requires the Scottish clergy to swear an oath of fidelity to the sovereign who is head of the Anglican Church. The restoration of patronage in the award of ecclesiastical benefices causes schism in the Scottish Church. In 1743 the Reformed Presbyterian Church breaks away, claiming to be the only true Church of the Covenanters.

The Jacobite "Attempts" to restore the Stuarts to the Scottish throne – still the focus of strong feelings in every Scottish breast – fail through lack of popular support, so great is the economic significance of the Union.

Jacobite Attempts

The Earl of Mar's Jacobite uprising fails; retribution is brutal.

1715

An act is passed forbidding the clans to carry arms. General Wade supervises the building of 220 miles/350km of roads through the Highlands.

1725

The first Highland Companies are formed, amalgamating in 1739 into the Royal Highland Regiment (the Black Watch). The formation of regiments serves to de-politicise many in the Highlands.

1729

Landing in Moidart, the 23-year old Charles Edward Stuart, "Bonnie Prince Charlie", grandson of James VII, wins over some of the clans to his cause. He captures Edinburgh and Perth where he proclaims his father King of Scotland; a Scottish government army is defeated at Prestonpans. Raising a largely Highland army he takes Carlisle and marches south as far as Derby. But the hoped-for rebellion by English Jacobites and Catholic supporters fails to materialise. Demoralised, the Highlanders retreat. Pursued north into Scotland by "Butcher" Cumberland they are crushed at Culloden in 1746. For several months the Prince is a fugitive in the Highlands before a French frigate arrives to take him abroad. In the aftermath of the rebellion, severe measures are taken against the clans (including a ban on the kilt and even the bagpipes!). These are relaxed only in 1782. The Jacobite movement is finished as a political force.

1745

1746
Culloden

"The Battle of Culloden" by David Morier – Cameron and Stewart clansmen confront the Hanoverian redcoats

History

Economic upheaval

After 1745 the economy of the Highlands undergoes far-reaching change. Clan chiefs increasingly forsake their patriarchal role for that of landlords, demanding ever higher rents which crofters with their traditional methods of cultivation are unable to pay. Potatoes, introduced in 1739, quickly become the staple food, especially in the Highlands. From 1760 onwards sheep rearing, the "Curse of the Highlands", begins to spread, undermining the crofters' subsistence economy. The gap between the underdeveloped Highlands and regions such as Lothian, Aberdeenshire and Galloway where modern farming methods have been practised since about 1715, widens after 1745. Many in the Highlands are forced to turn to seasonal work in the Scottish south and east or to collecting kelp (to be burned for fertiliser); others join the army, move permanently to the cities and towns, or emigrate.

Having survived an early threat posed by stiff English competition, the textiles industry becomes firmly established in Central Scotland.

1710

From 1710 onwards the manufacture of linen (and the famous Paisley fabrics) flourishes and in 1746 the British Linen Company is founded. After 1775 the cotton industry develops rapidly, particularly in the Greater Glasgow area. Arkwright's invention of the mechanical loom leads to the concentration of production in mills, one of which, the New

1786

Lanark Mill, opened in 1786, becomes the centre of a model industrial village, a project inspired by one of the mill's owners, Robert Owen. Meanwhile a woollens industry develops in the Scottish Borders.

1759

The first iron-works open at Carron; by 1800 there are blast furnaces in Glasgow, Lanarkshire and Ayrshire. Industrialisation stimulates construction of a canal system (1790; Forth and Clyde Canal).

Reforms

For four decades the French Revolution and its aftermath dominate political developments in Scotland, at first in the guise of the war with France (1793–1815) and subsequently by fuelling demands for constitutional and economic reform. In 1792 the "Society of Friends of the People" is founded and pressure for universal franchise grows. The much-disliked Secretary of State for Scotland, Lord Dundas, responds with repressive measures. Between 1808 and 1833 various reforms are introduced: the legal system is amended (1808, 1815, 1824), parliamentary constituencies are re-organised and seats in the House of

1831–1832

Commons redistributed (1831 Reform Bill; 1832 Scottish Bill for Parliamentary Reform). Changes are also made at local level in the administration of the burghs, including wider enfranchisement (1833 Burgh Reform Act).

Highland Clearances

While southern Scotland reaps the benefits of socio-political reform and growing industrialisation, the Highlands suffer economic and social decline. The clan chiefs, many of them increasingly "anglicised", need full purses to support the extravagancies of their new lifestyles as they strive to live up to the Romanticised image of a Celtic Highland prince. Clan lands are treated as private property to be exploited for maximum profit; entire areas are turned over to grazing and the raising of sheep. The traumatic Highland Clearances ensue: whole tracts are emptied of people, peasant farmers being systematically driven from their land and forceably resettled on the coast or compelled to emigrate (a measure supported by government and even by philanthropic societies). Families are evicted from their homes, often with cruel harshness, the thatched roofs being set alight above their heads.

1814

"Bliadhna an Losgaidh", the "Year of the Burning": height of the Highland Clearances in Sutherland (1807–20).

1853

The particularly brutal Glengarry Clearances.

1846

Potato blight affects Ireland; during the ensuing famines, considerable numbers of Irish people emigrate to Scotland.

1834

Many clergy accept the Clearances as "God's will", thus deepening the gulf between evangelicals and moderates in the Church of Scotland

and leading, in 1834, to the "Great Schism". Thomas Chalmer and as many as a third of his fellow clergy break away and establish the Free Church. Opposed to the patronage of landowners and to any state interference whatsoever, they regard the parish as the foundation of social life. The breach is partly healed in 1900 and fully only in 1929. Even then 150 Highland parishes remain "free" and continue to wield a powerful influence, mainly in the Islands.

Victorian Scotland

In the 19th c. the depth of Anglo-Scottish economic integration and the substantial contribution of Scots to the building of the Empire make Scottish history inseparable from that of Britain as a whole.

George IV visits Scotland. He is greeted with a pageant of traditional Scottish life – at the very time when the Clearances are convulsing the Highlands.

1822

Queen Victoria acquires Balmoral Castle as a private retreat ("Royal Deeside"). Scotland becomes fashionable and the Highlands a recreational mecca for English society. A cult of everything to do with the Highlands is born, based as much on folk myth as on reality; it gives rise to a craze for tartan which remains the bedrock of the Scottish tourist industry today. In his avidly-read novels Sir Walter Scott (1771–1832) recreates the landscape and history of Scotland for millions of British and continental readers.

1848

Despite its absorption into the United Kingdom, Scotland responds in its own fashion to the great issues of the century. The Scottish desire for reform is more broadly based and popular, even radical. Politics and religion are often found in harmony, as in the Temperance Movement. Above all, the feeling persists that Scottish interests are not sufficiently well-represented in Parliament.

From 1853 Scottish MPs campaign for universal franchise. In 1865 the Liberals, the country's major political force, press for proportional representation in Parliament. Disraeli's Reform Act of 1867 goes only part way towards fulfilling the demand; it is left to Gladstone's Reform Act of 1884–85 to increase the Scottish share of seats in the Commons to reflect the size of the country's population.

Reforms

1867

1884–85

In the process of nationwide educational reform, the Scottish Education Department is set up, a recognition of the distinctiveness of the Scottish education system. Gaelic disappears from the curriculum.

1072

Economic development in Scotland is increasingly shaped by external factors – overseas markets and Britain's colonies. By the end of the century only 200,000 are employed on the land (compared with 0.5 million in 1801). From 1840 the rail network is under construction. Heavy industry – coal, iron and steel, railway and other engineering and, above all, shipbuilding – replaces textiles as the mainstay of the Scottish economy. From the middle of the 19th c. the shipyards on the Clyde prosper to such an extent that by 1913 some 20% of the world's tonnage is launched on Clydeside. The population trebles to 4.5 million. At the outbreak of the First World War Scotland is one of the most prosperous countries in the world.

Economic development

Mounting social problems lead to the formation of the Scottish Labour Party.

1880

The plight of Highland tenant farmers leads to unrest, erupting in 1882 in the Crofters' Wars. The Crofters' Act of 1886 ensures security of tenure and fair rents.

1882

The Scottish Office is established. The country's economic strength fosters a new self-confidence and a series of Home Rule Bills are

1885

drafted. It seems only a matter of time before one is introduced, but the First World War intervenes.

Scotland in the 20th century

First World War
1914–18

Scotland loses more men (10% of those aged between 16 and 50) than any other part of the United Kingdom.

1918–39

1918

In the parliamentary elections of 1918 the Scottish Labour Party secures ten times more votes than in 1910 and demands separate Scottish representation in the peace negotiations at Versailles.

In the same year the Scottish Home Rule Association (SHRA) is re-formed. Founded in 1886, in the period leading up to the First World War it had served to unite Labour, the Liberals and the nationalist movements.

The social problems of the immediate post-war period lead to unrest on "red" Clydeside. Troops are called in to quell the "Bolshevik revolt".

1920–31

The worldwide recession in the 1920s hits Scotland harder than England. Over a period starting in 1921, 8% of Scots emigrate, bringing the first fall in population since 1801.

1928

The Scottish Nationalist Party (SNP) is founded in Bannockburn. Failing to gather support from the SHRA or Labour, it is consigned at the outset to the political fringe. Even so, separatism versus Home Rule is set to become a key issue in nationalist politics.

Second World War
1939–45

Government control of Britain's wartime economy leaves little scope for Scottish independence. As in the First World War, the British Home Fleet is based in Scapa Flow. Glasgow and the shipyards on the Clyde are the target of German bombing raids.

1945–79

1947

The Labour government of the early post-war years introduces the Welfare State, but is unpopular in Scotland.

A "Scottish National Assembly", meeting in Glasgow, begins work on a Covenant for Scotland which, in 1949, is adopted enthusiastically at a further meeting in Edinburgh. It calls for Home Rule within the United Kingdom, with a separate Scottish parliament. Although signed subsequently by two million Scots, the initiative peters out. Home Rule is not for the moment a major political issue – indeed Labour's 1950 election manifesto omits, for the first time any reference to Home Rule for Scotland. In the 1960s growing support for the SNP causes Labour to rethink and in 1974 Prime Minister Wilson declares himself in favour of Home Rule. As early as 1970, at the start of the so-called Decade of Devolution, a greater degree of control over its affairs is already being granted to Scotland.

1971

In the biggest demonstration of its kind in Scottish history, 700,000 people on Clydeside protest against government economic policy.

1974

Under sweeping changes to local government the old counties are abolished.

1977

In a speech marking her 25th Jubilee Queen Elizabeth II makes clear her opposition to Scottish nationalism and devolution. However the Scottish Devolution Bill is approved by Parliament and in 1978 receives the Royal Assent.

1979

In a referendum on the Bill, 1.23 million Scots vote for devolution and 1.15 million against, votes in favour falling short of the required 40% of those eligible to vote. The technicalities of the referendum are only one factor in the result however. Labour had pushed the Bill through Parliament without any real conviction, chiefly for electoral reasons. The Labour Party under Callaghan lacks popular support and the Scots regard the whole affair as an exercise in political manoeuvring. Attempts to salvage the Bill fail; the SNP brings down the Callaghan government on a motion of no confidence.

Margaret Thatcher's attempt to transform British society through radical Right-wing reforms meets with severe opposition in Scotland and provokes new calls for Home Rule. In 1987 the Conservatives suffer their worst election defeat in Scotland since 1910, winning only ten Scottish seats in Parliament. The view gains ground that the Thatcher government has "no mandate" in Scotland. Despite the relative prosperity of Scotland, which withstands the economic recession better than England, Scots are alienated from the state and government which they regard as too English-orientated. A Civil Politics Movement comes into being in parallel with similar developments in England such as Charter 88.

Thatcher Era (1979–90)

The Thatcher debate reaches a symbolic climax when the Prime Minister, addressing a meeting of the Scottish Church, defends her social and economic policies against criticism on religious grounds. The audience reject her measures as un-Christian; the Moderator (the leader of the Church, who is elected annually) presents the Prime Minister with a book on Christian economic policy.

1988

The introduction of the Poll Tax provokes widespread opposition in Scotland leading to 2.5 million prosecutions for non-payment by 1991. A Scottish Constitutional Convention (SCC) meeting in Edinburgh – without the participation of Scottish Conservatives or the SNP – produces detailed proposals for a Scottish parliament in the context of political reform in Great Britain as a whole.

1989

Labour adopts the SCC's proposals in its election manifesto. Against expectations the Conservatives are returned to power, creating an absurd situation: although 58 of the 72 Scottish members support the SCC's proposals, the Prime Minister John Major argues that Home Rule for Scotland would weaken Britain's influence in Europe and the world.

1992

In the same year the Scottish Labour leader John Smith becomes leader of the British Labour Party. In May 1994 he dies. His funeral in Edinburgh sparks off a show of national feeling and the desire for greater independence.

1994

In March Dunblane becomes the scene of a tragedy when a gunman runs amok at the school and kills more than half of the infants class. Edinburgh becomes the second British city to be nominated as a "city of culture" by UNESCO.

1996

Following the Labour Party's victory in the General Election a Referendum was held which gave overwhelming support for Devolution and a Scottish Assembly.

1997

Famous People

Listed in alphabetical order below are a selection of the men and women who, associated with Scotland by birth, residence or death, have achieved national or international recognition.

John Logie Baird
(1888–1946)

Baird, pioneer and co-inventor of television, was born in Helensburgh and studied electronics in Glasgow. Forced to abandon his career as an engineer by ill health, in 1922, at his new home in Hastings (Sussex), he began experimenting in a makeshift way with television. In London in 1926 he succeeded in transmitting the first television pictures, using a semitone frequency band and Nipkow screen with a 30-line raster at five frames a second. The following year he founded the Baird Television Development Co. and a year later made the first successful television transmission between London and New York. His system continued to be used by the BBC until 1937, by which time Marconi-EMIO had developed a superior technology. Baird also experimented with colour transmissions and stereoscopic imaging, and worked on an infra-red device for improving night vision.

Alexander Graham Bell
(1847–1922)

The British-American physiologist Alexander Graham Bell is known as "the father of the telephone". Born at 16 South Charlotte Street in Edinburgh, he worked as a teacher of the deaf and dumb before emigrating to Canada in 1870. In 1873 he was appointed professor at the University of Boston. There he experimented with the idea of converting sound into voltage fluctuations in an electric current, which could then be passed along a wire and the fluctuations converted back into sound. These experiments resulted in the first working telephone, patented by Bell in 1876. Brought to England in 1877, the design was later improved by Thomas Edison using a carbon microphone; but Bell's original concept remains the basis of telephone technology today. The Bell Telephone Co., founded in 1877, became the American Telephone and Telegraph Company (AT & T), now the largest private company of its kind in the world.

Robert Burns
(1759–96)

Sir Walter Scott apart, Robert Burns is indisputably Scotland's finest writer, a poet whose oft-quoted verses and ballads express a deep affinity with his native country and countrymen. Born in Alloway in Ayrshire, the eldest of seven offspring of an impoverished small farmer, Burns's life was both hard and short (he died aged 37 from inflammation of a heart valve). Despite the poverty in which he was brought up, he managed to teach himself the rudiments of literary skill. Notoriously he revelled in life and had more than an eye for a pretty girl, a weakness which inspired many of his verses. His earliest love poems were penned for his childhood sweetheart Peggy; others, including "My Jean", were written for Jean Armour, Burns's mistress of many years and latterly his wife. "Highland Mary" was Mary Campbell, a captain's daughter from Dunoon, and "Clarinda" his beloved Mrs MacLehose from Edinburgh.

When Burns was seven his family moved to a farm at Mount Oliphant. Despite exhausting days spent working on the land, he was able to read widely, having his love of poetry aroused by the folk songs and poems of Allan Ramsay and Robert Fergusson. In 1777 the Burnses moved yet again, this time to a farm near Tarbolton, but with no more success than before; shortly afterwards Burns's father died. Dogged by his inability to earn a living – his ventures included running Moss-giel Farm with his brother Gilbert – and his troubled love affair with Jean Armour, who gave birth to a child by him in Mauchline, the

Robert Burns

Andrew Carnegie

Sean Connery

27-year old Burns was on the point of emigrating when publication of his first volume of poetry "Poems chiefly in the Scottish dialect" brought instant fame. He was invited to Edinburgh where he was fêted by the capital's literati. Two years later he married Jean Armour, briefly taking on yet another farm (at Ellisland) before accepting appointment as an Excise collector – a job which also proved extremely hard work. Declining the offer of a post at Edinburgh University, in 1791 he moved house to Dumfries where, during the last five years of his life, he wrote a six-volume anthology of songs, "The Scots Musical Museum", and his delightful "Melodies of Scotland" ("A Select Collection of Scottish Airs for the Voice", 1793–1818).

Inspired by old Scottish folk-songs and legends and written mainly in the local dialect, most of Burns's verses are on traditional, homely themes. As well as earthy ballads like the one recounting the daring ride of "Tam o'Shanter", and highly original songs in praise of whisky and the haggis (see p. 328), he also wrote expressive lyrics about Nature and profoundly moving love-songs (including the well-known "A red, red rose", "To Mary in Heaven" and "My Jean"). The poet's deep sense of national pride found expression in "My Heart's in the Highlands" (see p. 257) and, of course, in "Auld Lang Syne", now sung at the end of happy gatherings the world over, as well as in his moving poem "The Cotter's Saturday Night".

Burns's sympathies with the ideals of the French Revolution and his keen satires against the puritanical despotism of the clergy brought him criticism from his patrons. His fame however had by this time spread abroad where he was acclaimed by leading writers such as Goethe and Herder. While opening the doors to popular understanding and breathing fresh life into the ballad, it was his lyric poems in particular which helped prepare the ground for British Romanticism. Today more than 100 Burns Societies throughout the world foster the memory of the poet with whom every Scot identifies. His birthday, January 25th, is celebrated annually the world over at Burns Night Suppers with haggis, Scotch and the skirl of bagpipes.

Like countless other hand-weavers, Andrew Carnegie's father lost his livelihood with the introduction of the mechanical loom. With no alternative but to emigrate, in May 1848 when Andrew was twelve years old, the impoverished family boarded a sailing ship in Glasgow bound for the United States, settling in Allegheny near Pittsburg. After working as a spool boy in a cotton factory and telegraph office delivery boy, Andrew's quick brain and cheerful willingness earned him the post of secretary to Thomas A. Scott, Controller of the Pennsylvania Railway in

Andrew Carnegie (1835–1919)

Pittsburg, who recognised the boy's exceptional acumen and pioneering spirit. At 24 Carnegie was put in charge of the Pittsburg rail department; most of his money however was made by successful investment in other companies. By 1865 the astute railway official had become a wealthy steel magnate, with business interests ranging from the manufacture of rolling stock and rails to bridge building, iron ore and coal mining, and oil. As a self-made man with a talent for management he recognised the importance of good accountancy – "Take care of your pennies, and the pounds will take care of themselves". He also had the happy knack of meeting the right people at the right time, almost all of whom became loyal colleagues and friends exercising a decisive influence on his life (a fact generously acknowledged by Carnegie himself in his memoirs). At the age of 33 he was already the uncrowned king of the American steel industry and one of the country's richest men.

But Carnegie was also by this time set on a philanthropic course, determined his wealth should further cultural progress and advance the public good. In 1901 he disposed of his business interests for $480 million and set about what he later described as the far more difficult task of giving away his money. Apart from establishing pension funds for factory workers and their families, he made a special point of supporting universities and other educational establishments. He made literally thousands of charitable endowments, funding such famous institutions as the Carnegie Hall in New York, the Carnegie Mellin University in Pittsburg, the Carnegie Institute in Washington and the Carnegie Foundation for International Peace, not to mention more than 2800 libraries worldwide.

Throughout his life Carnegie remained deeply attached to his native Scotland which reaped its fair share of his generosity – his birthplace Dunfermline alone received $1 million, worth about $25 million today, for various social and cultural projects. In 1898 Carnegie acquired Skibo Castle (now an exclusive private club) in the North of Scotland as a summer residence, intending to spend the last years of his life there with his wife Louise who was equally devoted to the country. But at the end of the First World War he returned to the United States where he died in Lenox, Massachusetts in 1919. By then he had given away more than $350 million in endowments; these were kept up by his wife and most are still in existence today.

Sean Connery
(b. 1930)

Sean Connery (real name: Thomas Connery) was born in Fountainbridge, a working-class suburb of Edinburgh. At the age of seven he was already earning money as a milk delivery boy, his daily round taking him past Fettes College which, by a strange coincidence, Ian Fleming chose to make the alma mater of his fictional hero James Bond, alias secret agent 007, in which role Connery was later to star. Leaving school at thirteen, Connery did various jobs to make ends meet before joining the navy at seventeen. Discharged for health reasons, he worked for the "Edinburgh Evening News" as a typesetter, was a lifeguard on a beach, and toyed with the idea of becoming a professional footballer. On holiday in London he joined a touring theatre company which, much to his amazement, engaged him for a musical.

Since then he has never left show business. He took lessons in acting and to begin with played only small parts. His first real break came with the television play "Requiem for a Heavyweight". This brought further contracts in England and the USA, although the films themselves (e.g. "Another Time, Another Place", 1958; with Lana Turner) were for the most part mediocre. Stardom came in 1961 when he was cast in the role of the indestructible James Bond. All the 007 films, from "Dr. No" (1962) to "Never Say Never Again" (1984), were major box-office hits. Connery also starred in several other successful movies including "The Longest Day" (1962; about the Normandy landings), Hitchcock's

"Marnie" (1964) and "Murder on the Orient Express" (1974). In later years he switched to character parts. His performance as a 1930s Chicago cop in the gangster film "The Untouchables" (1986) won him an Oscar, the film industry's most prestigious award. In 1987 he again shone as the Franciscan monk William de Baskerville in the film version of Umberto Eco's novel "The Name of the Rose" and as the wily grandfather in Sidney Lumet's "Family Business". As if that were not enough he was also voted "sexiest man of the year" by America's "People" magazine. In 1990 he played opposite Michelle Pfiefer in the film of John Le Carré's bestseller "The Russian House" and in the spy thriller "The Hunt for Red October". Now resident in Spain, Connery often spends time in Scotland where, among other things, he has founded the Scottish International Education Trust dedicated to the fostering of new talent.

Sir Arthur Conan Doyle, doctor and author, was born at 11 Picardy Place, Edinburgh, the youngest son of an alcoholic civil servant of Irish extraction. Required to help support his family even as a medical student, he attended lectures given by the psychiatrist Dr Joseph Bell (1837–1911), which equipped him not only with unusual diagnostic skill but also an uncanny ability to infer all manner of information about a person's life and character from observation of small, and to others insignificant, details. It was just such powers of deduction that he conferred on the resourceful hero of his ever-popular detective yarns, the master sleuth Sherlock Holmes, who made his debut in 1887 in a short story, "A Study in Scarlet", published in Beeton's Christmas Annual. With the aid of the steadfast companion and chronicler Conan Doyle so considerately provided for him – the physician Dr John H. Watson, late of Her Majesty's armed forces – the gaunt but exceptionally fit Holmes with his brilliant intellect and expert knowledge of chemistry, given to playing the violin and smoking pipefuls of cheap tobacco while pondering a difficult case, went on to solve one complicated mystery after another over the years. In 1882 Conan Doyle took up medical practice in England (at Southsea, near Portsmouth), continuing meanwhile to give his narrative talents full rein in several novels – "Micah Clarke" (1887), "The White Company" (1890), "The Sign of Four" (1890) and "Sir Nigel" (1906).

Sir Arthur Conan Doyle (1859–1930)

John Boyd Dunlop came from Dreghorn in Ayrshire. A vet by profession, he was also a keen cyclist, a hobby which led to his making his name as an inventor. In 1888, unaware of Robert Thompson's earlier patent (of 1845), Dunlop developed a tricycle for his children, fitted with pneumatic rubber tyres. The following year he set up a tyre and bicycle manufacturing company in Dublin, which later became the Dunlop Rubber Co.

John Boyd Dunlop (1840–1921)

Alexander Fleming was a native of Loudoun in Ayrshire. In 1928, while working as a bacteriologist at St Mary's Hospital Medical School (attached to the University of London), his attention was caught by a bacteria-free zone which had formed around a culture of a particular mould. This led him to the discovery of penicillin, the single most important advance so far made in the fight against infection – though it was another eleven years before production of the drug could begin. Fleming's pioneering work earned him the Nobel Prize for medicine in 1945.

Sir Alexander Fleming (1881–1955)

The philosopher, economist and historian David Hume was born in Edinburgh. Attending the university there, he was introduced to the work of John Locke and Isaac Newton, whose ideas were to have a decisive influence upon his life. In 1734 he withdrew to the relative peace of La Flèche in France where he wrote his three-volume "A

David Hume (1711–76)

Treatise of Human Nature". Far from bringing the acclaim for which he had hoped, the Treatise, as Hume put it, "fell still-born from the press". It was not until the publication in 1748 of the more accessible "An Enquiry Concerning Human Understanding" that he achieved the philosophical recognition he deserved. Other important treatises followed, including "An Enquiry concerning the Principles of Morals" and "Dialogues concerning Natural Religion". His six-volume "History of England" (1754–62) was to have a lasting influence on historiography in Britain.

Hume ranks alongside Locke as the leading representative of British Empiricism. His epistemology includes a profound critique of empirical knowledge, based on a fundamental distinction between impressions (sensation and feeling) and ideas (thought) and an analysis of the roles of memory and the imagination, in the course of which Hume expounds the argument for which he is perhaps most famous concerning the problem of induction (i.e. the problem of justifying inferences from the observed to the unobserved). In his moral philosophy, by holding morality to be grounded in feeling (rather than cognition) and virtues to be such on account of their social usefulness, Hume reveals himself a precursor of 19th c. Utilitarianism. His mercantilism, in contrast, identifies the politico-economic end as being, not the wealth of states but the affluence of their citizens.

John Knox
(1513?–72)

Giffordgate, now part of Haddington in East Lothian, was the birthplace of John Knox, the resolutely Puritan pastor who, from 1546 onwards, staunchly supported and ultimately led the Reformation movement in Scotland. Condemned by opponents as a trouble-maker and kill-joy, this fiery preacher with a consuming sense of mission was probably educated at St Andrews. When, in 1547, his mentor there, George Wishart, was burnt at the stake for heresy, Knox's voice was among the loudest raised in protest against the prosecutor, Cardinal David Beaton, champion of the Franco-Scottish alliance and himself later lynched by a Protestant mob. When the revolt was crushed Knox was taken prisoner, serving 19 months on a French galley. Following his release he spent some time in Berwick, Newcastle and London as a chaplain to Edward VI. But when the Catholic Queen Mary I came to the throne in 1554, he was forced to flee, escaping to Switzerland. By now almost 50 years old, Knox made his way to Geneva where he immersed himself in Calvinism. His return to Scotland in May 1559 was marked by a wave of iconoclastic violence before Calvinism was adopted as the established religion of Scotland by the "Reform Parliament". After 1560 Knox became minister of St Giles Cathedral in Edinburgh from the pulpit of which, in the course of an extended battle of wills with Mary Stuart, he delivered impassioned sermons against the papists (as a consequence of which he was twice forced to leave the country). His principal works are the "Confessio Scottica" and the "Book of Discipline", both published in 1560, in which he set down proposals for a nation-wide system of education aimed at universal literacy. The largely autobiographical "History of the Reformation of Scotland" appeared between 1559 and 1564.

Knox was twice married, first to Marjory Bowers (d. 1560), an Englishwoman, and second to Margaret Stewart, daughter of Lord Ochiltree. The house on Edinburgh's Royal Mile where he is said to have lived is now a museum dedicated to the life and work of this pugnacious reformer.

David
Livingstone
(1813–73)

The great African explorer David Livingstone was born in Low Blantyre on the banks of the River Clyde in Lanarkshire. Having decided to become a missionary in China he went in 1834 to Glasgow, where he spent two years studying Greek, theology and medicine. But the China project fell through and in 1841 he went instead as a missionary to

South Africa. His missionary zeal and thirst for knowledge led him to penetrate farther into "the dark continent" than any white man had done before, his first venture taking him as far as Lake Ngami in what is now Botswana. His second expedition, in 1854, was to the Zambesi and from there north-westward as far as Luanda. In the next two years he became the first European to cross Africa from the Atlantic in the west to the Indian Ocean in the east. In November 1855 he discovered the mighty falls on the Zambesi which, in honour of Queen Victoria, he named the Victoria Falls. Returning home he gave lectures about his journeys, which proved immensely popular. On his next expedition up the Zambesi between 1858 and 1864, he discovered Lake Nyasa (now Lake Malawi). Two years later he set out again, determined this time to find the source of the Nile. In 1869 his party reached Lake Tanganyika. Here Livingstone was taken ill, his companions quarrelled, and the expedition's supplies ran out; in Britain it was feared he was dead. It was at this point that Henry Morton Stanley, a correspondent on the "New York Herald", was dispatched by his editor to search for Livingstone, whom he finally tracked down on the shores of Lake Tanganyika on October 28th 1871. He is reputed to have greeted the explorer with the now immortal words "Dr Livingstone, I presume?". The two of them then set about exploring Lake Tanganyika. Having decided against returning to Britain, Livingstone died in Chatambo (Zambia) in 1873, his body being taken back to London for burial in Westminster Abbey. His life and work as a missionary is today documented in the David Livingstone Centre in Low Blantyre.

Allan Pinkerton, founder of the world's most famous detective agency, was born on August 8th 1819. Son of a Glasgow policeman, Pinkerton served his apprenticeship as a cooper before emigrating to Chicago in 1842. His career was launched when he secured the conviction of a gang of counterfeiters and received a sheriff's star. In 1850 he set up the National Detective Agency which, before long, was not only providing security for railway companies and supplying personal body-guards, but also hunting down such notorious Wild West outlaws as Jessie James, Butch Cassidy and the Sundance Kid. In 1861 the NDA saved President Lincoln from assassination and in 1866 apprehended a gang of criminals who had made off with $700,000 in a raid. Kate Warne, the United States's first woman detective, worked for the agency from 1858. After Pinkerton's death the NDA continued in family ownership until 1967. Today the firm has more than 50,000 employees and provides security services to such major companies as General Motors and Hewlett Packard as well as the security guards for the Oscar Awards ceremony in Hollywood.

Allan Pinkerton (1819–84)

Robert I the Bruce was born at Turnberry Castle, the son of Robert Bruce, Earl of Carrick and Annandale, and Marjorie, Countess of Carrick. He became Scotland's national hero after defeating Edward II at Bannockburn on June 24th 1314, so freeing his native land from English domination. His grandfather, also Robert, had been claimant to the Scottish throne when, in 1290, Edward I of England had installed John de Balliol as king, so tightening his own grip on the country. In 1297 Bruce joined forces with Sir William Wallace to drive out "Scotland's enemies", but the rebellion was crushed and Wallace executed. In February 1306 Bruce and his followers murdered Balliol's nephew, John "the Red" Comyn, a possible rival for the throne, in the monastery church at Dumfries. In March Bruce himself was crowned king of Scotland at Scone Palace near Perth. Years of campaigning followed during which English garrisons were driven from Scottish soil, until Bannockburn settled the issue once and for all. The remainder of his reign was devoted to uniting his country and ridding it of all who had supported England. The Treaty of Northampton (1328) recognised Bruce's title to the Scottish throne and his country's right to indepen-

Robert I the Bruce (1274–1329)

Sir Walter Scott

Adam Smith

Mary Stuart

dence. When in 1329 Bruce died on the family estate at Cardross, his heart was removed, as he had instructed, by Sir James Douglas and taken to the Holy Land on crusade, afterwards almost certainly being interred in Melrose Abbey. His body lies buried in Dunfermline Abbey, where a brass plaque marks the grave.

**Sir Walter Scott
(1771–1832)**

Scotland's greatest novelist was born in Guthrie Street, Edinburgh, the youngest of 13 children. Scion of an old Scottish family, he followed his father into the law, rising to become sheriff of the County of Selkirk and eventually a judge in the city of his birth. While still a student he became interested in German literature, translating Bürger's "Leonore" and Goethe's "Götz von Berlichingen". As a young lawyer he published the "Minstrelsy of the Scottish Border" (1802–03), a collection of embellished Anglo-Scottish Border ballads. Next he wrote a number of epic narrative poems combining the descriptiveness of the Scottish ballad with the romance of medieval chivalry; these included "The Lay of the Last Minstrel" (1805), "Marmion" (1808), "The Lady of the Lake" (1810) and "The Bridal of Triermain" (1813). All met with enthusiastic public acclaim. After that he turned to prose fiction, writing in rapid succession, at first anonymously, 27 historical novels, the "Waverley Novels". These too were a huge success and had an influence extending far beyond Scotland's borders on writers as famous as Alexander Dumas, Victor Hugo, Honoré de Balzac, Wilhelm Hauff and Carlo Manzoni.

The income from his writing enabled Scott in 1812 to buy and then refurbish Abbotsford House on the Tweed. It was here that he wrote his historical novels, recreating 500 years of Anglo-Scottish history, from the 13th to the 18th c., among the threads of which Scott wove his imaginary tales of adventure and romance; for although his heroes are fictional, they do battle in circumstances shaped as they were in reality by famous historical figures. Most of the novels are set in 17th and 18th c. Scotland, including "Rob Roy" (1817), "The Heart of Midlothian" (1818), "The Legend of Montrose" (1819), "The Bride of Lammermoor" (1819), "Chronicles of the Canongate" (1827) and "The Fair Maid of Perth" (1828), others, like "Ivanhoe" (1820), in the England of the Crusades or, like "Quentin Durward" (1823), Louis XIV's France. In 1820, while at the height of his success, Scott was knighted. Six years later a failed venture into publishing left him facing bankruptcy and the final years of his life were spent writing feverishly to pay off his creditors. He died in the autumn of 1832 from a heart attack and was buried in Dryburgh Abbey.

Scott did more than anyone to restore pride and self-belief to a people who had lived long under English domination, reviving his countrymen's faith in their own national identity. By making the Scottish language and its literature socially acceptable and throwing his weight behind every Scottish cause (the lifting of the ban on the kilt and plaid, for example), he contributed substantially to the renewal of Scottish culture which experienced its true renaissance under George IV and Queen Victoria.

Adam Smith, philosopher and political economist, was a native of Kirkcaldy in Fife. As a young man he became a member of the intellectual circle in Edinburgh centred around the philosopher David Hume and historian William Rutherford (1721–93). In 1751 Smith was appointed to the chair in logic at Glasgow University and four years later to the chair in moral philosophy which he held until 1763. From 1787 to 1789 he was rector of the university. His "Theory of the Moral Sentiments", published in 1759, sought to interpret social behaviour in terms of three basic virtues: enlightened self-interest (prudence), freedom under a state-guaranteed framework of law (justice), and concern for others (benevolence).

Adam Smith (1723–90)

In his *magnum opus*, "An Inquiry into the Nature and Causes of the Wealth of Nations" (1776), a systematic exposition in three volumes of 18th c. liberal economic theory, Smith laid the foundations of classical political economy. In opposition to the mercantilists who exaggerated the importance of the money supply, and the physiocrats who put the productivity of land before all else, Smith argued that labour and the distribution of labour were the true sources of national wealth. As a vigorous advocate of the free market economy his theories played an important part in its practical implementation. Smith is buried in the graveyard of Edinburgh's Canongate Church.

The author of "Treasure Island" (1883) and the mysterious case of "Dr Jeckyll and Mr Hyde" (1887) was born the son of a prosperous engineer in Howard Place in Edinburgh's New Town. Although most of his life was spent travelling, and much of it on the other side of the world, his Scottish homeland was never far from Stevenson's thoughts and it is there that some of his best stories are set. Thus when in writing "Kidnapped" (1886) Stevenson chose to have David Balfour kept captive on the Bass Rock and start out on his great journey of adventure from the Hawes Inn at South Queensferry, he was drawing on his recollections of the coastal scenery of East Lothian from a holiday of some years previous. The Stevensons' own little cottage in Swanston at the foot of the Pentland Hills also appears in the unfinished novel "St Ives" as a "tiny, labyrinthine cathedral".

Robert Louis Balfour Stevenson (1850–94)

Stevenson began to write at a young age, first trying his hand at plays and travelogues before devoting himself to narrative and his exciting adventure stories. From 1875, having completed his studies in law – though never practising as a lawyer – he travelled about Europe, during which time he met Fanny Osbourne, an American woman to whom in 1880 he was married in California. Within a few months ill health forced his return to Scotland where, in 1883 in Braemar, he wrote "Treasure Island", the most famous of his novels, inspired by a sketch of the small island of Fidra in the Firth of Forth. When his chest illness made a change of location imperative he went first to Switzerland, then to the South of France and finally to England. Many of his best-loved novels were written at this time. In 1887 he set out via America for the South Seas where, at the early age of 44, he died from tuberculosis in Western Samoa.

The Glasgow-born architect James Stirling attracted controversy wherever he worked – "crude", "too massive" and "post-modernist kitsch" are how some people reacted to his designs. He delighted in buildings which echoed other periods and the work of other architects

James Stirling (1926–92)

such as Le Corbusier and Aalto, of which his Staatsgalerie in Stuttgart, Germany is perhaps the most notorious example. Among his earlier projects in Britain, the Faculty of Technology Building in Leicester was an immediate success. Other major buildings by Stirling include the History Faculty Building in Cambridge, city centre complexes in Derby, the Olivetti Training Centre at Haslemere and the Clore Gallery in London. His last commission was the Tate Gallery in Liverpool's converted Albert Dock, opened in 1988.

Mary Stuart
(1542–87)

Mary Stuart's unhappy fate, controversy-filled life and ambivalent personality – passionate lover, murderess, Machiavellian schemer and royal martyr – have captured the imagination of countless historians and writers (Lopa de Vega, Schiller, Swinburne, Stefan Zweig and Wolfgang Hildesheimer to name but a few). Born at Linlithgow in 1542, Mary Stuart, or Mary Queen of Scots as she is also known, was the daughter of James V of Scotland and his French wife Mary of Guise, and the granddaughter of Henry VII of England. Her father died just a week after her birth leaving his country racked by political intrigue and religious turmoil and threatened by English pretensions to power. As a result Mary was hastily crowned queen of Scotland in Stirling Castle at the tender age of nine months. At the age of five she was sent to the French court and was brought up in the manner of a French princess. Married at sixteen to Francis II of France, on his death only two years later she returned to a by now Protestant Scotland governed by a suspicious nobility and in a ferment of Calvinist zeal inspired by the reformer John Knox. To many of her subjects she was an unwelcome Catholic stranger while to her cousin Elizabeth I she was her most serious rival for the English throne, being next in line and favoured by those in England who regarded Elizabeth as the illegitimate offspring of Henry VIII.

Mary incurred more heartache as a result of her marriage to her cousin Henry Stuart, Lord Darnley, a handsome but depraved ne'er-do-well. Barely a year had gone by before passion turned to hatred when in 1566 Darnley murdered her confidant David Rizzio in front of the pregnant queen. Following the birth of her son James, Mary tried to obtain a separation from her husband, finding an ally in the commander of her troops, James Hepburn, 4th Earl of Bothwell. In 1567 the house in which Darnley was staying, called Kirk o' Field, was blown up and Darnley himself was found strangled. Within three months Mary had married the principal suspect, Bothwell, so putting herself finally beyond the pale in the eyes of the Scottish nobility. The young couple spent only three weeks together, in Dunbar Castle, a time described later by Mary as the best of her life. On July 24th 1567 she was forced to abdicate and banished to an inaccessible island fortress in Loch Leven from whence, two years later, she managed to escape to England. There, ostensibly for having been implicated in Darnley's murder but in truth because of the threat she represented to Elizabeth's throne, Mary was again imprisoned. She remained incarcerated for the next eighteen years, a pawn in the struggle between Catholics and Protestants for the throne of England. The disclosure in 1586 of a plot to assassinate Elizabeth was the excuse for a charge of high treason against Mary. Sentenced to death she was beheaded at Fotheringhay Castle in Northamptonshire in 1587.

James Watt
(1736–1819)

The inventor James Watt came from Greenock on the Firth of Clyde. He studied precision engineering in Glasgow and London and from 1759 devoted himself to developing the steam engine. He vastly improved the efficiency of Thomas Newcomen's steam engine by adding a condenser separate from the main cylinder, an idea for which he was awarded a patent in 1769. In 1775 he and his partner Matthew Boulton founded the Boulton & Watt works at Soho near Birmingham where, from the mid 1780s onwards, they manufactured low-pressure rotary steam engines. Further innovations followed, including in 1788 the introduction of engines with centrifugal regulators and throttle-valves. Production of these engines played a vital role in the Industrial Revolution.

Art and Culture

Art History

Stone, Bronze and Iron Ages

For those with an interest in pre- and early history, Scotland's legacy of Stone and Iron Age monuments, many of unique archaeological importance, is a further rich source of fascination. Sited mainly on the coast, they are found in greatest numbers in the fertile north-east and Orkney and Shetland. Whereas in prehistoric times the highlands were thickly forested and inaccessible, coasts and islands offered land for cultivation and plentiful supplies of fish and game. Just about the only resource lacking in the Orkneys and Shetlands 6000 years ago was wood. Stone, of which however there was an abundance, was therefore used for building, as a result of which homesteads and even whole villages dating from the New Stone Age can still be seen. The oldest dwellings are a pair of semi-detached houses from the 4th millennium B.C. at Knap of Howar on Papa Westray in the Orkneys. The best known Stone Age village site, Skara Brae in Orkney, was completely buried beneath sand by a storm and thus preserved almost intact, together with stone furniture, tools and jewellery. Jarlshof in Shetland is an agglomeration of settlements dating variously from the Stone Age through to Viking times.

Cairns

As every hill walker knows, the word "cairn" (from the Gaelic "càrn" meaning "heap" or "hill") is the name given today to the piles of stones marking the footpaths and summits of Britain's mountains, the Scottish mountains included. But in Scotland it also has another more ancient use, referring to the country's numerous Stone Age barrows, the earliest of which date from around 3700 B.C. Several thousand of these artificial mounds are found in the Orkneys and Shetlands alone. Constructed without the use of mortar from carefully layered undressed stone covered over with earth, they are found in two basic types, gallery tombs (e.g. at Midhowe, Knowe of Yarso and Blackhammer in the Orkneys) and chamber tombs (e.g. at Quanterness, Wideford Hill and Maes Howe, also in the Orkneys). Gallery tombs have an entrance leading directly into a narrow rectangular burial-chamber with walls formed by large upright slabs and partitioned for individual burials; chamber tombs have a long entrance passage giving access to a principal chamber with a number of small burial chambers leading off it.

Menhirs and stone circles

The prehistoric stone circles of Britain still represent something of a mystery; even their dates are controversial. The most famous, Stonehenge near Salisbury in southern England, appears to have been built in three phases between 2800 and 1500 B.C. The circle at Callanish on Lewis, the largest in Scotland, with several rows of tall stones around a central monolith, was constructed between 2000 and 1500 B.C. There are several hundred other cruder circles and menhirs (single standing stones), often found in conjunction with one or more cairns. Although these stone circles were undoubtedly cult sites, almost nothing is known of the cults themselves. What *is* known however is that the larger circles were in effect solar and lunar observatories allowing precise calculation of key dates in the solar calendar. The people who built them must have been able to draw not only on the necessary astronomical and mathematical skill, but also the resources of a highly organised society; the huge blocks of stone, each weighing several tons, had to be transported considerable distances without the aid of a wheeled vehicle of any sort, and erected with great precision in their allotted positions.

Stone Age settlement, Skara Brae (Orkneys)   *Jarlshof in the Shetland Isles*

From about the 5th c., i.e. the middle of the Iron Age, the Celts began their settlement of Britain. "Dun" is the Gaelic word for fortification. Scotland's Iron Age hill forts are similar to those found throughout Europe, substantial ring works occupying rounded hilltops. However the fortified towers known as brochs are unique to Scotland. Dating mainly from the first centuries B.C. and A.D., they are found in large numbers in the Hebrides (especially Skye), in the Orkneys and Shetlands and in north-east Scotland; only a few isolated examples occur in the south. More or less round, they have walls 13–16ft/4–5m thick enclosing a space about 30–40ft/9–12m in diameter. Their most characteristic feature is the cavity construction of the walls, reinforced at regular intervals by stone slabs laid horizontally. The galleries thus formed presumably served for storage, though their main function appears to have been structural. The drystone construction was so skilfully executed that even as late as the 12th c. the Mousa Broch in Shetland was able to withstand a siege of several days without damage; it still stands to almost its full height today. Although the majority of brochs were plundered for building material in later centuries, in their own day they must have been virtually unassailable. Who exactly constructed these refuges and why they did so is yet to be satisfactorily explained. The brochs at Carloway (Lewis) and near Glenelg (opposite Skye) give a good idea of the typical wall construction; those at Gurness in the Orkneys and Clickhimin in Shetland are encircled by the remains of outbuildings and outer fortifications.

Hill forts, duns and brochs

The Romans left few traces in Scotland, just a handful of roads and military installations. Although in 84 A.D. Agricola pushed north as far as the Moray Firth, following his recall, the Romans were forced to retreat. Even the Antonine Wall, built in around 140 across the narrow neck of land between the Forth and the Clyde, was only held for about 40 years before the Romans finally withdrew behind the comparative

Roman period

Gurness Broch – ancient Celtic refuge in Orkney

safety of Hadrians Wall linking the Solway Firth and Tyne estuary. The best preserved Roman fort on the Antonine Wall is Rough Castle west of Falkirk. Ardoch Castle near Braco in Perthshire is one of the largest Roman camps in Great Britain.

Picts

"Picti", i.e. painted men, was how, at the close of the 3rd c., the Romans referred to the barbarian warriors from the north who proved a constant thorn in their side in the Scottish lowlands and blocked any further advance. Until the 9th c., except for Argyll where in the 6th c. the Scotti, incomers from Ireland, established their kingdom of Dalriada, the Picts controlled the whole of Scotland north of the rivers Forth and Clyde. Apart from a list of the names of their kings they left no written legacy; and because they buried nothing with their dead very few everyday items have survived. Only one or two Pictish dwellings, such as those at Gurness in the Orkneys, have come to light. The sole, entirely unique, testament to their culture are the intriguing Pictish relief stones. The oldest have abstract symbols, animals, mythical beasts and battle and hunting scenes carved into rough, undressed stone; others are smooth cleanly hewn slabs carved on both sides in high-relief, the front always having as the dominant motif a cross – for which reason they are known as cross-stones. Stones such as these must have been an omnipresent feature of the Pictish landscape because more than 200 can still be seen today in various parts of North and East Scotland. No other Western European tribe of this period left behind so extensive a legacy of stone sculptures. Since the same symbols appeared on the stones throughout the Pictish realm, it is safe to assume they had some standard signification. But what exactly? They may have been memorials to the dead, records of kinship by intermarriage or markers for tribal territories. In truth not even the age of these stones is known with any certainty, though some of the symbols have parallels in early illuminated manuscripts. The oldest stones are thought likely to date from the 6th c., the majority from the 7th c.

It was during that same period (6th–7th c.) that the Picts were gradually converted to Christianity. One or two Christian communities had already taken root in the romanised lowlands as early as late Roman times; St Ninian's monastery at Whithorn in Galloway was the first ecclesiatical foundation on Scottish soil. However the conversion of the Picts was the work of monks from the small island of Iona off the west coast of Mull, where St Columba landed on his missionary voyage from Ireland in 563. Foundations and remains of very early churches have been uncovered at Whithorn, Iona, one or two other islands on the West Coast and at Gurness and Birsay in the Orkneys. From the 8th c. onwards Tayside, the Pictish heartland, was a centre of the early Church. Some of the oldest church buildings are found there, as well as the great majority of Pictish cross-stones. Particularly fine examples of these stones can be seen at St Vigeans near Arbroath and in the museum at Meigle.

Conversion to Christianity

In Scotland as elsewhere it is usually only the towers of very early churches which have survived (or at least the lower portions). While the ruins of Restenneth Priory are largely 13th c., the base of the tower has been dated to the 8th c. Next oldest are the 11th c. round towers at Brechin and Abernethy, still their original height though capped with spires of later date. Almost completely windowless and with elevated entrances they served the dual purpose of belfry and keep. In Ireland there are as many as 80 round towers of this kind; the towers at Brechin and Abernethy testify to the continuing influence of the ascetic Irish monastic tradition in Scotland even as late as the 11th c.

Church architecture
Early Middle
Ages

At the end of the 11th/beginning of the 12th c. Malcolm III (Canmore) the anglicised Scottish king and Margaret his English queen initiated the reform of the Scottish Church, imposing the ecclesiastical structures and church–state relationships of the Roman tradition. As well as enhancing the power of the bishops, Malcolm founded several monasteries. The result was a number of fine Romanesque and Early Gothic buildings which, had it not been for later religious strife which left Scotland's monastic heritage in ruins, would certainly have stood comparison with those of England or continental Europe.

Romanesque

Among the earliest of these large Scottish Romanesque churches was Dunfermline Abbey, built between about 1130 and 1150. Although only the nave survives, neither the Late Gothic additions nor the vast, intrusive Neo-Gothic chancel can altogether disguise the splendour of the Norman Romanesque interior with its unmistakable echoes of Durham Cathedral. Stout cylindrical piers dominate the central space while the strongly projecting arcades seem almost weighed down under the burden of the walls, whose massiveness is reflected in the deep-set triforium arches above.

Of the four great Border abbeys – Kelso, Melrose, Jedburgh and Dryburgh – Kelso is the oldest. Originally with twin chancels and crossings on the model of the Carolingian and Romanesque churches of the Rhineland, today only the 12th c. west chancel and transept remain. The kirks at Birnie (Morayshire) and Dalmeny (Lothian) are typical of the small Romanesque parish churches built during this period.

The finest example of Early Gothic architecture in Scotland is the beautiful and remarkably little-altered Glasgow Cathedral, the chancel and vast crypt of which were constructed between 1233 and 1258. Although the nave took more than 200 years to complete, the builders stayed true to the original style, thus preserving the homogeneity of the whole. Elgin Cathedral, dubbed the "Light of the North", was completed in about 1300. Splendidly restored at the beginning of the

Gothic

15th c. after having been partly destroyed, this delightful mixture of High and Late Gothic is once again reduced to a ruin. However, of Scotland's many ruined churches, it was not Elgin but the Late Gothic Melrose Abbey with its elaborate carvings like a stone "herbarium scoticum" that Theodore Fontane considered the loveliest of all. Although its builders came from York, the east front shows evidence of French influence. Scotland's other Late Gothic churches – Dunkeld Cathedral, St Machars in Aberdeen and monastic buildings on Iona – appear provincial and dated by comparison.

Post-Reformation church architecture

The Reformation in Scotland was marked by considerable violence and a great many churches and especially their furnishings were destroyed. When the Presbyterians began to rebuild, persevering with a predominantly Gothic style well into the 17th c., they attached great importance to seating the congregation in a single space around the chancel. Hence single-aisled or hall churches were favoured. From the 17th c. onwards these often had a short wing or side aisle added in the right-hand corner, accommodating the laird's family burial vault and private gallery or "loft". Examples can be seen at Anstruther Easter and Tulliallan (both in Fife).

Castles
Norman forts

The secular counterparts of Romanesque churches were the motte and bailey forts which, having evolved in early 11th c. France, were introduced into Britain by the Normans following the Conquest in 1066. The motte was a tall mound in the shape of a truncated cone, around which a deep ditch was dug and on top of which was built a wooden tower surrounded by a stout palisade. The bailey was the area around the motte where the ancilliary buildings stood, encircled by an earth rampart and second ditch. Access to the motte from the bailey was via a steep, easily defended bridge. Since almost all motte and bailey forts were constructed of timber, there is little to be seen nowadays in most cases apart from ditches and ramparts. The Motte of Urr in Kirkcud-

Late Gothic ruins: Melrose Abbey

Typical Scottish Baronial: Craigievar Castle

brightshire and Urquhart Castle on the shores of Loch Ness are however still impressive. Duffus Castle (near Elgin, Morayshire) was later rebuilt in stone on the original plan.

Even as early as the 12th c. one or two fortified towers were already being built in stone. In the 13th c., as weapons became more powerful and siege techniques improved, the design of castles developed accordingly; in particular they became larger and more complex. Three basic types of structure made their appearance, capable of being combined in endless different ways – curtain walls, gatehouses and tower-houses. Massive stone curtain walls, high enough to prevent them being scaled using the newly developed aids, replaced the earlier wooden palisades. The walls themselves and any outworks (ditches, ramparts, palisades, etc.) could be defended by archers from the safety of projecting (corner) towers and protruding turrets. The simplest 13th c. castles consisted of little more than a massive curtain wall protecting the buildings within; Castle Roy in Inverness-shire and Castle Tioram in Ross and Cromarty are of this type. Gates were a weak point in any wall and required special protection, for which purpose the gatehouse was devised. In the 13th c. these generally took the form of a pair of tall towers flanking the entrance, usually rounded on the outside the better to withstand assault. Tantallon Castle (East Lothian) and Caerlaverock Castle (Dumfriesshire) are splendid examples, each dominated by its massive gatehouse, centrepiece of the entire complex. Built in the 14th c. and later onlarged, both castles are now in ruins. In lieu of – or sometimes in addition to – the gatehouse, more elaborate castles had a tower house or keep accommodating the domestic quarters (such keeps replaced the earth mound and wooden tower of the old motte and bailey fortress). In some instances a corner tower in the curtain wall was converted for the purpose. Bothwell Castle in Lanarkshire and Kildrummy Castle in Aberdeenshire, both early 14th c., are impressive examples of castles with all three features, curtain wall, gatehouse and keep.

The very simplest type of medieval fortified dwelling was the tower-house, examples of which are found throughout Europe, the oldest dating from the 12th c. In Scotland tower-houses were embraced in a unique fashion; over a period of more than 250 years, from the late 14th to the early 17th c., the vast majority of Scottish castles took that form. Virtually every laird or landowning member of the minor nobility built himself a tower-house on his farm between the midden and the pigsty; even the royal palace at Holyrood started life in that way. However great the differences in size or detail the basic design was always the same: larders and storerooms on the ground floor; above them a great hall; and above the hall the private apartments of the laird and his family. Access to all levels was via a spiral staircase in one corner of the tower, a kind of vertical entrance hall. The earliest tower-houses, of which Drum Castle (late 13th c.) in Aberdeenshire and Threave Castle (14th c.) in Kirkcudbrightshire are fine examples, were always rectangular or square. Later designs incorporated either one or two wings, giving rise to the familiar L- or Z-shaped ground plan of the typical Scottish tower-house. The wings were not only advantageous from the point of view of defence but also allowed more spacious, comfortable accommodation and more varied articulation of the exterior.

From the mid 16th c. onwards, fortification gradually took second place to comfort, though the tower-house form was more or less retained. So evolved the Scottish Baronial style. Continuing requirements of defence meant that ground floors remained fortress-like, often with embrasures; but whereas the older tower-houses had only a scattering of very small windows, light was now allowed to stream into halls and apartments through much larger openings. These, though still not evenly distributed, were nevertheless arranged with a view of the outside world very much in mind. The overall impression remained

13th and 14th c. castles

15th and 16th c. tower-houses

16th and 17th c. Scottish Baronial style

that of a stoutly built tower, an effect often whimsically heightened by confining external embellishment to the upper floors. And what external embellishment! Protruding cylindrical turrets with pointed pepper-pot roofs supported on ornate, multi-stepped corbelling running right around the building; projecting gables standing clear of the main roof in a manner similar to the turrets; dormer windows with their own little roofs and ornamental caps; even chimneys serving a decorative purpose. The Grampian Region is particularly well-endowed with castles in this uniquely Scottish style, the best known being Castle Fraser, Crathes Castle and Craigievar Castle, this latter being perhaps the finest of all.

Renaissance
façades

As its name implies, Scottish Baronial was the architecture of the minor nobility or barons. In the 16th c. the Scottish kings and one or two of the wealthier, more widely-travelled noblemen, were drawn to the prevailing international style. Consequently it is in Scotland that the earliest examples of Renaissance architecture in Britain are found. As early as 1538, James V, newly married to Mary of Guise, embellished the wings of the royal palace at Falkland (Fife) with Renaissance façades. Afterwards the workforce, some of whom had been brought over from France, moved on to Stirling, constructing a Renaissance palace on a courtyard plan within the existing castle. Other Renaissance façades can be seen at Caerlaverock Castle (Dumfries) and Crichton Castle (Lothian). Generally speaking however these developments had little influence on Scottish architecture as a whole.

Architecture in the 17th and 18th c.

Palladian,
Neo-Classical,
and Georgian

In the 17th c. a distinctive English style of architecture was developed by Inigo Jones and Christopher Wren, initially inspired by the work and ideas of the Italian Andrea Palladio (1508–80) who had himself revived and breathed new life into the classical architectural canons of ancient Rome. Introduced into Scotland by Sir William Bruce, Bruce's pupil James Smith and also William Adam the Elder, the Palladian style was characterised by symmetrical ground-plans and restrained articulation of strictly uniform façades. Starting in 1671 Bruce systematically rebuilt Holyrood Palace, retaining only the existing north-west wing which he incorporated into a new symmetrical façade. Floors Castle (near Kelso) and Mellerstain House (Berwickshire) are examples of the work of William Adam the Elder.

Robert Adam (1728–92), son of William Adam the Elder, was the leading British architect of the 18th c. As well as establishing a highly successful architectural practice in London, he received numerous commissions in his native Scotland, including Hopetoun House in Lothian and Culzean Castle in Ayrshire. The strict symmetry and clear lines of his buildings are skilfully and elegantly relieved by the use of curves. Adam designed not only buildings but décor and furnishings as well, everything from furniture, carpets and stucco-work to items such as door-knobs. To provide an outlet for his products he and his three brothers founded William Adam & Co., with a staff sometimes numbering as many as two thousand. His designs continued to be used well into the 19th c. "Adam" rooms are characterised by their delightful combination of filigree stucco-work (often inspired by Roman grotesques), bust medallions and classical figurative friezes, all in gentle pastel shades producing a porcelain-like effect.

Town planning

In the 18th c. town planning provided a new challenge for architects. Terraces, squares, even entire districts, came to be conceived as integrated wholes. Edinburgh New Town, construction of which began in 1767 to plans by James Craig, is a magnificent case in point. The fronts of the individual terrace houses combine to form palatial façades, their centrepieces and end pavilions emphasised by being projected slightly forward, creating both symmetry and movement. Wide streets and lots of squares, many of them circuses or elliptical in shape, often with small gardens, typify this new-style townscape.

Floors Castle, Kelso: Georgian design by W. Adam the Elder

In British art history, the years from the end of the 17th c. to the early part of the 19th are known as the Georgian period after the four Hanoverian kings, all named George, who reigned over the country from 1698 to 1830. Georgian architecture is by no means exclusively Neo-Classical and in Scotland architects commissioned to build castles quickly reverted to medieval forms. Inveraray Castle (1745–61), designed by Roger Morris, is a fine, early example of the Neo-Gothic style, while in the design of his later castles, Culzean in particular, Robert Adam successfully combined Neo-Classical elements with Neo-Gothic.

As on the continent, great architectural diversity prevailed in Victorian Britain well into the 19th c. Architects felt free to draw on almost any period, allowing the function of a building to determine its style. Thus churches were generally Neo-Gothic, schools and railway stations – for which there were no obvious precedents – masqueraded as Renaissance palaces, and Greek temples appeared in numbers, often dedicated to some muse (the National Gallery of Scotland in Edinburgh is a case in point). Far from pursuing strict symmetry, the designers of castles strove for picturesque effect, making bold use of irregular dimensions and decorative elements borrowed chiefly from Gothic. The distinctively Scottish variation on this historicist theme in castle architecture was the New Baronial style, reviving the 16th c. towerhouse though in a more ornate and considerably more comfortable form.

19th c architecture

Painting only began to flourish in Scotland, and also in England, from the mid 18th c. onwards, when the puritanical stranglehold of the Church with its hostility to imagery was loosened by the spread of Enlightenment ideas. At the same time the British upper classes were beginning to accumulate considerable wealth, the result, in roughly

Painting in the 18th and 19th c.

equal measure, of agrarian reform, colonial expansion and burgeoning industrialisation. Portraiture came greatly into demand. One of the most talented early portraitists was Allan Ramsay (1713–84). After a number of years spent studying in Italy, he settled in London, but for a while maintained a second studio in his native city of Edinburgh. Ramsay's portraits are exceptionally vivid and very finely executed, in marked contrast to the rapid, vigorous brush strokes of Henry Raeburn (1756–1823). Like Ramsay, Raeburn grew up in Edinburgh, becoming, in the latter part of the 1780s, the leading portraitist of his day. His contemporary Alexander Nasmyth (1756–1840), another native of Edinburgh, is considered the father of Scottish landscape painting.

The principal Scottish landscape artists of the 19th c. were, in chronological order, John Thomson, Horatio McCulloch and William McTaggart. While Thomson (1778–1840) and McCulloch (1805–67) interpret the Scottish landscape in a manner typical of Romanticism, McTaggart's (1835–1910) early pictures are reminiscent of Hans Thomas's rural scenes; his later work was influenced by French Impressionism. David Wilkie (1785–1841), a minister's son from Cults in Fife, caused quite a stir in London with his genre scenes of Scottish country life. In the second half of the 19th c. Glasgow superseded Edinburgh as the focal point, not only of the new industrially-based prosperity, but of artistic innovation as well. The "Glasgow Boys", a group centred round James Guthrie, James Paterson, George Henry and Edward A. Hornel, would set off into the Scottish countryside to paint, their work being much influenced by French Realism and also by Whistler. In 1893 the so-called "Four" – the Macdonald sisters, Margaret and Frances, and two budding architects, Herbert MacNair and Charles Rennie Mackintosh – came together at the Glasgow Academy of Art where, working at first in graphics, metal and textile design, they began to develop a distinctive new style, a Scottish variant of Art Nouveau with which the name of the gifted designer and architect Charles Rennie

Hill House in Helensburgh: Art Nouveau villa by Charles Rennie Mackintosh

Mackintosh has become almost synonymous today (see Baedeker Special, "Mackintosh – Art Nouveau Glasgow-style").

As in the closing years of the 19th c., in the first half of the 20th c. painting in Scotland was heavily influenced by French art. The Scottish Colourists – John D. Fergusson (1874–1961), Samuel J. Peploe (1871–1935), Francis C. B. Cadell (1883–1937) and Leslie Hunter (1877–1931) – were guided by Cézanne, Matisse and Les Fauves. Robert Colquhoun (1914–62) and Robert MacBryde (1913–66), both of whom studied in Glasgow and later worked together in London, were influenced by Cubism. So too was William Gillies (1898–1973), who became Principal of the Edinburgh College of Art, a post he held until 1946. But Gillies, like his Edinburgh colleagues, later turned to "la belle peinture", colourful oil paintings in the manner of Bonnard and the Scottish Colourists.

20th c. painting and sculpture

Influence of French art: Colourists and Cubists

The abstract movement is represented in Scotland by William Gear (b. 1915). In the post-war years he became associated with Appel's Cobra Group in Paris and, together with Pollock, exhibited in New York. Alan Davie (b. 1920), whose paintings draw inspiration from magic and myth, is another Scot to achieve international recognition. The best known Scottish woman painter of the 1950s and early 1960s was Joan Eardley (1921–63), most of whose landscapes, though painted out of doors, are examples of free association in the sense of American abstract Expressionism.

Abstract art

Eduardo Paolozzi, born in Edinburgh in 1924 to Italian parents, studied in Edinburgh and London where he has worked since the 1950s. He was one of a group of young British artists who, in the 1950s, earned widespread recognition with their metal sculptures of varying degrees of abstraction. Paolozzi's bronzes, cast from plaster of Paris moulds of *objets trouvés*, and also his collages of magazine pictures and advertisements, have established him as a leading exponent of Pop Art. Since the early 1970s Bruce McLean, born in Glasgow in 1944, has experimented with sculpture as performance, making the traditional activities of artists the target of his satire.

Sculpture

Language and Literature

Scotland has its own long-established literary tradition, a fact which linguistic diversity – the use of Gaelic, Scots, Lallan (a form of broad Scots deliberately developed by 20th c. writers) and English – has always tended to conceal.

Gaelic, Scots, Lallan and Scottish English

The ancient Picts spoke in a dialect of the so-called P Celtic group, to which Welsh also belongs. The Scots in contrast, coming from Ireland, spoke Gaelic, a Q Celtic tongue. When the Scottish chieftain Kenneth MacAlpin became king of the Picts in 843, Gaelic took over as the language of the new, unified Celtic kingdom. After 1069 however, the introduction of feudalism and the anglicisation of Scotland under Malcolm III, led to Anglo-Saxon being adopted as the language of administration and the court, a development which marked the beginning of Scotland's polarisation into Celtic Highlands and "English" Lowlands. At first the idiom of Anglo-Saxon Lothian was dubbed "Inglis" while Gaelic was known as "Scottis"; but towards the end of the 15th c. usage altered and "Scottis" came to refer to Inglis. Thus it was that "Scottis" (i.e. Scots) became the language of Scotland's non-Gaelic medieval literature. Though the Reformation severely diminished the standing of Scots, it continued to be the language of everyday use, the idiom of domesticity, feeling and humour – precisely the position it retains today in the nation's linguistic consciousness.

The corollary of all this was that Gaelic progressively lost its place as the national tongue, eventually being reduced almost to myth – as the language of a lost Celtic paradise. But it never quite died out in the Highlands and Islands, and since the 1970s strenuous efforts have been made to revive it. Signposts in the Highlands are now bi-lingual and so are many official publications. A command of Gaelic is increasingly an advantage and in some cases a requirement for certain public appointments. It is well on the way to restoration as a living minority language.

Scottish English has also seen something of a resurgence in the 20th c. Scots, having been in decline since the Reformation, was restored to literary respectability alongside the nation's other languages by Robert Burns and Sir Walter Scott.

Middle Ages

John Barbour

Although the written tradition in Scottish literature is recognised as having begun in the late 13th c., the first major figure was John Barbour (c. 1316–95). His patriotic verse epic "The Bruce" (1375) recounts, in 14,000 lines, in the manner of the French chanson de geste, the life and exploits of Scotland's national hero.

Makars

"The Makars" (i.e. Makers) is the title given to the great Scottish poets of the centuries prior to the union with England. Despite borrowing the courtly content of their writing from Geoffrey Chaucer and their style from Europe, they laid the foundations of a distinctively "Scot-

Robert Henryson

tish" poetic tradition. Chief among them were: Robert Henryson (c. 1435–1506), author of "The Testament of Cresseid" (a continuation of Chaucer's "Troilus and Cressida"), "Robene and Makyne", and "The

William Dunbar

Morall Fabillis of Esope"; William Dunbar (c. 1460–1521), leading figure of the "Golden Age" during the reign of James IV, notable especially for his poetic scolding-matches known as flytings, e.g. "The

Gavin Douglas

Flyting of Dunbar and Kennedie"; Gavin Douglas (c. 1474–1522) who, in his "Eneados", a translation of Virgil's "Aeneas", was the first to refer to his native tongue as "Scots" (the work itself being nothing less

David Lindsay

than a dictionary of the language as it was at that time); and David Lindsay (1490–1555), whose writings were the most published and widely read of all the Makars, surpassed by none until Sir Walter Scott. Although employed at court he addressed himself explicitly to country folk. His principal work, "Ane Satyre of the Thrie Esteits (1533), is a allegoric morality play.

By the eve of the Reformation the language of Scottish literature was already fully shaped and part of the language of European literature as a whole. The vigorous growth of a floridly rhetorical, magniloquent style reflected, not only a closeness to the Gaelic-bardic tradition, but also the gift for oratory for which the Scots, Irish and Welsh are still known today.

Reformation

In the grip of Calvinism

The Reformation absorbed all intellectual energy. Calvinism proved a barrier to any secular literature or public theatrical tradition, the puritan hostility towards art exerting a negative influence on Scottish culture until well into the 20th c. Religion held a monopoly of the period's powerful prose (e.g. John Knox's "The First Blast of the Trumpet against the Monstrous Regiment of Women", 1558) and such secular writers as there were fall into the category of "Minor Poets". Though masters of lyric form and obeying the canons of the European Renaissance, they continued the "local" tradition of poems about-nature. Just occasionally there are echoes of the Makars' more militant style, as in Montgomerie's verses "The Cherrie and the Slae", one of the most popular of all Scottish poems.

17th century

The removal of the Scottish court to London in 1603 had the effect of
further anglicising the Scottish literary scene, bringing a widening gulf
between "high" culture and the folk tradition. The latter continued to
be passed down orally, particularly in the form of folk ballads which,
flourishing throughout the period from the 16th to the 18th c., were
finally recorded and anthologised in the 19th c., most notably by
Sir Walter Scott (from 1802) and F. J. Child (1848). The ballads fall into
three main categories: (1) the Border Ballads, of which 60 have been
handed down, originating, as the name implies, from the Anglo-
Scottish marches and drawing on historic border incidents for their
themes, e.g. "The Battle of Otterburn"; (2) ballads of the supernatural,
a genre more common in Scotland than elsewhere, of which "Thomas
the Rhymer" is an example; (3) romantic or traditional ballads with no
specifically Scottish significance, often more realistic, gloomier and
more tragic than, for example, their English counterparts, e.g. "The
Twa Corbies" (compare the English "The Three Ravens"). Many of
these ballads continue to be heard, particularly since the revival of folk
singing in the 1960s.

Folk ballads

18th century

The union with England in 1707 further weakened Scotland's home-
grown literary tradition. The Scots language became increasingly
anglicised and Scottish writers were deprived of aristocratic patronage
and the stimulus provided by a court. Facing a loss of identity, some
Scots turned to the literature of the past. The central figure in this
movement was Allan Ramsay (1684–1758) who, by publishing Scottish
poems written before 1600 and ballads "ancient" as well as new, made
the old texts available again for the first time. His lending library in
Edinburgh, opened in 1728, quickly became a meeting place for Scotland's literati, and in 1736 he opened the first real theatre in the Scottish
capital. But at the same time Edinburgh epitomised the cultural hiatus
developing in 18th c. Scotland; for in this "Athens of the North", the
finest minds of the Scottish Enlightenment – Francis Hutcheson, David
Hume, William Robertson, Hugh Blair and Adam Smith – were philoso-
phers, historians and political economists rather than poets, and wrote
moreover in English.

Allan Ramsay

One of those who did most to re-establish continuity with pre-
Reformation literature was Robert Fergusson (1750–74). He re-
invigorated Scots as a literary language by his resurrecting of the
flytings and portrayals of Edinburgh life.

**Rediscovery
of Scottish
literature**

All the different strands of the revival came together in the work of
Robert Burns (1759–96; see Famous People). Like Ramsay he collected
and embellished numerous Scottish folk songs and, from 1786, published hundreds of songs of his own on popular themes – love, work,
sociability, festivities, the joys of life in general (e.g. "My Luve's like a
Red, Red Rose", "To a Haggis", etc., see Baedeker Special, "Chieftan o'
the Puddin-race!"). He combined an intuitive understanding of Scotland's literary heritage with an informed political awareness, speaking
out for the ideals of the French Revolution. His influence was immense.
His songs and ballads, such as "Tam o'Shanter", are a core part of the
Scottish literary canon and many, like "My Heart's in the Highlands"
(see p. 257), have become folk songs in their own right. Burns is much
more than Scotland's national poet; he is the figure around whom
Scotland's cultural identity as a whole crystallises.

Robert Burns

The second outstanding personality of the Scottish literary revival was
Sir Walter Scott (1771–1832; see Famous People). He too collected and
recorded the oral tradition, finding in it a source of inspiration for his

Sir Walter Scott

own work. His verse narratives ("Minstrelsy of the Scottish Border", "The Lay of the Last Minstrel", "The Lady of the Lake", etc.) combine the setting and atmosphere of the border ballads with themes from the great epics of medieval chivalry. In the "Waverley Novels", the first of which appeared in 1814 and of which there are 27 in all ("The Heart of Midlothian", "The Bride of Lammermoor", "Ivanhoe", etc.), Scott powerfully recreated the rich panoply of 500 years of Anglo-Scottish history and in so doing gave birth to the historical novel. The Scotland he portrays is a romantic country, a country steeped in history. For Scott – and indeed for the Scots as a nation – history is no mere insubstantial backcloth to the present, but a living force forever shaping the actions and fate of men. In the novels it is seen through the eyes of ordinary folk, the many "characters", real and imaginary, who are the heroes of Scott's tales. The history of which they tell is likewise that of ordinary people, people whose tongue is Scots, the language of the heart, not the English of the narrator. Scott's literary achievement was immense; as lyricist, novelist, journalist, historian, collector and publisher, his place is among the most successful writers of all time; he was, it could be said, the first best-selling author.

19th century

Burns and Scott established once and for all Scotland's claim to literary independence. But so great was Scott's influence that critics are wont to dismiss his contemporaries and the subsequent two generations of writers as merely imitative. In practice it is often difficult to recognise anything specifically Scottish in the work of Scottish authors – indeed many people fail to realise that e.g. Byron, Macaulay and Kipling were of Scottish birth.

John Galt
James Hogg

While John Galt (1779–1839) depicted the effects on village life of the cultural, social and economic upheavals of his time, the work of James Hogg (1770–1835) is proof that Scott and his followers did not entirely exhaust every "Scottish" topic: "The Private Memoirs and Confessions of a justified Sinner" (1824), ostensibly an analysis of religious fanaticism exemplified by two very different brothers, is actually a classical study of totalitarian thought and as such very modern in its theme. The contradictions in the character of Robert, the hero of the novel, illustrate the divided nature of Scottish society.

Robert Louis
Stevenson

In "The Strange Case of Dr Jekyll and Mr Hyde" (1886), Robert Louis Stevenson (1850–94; see Famous People) explored the subject of split personality in a classical literary fashion. Having completed "Kidnapped" (1886) and "The Master of Ballantrae", it was not until he embarked on the unfinished "Weir of Hermiston" (1896) that Stevenson wrote again about Scotland. Skilfully deploying the methods of the first modern writers, he conducts his psychological probing of his characters in a novel typically Scottish in subject matter and themes.

The regional novel
Kailyard School

Towards the end of the 19th c. the Scottish literary scene was dominated by the regional novel. Writers of the Kailyard School (kailyard = herb garden) such as J. M. Barrie, S. R. Crockett and Ian MacLaren, achieved wide circulation in Britain and the USA. Writing extensively in Scots and on innocent, homely themes, they draw a sentimental picture of Scottish small town life seen, so to speak, from the manse – both Crockett and MacLaren were ministers. "The House with the

George Douglas
Brown

J. MacDougall
Hay

Green Shutters" (1901) by George Douglas Brown (1869–1902), was written as a deliberate counterblast to the complacency of the regional novel; while it too is set in a small provincial town, the story it tells is one of family tragedy. In "Gillespie" (1914), J. MacDougall Hay (1881–1919) portrays life in a little town in the West of Scotland.

The "Scottish Renaissance" · 20th century

True modernity entered Scottish literature with the emergence of a fundamentally new approach to language, literature and cultural identity.

The central figure in this was Hugh MacDiarmid (1892–1978) to whom English "ascendancy" represented an injustice to be strenuously opposed in all its forms. He propounded the idea of an all-embracing Scottish culture in which art was indivisible from nationalism and politics. Regarding English as a forcibly imposed foreign tongue, he developed a synthetic form of Scots (later called Lallan) by the use of which, from 1925 onwards, he sought to render every aspect of modern European writing accessible to the Scottish lyric. His figuratively complex poems are journeys of exploration in search of a new Scottish identity. "A drunk Man looks at the Thistle" (1926) expounds Mac-Diarmid's own vision of Scotland reborn. As the protagonist unsteadily makes his way home, his drunken monologue turns into an odyssey, which ends after frequent interruptions and detours in a Scotland freed from defeatism.

Writing in English as well as Scots, William Souter (1889–1943) is known especially for his scurrilous but highly original children's poems. Sidney Goodsir Smith (1915–75) was Edinburgh's latter-day Robert Fergusson, rendering modern themes in old Scottish. His "Under the Eildon Tree" (1948) is generally considered the most important lyric work since the poems of MacDiarmid. Edwin Muir (1887–1959) provided a much-needed counterbalance to MacDiarmid, proving that for a Scot to write in English was not necessarily a betrayal of the national cause. Although working within the high lyric tradition of "British" English-language poetry, Muir's theme too is Scottish identity in the modern world ("Scotland 1941"). In his important autobiography, published in 1954, he portrays the lost paradise of his Orkney childhood.

Much of the heat was taken out of the linguistic debate by the growing self-confidence engendered by the Scottish independence movement in the post-war years. By 1960 Scots had become firmly established as the language of the Scottish lyric, and in place of Mac-Diarmid's linguistic purism, writers felt free to work in whichever language they chose. This new linguistic freedom also benefited Gaelic literature. Sorley MacLean (b. 1911), the most important Gaelic poet this century, deals with the momentous events of the age and its social problems against the background of the timeless rhythm of nature in his native Hebrides. MacLean is only one, albeit the most influential, of several poets who, in an effort to bridge the cultural divide between the Highlands and Lowlands and foster a sense of Scotland's identity as a whole, have enriched the country's literature by their Highland background and motifs. Edwin Morgan's Glasgow city poems and Sorley MacLean's landscape poems from Skye testify to the immense diversity of Scottish poetry today, another notable feature of which is the interplay of literature and politics, e.g. in the work of Douglas Dann.

In the 1960s a new generation of voices began to be heard. Authors such as Tom Buchan and Alan Jackson look across the Atlantic for inspiration, refusing to become too preoccupied with the recurrent, purely Scottish themes.

The contemporary Scottish scene is marked by extraordinary vitality and diversity. Young Scottish writers, especially women writers such as Carol Ann Duffy, are drawing acclaim not only in Scotland but in England too. Colloquial in its language ("Strath Scots"), their work is shaped thematically and formally by an extended concept of literature. Liz Lochhead (b. 1947) is a notable example, her poems and short prose pieces on keenly observed everyday themes, amusing, snappy, brash and brilliant all in one, exploit her mastery of current jargon and breadth of linguistic range ("Bagpipe Muzak", 1991). The link with the old oral traditional is also strong. Having lingered on, in the Highlands and Islands especially, it has since been revitalised by the topical songs of folk singers such as Hamish Henderson and Ewan MacColl. Glasgow football and street songs and the Clydeside workmen's song (Matt McGinn) are all part of this same live tradition.

Drama

One of very few Scottish theatrical productions to have created a stir in recent decades was a dramatic reconstruction of the 19th c. Highland Clearances – "The Cheviot, The Stag and the Black, Black Oil". This uninhibited mélange of traditions, forms and styles, was taken on tour in 1973 by John McGrath's theatre company "7:84", playing to audiences throughout Scotland.

Scotland has a lively music-hall tradition and a near-professional amateur theatre circuit in which the universities play a major role. Calvinist antipathy to the theatre hindered its development until into the 20th c. Even now there is no national theatre and only a handful of permanent theatres; these include Glasgow's Citizens' Theatre and Edinburgh's Lyceum and Traverse Theatre Club. But in any case the language is an insuperable barrier to international success as far as any truly authentic Scottish drama is concerned, as even J. M. Barrie (1860–1937) and James Bridie (1888–1951), whose plays were highly acclaimed in their own time, found. The impact of Scottish plays – whether by earlier dramatists such as Joe Corrie (1894–1968), Robert McLellan (b. 1907) and S. G. Smith, or playwrights of the 1970s like Bill Bryden, Roddy McMillian, Hector McMillan and others – is inevitably limited to a single small country with a barely subsidised theatrical scene, which is the main reason why ambitious producers like Bill Bryden move to London.

Prose
fiction
Lewis Grassic
Gibbon

The most important Scottish novel of the 1930s is "A Scots Quair" by Lewis Grassic Gibbon (1901–35). In the form of a trilogy each volume of which ("Sunset Song, 1932; "Cloud Howe, 1933; "Grey Granite", 1934) is centred upon a particular historic event, it tells the story of Chris Guthrie whose life takes her away from Kinraddie, a small farming community in north-east Scotland, first to the town and eventually the city. As the novel progresses Chris, who never relinquishes the memories of her farming roots and childhood home, becomes a symbol of Scotland. Her awareness of continuity with a timeless world of ordinary people infuses the novel's analysis of contemporary politics, introducing a third, mythical level complementing the personal and social.

Highland
Clearances

Neil M. Gunn

The idea of a golden age, a pre-industrial Scotland with communal values and integrated way of life, is a theme which, in the last 50 years, has been thoroughly explored in a number of novels about the Highland Clearances. In particular it is the subject of several books by Neil M. Gunn (1891–1934; "The Lost Glen", 1932; "Butcher's Broom", 1934 and "The Silver Darlings", 1941); others who have written on the same theme include Ian MacPherson ("Land of Our Fathers", 1933), Fionn MacColla ("And the Cock Crew", 1945) and Iain Crichton Smith ("Consider the Lilies", 1968). For these authors the Clearances are not just the historical reality responsible for the problems facing the Highlands today, but the root cause of Scotland's trauma as a nation and the origin of the country's loss of identity and sense of alienation.

The Highland Clearances are also the background to novels like "Greenvoe" (1972) by George Mackay Brown (b. 1921). As an Orkney writer Brown ranks second only to Edwin Muir. His accurate observations of Orkney life are set in a context of myth going back to prehistory. Eric Linklater (1899–1974) has also written about the Orkneys (e.g. "White Maa's Saga", 1929), though his stories mainly concern the present day and lack historical depth. His Magnus Meriman (in the 1934 novel of that name) is a Scottish Don Quixote and the book a satirical roman à clef in which many representatives of the Scottish Literary Renaissance appear. Linklater's best novel ("Private Angelo", 1946) is a comic portrayal of the immediate post-war period in Italy.

Muriel Spark (b. 1918) is one of the best known of present-day Scottish authors. Although regarded as a "British" writer, the Scottish background to the frequently morbid themes of her stylistically faultless novels is unmistakable (e.g. "Memento Mori", 1959; "The Ballad of Peckham Rye", 1960). In "The Prime of Miss Jean Brodie" (1961) and "The Girls of Slender Means" (1963), the character of Jean Brodie projects the claustrophobic world of an Edinburgh girls' school. Spark's brilliant autobiography ("Curriculum Vitae", 1992) traces the formative influence of Judaism and Calvinism during her Edinburgh childhood and is among the most astute of all the analyses of Scottish identity.

Muriel Spark

Calvinism is a constantly recurring topic in many Scottish novels. Hypocrisy (Parson Gibbon in L. G. Gibbon's "Sunset Song"), the doctrine of the Elect (Robin Jenkins's "Fergus Lamont"), the clergy's acquiescence in the traumatic Highland Clearances and Calvinism's life-denying image of man as a corrupt, eternally sinful being, with its warping effect on the Scottish psycho (e.g. in "Greenvoe") are among the many themes.

Calvinism

Urban man's quest for meaning and self-realisation takes different forms. Glasgow has inspired several novels in which sensitive characters in search of identity struggle against a culturally hostile, philistine environment, e.g. "A Green Tree in Gedde" (1965) by Alan Sharp (b. 1934), with stylistic echoes of James Joyce, and "The Dear Green Place" (1966) by Archie Hind (b. 1928), the autobiographical story of a "working class boy" who is determined to write a novel. In these "proletarian" novels the quest for personal fulfilment and secure values proves to be in vain. Despair engendered by failure in both love and art is likewise the eventual fate of Duncan Thaw in "Lanark" (1981) by Alasdair Gray (b. 1934). With his uninhibited, inventive use of language and obvious delight in narration, Gray weaves together the stories of Lanark, of Duncan Thaw, of Unthank and of Glasgow in a work hailed by Anthony Burgess as the most important in Scottish literature since Scott's Waverley Novels. Glasgow is also the focus of novels and short stories by James Kelman (b. 1946) who enjoys something of a cult status in the city today. For Kelman, Glasgow is a city of the unemployed and layabouts, dropouts and boozers, whose frustrations and tragedies he analyses in hard, forensic prose. Kelman's characters are prisoners in a situation without hope (e.g. "A Disaffection", 1989, and the short stories "Lean Tales" and "Greyhound for Breakfast").

Urban novels

The hankering after solidarity and a community of values and aims, is a recurrent theme in these Glasgow novels of the Thatcher era (e.g. also Jeff Torrington's "Swing, Hammer, Swing", 1991), as indeed of contemporary Scottish writing as a whole. While the world they reveal is riven by conflict, it is portrayed with immense linguistic and social vitality, avoiding cliché and patently innovative. For such a small country, Scotland's modern-day literature displays a quite extraordinary cultural and thematic diversity, embracing not only the urban working-class world of the Glaswegian writers and the middle-class Edinburgh of Muriel Spark and Joan Lingard, but also the rural landscapes of the Highlands and Islands and the country's far North-east.

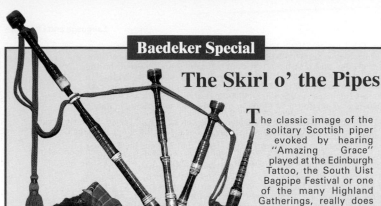

The Skirl o' the Pipes

The classic image of the solitary Scottish piper evoked by hearing "Amazing Grace" played at the Edinburgh Tattoo, the South Uist Bagpipe Festival or one of the many Highland Gatherings, really does scant justice to the instrument's history. Bagpipes in fact originated with the pastoral tribes of Asia and North Africa, and were introduced throughout Europe by the Romans in the 1st c. A.D. On the continent they were soon discarded in favour of other instruments, but in the highlands of Scotland bagpipes retained their popularity together with the Celtic harp.

As well as agile fingers and capacious lungs, pipers must surely be endowed with a passion for the pipes, a passion moreover inborn, for the sound takes some getting used to! The bag itself is made from impregnated goat's or sheep's hide and the pipes from hardwood – the harder the wood the better the tone – embellished with silver, ivory or, nowadays, white plastic. Held under the arm, the bag is kept inflated by blowing into a short mouthpiece while air is simultaneously expelled through the pipes by rhythmic pressure of the elbow. Three pipes of fixed pitch known as "borduns" emit a steady, sonorous drone. The melody is played on a fourth, flute-like pipe with six finger-holes, called the chanter. The bass note is sounded by the longer of the

Highland Games, Festivals and Folk Music

Highland Games

History

When in the 11th c. King Malcolm III needed a suitably sturdy runner to be his new personal messenger, he arranged a race from Braemar up Creag Choinnich, with the winner to receive the Baldric (an ornate belt buckle) and the royal appointment. Folk from Braemar and further afield met together to take part in contests of the kind now associated with Highland Games – pitching tree trunks ("tossing the caber"), heaving rocks ("putting the shot") and hurling hammers ("hammer throwing") – all doubtless wearing the plaid and accompanied by the skirling of pipes.

Although the exact origin of the Games lies shrouded in the mists of time, these tournament-style meetings probably began by serving a number of different purposes, martial, sporting and religious. They may well have been initiated by clan chieftains with an eye to recruitment: powerful runners make good couriers, strong men good bodyguards and hammer-throwers could propel a nail-studded flail deep three borduns, the other two being tuned higher by fifths to produce the familiar, penetrating tone. Whereas the Irish pipes can be played seated, Scottish pipers must stand or march about whilst playing because of the size of the large bordun.

The first official bagpipe school in Scotland is supposed to have been founded in about 1500 by the MacCrimmons of Boreraig on Skye. Nowadays to train as a master piper takes seven years, at the end of which the successful "graduate" is expected to be able to play by heart at least 300 classic pibrochs and laments as well as the reels and strathspeys which accompany Highland dancing. Originally pipers put their talents to purely peaceful use, for example providing entertainment at court; but from the mid 16th c. they also appeared in a military role. Wherever the Scots took up arms, the sound of the pipes would be heard. By the mid 18th c. the clans could boast generations of valiant pipers whose stirring tunes would rally their men in the heat of the skirmish and strike fear into enemy hearts. Many of these pipers were possibly taught their trade by the MacCrimmons of Skye, as suggested by a document of 1743, a piping indenture mentioning the MacCrimmons; this tradition is supported by a statement of one of Queen Victoria's pipers, Angus Mackay. But whatever the truth of the past, the MacCrimmon Piping Heritage Centre in Boreraig remains a mine of information on the history of the instrument and the MacCrimmons's bagpipe school. The master pipers of today are trained in tried and tested fashion at the Glasgow College of Piping, opened in 1945.

After Bonnie Prince Charlie's crushing defeat at Culloden in 1746, the bagpipes were proscribed, together with the wearing of the kilt and tartan, delivering a severe blow to Highland culture. But when Britain's first Highland Regiment was raised in 1757, the pipes and drums were able to sound again. In the 19th c., as successive waves of migration depopulated the Highlands and scattered tens of thousands of Scots around the world, the distinctive strains of the bagpipes experienced a real renaissance, becoming a symbol of national identity and an expression of the exiled Scot's nostalgia for his Highland home.

into enemy ranks. In time the contests became an established tradition in the Highlands where, at the annual "gathering" with its competitions, music and dancing, village measured itself against village and clan against clan.

The spectacle greeting visitors today however really goes back no further than the 19th c. when Queen Victoria with her notoriously sentimental attachment to Scotland, greatly contributed to the revival of its customs. Familiar with Highland Games from reading the novels of Sir Walter Scott, she stimulated new interest in them when, in 1848, she visited the Braemar Gathering for the first time, thus giving it her royal blessing. Among the first of the many legendary Champions of the Games was Donald Dinnie whose records remained unbroken for decades. Then at the turn of the century came A. A. Cameron, the most famous "heavie" in the annals of the Games; in 1986 "Big Bill" Anderson celebrated 30 years as "Champ". Today Highland Games are held at more than 100 different locations in Scotland. The summer 1994 calendar published by sponsors Glenfiddich listed no less than 54 such Gatherings in the Highlands and Islands, starting with Poolewe Mini Games on June 3rd and ending with the Invercharron Highland Games on September 17th at Ardgay/Bonar Bridge.

Highland Games, Festivals and Folk Music

Braemar Royal Highland Gathering

The most famous of the Highland Games is the Braemar Royal Highland Gathering held on the first weekend in September, a highlight of which is the tossing of the legendary Braemar caber – a tree trunk over 19ft/6m long weighing 145lb/66kg. Just lifting and balancing the caber against the shoulder requires great strength and skill. But that is the least of it! A successful throw requires a fast, controlled run-up and abrupt halt before pitching the caber forward and upward with both hands. Distance is of secondary importance. What matters is for the "toss" to be completed in the approved manner, the caber somersaulting through 180° before coming to rest, ideally in the "twelve o'clock" position, i.e. pointing straight ahead of the thrower. Few competitors are 100% successful, but those who are are greeted with thunderous applause. Tugs-of-war, gymkhana events, sheep dog trials, livestock shows and markets, piping and Highland dancing competitions in various categories – pibroch (pinnacle of the solo piper's art based on traditional classic melodies), marches, strathspeys and reels as well as the Highland fling (once danced on a targe) and the sword dance (during which the dancer's nimble feet must not disturb the crossed swords laid on the ground) – all go to make the Highland Gathering a colourful cacophony of sound, a folk spectacle and fête at the centre of which are those kilt-clad heavyweights. Though certainly not to everyone's taste, anyone who enjoys this kind of jamboree, rustic, vibrant and noisy, will find it all good fun.

Nowadays Highland Games are held in places far removed from the Highlands of Scotland; the Fair of Blair (Blairgowrie Highland Games), revived in 1974, has a counterpart halfway round the world – the Santa Rosa Highland Gathering in California. Also, today's muscular competitors include women as well as men. Nor do they come just from the Highlands, or even from Scotland; Australia, New Zealand and America provide many participants and many champions too, especially at the larger, better-known gatherings like the two-day Argyllshire Highland Games held in Oban in August (where the Oban Ball is the high-point of the Highland season) and, of course, the Royal Highland Gathering at Braemar, not far from Balmoral. Queen Elizabeth II will allow nothing to keep her away from the Gathering which she has attended every autumn for the last 50 years. The race up Creag Choinnich instituted by Malcolm III almost a millennium ago is still the principal attraction of the Games.

Feast days and festivals

Traditional feast days

Scotland abounds in traditional feast days and colourful festivals, many of them Pictish, Scandinavian or Celtic in origin. Religious festivals, part of the seasonal cycle, are the backbone of a crowded calendar stretching from Hogmanay (December 31st, seeing in the New Year with helpings of haggis and much merrymaking) and Up Helly-Aa (late Jan.) through Imbolc (Feb. 1st), Beltane (May 1st), Lugnasad (Aug. 1st) and Samhuinn (Nov. 1st) to the Feast of Martinmas and Yuletide. Observance of many of these festivals lapsed during the 18th and 19th c. but the last few decades have seen a remarkable revival – a sign not only of a more leisured society and the growing significance of tourism, but also Scotland's heightened nationalism. It would be quite impractical to list all the festivals here, there are as many as 125 in June alone! The Scottish Tourist Board publishes a useful brochure called "Events in Scotland". Alternatively visitors can make enquiries locally "on the ground" to discover what is on. Among the major events in the Scottish calendar however are:

Burns Night

January 25th: The birthday of Scotland's national poet Robert Burns (see Famous People) is marked by an ever-increasing number of gatherings of his many fans for a celebratory feast known as Burns's

Supper – a custom which began in his birthplace Alloway in 1801 and since 1859 has spread throughout Scotland and further afield wherever there are Scots. The supper itself consists of Scotch broth or cock-a-leekie soup and, of course, the haggis, subject of a eulogy in verse by the poet (see Baedeker Special, "Chieftan o' the Puddin-race!"); it is traditionally followed by toasts to the head of state, the immortal memory of the bard himself and finally the guests. Afterwards there is singing, usually a selection from the more than 300 songs written or adapted by Burns. Naturally no Burns's Supper would be complete without a rendering of "Auld Lang Syne" at the close.

January 31st: Held in Lerwick in the Shetlands the midwinter festival of Up Helly-Aa rekindles the islands's Viking past with the ceremonial burning of a Viking ship followed by suitably Nordic celebrations.

Up Helly-Aa

Two traditional football games known as the Boys' and Men's Ba' Games take place on Christmas and New Year's Day in Kirkwall in the Orkneys. Both start from Kirk Green and are played in the streets with the onlookers participating.

Yuletide

Between June and August a series of festivals take place in the Scottish Border towns the centrepiece of which is the ceremony of riding the marches. These equestrian celebrations are a relic of the ancient custom of re-marking the local boundaries each year. The Common Ridings or Ridings of the Marches have a prescribed ritual and costumed riders, but are usually combined with musical festivals, agricultural shows, processions, parades and funfairs. Among the many events of this kind are the West Linton Festival and Saturday Rideout (beginning of June), the Hawick Common Riding (mid June), the Selkirk Common Riding (mid June), the Melrose Festival (third week in June), the Peebles Riding of the Marches and Beltane Festival (mid June), the Galashiels Gathering (end of June), Duns Reivers Week (first week of July), the Callants' Festival in Jedburgh (first two weeks of July), Kelso's Yetholm Ride and Civic Week (mid June), the Langholm Common Riding (mid July) and Coldstream Civic Week (first week in August).

Common Ridings

The Edinburgh International Festival, founded in 1947, is still a dominant force in Scottish cultural life. Held in the last three weeks of August, it is an international showcase for the best in European and British culture. Important though the "official" festival is, it comes close to being upstaged by the so-called "fringe" festival attracting more than 1000 different theatre companies, cabaret artists, comedians, musical groups and a variety of other performers, all vying for the public's favour. The Fringe Firsts (prizes awarded by the Scotsman newspaper for the best theatrical production) are highly sought after by troupes from all over Britain and even overseas. A relative newcomer to the festival scene but now very popular is the Glasgow May Festival, established in the 1980s. Local in orientation, it aims to further the traditions of the workers' movement and its culture e.g. by fostering cultural interchange both national and international. St Andrews has a biennial festival which takes place in mid February, with music, theatre, cabaret, a film festival and art exhibitions.

Festivals

Many coastal towns have festivals associated with fishing or the sea, most notably Eyemouth's Herring Festival (end of July/beginning of August) and the Fisherman's Walk in Musselburgh (beginning of September), a parade marking the end of the fishing season even though the last herring boat left Musselburgh long ago. City Festivals are held in Dundee (July) and Stirling (end of July/beg. of August) with hundreds of events including jazz, folk, theatre, film and sport. Every year between April and October Pitlochry holds a big theatre festival. In June Kirkwall in the Orkneys hosts the annual St Magnus Festival, a six-day international gala featuring excellent programmes of music, literature, theatre, film and the arts in general. Last but by no means least, in August there is the colourful St Andrews Lammas Fair, one of the oldest fairs of its kind in Scotland with roots going back to the Middle Ages.

Folk music

Live
tradition

The solitary kilt-clad piper silhouetted against magnificent Highland scenery, and the stirring sound of the pipes and drums at the Edinburgh Military Tattoo, are only one strand in the rich fabric of "Scottish music". Less familiar perhaps, but no less part of that fabric, are Scotland's traditional ballads, songs passed down orally from generation to generation, new songs, folk bands and innovative groups with their fusion of Scottish-Celtic music and rock, pop or jazz. The image of the piper, aural as well as visual, does nevertheless have a special significance. The Highlander with his Great Highland Pipes represents the romantic Scotland, the Scotland which, at the beginning of the 19th c., Sir Walter Scott (see Famous People) created in his historical novels. With Scott the Highlands ceased to be de facto wild and became romantically wild, the Highlander no longer savage but noble and loyal. Scott's anthology "The Minstrelsy of the Scottish Borders", secured his place alongside the greatest of all Scottish songwriters Robert Burns (see Famous People), who supplied new words for more than 300 traditional Scottish melodies including "My Luve's like a Red, Red Rose" and "A Man's a Man for a' That". By singing the praises of "plain folk", farmers and farm labourers, and by erecting a memorial in verse to the loyal Jacobite support for Bonnie Prince Charlie, Burns delivered an encomium striking a chord in every heart: to the workers' movement he was the hard drinking dissident and outspoken critic of Church and state; to the moneyed landowning aristocracy he was the minstrel of Jacobite sympathies; to the small Lowland farmer he was the poet of the simple, rural life; and to the Highlander he was the high priest of Highland culture. Together with James Macpherson the "translator" of Ossian, Burns and Scott created a Scottish past, a past moreover which, musically speaking, captured the imagination of Europe. Beethoven, Rossini, Mendelssohn, Chopin, Schumann and Shostakovich all took inspiration from Burns's songs. In Scotland itself in the 19th and 20th centuries, folk music ran the risk of becoming caught up in the prevailing "Highland nostalgia". But the Celtic Renaissance at the end of the 19th c. together with the vitality of the workers' movement and, in due course, the folk revival of the 1960s, not only restored continuity with, and breathed new life into, the folk tradition but also gave Scottish folk music new shape and fresh direction.

Traditional
musical
instruments

The National Mod, a festival designed to foster Gaelic culture, inaugurated in 1892, is one place where it is possible to hear Scotland's oldest instrument, the little Celtic harp (clarsach). Introduced in the 9th c., it had almost totally disappeared by the 18th, before being "rediscovered" at the end of the 19th c. The leading performers on the harp today are a group called Sileas. Most widespread of all the traditional instruments is the fiddle, which has experienced a notable renaissance, especially in the Shetlands. Next of course come the pipes, or more precisely the Great Highland Pipes (see Baedeker Special, "The Skirl o' the Pipes"), played either as a solo instrument or in a pipe band. As the pinnacle of the piper's art the pibroch, a slow air consisting of theme and elaboration, is dubbed ceol mor (great music) while marches and dance music – strathpeys, reels and jigs – are known as ceol beag (little music). Mouth music or lilting is music without instruments, the rhythmic stringing together of nonsense syllables. If for dancing it is known as puirt a beul, otherwise canntaireachd or simply diddling (fiddle or pipe tunes).

On parade at the Braemar Royal Highland Gathering

"Little music" is the music of the traditional ceilidh, the informal Scottish get-together, an evening of music, singing and dancing with everyone joining in.

Ceilidh

Scottish songs and ballads fall into three categories: Gaelic, English and Scots Lallan songs. Gaelic songs were systematically suppressed following the defeat at Culloden in 1746. Scottish and English-language songs were elevated to literature by Burns and Scott, while the Highland and Lowland ballads were collected by Harvard professor Francis James Child. His five-volume anthology "The English and Scottish Popular Ballads" (1882–98) is the bible of the órain mhór (muckle or "great" songs), multi-verse ballads, originally sung by itinerant folk singers, of which Jeannie Robertson was one of the finest recent interpreters. The songs include the bothy ballads of North-east Scotland describing the life of labourers on the land. The cultural awareness stimulated by the workers' movement inspired a new generation of folk song collectors and historians as well as musicians who wrote and performed their own topical songs. Best known among the latter are Ewan McColl (1915–89), whose "Dirty Old Town" has become a popular classic, Hamish Henderson (b. 1919), composer of the "alternative" Scottish national anthem "Freedom Come All Ye", and Norman Buchan and Peter Hall who, in 1973, published their collection "The Scottish Folksinger". The folk revival of the 1960s was heavily influenced by the American civil rights movement, an important consequence of which was that renewed interest in old songs was accompanied by the writing of many new ones, enriching the repertoires of groups such as the immensely successful Corries – one of whom wrote "The Flowers of the Forest" – and the McCalmans and of singers and song-writers like Ian Mackintosh, Hamish Imlach, Archie Fisher and in particular Brian McNeill and Dick Gaughan. Hamish Henderson's "Freedom Come All Ye" is a prime example of the new

Songs and ballads

generation of "protest" songs, socio-political commentaries on the past and present condition of the country and its people. These songs, written in Scottish English or Lallan, aim to hasten the coming of better times in Scotland and around the world. Henderson sings of the "winds of change" blowing over (not only) Scotland, sweeping away those responsible for exploitation and war and heralding a new dawn in which, with militarism banished, poverty will be unknown in a multi-cultural society from which none will be driven or feel the need to escape.

Folk bands

In the 1960s some folk bands such as the internationally-acclaimed Tannahill Weavers and Scotland's currently most successful folk group the Battleship Band, began to feature the bagpipes in their music. This willingness to mix different musical genres is typical of the contemporary Scottish scene: Run Rig blend Gaelic songs and traditional elements with rock; the Proclaimers, singing in broad Scots, marry Country and Western with early folk-revival; Big Country are a rock band whose Scottish roots also find expression in a leavening of folk. One of the most interesting combinations is the Scottish-Irish group Boys of the Lough: Aly Bain is currently the best-known performer on the Shetland fiddle, Cathal O'Connell represents the (Northern) Irish vocal tradition, and Christy O'Leary plays the Irish bagpipes or uillean pipes. While maintaining Scotland's long musical tradition, groups such as these are also a lively, critical, sometimes politically committed voice in the assertion of Scottish identity. They have a following which extends far beyond the folk clubs. When the Battlefield Band put "Forward with Scotland's Past" on their banners they spoke for a whole generation of young folk musicians.

Quotations

Shall I tire you with a description of this unfruitful country? where I must lead you over their hills all brown with heath, or their valleys scarce able to feed a rabbet? Man alone seems to be the only creature who has arrived to the naturall size in this poor soil; every part of the country presents the same dismall landscape, no grove nor brook lend their musick to cheer the stranger, or make the inhabitants forget their poverty; yet with all these disadvantages to call him down to humility, a scotchman is one of the prowdest things alive.

Oliver Goldsmith
(1730–74)

Letter to Robert Bryanton, September 26th 1753

The doctor accompanied us to Kingsburgh, which is called a mile farther; but the computation of Sky has no connection whatever with real distance.

I was highly pleased to see Dr. Johnson safely arrived at Kingsburgh, and received by the hospitable Mr. Macdonald, who, with a most respectful attention, supported him into the house. Kingsburgh was completely the figure of a gallant Highlander exhibiting "the graceful mien, and manly looks", which our popular Scotch song has justly attributed to that character. He had his Tartan plaid thrown about him, a large blue bonnet with a knot of black ribband like a cockade, a brown short coat of a kind of duffil, a Tartan waistcoat with gold buttons and gold button-holes, a bluish philibeg, and Tartan hose, He had jet black hair tied behind, and was a large stately man, with a steady sensible countenance.

James Boswell
(1740–95)

The Journal of a Tour to the Hebrides with Samuel Johnson, (1786)

Breathes there a man with soul so dead,
Who never to himself hath said,
This is my own, my native land!
Whose heart hath ne'er within him burn'd
As home his footsteps he hath turn'd
From wandering on a foreign strand!

Sir Walter Scott
(1771–1832)

The Lay of the Last Minstrel, 1805

Old Edinburgh would not be what it is if it weren't for its haunted houses. Anyone who has walked up the High Street will possibly have wondered whether he should regard the fog hanging above the houses as a city that has vanished or the grey town as solidified sediment deposited by fog. The feeling exists that this is a fortress in which a ghosts' army would probably try to put up their last stand, when the rest of the world had taken the decision many years ago to finish once and for all with witches, elves, imps, sprites, poltergeists and hob-goblins. What is true of the whole country is true of the capital; along with Puritanism and the steam engine, old national superstitions remain in force. You will meet them everywhere you go. Of course, the Scots have become so refined about them that books and newspaper columns are no longer filled with the old tales and gloom of the Middle Ages, but you do not have to look around you for long to see just how thin that bed-cover is beneath which these favourite figures sleep. Ghosts seem to be a product of the country here.

Theodor Fontane
German writer
(1819–98)

In fact, I would like to see that person who would ride at night past Scone and Dunsinan, the open countryside and fields of stone in the county of Inverness without encountering any ghosts. For miles there is not a tree, not a shrub. The Grampians to the right, a mountain stream to the left, nothing audible other than the rushing water and horses' hooves. Mountain shadows fall across the path and a ptarmigan flies off. Anyone who can make such a journey without seeing Macbeth's witches emerging from a rock face, has made his own judgement. The world of spirits is closed to him.

All Scottish writers have joined wholeheartedly in the superstitions of their fellow-countrymen. Burns, it could be argued, ridiculed the people's fear of ghosts with some exaggerated jokes in "Tam O'Shanter", but you know what to make of those jokes; it was alright for him in daylight, but at night he would whistle and sing on the lonely wooded paths.

Jenseits des Tweeds, 1860. Copyright Insel Verlag, Frankfurt am Main 1989.

Robert Louis
Stevenson
(1850–94)

There is no special loveliness in that grey country, with its rainy, sea-belt archipelago; its fields of dark mountains; its unsightly places, black with coal; its treeless, sour, unfriendly-looking cornlands; its quaint, grey, castled city, where the bells clash of a Sunday, and the wind squalls, and the salt showers fly and beat. I do not even know if I desire to live there; but let me hear, in some far land, a kindred voice sing out, "O why left I my hame?" and it seems at once as if no beauty under the kind heavens, and no society of the wise and good, can repay me for my absence from my country. And though I think I would rather die elsewhere, yet in my heart of hearts I long to be buried among good Scots clods. I will say it fairly, it grows on me with every year: there are no stars so lovely as Edinburgh streetlamps.

The Silverado Squatters, 1883

Baedeker's
Great Britain
(1899)

Glasgow specialises in the building of ships, the largest of ocean-going steamers as well as fast, pleasantly-appointed river steamers on American lines. Here in 1763 Glaswegian-born James Watt constructed the improved steam-engine of the type still in general use today. In Glasgow in 1812 Henry Bell launched the first steamer to ply the Clyde between Glasgow and Greenock. Two thirds of all British steamers are built or fitted out with engines here. Of the many factories in or near Glasgow the most notable are: St Rollox Chemical Works, a vast establishment covering 6 hectares, with a 130m high chimney which is visible all around (near by, rising even higher by another 12m, is the Townsend factory chimney, certainly the world's tallest); the Steel Company of Scotland's works in Newtown (railway from Central Station in 15 minutes) and Blochairn; and the shipbuilding yards in Govan. The Singer Manufacturing Co. of New York (makers of sewing machines), has splendid factories in Kilbowie (20 minutes by train from Queen Street Station). Glasgow's other principal manufactures and branches of industry are iron goods, cotton and woollen fabrics, yarn, pipes and boilers, printed cottons, glass and earthenware, bleach, Turkey red dyes, muslin weaving and carpets. The coal trade is also very important.

Glasgow is one of the best administered cities in Great Britain. The gas and waterworks, trams, parks, etc. are controlled by the municipal corporation, which has also erected model homes and public baths and wash-houses and has in every respect rendered outstanding service in regard to the health of the city. Ample supplies of excellent water come from Loch Katrine 42 miles away. The pipeline cost almost £2½ million sterling and is about to be extended still further.

Ruskin truly observes that every bright boy in Edinburgh is influenced by the sight of the Castle. So is the child of Dunfermline, by its noble Abbey, the Westminster of Scotland, founded early in the eleventh century (1070) by Malcolm Canmore and his Queen Margaret, Scotland's patron saint. The ruins of the great monastery and of the palace where kings were born still stand and there, too, is Pittencrieff Glen, embracing Queen Margaret's shrine and the ruins of King Malcolm's Tower. [. . .] Fortunate, indeed, the child who first sees the light in that romantic town, which occupies high ground three miles north of the Firth of Forth, overlooking the sea, with Edinburgh in sight to the south, and to the north the peaks of the Ochils. All is still redolent of the mighty past when Dunfermline was both nationally and religiously the capital of Scotland.

Andrew Carnegie
(1835–1918)

Autobiography (1920)

**Sights
from A to Z**

Information

Many of Scotland's famous castles, fortresses and historic sites are now administered by two independent bodies, the National Trust for Scotland (NTS) and Historic Scotland (HS), although they are both ultimately the responsibility of the Department of the Environment. The guide will state which organisation runs a particular site, but visitors who are taking a long holiday in Scotland would be well advised to acquire a Great Heritage Pass or a Scottish Explorer Ticket. (See Practical Information, Castles and Historic Sites.)

Aberdeen   G 4

Region: Grampian
Population: 215,000

★ Flower city and
oil metropolis

Aberdeen, "The Flower of Scotland", lies in a picturesque spot on the North Sea coast between the Dee and the Don. The capital of the Grampian Region (see entry) is Scotland's biggest fishing port and has, since the end of the 1960s when oil was first discovered in the North Sea, developed into an important centre for Europe's offshore oil industry. Even in the early days of the oil boom Aberdeen was an obvious choice as offshore capital of Europe, not just because of its proximity to the oil fields in the North Sea, but also for its central position on the eastern coastal plain, its infrastructure with good road and rail links and also its plentiful supply of labour.

Aberdeen, Scotland's third-biggest city, whose name derives from the juxtaposition of "aber" meaning "mouth" and the combination of Dee and Don, has a rich cultural tradition plus modern facilities and a range of industries. The port is an important commercial and shopping centre with many sights of interest and a number of well-tended parks and gardens. Visitors will find some 2 miles/3km of sandy beach, the Beach Leisure Centre swimming pool with wave machine, superb golf courses, performances of ballet, plays and opera in His Majesty's Theatre, concerts by top-class orchestras in the Music Hall, experimental drama productions in the Arts Centre and Theatre as well as a variety of arts festivals during the summer months. The silver-grey granite from nearby quarries gives the city a distinctive character, although the last quarry in Rubislaw was closed in 1971. St Machar's, the oldest granite cathedral in the world, was built with stone from Rubislaw. When the sun shines, the mica in the granite sparkles, hence "Silver City" has become a popular description for Aberdeen. "Flower City" refers to the splendid flower beds and displays, which have repeatedly brought the city success in the "Britain in Bloom" competitions.

Communications

Aberdeen's airport serves all the main regional airports in Britain and lies 6 miles/9.6km north-west of the city in Dyce (Bus No. 27). InterCity rail services from Aberdeen station in Guild Street serve Glasgow and Edinburgh via Dundee (see entries) with connections to London. There are also direct trains to Inverness (see entry). From Guild Street bus station good bus services connect Aberdeen with Dundee, Edinburgh, Glasgow (Citylink) and the whole Grampian Region. Ferries to the Orkney and Shetland Islands (see entries) leave regularly from Jamieson's Quay.

History

The exact date when the city was founded is not clear, but it is known that St Machar established a Celtic chapel here in the 6th c., that Alexander I made Aberdeen his main residence in the 11th c. and in a charter of 1179 William "the Lion" granted the burghers the rights of a "free hanse". The famous bridge over the Don to the east of the "crook" in the river was started in 1285 but this crossing point which spans the river with a steep Gothic arch was not finished until 1320. After the Aberdonians supported Robert the Bruce (see Famous People) in the War of Independence at the beginning of

◀ *Inveraray Castle, Highland seat of the Dukes of Argyll*

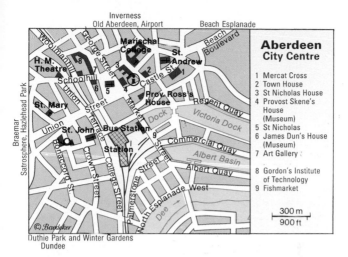

Inverness
Old Aberdeen, Airport   Beach Esplanade

Aberdeen City Centre

1 Mercat Cross
2 Town House
3 St Nicholas House
4 Provost Skene's House (Museum)
5 St Nicholas
6 James Dun's House (Museum)
7 Art Gallery
8 Gordon's Institute of Technology
9 Fishmarket

300 m
900 ft

© Baedeker

Braemar
Satrosphere, Hazlehead Park

Duthie Park and Winter Gardens
Dundee

the 14th c., they received as a reward hunting land and a coat-of-arms with the motto "Bon Accord". During the industrial revolution, Aberdeen saw the construction of textile factories and paper mills and the clippers from the Footdee wharf came to be regarded as the fastest sailing ships of their time. Steam-driven fishing boats gave the fishing industry a new impetus and large fleets of trawlers based in Aberdeen went in search of herring, cod and haddock. Two town planners by the name of Archibald Simpson and John Smith created the now unmistakeable character of the ambitious "Granite City", constructing administrative buildings and housing around Union Street from the local granite. But 1969 was perhaps the most important year in Aberdeen's history when "Montrose Field", the first British oil field, was opened. By 1995, almost 50 oil and gas fields were in production and this brought a massive boom to the local economy as many oil and gas-related companies moved to Aberdeen to supply and maintain the North Sea oil platforms.

Sights

Given the shortage of car parks, it is fortunate that central Aberdeen can easily be visited on foot. Start the tour north of the harbour at the east end of busy Union Street, in Castle Street which, as Castlegate, was the centre of Aberdeen in the olden days and is today still the focal point of the town.

Castle Street

The castle itself no longer exists, but the tower of the Tolbooth (14th c.), formerly the town hall and prison, is the city's oldest building.

Tolbooth

Diagonally opposite and adorned with a white unicorn stands the Mercat Cross, a medieval symbol of the town's right to hold a market. On the town cross which was built in 1686 by Aberdeen's guild of merchants, the portrait medallions show the heads of the ten Stuart monarchs from James I through to James VII, Charles I, Charles II and Mary Stuart.

Mercat Cross

Only a few yards away stood the town residence of the Earl Marischal from whose window in 1562 Mary Stuart (see Famous People) is said to have watched the execution of her cousin and admirer Sir John Gordon of Findlater. He had threatened Mary with a forced marriage but later found himself a victim of the "Aberdeen Maiden", a Scottish variation of the guillotine.

Castlegate – Aberdeen town centre since medieval times

Peacock Artspace	The Peacock Gallery exhibits works by local and international artists (open: Mon.–Sat. 9.30am–5pm).
St Andrew's Cathedral	To the north in King Street stands the sandstone episcopal church of St Andrew which was first consecrated in 1816. Built in Perpendicular style, it was one of the first creations of city architect Archibald Simpson (open: May–Sept. Mon.–Sat. 10am–4pm).
Union Street Town House	Some notable granite edifices by the civic architects Archibald Simpson, William Smith and James Matthew line Union Street, Aberdeen's busy main street. It celebrated its 200th anniversary in 1994. As well as all the modern shops, pubs and shopping arcades along the "Silver Mile", the corner with Broad Street is overlooked by the Victorian-style Town House, which was built between 1868 and 1874.
★**Provost Skene's House** Open: Mon.–Sat. 10am–5pm	Follow Broad Street northwards and then fork left along the short Guest Row to Provost Skene's House just past the modern Tourist Information Centre. Sir George Skene of Rubislaw was a prosperous merchant whose wealth was derived from trade with what is now the Baltic port of Gdansk. He was provost from 1676 to 1685. His home, the oldest standing residence in Aberdeen, now houses the Municipal Museum. Several floors contain locally-excavated artefacts and these help to document the town's history from the Cromwell era to Victorian times. The plasterwork in the old bedroom (1676) and the painted wooden ceilings (17th c.) in the picture gallery are of note. The "Maiden" Guillotine on the upper floor is a reminder of Aberdeen's darker side.
★**Marischal College**	On the other side of Broad Street stands the Marischal College. Founded in 1593 by George Keith, the 5th Earl Marischal of Dunnottar, it is the second-largest granite building in the world after Spain's El Escorial. Keith sought a Protestant counterbalance to the Catholic King's College in Old Aberdeen.

Work started on the present college in 1837 with the 235ft/72m Mitchell Tower. Archibald Simpson supplied the plans for the huge four-winged edifice but the Neo-Gothic west front was designed by A. Marshall MacKenzie and was built between 1890 and 1906. The Marischal Museum in the college possesses a superb anthropological collection, including exhibits from Egypt, Nigeria, Papua New Guinea, Hawaii and Tibet. However, the main emphasis in the museum is on the north-east of Scotland (open: Mon.–Fri. 10am–5pm, Sun. 2–5pm).

By the time the Cutty Sark Tall Ships race returns to Aberdeen Harbour in 1997, Aberdeen will have a brand new Maritime Museum. The new museum, which will open in spring 1997, will be 5 times the size of the present development in Provost Ross's House, after a £4 million re-development. The new exhibitions will highlight the drama of the North Sea industries: offshore oil, fishing and shipping. The vast scope of the museum's fine collections of models, paintings and objects will be seen to good effect. A new dimension will be available through extensive use of multi-media displays, including touch-screen consoles, computer visual databases, audio visual theatre and hands-on exhibits.

★**New Aberdeen Maritime Museum**

For further information telephone John Edwards on: (01224) 646333.

The biggest parish church in Scotland is St Nicholas in Back Wynd, but it is better known as East and West Churches as during the Reformation it was divided into two separate chapels. The West Church, which was built between 1741 and 1755 in Renaissance style under the direction of the church architect James Gribbs, contains four wall tapestries and some fine wooden carvings dating from the 17th c., while, beneath the East Church, badly damaged by fire in the 19th c., lies an old crypt, St Mary's Chapel (c. 1420). During the 17th c. it was used as a prison for women thought to be witches. St John's Chapel, part of which originated in the 12th c., is now dedicated to the oil industry.

★St Nicholas

The neighbouring Shopping Centre, as it is known, offers a wide selection of shops and is a welcome refuge in bad weather.

Shopping centre

James Dun's House, a Georgian-style building, lies to the west of the town centre on Schoolhill and is used for touring art exhibitions (open: Mon.–Sat. 10am–5pm).

James Dun's House

On the north side of Schoolhill stands the Neo Classical Art Gallery which was built in 1884 to a design by A. Marshall MacKenzie. It houses a comprehensive collection of 17th–20th c. paintings.

★**Art Gallery**

Open:
Mon.–Sat.
10am–5pm
Thur. until 8pm
Sun. 2–5pm

Among the most famous are portraits by Raeburn and works by William Turner ("Ely Cathedral", 1796), William Daniell ("Dunnottar Castle", c. 1800), Dante Gabriel Rossetti ("Mariana", 1870), Ford Madox Brown ("The Romans Build Manchester", c. 1879), Ben Nicholson ("Still Life, March 14–47", 1947) and David Hockney ("Blue Guitar No. 1", 1976). Impressionists such as Monet, Sisley, Bonnard, Pissaro and Renoir are also represented. Scottish artists with work displayed here include William Dyce ("Titian's First Essay in Colour", 1857), Thomas Faed ("Highland Mary", 1857), John Philip ("A Scottish Fair", 1848), Allan Ramsay ("Miss Janet Shairp", 1750), Charles Rennie Mackintosh ("Berberis", 1915) and other representatives of the Glasgow School. George Jameson (1589–1644) also has works exhibited here. Jameson was Scotland's first portrait painter and his studio was situated nearby. Sculptures by Barbara Hepworth and Jacob Epstein are on display in the well-lit entrance hall. The museum possesses interesting collections of British silver, glass and ceramics.

Market Street leads down to the harbour which provides sufficient depth for large ocean-going vessels up to Victoria and Upper Dock. At the eastern end of the harbour complex, the huge tanks serve to demonstrate the economic significance of North Sea oil. The fish market, between Commercial Quay and Albert Basin, opens on weekdays at 4am. Allow plenty of time for a visit as the fish auction lasts until 7.30am.

Port

Fish market

Aberdeen

Footdee

Images of times past still remain at the eastern end of the harbour. The Footdee (pronounced "Fittie") cottages near Pocra Quay were built at the beginning of the 19th c. by local fishermen.

Satrosphere

At no. 19 Justice Mill Lane near the western end of Union Street stands a centre for science and technology where visitors can test for themselves some of the laws of science and nature (open: Apr.–mid Oct. Mon., Wed.–Sat. 10am–5pm, Sun. 1.30–5pm; mid Oct–Mar. Mon., Wed.–Fri. 10am–4pm, Sat. 10am–5pm, Sun. 1.30–5pm).

★Old Aberdeen

Up until the last century, medieval Old Aberdeen in the area around St Machar's Cathedral had its own market charter. Today it has a host of protected buildings, the oldest of which dates from the 16th c. and the quarter has become a popular meeting place for students who frequent the pubs and restaurants near the university.

King's College

The Catholic King's College in the High Street received its charter from King James IV. This seat of learning was founded in 1495 by Bishop William Elphinstone. Union with the Protestant Marischal College followed in 1860. The latter was a centre for the natural sciences, while the former was an arts stronghold. One of the college's identifying features is its huge tower (1633) and an elegant stone dome. Apart from St Giles (see Edinburgh), it is the only remaining dome of its kind in Scotland. A stone replica of the imperial crown of Charlemagne sits on top of the dome. The oak choir stalls and the wooden ceiling in the chapel (c. 1505) are preserved in their original form. Portraits of the Stuart monarchs, similar to those around the Mercat Cross, can be seen here, but they are carved out of wood.

Old Town House
Cruickshank
Botanic Gardens

At the end of High Street stands the Georgian Old Town House (1788). It now houses a branch library. Follow the nearby Chanonry further north to the botanical gardens on the left. Among the plants on display are some interesting alpine and sub-tropical collections. There is also an arboretum and a delightful water garden (open: all the year round Mon.–Fri. 9am–4.30pm, May to Sept. also Sat. and Sun. 2–5pm).

★St Machar's
Cathedral

The Cathedral of St Machar is thought to have been constructed about 1136 on the site of a Celtic chapel (581) built by St Machar (died c. 594). Consecrated about 1440 by Bishop Leighton, the most striking features of this granite edifice are the two west towers with their sandstone spires. These were completed between 1518 and 1530 under Bishop Dunbar, who was also responsible for the nave's splendid oak ceiling and its coats-of-arms. Both Leighton and Dunbar are buried in the cathedral (open: daily, 9am–5pm).

Seaton Park
Brig o'Balgownie

A walk through Seaton Park down to Brig o'Balgownie is well worth the effort. This bridge, the oldest in Scotland, was built on the orders of Robert Bruce (see Famous People) and was restored in 1607. From 1329 and for the next 500 years, it served as the Don's main crossing point. Lord Byron, who went to school in Aberdeen for a short time, referred affectionately to the single span bridge in the tenth chapter of his "Don Juan".

★Duthie Park and
Winter Gardens

Riverside Drive leads south of the harbour by the banks of the Dee to Duthie Park. This park is famous for one of the largest Winter Gardens in the world and also for much-acclaimed flower beds. One hill is devoted entirely to roses (open: daily, 9.30am until dusk).

Brig o'Dee

Follow the Dee upstream as far as the seven-arched Brig o'Dee. Commissioned by Bishop Dunbar it was built between 1520 and 1527. It is decorated with coats-of-arms and inscriptions.

Surroundings

Newburgh

About 13 miles/20.8km north of the River Ythan estuary lies the fishing village of Newburgh. A pearl found in one of the local mussels was incorporated into the Scottish crown.

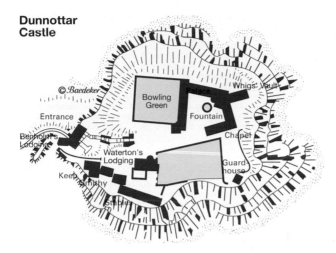

Dunnottar Castle

Bowling Green

Whigs' Vault

Palace

Entrance

Fountain

Benholm's Lodging

Chapel

Waterton's Lodging

Guard house

Keep

Smithy

Stables

© *Baedeker*

To Arbroath via Stonehaven and Montrose

The fishing port of Stonehaven (pop. 9300) some 15 miles/24km south of Aberdeen on the border between the Highlands and Lowlands is a popular holiday resort that can offer some fine cliff walks. Sea angling is another popular pastime among locals and holidaymakers alike.

Stonehaven

Just under 1½ miles/2.4km south of Stonehaven stands Dunnottar Castle. The dramatic ruins were chosen by Franco Zeffirelli for his film of "Hamlet". The imposing castle is surrounded on three sides by water and sheltered on the land side by a gap in the cliffs. The L-shaped belfry dating from the 14th c. is well preserved. The prefix "dun" indicates that the site was used by the Picts (see Art History). The massive gatehouse and the four-winged palace with a completely restored drawing room and chapel give at least an idea of the original size of the fortress, which was for many years reckoned to be impregnable. During 1685 the infamous Whig's Vault was used to incarcerate 167 Covenanters, including 45 women, for two months. The bakery, the stables and the vaulting in the kitchen are also of interest. One of the most important events in Scottish history took place here in 1652. While the castle was under siege by Cromwell's army, the royal regalia of Scotland were smuggled out by the wife of the priest of Kinneff (6½ miles/10.4km to the south). A monument records her part in this heroic event.

★**Dunnottar Castle**

Open:
Easter–Oct. Mon.–Sat. 9am–6pm,
Sun. 2–5pm;
Nov.–Easter Mon.–Fri. 9am until dusk

The distillery at Fettercairn, 12½ miles/20km south-west of Stonehaven, is one of the oldest whisky distilleries in Scotland. Guided tours of the factory provide background information on the production of scotch (see Baedeker Special, "Scotch Whisky") and also the history of the Mearns (open: May–Sept. Mon.–Sat. 10am–4.30pm).

Fettercairn
Distillery

In 1829 Sir John Gladstone acquired the splendid mansion (1809) that lies half a mile (1km) north of Fettercairn (B974). It thus became the Gladstone family home with William Gladstone, who was four times British prime minister during the reign of Queen Victoria, the most famous resident. Little has changed "below stairs" in the servants' quarters and much can be gleaned about life in Victorian times from a tour around the kitchen, wash-room and bakery. A self-supporting staircase leads "upstairs" to the ele-

★Fasque House

gant chambers that were used by the prime minister (open: May-Sept. daily 11am–5.30pm).

Edzell Castle and ★Garden

Follow the B966 south towards Brechin. Six miles/9.6km north of the town stands the seat of the Lindsays of Glenesk. A closer look is worthwhile not just for the castle's fortifications but also for the marvellous 16th c. Renaissance gardens that were laid out in 1604 by Sir David Lindsay. In the summer a colourful display of blooms in the colours of the Lindsay coat-of-arms decorates the red enclosure walls. A Neo-Gothic summer house and an attractive ruined 17th c. bath house are among the delights of the garden (HS; open: Apr.–Sept. Mon.–Sat. 9.30am–6.30pm; Sun. 2–6.30pm; Oct.–Mar. Mon.–Wed. and Sat. 9.30am–6.30pm, Thur. 9.30am–noon; Sun. 2–4.30pm).

Caterthuns

The remains of Iron Age fortifications with ramparts and ditches are situated about 5 miles/8km north-west of Brechin.

Brechin
Round Tower

The Round Tower built in Irish-Celtic style during the 11th c. is perhaps the most interesting sight in this small town. The only other comparable tower is in Abernethy (see Fife). The narrow doorway some 6ft/2m above ground proves that it had a double function: as an early Christian church and also as a place of refuge. The nearby cathedral was founded in 1150 by David I, but the tower (c. 1360), the early Gothic west portal and a few interesting gravestones all date from the Middle Ages.

★★House of Dun

Open: Easter,
May–Sept. daily,
1.30–5.30pm;
Oct. Sat., Sun.
1.30–5.30pm

Slightly less than 4 miles/6km outside Montrose stands a jewel among Georgian country houses. The House of Dun was built for Lord David Erskine between 1730 and 1742. Since 1980 it has been in the possession of the National Trust for Scotland. William Adam designed this two-storey Palladian building in the style of the Château d'Issy near Paris. The Dutchman Joseph Enzer was responsible for the extravagant allegorical stucco-work in the Great Drawing Room. The Scottish lion and Mars (a reference to the earls of Mar, the king's sword-bearers) guard the Scottish regalia, flanked by national emblems serving as symbols of the "Auld Alliance" with France and the "Grand Alliance" or "Union of Crowns" with England. The Neo-Baroque Dining Room (19th c.) and the Flemish tapestries (17th c.) in the Tapestry Room are of interest. Demonstrations of traditional cloth weaving on old handlooms take place in the courtyard buildings.

Montrose
Museum and
Art Gallery

A mile-long (1.5km) sandy beach is one attraction in this fishing port (pop. 11,000). Montrose Museum and Art Gallery by Panmure Place contains a comprehensive collection of artefacts documenting the history of the region. Exhibits include Pictish stones and traditional whaling equipment as well as pictures and sculptures by local artists (open: Mon.–Sat. 10am–5pm).

Arbroath

The inhabitants of this pretty little harbour town (pop. 23,000) earn their living from fishing and tourism, although it is the "Arbroath smoky", a type of smoked haddock, for which the town is best known. A nature trail which takes in some magnificent views starts at the north end of the promenade. The highlights of the trail are a number of notorious smugglers' caves and a fascinating cliff landscape.

★Abbey

The Benedictine abbey was built out of red sandstone in 1178 by William the Lion. In 1320 it played an important part in Scottish history when six years after the decisive Battle of Bannockburn (see Bannockburn) noblemen and clergy met in the tower of the gatehouse to sign a letter to Pope John XXII, the so-called Declaration of Arbroath, which resulted in Robert the Bruce (see Famous People) becoming king. Only sections of the richly-ornamented Romanesque west portal, the south transept of the sacristy and the presbytery survive from this once vast, cruciform abbey. Some of the original vaulting remains in the sacristy where capitals imaginatively decorate the surrounding blind arcades. The "O of Arbroath", a rose

Arbroath Abbey

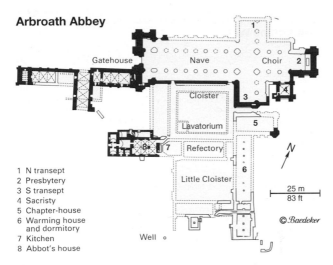

Gatehouse · Nave · Choir

1
2

Cloister
3
4

Lavatorium
5

Refectory
8 · 7
6

Little Cloister

25 m
83 ft

© Baedeker

Well o

1 N transept
2 Presbytery
3 S transept
4 Sacristy
5 Chapter-house
6 Warming house
  and dormitory
7 Kitchen
8 Abbot's house

window which faces out to sea above a round-arched triforium in the south transept, served as a beacon for vessels out at sea during the Middle Ages. The restored hall in the old Abbots House is now a museum where exhibits include medieval frescos and a copy of the Declaration of Arbroath (HS; open: Apr.–Sept. Mon.–Sat. 9.30am–6.30pm, Sun. 2–6.30pm; Oct.–Mar. Mon.–Sat. 9.30am–4.30pm, Sun. 2–4.30pm).

Antonine Wall

Regions: Strathclyde and Central

Situation

The Antonine Wall, also known as the Roman Wall, Graham's or Grim's Dyke, was a Roman border fortification with nineteen forts that stretched from the Firth of Forth to the Firth of Clyde or, more precisely from Dunglass Castle, Dunglass Point near Clydebank to Borrowstounness. Measuring 39 miles/62.4km in length, it is made of earth and clay on stone foundations. On the north side of the wall, a ditch 20ft/6.1m deep and 40ft/12.2m wide was dug, while to the south ran a stone path at a height of 10ft/3.04m and 14ft/4.3m in width.

History

The wall was built by legionnaires in A.D. 142. A model in Glasgow's Hunterian Museum (see entry) shows clearly how the sections of the wall were built and other exhibits include finds from the forts.

Unlike England, Scotland was never ruled by the Romans, although they occupied it for a time to protect their province of Britannia. Agricola entered Scotland in A.D. 80, annihilated the inhabitants on Mons Graupius – thought to be in the south of Perthshire – in 84 and then built a number of fortresses. His successor Quintus Lolius Urbicus was responsible for constructing the wall and he named it after the emperor at that time Titus Aurelius Antonius. Gauls, Belgians, Syrians and Thracians were sent to man the forts. About 40 years after the completion of the wall (c. 185), it was abandoned.

Tour
Kirkintilloch
Falkirk

Parts of the ditch remain and six of the forts have been uncovered. For a good view of the forts go to either Kirkintilloch (pop. 23,200; also known as Caerpentulach) or Rough Castle near Falkirk (pop. 42,800), a coal and steel

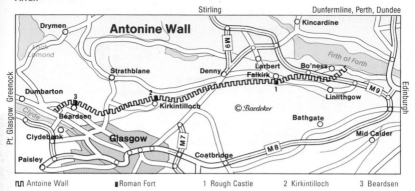

| ⋔ Antoine Wall | ■ Roman Fort | 1 Rough Castle | 2 Kirkintilloch | 3 Beardsen |

Bearsden

town. As for the Antonine Walls, they remain in a reasonably good state near Callendar House, to the east of Falkirk. Another good place to see the remains is to the north-west and north-east of the town of Bearsden (pop. 26,000), north-west of Glasgow.

Arran

D 6

Region: Strathclyde
Population: 3600

Situation and ★ topography

The delightful island of Arran lies 12 miles/19.2km off the Ayrshire coast and measures 20 miles/32km in length, 11 miles/17.6km in width. Covering an area of 101sq.miles/264sq.km, it is the biggest and at the same time most varied of all the islands in the Clyde. The rugged north is characterised by hills – of granite, volcanic rock and red sandstone – deep valleys and broad moorland. South of the Highland Boundary Fault fertile soil and lower slopes predominate, so it is much more like the "Lowlands". In fact, the island is sometimes described as "Scotland in Miniature". Geologists in particular are fascinated by the island for it possesses, within a relatively small area, nearly all the different types of rock found in Scotland. Amateur archaeologists will find tumuli and monoliths to investigate and walkers can choose from many footpaths offering spectacular views. Thanks to the favourable climate provided by the Gulf Stream, azaleas, fuchsias, rhododendrons, palms and many rare mountain species thrive on the island. Anglers make for Drumadoon Bay in large numbers and there are also opportunities for pony trekking, tennis and watersports. The island has a total of seven golf courses.

Ferries

Several car ferries a day cross to Brodick from Ardrossan. In summer there are also ferries between Claonaig (Kintyre) and Lochranza (see Practical Information, Ferries).

Island tour

Brodick

The String (A841), as the locals call it, follows the coast right round the island. Situated on the east coast overlooking a bay of the same name lies Brodick (pop. 860), the island's main port with a jetty for ferries and the starting point for this tour. An exhibition on the history of the island is held at the Arran Heritage Museum (Rosaburn) between May and September. Also on display here is a "smiddy", a cottage built in "turn-of-the-century" style. The Transport Museum in the Old Courthouse (Claydach) specialises in the development of maritime transport and communications in the region (open: daily, in summer 10.30am–7pm).

Close on 2 miles/3km north of Brodick stands the red-sandstone Brodick Castle. It was once the home of the dukes of Hamilton and is now owned by the National Trust for Scotland (open: Apr.–Oct. daily, 11.30am–5pm; garden and park daily 9.30am–dusk). Originally built in the 13th c. to defend the Clyde estuary it underwent many changes in the 16th and 17th c., with the most recent alterations taking place in the middle of the 19th c. Six paintings by James Pollard hang in the Victorian entrance hall, while the chambers upstairs, designed by James Gillespie Graham, contain a fine collection of period furniture, silver, porcelain and ivory, together with more paintings, including sketches and portraits by Thomas Gainsborough, landscapes by William Turner and two pictures by Antoine Watteau. Colourful rhododendron bushes, azaleas, magnolias and some rare trees flourish in the extensive parkland.

★Brodick Castle Gardens and Country Park

Goatfell (2866ft/874m) is the highest peak on Arran and can be reached from Brodick. On a clear day the summit affords a clear view of the Clyde estuary and beyond. Allow about five hours for this excursion. The return journey can be interrupted at Corric.

★Goatfell

A detour along the pretty valley of Glen Rosa is well worth the effort.

Glen Rosa

The tiny island of Holy Island (1 mile/1.6km in length) lies 5 miles/8km to the south of Brodick off Lamlash Bay. The changing landscape, dominated by a hill (1030ft/314m), is ideal for bird-life and the island has become a popular spot for ornithologists. According to legend St Molaise, a pupil of St Columba, lived here and the walls and roofs of the caves in the west of the

Lamlash Bay
Holy Island

Brodick Castle, set in delightful gardens

Isle of Arran – Scotland in miniature

island are covered with runic symbols and inscriptions that date from different periods. A 7ft/2m sandstone block marked all around with man-made indentations is revered as the saint's seat of judgement.

Lamlash

Lamlash (pop. 620) is the second-largest village on the east coast. It is a popular resort with a sailing school, yachting club, fishing centre and an attractive sandy beach.

Whiting Bay

At the southern end of Lamlash Bay lies the village of Kingscross and beyond here is Whiting Bay and a golf course. Just a little further south the road passes two waterfalls near Glen Ashdale.

Kildonan Castle

Kildonan Castle was once a royal hunting lodge when Arran belonged to the royal family. Scottish kings often came here to hunt the imported red deer. The dilapidated castle stands in an exposed but picturesque spot with a view over the sea.

Bennan Head

Bennan Head marks the southern tip of the island and the Struey Rocks are well worth a closer look. The 82ft/25m deep "Black Cave" extends almost 150ft/46m under the cliff.

Lagg

Carry on through Lagg, a peaceful resort with the pre-historic Kilmory Cairns, and on to Sliddery where the remains of a watchtower on Castle Hill overlook the western Firth of Clyde. The pretty valley of Glen Scorrodale leads back across the island to Lamlash.

Blackwaterfoot

Blackwaterfoot with its twelve-hole golf course, riding centre and good watersport facilities is situated on the south-west coast looking out to Kilbrannan Sound.

King's Cave

King's Hill lies to the north of Drumadoon Bay. The caves in the vicinity were used as hideaways by Robert the Bruce and his men (see Famous

People) at the beginning of the 14th c. The biggest of the caves is called King's Cave after Scotland's national hero.

To reach the six Bronze Age stones (granite, old red sandstone) known as the Machrie Moor Standing Stones turn inland about 3 miles/4.8km further north near Tormore, taking Moss Farm Road by Machrie Water. The stones are thought to date from c. 1600 B.C.

Machrie Moor Standing Stones

About 2½ miles/4km further north stands another prehistoric site. The Auchagallon Stone Circle by Machrie Bay now consists of about fifteen red sandstone blocks.

Auchagallon Stone Circle

The ferry port of Lochranza lies beyond Auchencar and Catacol. A golf course and the 400-year-old ruins of Lochranza Castle, once a hunting lodge for Scottish kings overlook the pretty bay. Cock of Arran, another 2 miles/3.2km past Lochranza, is the northernmost tip of the island.

Lochranza
Castle

Leave the northern coast and follow Glen Chalmadale through to Sannox Bay on the east coast. Glen Sannox leads inland from here to become one of Arran's wildest glens. The dramatic landscape that can be viewed from Fallen Rocks along the north coast emerged during the last Ice Age. Return to Brodick (6 miles/9.6km) via Corrie with its golf course and trekking centre.

★ Glen Sannox Corrie

Ayr   E 6

Region: Strathclyde
Population: 48,000

Ayr is not only a good shopping centre but also a good base for exploring the Lowlands. It faces the island of Arran and is the main town in the county of Ayrshire. Robert Burns (see Famous People) described the local people as "honest men and bonnie lasses". A memorial at the station, Tam o'Shanter Inn and Rabbies Bar are just a few examples of the Burns legacy in the region. Devotees can even follow the Burns' Heritage Trail, a literary tour through south-west Scotland as far as Dumfries (see Dumfries and Galloway), that takes in all the places connected with Burns. Ayr boasts an important racecourse, no fewer than three golf courses and a long sandy beach.

Situation and characteristics

★ The Burns' Heritage Trail

The thatched house where Burns was born is situated in Alloway, a suburb to the south of Ayr. It was built by his father and Burns spent the first seven years of his short life here. Exhibits include memorabilia, manuscripts and the old family Bible (open: June–Aug. Mon.–Sat. 9am–6pm, Sun. 10am–6pm; Apr., May, Sept., Oct. Mon.–Sat. 10am–5pm, Sun. 2–5pm; Nov.–Mar. Mon.–Sat. 10am–4pm).

Alloway
★ Burns' Cottage and Museum

A few yards further on, an account of Burns' life and times is given with the help of an audio-visual presentation (open: daily, 10am–5pm).

Land o'Burns Centre

Tam o'Shanter is said to have looked out of a window in the Auld Kirk (early 16th c.) and seen the devil at a witches' sabbath. The grave of Burns' father, who died at the age of 63, lies at the entrance to the cemetery.

Auld Kirk

There is a fine view over the River Ayr and its two bridges from the Burns' Monument (1823) where more than 600 exhibits relating to the celebrated Scottish hero are displayed (by the B7024; open: June–Aug. daily, 9am–6pm; Apr., May, Sept., Oct., Mon.–Sat. 10am–5pm, Sun. 2–5pm; Nov.–Mar. Mon.–Sat. 10am–4pm).

Burns' Monument

It was across one of the bridges, the 13th c. "Auld Brig", that Tam o'Shanter fled from the witches – he remembered that they were not allowed to cross

Ayr Bridge

flowing water – only his horse's tail remained in the hands of his pursuers. In line with Burns' prophecy, the bridge of 1788 had to be rebuilt in 1877.

Tarbolton
★Bachelor's Club

Tarbolton (8 miles/12.8km north of Ayr) owes its fame to the fact that Burns and his friends founded the Bachelor's Club here in 1780 and then a year later he joined the local Freemason's Lodge (NTS; open: Apr.–Oct daily, noon–5pm).

Mauchline
Poosie Nansie's
Tavern
Burns' House
Burns' Memorial
Tower

It was in Poosie Nansie's pub that Burns met his future wife Jean Armour. The Castle Street cottage in Mauchline where they lived after their marriage in 1788 is now the Burns' House Museum (open: Easter–Sept. Mon.–Sat. 11am–12.30pm, 1.30–5.30pm, Sun. 2–5pm). At the north end of Mauchline stands the Burns' Memorial Tower and to the west lies Mossgiel Farm which Burns managed for four years.

Auchinleck
Boswell Museum

Take a detour to Auchinleck about 6 miles/9.6km to the south-east. The Boswell Museum in the old parish church documents the life of the village's most famous son, James Boswell (1740–95). He is best known for his association with the English man of letters Dr Samuel Johnson (1709–84). Boswell accompanied Johnson to the Hebrides and he wrote a diary about their travels (see Scotland in Quotations) which was the forerunner for his biography of Dr Johnson (for information on opening times, telephone (012190) 20931).

Kirkoswald
★Souter Johnnie's
Cottage

Souter Johnnie's Cottage in Kirkoswald is in fact a museum dedicated to the souter (cobbler) John Davidson who with his drinking friend Douglas Graham is immortalised in Burns' narrative poem "Tam o'Shanter". Tam o'Shanter and Souter Johnnie sit in the museum garden as life-sized statues, both the work of James Thorn (1802) who later emigrated to America and became an architect (open: Apr.–Oct. daily, noon–5pm).

Burns' Centre House, Mausoleum. See Dumfries and Galloway, Dumfries.

Cobbler's workshop in Souter Johnnie's Cottage

North of Ayr

The industrial heartland of Ayrshire is centred on Kilmarnock (pop. 50,000). The town's name is derived from the early Christian missionary St Marnock. The prefix "Kil" is a Celtic word for "church". In Kay Park another monument commemorates the celebrated poet. Burns' first anthology of poems, the Kilmarnock edition, is among the exhibits in the museum (closed temporarily).

Kilmarnock

Burns' Monument

Dean Castle and its splendid country park to the north of the town are worth a visit. The castle (14th/15th c.) was once the seat of the Boyd family. Medieval weapons, Burns manuscripts and a collection of early European musical instruments are among the most interesting items on display (open: daily, noon–5pm).

★Dean Castle

Whisky drinkers will not want to miss the tour of the Johnnie Walker Distillery in Hill Street. Established in 1820, the business today produces the well-known blended whisky – "The day goes, Johnnie Walker comes" (guided tours by arrangement only, tel. (01563) 523401, fax 536744; see Baedeker Special "Scotch Whisky").

Johnnie Walker Distillery

Trawlers, lifeboats and tugs are among the vessels on display in this maritime museum. Exhibits at the Victorian Linthouse Building at the end of the harbour include a collection of model ships (open: Apr.–Oct. daily, 10am–5pm).

Irvine
Scottish Maritime Museum

The museum's premises on the Dalry Road (A737) date from 1753. The old mill has recently undergone careful restoration and its displays now record country life in Ayrshire. Fresh bread made from flour ground at the mill is sold in the bakery (open: Mon.–Sat. 10am–5pm, Sun. 12.30–5pm).

Kilwinning
Dalgarven Mill

Saltcoats has a fine beach. The town's Martello tower dates from 1800. Ferries for Arran (see entry) leave from Ardrossan. The 12th c. castle was destroyed by Cromwell's troops and little now remains.

Saltcoats
Ardrossan

The Pencil Monument in the sailing centre of Largs (pop. 11,200) was erected to commemorate the decisive battle of 1263, which resulted in the Hebrides, for centuries under Norwegian domination, being captured by the Scots.

Largs
Pencil Monument

Well-maintained footpaths, rare giant trees, waterfalls, beautiful views and pony trekking for children are just a few of the attractions on offer at Kelburn Country Centre (open: Apr.–Oct. daily, 10am–6pm). The residents at Kelburn Castle only open their doors to visitors in July and August.

Kelburn Country Centre

South of Ayr

Culzean Castle is one of Scotland's most popular castles. It is managed by the National Trust for Scotland and lies in a picturesque spot on the clifftops

★★Culzean Castle

Open:
Apr.–Oct daily,
10.30am–5.30pm

about 12 miles/19.2km south of Ayr. A fortress had stood on this spot since the 14th c., but in the 18th c. it was transformed into a "picture-book" castle. The 9th Earl of Cassillis Sir Thomas Kennedy had a new wing added on the seaward side and in 1777 his brother David the 10th Earl of Cassillis commissioned Robert Adam the celebrated Classical architect to rebuild it in Italian style. Two wings were soon added complete with small corner towers, parapet and ornate window sills. In 1785 the "Sir Thomas" wing with a huge drum tower was built to overlook the cliff. Adam's strength lay in his ability to combine the elegance of Georgian symmetry with attractive Romantic features.

Sundial at Culzean

The Italianate Culzean Castle   *Ailsa Craig – granite outpost*

Enter the castle through the Front Hall (1870) and pass the Armoury with its extensive collection of pistols before reaching the old Dining Hall where the ceiling is decorated with paintings by Antonio Zucchi. The furniture in the dining hall is in Chippendale style and dates from the early 19th c. Delicate pastel shades and a Classical balustrade with Doric, Corinthian and Ionic columns enhance the light, oval staircase beneath a round dome. From the circular Saloon the view of the sea, sky and mountain contrasts strikingly with the serene elegance of the immediate surroundings. The pink tones of the locally woven carpet complement the pastel arabesques on the stucco ceiling which were restored between 1968 and 1974 based on Robert Adam's original watercolour. The watercolour hangs by the door to the Saloon. Lord Cassillis' chamber with Chippendale and Regency furniture is characterised by warm beiges and greens. Pleasing colour combinations enhance the other rooms such as the recently renovated Best Bedroom and the Picture Room, hung with a view of Culzean by Alexander Nasmyth and a portrait (1764) of the 10th Earl of Cassillis painted by Pompeo Batoni in Rome. There is a guest suite on the first floor. President Eisenhower was granted the right to stay in Culzean Castle whenever he wished and a portrait of the general hangs in a side room, together with other Eisenhower memorabilia.

Park

The 568 acre/230ha. park at Culzean Castle was Scotland's first country park (1969) with the farmhouse, another creation of Robert Adam, serving as the reception and information centre for visitors. The most striking features are the Fountain Court, the Walled Garden with some colourful flower beds and Sir Herbert Maxwell's Scottish Garden (open: daily, 9am until dusk).

Turnberry
Castle

Turnberry is synonymous with golf. As well as two golf courses, the "Ailsa" and the "Arran", a top-class hotel has also been built there (see Practical

Information, Hotels). Turnberry Castle (2 miles/3.2km to the south) was the birthplace of Robert the Bruce (see Famous People).

One of Scotland's few Cluniac monasteries is situated about 5 miles/8km to the east near Maybole. The foundation stone for Crossraguel Abbey was laid in 1244 by Duncan, Earl of Carrick, but the monastery was destroyed by Edward I in the 13th c. It was rebuilt in the 15th c. and the monks even acquired the right to mint coins. The well-preserved ruins of the monastery testify to the high status that this abbey once enjoyed (HS; open Apr.–Sept. Mon.–Sat. 9.30am–6pm, Sun. 2–6pm).

Crossraguel
Abbey

Girvan is a popular holiday resort which every year hosts an international jazz festival. Boat trips to Ailsa Craig leave from the harbour.

Girvan

A huge granite rock some 1114ft/348m high and 2 miles/3km in circumference is visible from Girvan. It lies 10 miles/16km offshore and is now a haven for birds. Ailsa Craig, Gaelic for "Fairyland Rock", is famous for the quality of its granite, known as "Ailsite" which is used, among other things, for making curling stones. A ruined medieval tower occupies a prominent position on the rock.

★Ailsa Craig

Bargany Gardens are noted for their colourful displays of azaleas, rhododendron and narcissi. They are situated 4 miles/6km north-east of Girvan (open: Mar.–Oct. daily, 9am–7pm).

Bargany Gardens

The powerful Kennedy family once resided in this castle which lies 5 miles/8km to the south of Girvan. According to the May Culean ballad, the knight Bluebeard once lived here. He disposed of his first seven wives by pushing them off the cliff. However, his eighth wife May was stronger than him and she threw him off first.

Carleton Castle

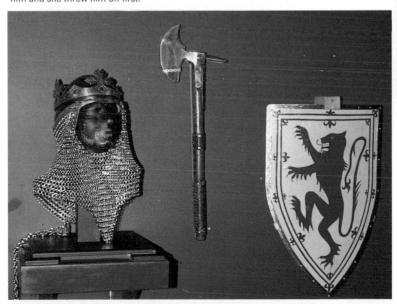

Medieval battle gear: helmet, battleaxe and shield

Independence for Scotland

The struggle for power in Scotland flared up at the end of the 13th c. amid the confusion that surrounded the succession after Alexander III's death. When Edward I, "the Hammer of the Scots", comprehensively defeated the Scottish army in 1298, the country was occupied and a garrison of English soldiers was established in practically every town between Annan and Dingwall. A rebellion led by William Wallace changed nothing. He was taken prisoner and cruelly executed in London in 1305.

A year later Robert I was crowned at Scone and the long battle for freedom commenced. One English fortress after another fell to Scottish troops and by the spring of 1314 only a few bastions remained in English hands, one of which was the strategically important Stirling Castle. Under an agreement between the English governor Sir Philip Moubray and the brother of the king, the besieged castle was to surrender if it had not been relieved by Midsummer Day 1314. To ensure that the castle was liberated in time and also to force the Scots to abandon their guerilla tactics and engage in open battle, Edward II and a huge army of heavy cavalry (about 2000 knights), archers and infantry (about 17,000 men) marched north from Wark near Berwick. They were opposed by 5500 trained soldiers, including 500 knights and about 2000 civilians (citizens and artisans) under the leadership of Robert I. Randolph, Earl of Moray, commanded the first division, which a few months earlier had captured Edinburgh Castle. The second wave was led by the king's brother Edward Bruce and the third by senior government figures. The fourth and strongest battalion, was led by the king himself but it consisted of fierce clansmen from the west under the leadership of the legendary Angus Og, MacDonald of the Isles. All the clans were represented among the knights and civilians – Cameron, Campbell, Chisholm, Fraser, Gordon, Grant, Gunn, MacKay, MacKintosh, MacPherson, MacQuarrie, MacLean, MacDonald, MacFarlane, MacGregor, MacKenzie, Menzies, Munro, Robertson, Ross, Sinclair, Sutherland – and all were determined to win independence for Scotland even if it meant laying down their lives. The words of the Declaration of Arbroath, signed six years later, establishing the independence of Scotland, recalled these men's courage in the face of the overwhelming superiority of the English army:

For so long as there shall but one hundred of us remain alive, we will never give consent to subject ourselves to the Dominion of the English. For it is not Glory, it is not Riches, neither is it Honour, but it is Liberty alone that we fight and contend for, which no Honest man will lose but with his life.

The two armies came face to face on 24th June in the lowland plain between the Pelstream and Bannockburn, known to the Scots as "The Carse" and the

---

Bannockburn   **F 5**

Region: Central

Situation and
characteristics

Barely 2 miles/3km south of Stirling (see entry) on the A872 between the Pelstream and Bannockburn rivers lie the fields and meadows where in

For ever confronting England: the Robert the Bruce memorial at Bannockburn

English as "The Pools". Marshland formed a boundary to the north of the Pelstream near the Forth, while the 50ft/15m wide Bannockburn also flowed through boggy terrain. Robert the Bruce skilfully exploited the advantages of this spot by laying traps in the uneven quagmire of pools and ditches, so that the English army could not spread out or manoeuvre through the narrow front. Slowly but inexorably the Scottish spear throwers and archers pushed forward, driving the enemy back upon themselves and preventing the rest of the English army from joining in the fray. Finally the English line yielded. Edward II, who saw that the battle was lost, fled with a small escort back to Berwick, while his soldiers met their death in the Forth or else drowned at high tide by the muddy banks of the Bannockburn.

The glorious victory over the English guaranteed Robert I a heroic place in Scottish history. He was, and still is, regarded as a standard bearer for Scots who see Scotland as a separate nation. England did not acknowledge the greatest victory that the Scots had ever won until 1328 when the Treaty of Northampton was signed. The symbolic significance of this decisive battle can be understood in the much-quoted lines of Robert Burns about Bruce and his army. The Battle of Bannockburn still features in such popular songs as the "Flower of Scotland" by the Corries, renderings of which are often struck up when England meet Scotland in the sports stadium.

1314 the great battle for Scottish independence took place. This historic site has been managed by the National Trust for Scotland since 1932. The area is now pleasantly laid out and a Visitor Centre providing background information on the battle has been built.

A flag-pole and the stone "Borestone" within the Rotunda mark the spot where it is believed Robert the Bruce (see Famous People) set up his ★Robert the Bruce memorial headquarters on June 23rd 1314. The following day he and his army inflicted a heavy defeat on the English army under Edward II. The victory memorial which shows Robert the Bruce on a bronze horse, protected by chain mail and armour, battle-axe aloft and looking south towards the approaching English foe was unveiled by the Queen Elizabeth II on the 650th anniversary of the battle.

★Bannockburn Heritage Centre

Open:
Apr.–Oct. daily,
10am–5.30pm
Mar., 11 Nov. to
23 Dec. daily
11am–3pm

Opened in 1987, the Bannockburn Heritage Centre documents Scottish history from the Wars of Independence to the Union with England at the beginning of the 17th c. "The Kingdom of Scotland" exhibition uses pictures and models, while in an annexe the course of the Battle of Bannockburn (Gaelic = "Blar Allt a'Bhain-Chnuic") is explained using audio-visual techniques.

Models include knights from William Wallace's entourage and a statue of the victorious king Robert I on his throne and information is also available on the "Lords of the Isles", those clans who once controlled the west of Scotland from Glenelg to the Mull of Kintyre. A section entitled "The Marriage between Thistle and Rose" covers the union between James IV and Margaret Tudor and also details the fragile peace that followed. Other topics covered in the Heritage Centre include the Scottish legal system, the Reformation in Scotland and the Stuart kings up to James VI.

Borders   F/G 6

Situation
and characteristics

Unspoilt nature and breathtaking scenery, beautiful beaches, busy fishing ports, picturesque villages tucked away on the hillsides, many grand castles and other historic sites make up the south-eastern corner of Scotland, often known as the Borders. The history of this region north of the Scottish–English border, which comprises the area around the Tweed valley south of the Pentland, Moorfoot and Lammermuir Hills, was greatly influenced by four famous abbeys which came into being during the reign of David I (1124–53). Despite many attacks from across the border, the monasteries developed into important cultural and economic centres – even the king sometimes sought financial assistance from them. Agriculture, cattle, handicrafts and

commerce all played an important role in the region's prosperity. When, in the middle of the 16th c., the English under the Earl of Hertford razed the monasteries to the ground, destroyed the crops in the fields, drove away the cattle and took everything that was not nailed to the floor, the local economy was shaken to its foundations.

The Lowlands were discovered by tourists much later than the ever popular Highlands so beloved by the Romantics, even though there is no shortage of natural beauty and the region can boast many fine, historic buildings. The waymarked Southern Uplands Way that stretches 212 miles/340km from Cockburnspath on the east coast to Portpatrick on the west is a favourite route with walkers.

Agriculture, mainly sheep farming, combines with textiles to form the backbone of the local economy. The Borders region enjoys an international reputation for quality woollen goods and woven materials. Hawick and Galashiels are the main centres for the textile industry, while Innerleithen and the surrounding area are best known for knitwear. Visitors can discover for themselves the beauty of the Lowland hillsides by following the signposted round tour between Hawick, Peebles and Kelso. Museums and factories provide an insight into the production of woollen goods starting with the rearing of Cheviot sheep through to the finished tweed.

★Woollen Trail

The A68 leads through the Cheviot Hills and the English county of Northumberland with Carter Bar (1371ft/418m) marking the boundary between the two countries. Look out for the road sign with the red lion of the Stuarts. The scenery is magnificent and it is easy to understand the nostalgic sentiments Bordermen and women feel when they return home.

★Carter Bar

Everyone will enjoy a tour of Jedforest Farm (5 miles/8km south of Jedburgh), a working farm with sheep, cows, horses, chickens, ducks and red deer. Visitors can take a horse or tractor ride around the fields (open: May–Oct. daily, 10am–5pm).

Jedforest Deer and Farm Park

Ferniehirst Castle is a typical example of a Borders fortress. It is situated 1½ miles/2.4km south of Jedburgh and is the seat of the Kerr family. A few years ago the 16th c. castle, fortified with small round towers, was fully restored. Information about the changing fortunes of the Borders country is available in the 17th c. stables.

Ferniehirst Castle

Open: May–Oct. Wed. 1.30–4.30pm

Jedburgh

The fine three-arched Canongate Bridge crosses the River Jed in the heart of this pretty little town (pop. 4100) some 10 miles/16km north of the border. It was the weavers of Jedburgh who used two different yarns to create the original "Tweedy" look, a style that was soon copied by other spinning mills in the vicinity. Knitwear and textiles production remain important aspects of the local economy.

Situation and characteristics

Kirkwall (see Orkneys) is the only other place in Scotland where people still play this ancient team game which requires more than 200 participants. In Jedburgh the game serves as a reminder to the residents of their bloody conflicts with their southern neighbours. The "Uppies", who live above the Mercat Cross compete against the "Downies" from below the cross. Starting on Castlehill, the winning team is the first to convey the small, straw-filled leather ball, symbolising the head of an Englishman, through the lanes, front gardens and backyards of Jedburgh to the end of High Street.

Hand Ba' Game

The principal sight in Jedburgh is the ruined abbey (HS). It is one of the four main Border abbeys which were founded around 1118 and then destroyed by the English in 1544. Two Norman arches and the west front with its magnificent rose window, the "St Catherine's Wheel", are the highlights of this sandstone church that stands on the crest of a hill looking south towards England. The arcades in the three-storey main nave and the window tracery are also worth a look. Excavations to the south side have unearthed a part of the monastery site, while the Visitor Centre has an exhibition explaining the day-to-day life of the monks.

★★**Jedburgh Abbey**

Open: Apr.–Sept. Mon.– Sat. 9.30am–6pm Sun. 2–6pm; Oct.–Mar. Mon.– Sat. 9.30am–4pm, Sun. 2–4pm

In 1987, to mark the death 400 years earlier of Mary Stuart (see Famous People), the T-shaped tower house was opened as a museum. It details the tragic fate of the Queen of Scots. Here on November 9th 1566, she received news that her lover, the Earl of Bothwell, was lying with gunshot wounds in Hermitage Castle (see below). After a day's ride to see the earl, she returned

Mary Queen of Scots House

Open: Mar.–mid Nov. daily, 10am–5pm

Castle Jail

exhausted and had to stay in Jedburgh for a month to recuperate from fever.

In 1823 the medieval fortress was turned into a prison and it now houses a museum (open: Easter–Oct. Mon.–Sat. 10am–5pm, Sun. 1–5pm).

Hawick

Hawick (pop. 15,700) is the biggest town in the Borders region and lies 11 miles/17.6km to the west of Jedburgh. It is an important textiles centre and is closely linked with the fashionable names of Pringle, Braemar and Peter Scott. The equestrian statue in High Street commemorates the recapture of the town flag after the Battle of Flodden Field (1513). The museum, opened in 1995 in Drumlanrig's Tower, documents the effect of the turbulent Middle Ages on the region.

Museum and Scott Gallery

In Wilton Lodge Park on the banks of the Teviot, a museum details the development of the woollen industry. There are also a number of paintings by 19th and 20th c. Scottish artists (open: Apr.–Sept. Mon.–Sat. 10am–noon, 1–5pm, Sun. 2–5pm; Oct.–Mar. Mon.–Fri. 1–4pm, Sun. 2–4pm).

★Hermitage Castle

This huge fortress (HS; 10 miles/16km south of Hawick) was built during the 13th/14th c. and has an unusual H-shaped layout (open: Apr.–Sept. Mon.–Sat. 9.30am–6pm, Sun. 2–6pm; Oct.–Mar. Sun. only). The castle is best known for Mary Stuart's daring ride to see her lover Bothwell. (see Jedburgh).

★★Dryburgh Abbey

Follow the A68 north out of Jedburgh to Dryburgh Abbey (HS; 8 miles/13km) which lies among old trees by the banks of the Tweed. The monastery was founded in 1150 by Hugh de Morville for monks of the Premonstratensian order. Thanks to donations and hard work by the

Dryburgh Abbey

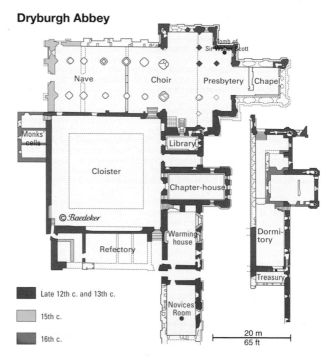

Late 12th c. and 13th c.

15th c.

16th c.

20 m
65 ft

monks, the monastery soon became a prosperous centre and wielded considerable influence. During the 14th c. it was repeatedly plundered by the English and was finally destroyed in 1544. Little remains of the Gothic abbey, but of particular interest are the marvellous west portal, the rose window at the west end of the refectory, the chapterhouse and St Modan's chapel – St Modan, it is said, was the abbot of a monastery that stood on this spot in the 6th c. In a granite sarcophagus designed by Chantrey and situated in the northern transept lies the body of Sir Walter Scott (see Famous People). For him Dryburgh Abbey was the "most romantic ruin".

Open:
Apr.–Sept. Mon.–
Sat. 9.30am–6pm,
Sun. 2–6pm;
Oct.–Mar. Mon.–
Sat. 9.30am–4pm,
Sun. 2–4pm

Melrose

Melrose (pop. 2300), a pleasant little town and a good starting point for tours of the central Borders region, nestles between the Tweed, much-favoured by anglers, and the Eildon Hills.

Situation and
characteristics

Many regard Melrose Abbey (HS) as the finest of the Borders region abbeys. Built from red sandstone for Cistercian monks in 1136, it was later plundered and desecrated on several occasions with some of the stones re-used in other buildings nearby. However, what remains – mostly from the 15th c. – makes an impressive sight. The artistic stonework, the ornate carving on the capitals and sculptures including a well-known water fountain in the form of a bagpipe-playing pig are particularly fine. The tracery for the transept windows and the east window are also much admired. The German writer Theodor Fontane spoke in glowing terms of the "herbarium scoticum in stone" containing flowers, leaves, lilies, thistles, oak leaves and clover leaves. The heart of Robert the Bruce (see Famous People), who authorised the reconstruction of the abbey after its destruction by Edward II, is said to have been buried beneath the east window – a mummified heart was in fact found in the chapterhouse in 1920. Part of the popularity of

★★Melrose Abbey

Open:
Apr.–Sept. Mon.–
Sat. 9.30am–6pm,
Sun. 2–6pm;
Oct.–Mar. Mon.–
Sat. 9.30am–4pm,
Sun. 2–4pm

Lovely decorative stonework . . .

. . . at the ruined Melrose Abbey

the abbey stems from William Turner's evocative drawings and Sir Walter Scott's "Lay of the Last Minstrel".

Motor Museum

Vintage cars in the motor museum in Annay Road include a 1909 Albion and a 1926 Arrol Johnston both of which were built in Scotland (open: May–Oct. daily, 10.30am–5.30pm).

Teddy Bear Museum

Pooh, Rupert, Bully, Paddington and many other children's favourites from 1900 onwards are among the exhibits in the High Street museum (open: Mon.–Sat. 10am–5pm, Sun. 2–5pm).

Newstead

A monument on Leaderfoot Hill in neighbouring Newstead marks the spot where the Roman Trimontium camp once stood. Finds from here are displayed in the national Museum of Antiquities (see Edinburgh).

★Scott's View

Scott's View, the famous novelist's favourite panoramic viewpoint, lies about 2 miles/3.2km east of Melrose and should not be missed. The scenery includes the Eildon Hills and the green Tweed valley, where in spring the slopes are smothered in yellow broom.

Eildon Hills

Michael Scott is also linked with the Eildon Hills, a three-pointed peak of volcanic origin that rises to a height of 1387ft/423m. The magician/mathematician is said to have caused the hill to break into three. The view from the top is truly magnificent.

★Smallholm Tower

On a small hill about 2 miles/3.2km east of Scott's View stands a 16th c. rectangular peel tower about 60ft/18m in height, which appears in one of William Turner's sketches. An exhibition inside contains dolls and wall hangings that relate to Scott's "Lay of the Last Minstrel". (HS; open: Apr.–Sept. Mon.–Sat. 9.30am–6pm, Sun. 2–6pm).

Gorse in flower below the Eildon Hills

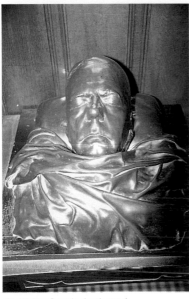

Sir Walter Scott's death mask . . .   *. . . and study*

At the heart of "Scott's country", as the Borders are sometimes known, lies Abbotsford, a house by the banks of the Tweed where Sir Walter Scott (see Famous People) wrote the majority of his poems and historical novels and where, in 1832, as a consequence of years of overwork he finally died. As the estate and ford below the house once belonged to the abbots of Melrose, Scott called it Abbotsford.

★★Abbotsford House

Open: mid-Mar.–Oct. Mon.–Sat. 10am–5pm, Sun. 2–5pm

The royalties from his highly-successful novels went towards converting the farmhouse into a Scottish-style mansion or in his own words a "romance in stone and mortar". William Atkinson was enlisted as architect and he added the little oriel windows and turreted corner towers.

The entrance is in the style of the main portal at Linlithgow Castle, part of a door came from the Tolbooth in Edinburgh, the courtyard wall resembles the cloisters at Melrose Abbey and the wooden ceiling in the library is a copy of Rosslyn Chapel. The house is crammed full of reminders of the best-selling writer, including manuscripts, Border ballads, portraits and curiosities such as "Bonnie Prince Charlie's" scotch glass (quaich) and the sword reputedly used by the outlaw Rob Roy of the Trossachs. There is also a collection of weapons and armour and in the study Scott's death mask can be seen.

Thirlestane border fortress lies 11 miles/18km north of Melrose and was built in the 13th c. In the 16th c. it was converted for use by the Maidlands family. This picture-book castle is fitted out with splendid 17th c. wooden ceilings and now belongs to the Lauderdale family. It houses a collection of old toys and the Border Country Life Museum that documents in some detail the turbulent past of the Borders region (open: July, Aug. Sun.–Fri. 2–5pm; Easter, May, June, Sept. Wed. Thur. Sun. 2–5pm).

★Thirlestane Castle

Thirlestane – picturesque Border castle

Selkirk

Situation	The little town of Selkirk (pop. 5900; 6 miles/9.6km south-west of Melrose) sits on a hill overlooking the River Ettrick.
Halliwell's House	The full history of the town from the Stone Age to modern times is documented in Halliwell's House by the market place (open: Apr.–Oct. Mon.–Sat. 10am–5pm, Sun. 2–4pm; July, Aug. daily, until 6pm; Nov., Dec. 2–4pm). The textile factories of Selkirk are located in the valley. It is possible to watch the weavers at work on rugs, ties and coat material. The courthouse where Scott worked as sheriff-depute can also be visited.
Selkirk Glass	In the Visitor Centre at Selkirk Glass (by the A7 to the north of the town), the craftsmen who create the intricate designs for the inside of glass paperweights can be seen at work (open: Mon.–Fri. 9am–5pm, Sat. 10am–4.30pm, Sun. noon–4pm).
Aikwood Tower	A 16th c. fortified tower in the Ettrick valley houses a recently opened exhibition on the life and work of James Hogg, the "Ettrick Shepherd". A contemporary of Sir Walter Scott, he taught himself to read and write and then while out on the hillsides with his sheep passed the time by composing poems and writing novels (open: Easter until Sept. Tue., Thur., Sun. 2–5pm).
★★Bowhill House Open: July daily 1–4.30pm	Bowhill House, the seat of the Duke of Buccleuch and Queensberry, is situated about 3 miles/5km west of Selkirk. This Victorian country house contains a fine collection of paintings, including an enchanting child study of Lady Caroline by Reynolds entitled "Winter" (1777) and landscapes by Claude Lorrain and Ruisdael. Family portraits by Gainsborough and Reynolds hang in the Drawing Room, while in the Entrance Hall there are seven Van Dyck portraits and works by Canaletto, Guardi, David Wilkie, Hans Holbein and Samuel Cooper. A plaid and other Scott memorabilia can be seen in the Study, together with a portrait of Scott by Raeburn (1808).

Meissen and Sèvres porcelain, Flemish tapestries and some marvellous French furniture form another part of the collection.

Take a detour along the A708 towards Moffat and the delightful St Mary's Loch where during her 92 years Isabella Richardson gathered around her many of Scotland's literary heroes including Sir Walter Scott, Robert Louis Stevenson, the historian Thomas Carlyle and the poetry-writing shepherd James Hogg (for Tibbie Shiels Inn, see Practical Information: Restaurants).

★St Mary's Loch
Tibbie Shiels
Inn

The name Galashiels (pop. 13,800; 6 miles/9.6km north of Selkirk) derives from "shielings", traditional shelters for shepherds by the banks of Gala Water. Since the Industrial Revolution, Galashiels has been the centre of the Scottish woollen industry.

Galashiels

During the months from April to October there are several tours each day around the Peter Anderson Mill in Huddersfield Street. The museum goes into some detail about the manufacture of tweed and tartan (open: Mon.–Sat. 9am–5pm; June–Sept also Sun. noon–5pm).

Peter Anderson
Mill

Innerleithen

The important textiles town of Innerleithen (pop. 2600) lies about 15 miles/24km north-west of Selkirk. At nos. 7–9 High Street the National Trust for Scotland has faithfully restored a Victorian printing works to full working order. Visitors are sometimes invited to set and print their own papers (open: Mon.–Sat. 10am–1pm, Sun. 2–5pm).

Situation and
characteristics
Robert Smail's
Printing Works

Traquair House near Innerleithen is one of the oldest inhabited mansions in Scotland. It was used by the Scottish royal family as a residence and hunting lodge from as early as the 10th c. The iron gates, known also as the Bear Gates as they are guarded by two stone bears, were closed behind "Bonnie Prince Charlie" in 1745 and he vowed not to re-open them until a Stuart had been restored to the Scottish throne – and so they remain closed. Traquair House beer, it is said, was first brewed in 1566 when Mary Queen of Scots visited the house and the brewers still use the same recipe.

★ **Traquair House**

Open:
Easter, May, June,
Sept. daily, 1.30–
5.30pm; July–Aug.
daily, 10.30am–
5.30pm

About 1¼ miles/2km outside Innerleithen near Walkerburn, the A72 passes the Tweedvale Mill and the Scottish Wool Museum, which specialises in displaying materials, designs and old documents illustrating the development of wool-based fabrics (open: Apr.–Oct. Mon.–Sat. 9am–5pm).

Scottish Museum
of Woollen
Textiles

Kailzie Gardens about 2½ miles/4km from Peebles is noted for its colourful roses, azaleas, rhododendrons and narcissi (open: mid-Mar.–Oct. daily, 11am–5.30pm).

Kailzie Gardens

★ Peebles

At the confluence of the rivers Eddleston and Tweed lies the busy textiles town of Peebles (pop. 7100). The Tweedsdale Museum in the High Street details the cultural development of the town and also the growth of the wool industry (open: Mon.–Fri. 10am–1pm, 2–5pm, Sun. 2–5pm).
The L-shaped Fraser Castle above the Tweed (1 mile/1.6km to the west) dates from the late 14th c. and was destroyed by Cromwell's troops. In some places the walls are 10ft/3m thick (open: Easter–Sept. Mon.–Sat. 11am–5pm, Sun. 1–5pm).

Situation
Tweedsdale
Museum

Neidpath Castle

These gardens are in fact an outpost of the Royal Botanic Garden in Edinburgh (see Edinburgh). Rare giant trees and splendid rhododendrons are among the flora on display here (open: Mar.–Oct. daily, 10am–6pm).

Dawyck Botanic
Gardens

★ Kelso

Situation and
characteristics

The attractive market town of Kelso (pop. 6100) 10 miles/16km east of Melrose was described by Scott as the "prettiest, if not the most romantic village in Scotland". The main roads converge on the Georgian market square where every night a tattoo is sounded at the courthouse. The five-arched bridge over the Tweed was built in 1803 by John Rennie and it offers a fine view of the ruined abbey. In September, farmers from far and wide gather for the famous Ram Market.

★★ Kelso Abbey

The biggest and, at the end of the 12th c., the richest of the four Border abbeys was founded in 1128 by monks from Picardy. It shared the same fate as the other abbeys and was destroyed in the 16th c. Once again it was the Earl of Hertford who during the Reformation, at the behest of Henry VIII, burnt the town and abbey to the ground. The transept and, above all, the west tower, which is rather reminiscent of a castle keep, are the best-preserved sections of this late Norman sandstone construction (HS; open: Apr.–Oct. Mon.–Sat. 9.30am–6pm, Sun. 2–6pm; Nov.–Mar. Mon.–Sat. 9.30am–4pm, Sun. 2–4pm).

Turret House

Turret House by Abbey Court is one of the town's oldest buildings. It houses a small museum on local commerce, textiles and the history of Kelso (NTS; open: Easter–Oct. Mon.–Sat. 10am–noon, 1–5pm, Sun. 2–5pm).

★★ Floors Castle

Open:
Apr.–Sept. Sun.–
Thur. 10.30am–
5.30pm;
July, Aug. daily
10.30am–5.30pm;
Oct. Sun., Wed.
10.30am–4.30pm

Floors Castle lies at the western end of the town and enjoys a fine view over the Tweed. This fairy-tale castle topped with small towers, ornate turrets and chimneys was built in Georgian style around 1721 by Robert Adam for the first duke of Roxburghe. Some 120 years later it was extended in decorative Tudor style by William Playfair for the 21-year-old sixth duke. The gatehouse and the imposing main gates which bear the family coat-of-arms were added in 1929 following the designs of Reginald Fairlie. The entrance to the castle is via an oak-panelled lobby on the north side of the castle. One of Raeburn's portraits depicts the fifth duke of Roxburghe and

Fairy-tale Floors Castle, seat of the Dukes of Roxburghe

there are further works by Van de Velde and Ruisdael. Above the fireplace in the Ante-Room hangs a Brussels tapestry with family portraits by Reynolds and Godfrey Kneller alongside. Duchess May, the American wife of the eighth duke, brought the 17th c. Brussels tapestries from Long Island and she furnished the room in Louis XV style. A room in the Palace of Versailles was the model for the Louis XVI-style Needle Room. The Ballroom was also lavishly decorated by Duchess May with 17th c. Gobelin tapestries and carvings in Grinling Gibbons style. The valuable collection of porcelain includes Dresden and Meissen ware, Davenport tableware and also items dating from the Chinese Ming dynasty. Portraits are by Gainsborough, Kneller and Reynolds. The Bird Room contains some rare exhibits including great bustards and osprey. Among the curiosities displayed in the Gallery is a hoard of treasure found buried near Kelso. It was only discovered in 1991 and consists of 1400 silver and gold coins that probably belonged to a wealthy nobleman *c.* 1643. The dining table in the Dining Room is laid with gilded silver cutlery and on the ground floor is a model of the castle made from matchsticks and icing. It is also worth having a look at the collection of Victorian coaches, prams and bathing machines, before taking a stroll through the beautiful gardens. One of the trees in the extensive parkland is said to mark the spot where James II was fatally wounded by a bullet during a siege of the castle in 1460.

The Georgian Mellerstain House, 6 miles/9.6km north-west of Kelso, was begun in 1725 by William Adam and then completed a few years later by his son Robert Adam. In 1909 Sir Reginald Blomfield designed the terraced gardens in Italian style. Chippendale, Sheraton and Hepplewhite furniture adorn the rooms, together with a valuable collection of paintings by Ramsay, Van Dyck, Aikman, Constable, Nasmyth and Gainsborough, but the Library, painted in delicate green and pink tones, with an exquisite stucco ceiling is probably the highlight of the house.

★★**Mellerstain House**

Open:
Easter, May–Sept.
Sun.–Fri.
12.30–5pm

Vintage cars in the gardens of Mellerstain House

Borders

From Coldstream to Eyemouth

Coldstream Museum

The museum by the market place in Coldstream (pop. 1700; 9 miles/12.6km north-east of Kelso) is concerned with local history (open: Easter–Oct. Mon.–Sat. 10am–1pm, 2–5pm, Sun. 2–5pm).

The Hirsel

At the west end of the town the park on the estate of Lord Home of the Hirsel is worth a visit in late spring to see the rhododendron bushes. In an old farmhouse and stables, a small museum details agricultural methods and the Home family's history. A craft centre is housed in an adjoining building (open daily).

Flodden Field

On the English side of the border in a field near the village of Branxton (5 miles/8km to the south-east), a granite memorial plaque commemorates "The Brave of Both Nations", the thousands of soldiers who gave up their lives in 1513 for England or Scotland. In 1503, hoping to cement a lasting peace with England, James IV had married Margaret Tudor, the daughter of Henry VII, and had brought her to Edinburgh. Despite a promising start, James IV's reign ended tragically. Under the terms of the "Auld Alliance", in the event of war he was obliged to come to the aid of France. When Henry VII attacked France, the Scots reacted by invading England. But on September 9th 1513, the Scottish army and the nobility were wiped out on Flodden Field. An old Scottish ballad "The Flowers of the Forest" which laments the terrible losses Scotland suffered was played by a piper of the Scots Guard when the coffins of the dead from the 1982 Falklands conflict returned to Great Britain.

Duns Jim Clark Room

In 1993 on the 25th anniversary of Jim Clark's death, a small museum about the racing driver was opened at no. 44 Newtown Street in Duns (pop. 2300). It tells the life story of the popular figure who twice won the Formula 1 championship (open: Mon.–Sat. 10am–1pm, 2–5pm, Sun. 2–5pm).

★ Manderston House

Open: May–Sept. Thur., Sun. 2–5.30pm

The Edwardian country house at Manderston (15 miles/24km north-east of Kelso) presently owned by the Palmer family is surrounded by a magnificent garden with beautiful rhododendrons. John Kinross designed the building at the turn of the century for a wealthy businessman called Sir James Miller. The marble staircase with gilded banisters is a particularly impressive sight.

Edin Hall's Broch

The remains of an Iron Age broch, a hollow round tower (HS) stand on a mound some 4 miles/6km to the north. In places the tower reaches a height of 5ft/1.5m.

★ Paxton House

Open: Easter–Oct. daily, noon–5pm

Paxton House (3 miles/4.8km west of Berwick-upon-Tweed) features in a romantic love story. While studying in Germany the young Patrick Home of Billie fell in love with the illegitimate daughter of Frederick the Great. In Berlin's Charlottenburg Castle in 1749, the young lady presented Patrick with a ring and a pair of silk gloves as a symbol of her love and these are on view in Paxton House to this day. After some initial hesitation, Frederick the Great gave his approval to the liaison but requested that Patrick transfer his assets to Prussia and live in Berlin, whereupon Patrick's mother threatened to disinherit her son. He returned to Scotland and sought the help of the king, who presented Home with Paxton House as a fitting residence for his future wife, but in the end they did not marry.

The mansion was built by John and James, two brothers of the celebrated Adam family. The Palladian-style country house is noted not only for its elegant Chippendale furniture but also its painting gallery in delicate pastel shades and topped with a glass dome. This and the library were designed by Robert Reid in 1811. The Regency-style rosewood furniture came from the workshops of the Edinburgh craftsman William Trotter. Paxton House once possessed the biggest private collection of any Scottish country house but the works of art have had to be sold to pay for the upkeep of the property. The current exhibits have been loaned by the National Gallery of Scotland.

Paxton House: Palladian design by John and James Adam

The harbour at Eyemouth

Eyemouth

Ayton Castle

The pretty little fishing port of Eyemouth (pop. 3500) is situated 8 miles/
12.8km north of Berwick-upon-Tweed. The Victorian Ayton Castle stands
beside the A1 just before the village. After extensive renovation work the
castle is once again inhabited (open: May–mid-Sept. Sun. 2–5pm).

★St Abbs Head

St Abbs Head, a nature reserve under the stewardship of the National Trust
for Scotland, is within walking distance from Eyemouth. Many different
species of sea bird such as guillemots, fulmars, kittiwakes and shags breed
on the ledges of the red sandstone cliffs. The lawn of Hotel Heaven offers
not only welcome refreshment but also splendid views of the bay.

Bute

See Cowal and Bute

Cairngorm Mountains   E/F 4

Region: Grampian

★★**Regional Park
and Skiing**

The ski runs in the Cairngorms are undoubtedly the best in Scotland. The
slopes are situated to the west of Braemar (see Dee Valley) and the Cairngorms are the highest mountains in the Grampian region (see Grampians).
The mountain range consists of peneplain with fissured moorland granite

★Ben Macdui

plateaux, dominated by a number of huge elevations with Ben Macdui
(4300ft/1310m) the highest peak in the Regional Park. One of the most

★Cairn Gorm

spectacular high-level footpaths runs from the mountain peaks – accessible all the year round by chairlift – via Cairn Gorm to Glenmore Lodge
(6.5 miles/10.4km from Aviemore). Cairn Gorm has lent its name to the
whole region but, at 4084ft/1245m, it is only the fourth-highest peak after
Ben Macdui, Braeriach (4248ft/1295m) and Cairn Toul (4241ft/1293m). The
easiest route to the summits is by the White Lady chairlift. Several lochs
including Loch Avon and Loch-an-Eilean lie between the pinky red granite
mountains which emerged during the Ice Age. The summits of Braeriach,
Cairn Toul and The Devil's Point probably offer the most impressive views.
Heather moorland, partly wooded with birch trees, provides good breeding
grounds for some rare bird species such as ospreys, ptarmigan, golden
eagles, peregrine falcons and merlins. Mammals such as the pine marten
and reindeer, introduced from Swedish Lapland in 1952, can sometimes be
seen in Glen More Forest.

★Hill walking

This part of Scotland is very popular with serious walkers. The 30-
mile/48km route from Aviemore to Braemar via Larig Ghru includes some
breathtaking views. Another path – about as long – runs from Braemar to
Blair Atholl (see Pitlochry), while a shorter, but still very pretty walk starts in
Aviemore, crosses the Revoan pass via Loch Avon and finishes in Nethy
Bridge, a popular base for skiers, anglers and golfers.

Aviemore

Aviemore (pop. 2400) is Scotland's leading ski resort. It nestles between the
Cairngorms and the Monadhliath Mountains and makes a good base for
excursions into the surrounding countryside. But Aviemore can offer more
than just hotels, chalets, skating rinks and swimming pools. Single malt

Whisky Centre
Loch Garten
Reserve

and blended whiskies can be sampled at the Cairngorm Whisky Centre and
Loch Garten Reserve, a protected area where extremely rare ospreys
breed, can be reached via the Strathspey Railway that links Aviemore and
Boat of Garten.

The distillery at Tomatin (15 miles/24km north-west of Aviemore) with its 23 stills accounts for about 12 million litres of Scotch production. The present owners Takura Skuzo and Okurra are Japanese (open: Mar.–Oct. Mon.–Fri. 9am–4.30pm; June–Oct. Mon.–Fri. 9am–4.30pm, Sat. 9.30am–12.30pm; see Baedeker Special "Scotch Whisky").

Tomatin
Distillery

The ruined "Wolf of Badenoch" castle rises out of the middle of Loch-an-Eileann, a secluded and picturesque lake 3 miles/4.8km south of Aviemore.

★ Loch-an-Eilean

Kingussie (12 miles/19km south-west of Aviemore) was the birthplace of James Macpherson (1736–96). This son of a Spey valley peasant claimed to have produced the first translation of a Gaelic manuscript ascribed to Ossian, the son of the Scottish king Fingal. Fifteen years after a disastrous defeat at Culloden (see entry), he provided the Scots with a heroic epic shrouded in mysticism, a monument of literature that soon won enthusiastic acclaim throughout the whole of Europe among artists and literati. Many of the latter including Herder, Brahms, Mendelssohn-Bartholdy (see Hebrides, Staffa), Turner and others found inspiration in the writings of Ossian. Although Macpherson failed to produce the original manuscripts, his Ossian verses sold well and he was able to afford a mansion in the Scottish Highlands. After his death the controversial Scot was granted a place alongside Britain's most celebrated poets in Westminster Abbey's Poet's Corner. However, it later transpired that Macpherson had been a brilliant forger. He had closely studied the Gaelic sources of the Fingal legend and combined them with his own composition.

Kingussie
James
Macpherson

Exhibits at this open-air museum include a Victorian salmon smokehouse, an old mill and a thatch-covered Black House typical of the Western Isles (see Hebrides, Outer). It also illustrates traditional life in the Scottish High-

★ Highland
Folk Museum

Thatched Hebridean cottage: Kingussie highland Folk Museum

115

The Loch Ness Monster

The Irish missionary St Columba is said to have been the first person to encounter the oldest inhabitant of Loch Ness or at least that was what his biographer Adamnan wrote in 565. A funeral on the lake was disturbed by the monster. "Go thou no further. Quick! Go back," cried St Columba and the creature disappeared into the impenetrable depths. In the 16th c. Hector Boece mentioned in "The History of Scotland" that a "terrible being" had suddenly emerged from the water and swallowed three men. The next sighting was in 1933 when the A82 was under construction. A Mr and Mrs Spicer were sitting on the north bank admiring the lakeside scenery when a strange, writhing creature crossed the road in front of them. This gave rise to wild speculation that a plesiosaur had survived from prehistoric times and was living in the lake.

The most famous picture of *Nessiteras Rhombopteryx*, to give Nessie its full name, came from the camera of the London gynaecologist Robert Wilson. On April 19th 1934 Wilson reported seeing "something on the water" and took a snap: a long neck of the monster had just emerged from the ice-cold water. But it later turned out that Wilson belonged to a team of five who had set out to play a trick on the media. Shortly before his death in 1993, Christian Spurling, one of the "conspirators", explained his part in the great deception to Loch Ness researchers David Martin and Alastair Boyd. Marmaduke Wetherell, a film producer, although at the time a reporter for the *Daily Mail* investigating the existence of Nessie, his son Jan and the insurance agent Maurice Chambers were also present. According to the *Sunday Times* Spurling, an amateur wood-worker, had rigged up a dinosaur dummy on a toy submarine. The ruse worked perfectly.

A host of snapshots and eye-witness reports followed, not to mention a grow-ing stream of visitors. Most descriptions of the beast say it resembles a large sea reptile from the era of tropical dinosaurs. It is said to have a long neck, a small head, fins and several humps, but these features match those of certain species of sea snake.

lands (open: Apr.–Oct. Mon.–Sat. 10am–6pm, Sun. 2–6pm; Nov.–Mar. Mon.–Fri. 10am–3pm).

Newtonmore
Clan Macpherson
Museum
Waltzing Waters

The Macpherson Museum in neighbouring Newtonmore documents the turbulent history of the Macpherson clan. One of the exhibits is a first edition of the "Fingal translation". "Waltzing Waters" offers a 50-minute water display (open: daily, 10am–4pm, sometimes 8.30pm).

Caledonian Canal   D 5–E 4

Region: Highland

★★ Situation and
history

The Caledonian fault (see North-West Highlands) has only been used for transport since the beginning of the 19th c. Thomas Telford set to work on the canal in 1803 and it was finally completed in 1849. As a result, shipping was spared the hazardous northern route through the Pentland Forth

Despite all the denials, many dedicated Nessie fans continue to search for the illustrious creature. In return for about £75, enthusiasts can take an hour-long dive in a miniature submarine and try to seek out the monster for themselves. However, as with Dr. Jonathan Demsey in the wildly romantic Hollywood film "Nessie" (1996); perhaps the preservation of the legend is the most attractive part.

The official monster exhibition ar Drumnadrochit uses audio-visual techniques to recount the evolutionary history of the region and visitors can also read up on the least developments in the

Loch Ness Monster – fact or fiction?

search for the monster. Other exhibits include the first photos, newspaper headlines, underwater photos using sonar and the results of "Operation Deepscan" in 1987. Various readings from the murky waters of Loch Ness did point to the existence of something down there and and at least did not rule out the existence of the beloved monster (open: June–Sept. daily, 9am–9pm, Oct–May daily, 9am–6pm.

Outside the Visitor Centre stands a bronze statue of Scotland's mythical beast. Perhaps it is simply too shy to reveal its secrets to the world.

between the Scottish mainland and the Orkneys (see entry). Since then, the rail and road network has carried most of the east–west freight but a number of small vessels ply up and down the canal. But today it is the leisure industry which makes most use of the canal with holidaymakers in hired boats and canoes enjoying the magnificent scenery along the waterway. Only a third of the canal's length is man-made. The major part of it consists of narrow lochs. After Loch Linnhe, which is actually a fjord, i.e. a valley with steep sides formed by glaciation and then flooded by the sea, comes Loch Lochy, the small Loch Oich and then the longest – and best-known – the 24-mile/38.4km Loch Ness. The full Caledonian Canal including lochs extends for 60½ miles/96.8km, reaches a depth of on average 16ft/4.87m and passes through no fewer than 29 locks. The main difficulty in the canal's construction arose near Corpach on Loch Lochy where it was necessary to lower the level of the lake by 93ft/28.5m to sea level. Each of the eight locks, known collectively as Neptune's Staircase, overcame a difference of 8ft/2.44m – a great technological feat at the time. The canal starts in the west at Fort William (see entry) and ends in the east at Inverness (see entry).

Neptune's Staircase

Caledonian Canal

Fort William	See entry

Spean Bridge

The road from Fort William to Inverness (A82) offers a splendid panorama of the Caledonian fault. The stretch as far as Spean Bridge affords many superb views of the northern side of Ben Nevis (see Fort William, Surroundings). More feats of engineering were required when water from Loch Treig was diverted to generate electricity. Spean Bridge makes an excellent base for walks through the Glen Roy nature reserve. "Parallel Roads", as the terraces which run along the slope are called, indicate the various levels reached by the water of a Pleistocene lake which was dammed up by Ice Age glaciers.

Loch Arkaig
Loch Lochy
Loch Oich

North of Gairlochy, where a by-road forks off west to Loch Arkaig, the main highway follows Loch Lochy past caves where "Bonnie Prince Charlie" sought refuge after defeat at Culloden (see entry). The small islands in Loch Oich set against a backdrop of steep hillsides make a picturesque sight.

Well of Seven Heads

On the west bank of Loch Oich near a spring known as Tobar nan Ceann stands a remarkable memorial to a bloody incident that took place in the 17th c. Seven brothers were executed for the deaths of two members of the Keppoch family. Their heads were washed in the spring before being presented to the clan chief.

Invergarry

Invergarry is another good base for hill walkers and also a popular centre for anglers. It is here that the A87, the panoramic "Road to the Isles", branches off via Loch Garry and Loch Duich to the Kyle of Lochalsh (see North-West Highlands) where ferries cross to Skye (see Hebrides).

★Loch Ness

Fort Augustus
Abbey

Foyers

Fort Augustus (pop. 890) at the south end of Loch Ness is a favourite spot for tourists. The fortress which gave the place its name was built in 1715 and it became the headquarters of the English general Wade in 1729. After changing hands a number of times the greater part of it was demolished in 1876. Benedictine monks have since built an abbey and a highly-regarded school on the site. The Great Glen Exhibition documents the military past of the glen, the arrival of the religious orders and also tales of the Loch Ness monster (open: May–Sept. Mon.–Sat. 10am–12.30pm, 1.30–5pm, Sun. 1.30–5pm). The main road (A82) now continues towards Inverness along the north bank of Loch Ness, while the B862/B852 follows the south bank, passing close to the magnificent waterfall at Foyers. With pretty woodland lining both sides of the road, the southerly route is probably the more scenic.

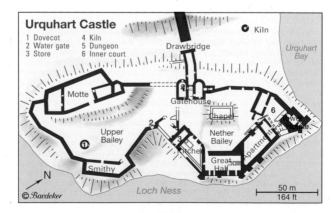

118

Follow the A82 about halfway along Loch Ness and just before the "Monster Exhibition" at Drumnadrochit the remains of Urquhart Castle appear standing on a tongue of land jutting out into the lake. Set against the backdrop of lake and mountain the castle is at the centre of many ancient myths. Dating from the 12th c. it was once a typical example of a motte and bailey fortification, but in the 14th c. stone walls replaced the original wooden structure. In 1509 James IV gave the castle to John Grant of Freuchie, whose family commissioned James Moray to extend the keep. At the end of the 17th c. the fortified castle fell victim to a fire (open: Apr.–Sept. daily, 9.30am–6.30pm; Oct.–Mar. Mon.–Sat. 9.30am–4.30pm, Sun. 11.30am–4.30pm).

★Urquhart Castle

At the north end of Loch Ness, a 3 mile/4.8km section of canal joins the narrow lake to Inverness (see entry) and the Moray Firth.

Moray Firth

Castle Trail

G 4

Region: Grampian

The Castle Trail is a circular tour of castles in the Grampian Region (see entry) starting from Aberdeen (see entry). White signs with blue writing refer to castles which are still intact. Blue signs with white writing refer to ruined castles.

Situation and description of the ★★ Castle Trail

Castle Fraser, built between 1575 and 1636, lies about 16 miles/25km north-west of Aberdeen on the A944. The huge stronghold was owned by the Fraser family until 1921 and has been run by the National Trust for Scotland since 1976. Like Crathes and Craigievar Castle, round towers, graceful conical roofs, oriel windows and decorative dormers create an impressive picture. The medieval belfry was extended in the late 16th c. with a five-storey wing, a square tower and a seven-storey round tower to create a Z-shaped structure. Two further low-level annexes were added in the 17th c. with stonemasons Bel and Leiper leaving behind their distinctive stamp. Some alterations made during the Victorian period have been reversed by the National Trust. Inside, the Great Hall and the "Laird's Lug", a secret chamber from which a spy could hear even whispered exchanges, are particularly interesting.

★Castle Fraser

Open: Easter, May, June, Sept. daily 1.30–5.30pm; July, Aug. daily 11am–5.30pm; Oct., Sat., Sun. 1.30–5.30pm

Craigievar Castle is situated 10 miles/16km further west. This delightful castle with small towers, crowstepped gables, round oriel windows, quaint conical roofs, ornamental stone cannons and a decorative zigzag console is proof that fairy tales can come true. The estate was first mentioned in documents dating from 1457 when it was owned by the Mortimer family. Work on the L-shaped tower house began at the end of the 16th c., but as a result of financial difficulties the castle had to be sold to William Forbes. "Danzig Willie" as the new owner was nicknamed had acquired his fortune from trade with the Baltic ports. Like Crathes and Castle Fraser, the towering seven-storey residence is not only a symbol of authority and wealth but it also has a practical function. Wood for building was in short supply in the Highlands, so architects exploited every inch of space under one small roof. The plasterwork in the Great Hall, the huge Stuart coat-of-arms above the fireplace and the carvings on the wall panelling were created in Renaissance style. A secret flight of steps leading up to a small room above a window in the Great Hall forms a part of a complicated system of stairs within the tower.

★★ Craigievar Castle

Open: May–Sept. daily, 1.30–5.30pm

En route to the next castle, it is worth calling in at Alford (pop. 1400) on the A980. The Grampian Transport Museum houses a collection of historic cars, cycles and carriages (open: Apr.–Nov. daily, 10am–5pm).
A narrow gauge railway runs from the restored Alford Station to Haughton Country Park, an ideal place for relaxing walks.

Alford
Grampian Transport Museum, Haughton Country Park

Castle Fraser: pepper-pot turrets and gabled dormers

★ Kildrummy Castle and Gardens

Open:
Apr.–Sept.
Mon.–Sat.
9.30am–6.30pm;
Oct.–Mar. Sat.
9.30am–4.30pm,
Sun. 2–4.30pm

Kildrummy Castle (HS; 8 miles/13km west of Alford) dates from the 13th c. Only scanty ruins remain but, surrounded by a wide moat, they nevertheless create a striking impression. Botanists will be interested in the water garden and rare trees. Built for Alexander II c. 1245, the castle has seen turbulent times. The English and Scots long disputed this strategic spot, besieging and destroying it more than once. On each occasion it was rebuilt but the edifice was finally dismantled in 1715 after the failed Jacobite uprising and the stonework was used elsewhere. The keep in the curtain wall, frequently a final refuge, possesses its own spring. The chapel's gable (1250) with three fine lancet windows is of particular interest.

Corgarff Castle

Open:
Apr.–Sept.
Mon.–Sat.
9.30am–6.30pm,
Sun. 2–6.30pm

Corgarff Castle (HS) stands on a hilltop by the Lecht pass (A939) about 16 miles/26km further west. The faithfully restored tower house was built in 1537 and star-shaped ramparts were added in 1738. The old Highland ballad "Edom o'Gordon" tells the tale of the tragic death in 1581 of Margaret Campbell, the wife of the laird Alexander Forbes, who perished in flames with her children and servants while the castle was under siege by the Gordons. After the Jacobite rebellion in 1748 Hanoverian troops used the castle as their barracks. They were followed by the English redcoats who had the unpopular job of putting a stop to whisky smuggling.

★ Leith Hall

Open:
May–Sept.
daily, 2–6.30pm;
Oct. Sat.–Sun.
2–5pm

Leith Hall lies at the heart of a 281 acre/114ha park 34 miles/55km northwest of Aberdeen and from 1605 it served for generations as the estate of the Leith family before passing to the National Trust for Scotland in 1945. An exhibition entitled "For Crown and Country" documents the history of the lairds who generally followed military careers. One of the exhibits is a present given by "Bonnie Prince Charlie" on the eve of the Battle of Culloden (see entry) in 1746. The Z-shaped 17th c. tower house and the 18th and 19th c. wings enclose an inner courtyard. It is worth having a quick look at the 18th c. stables and then taking a relaxing stroll through the extensive parkland with its lakes, viewpoint, Highland

Dinning room at Leith Hall

cattle and rare Soay breed of sheep, only found here or on St Kilda (see entry).

The imposing ruins of Huntly Castle (HS) barely 7 miles/11km further north stand on the site of the medieval Strathbogie Castle, which was until the middle of the 16th c. the seat of the Gordon family, the most powerful family in the region. The first Norman castle was burnt down in 1452 by Moray, but was rebuilt by the 4th Earl Gordon of Huntly starting in 1554. Forty years later it was destroyed again. The main section of the ruin dates from the restoration of 1602 undertaken by the 1st Marquis of Huntly. The entrance hall is decorated with weapons and heraldic ornamentation. Above the fireplace in the palace hang two portrait medallions of the 1st marquis George Gordon and his wife Henriette Stewart. The 15th c. tower house is the oldest part of the complex, but the brewery, bakery, east and west wings and stables were added in the 16th and 17th c.

★ Huntly Castle

Open:
Apr.–Sept.
Mon.–Sat.
9.30am–6.30pm,
Sun. 2–6.30pm

Five families have played their part in the history of Fyvie Castle (15 miles/24km to the east of Huntly) and the five towers bear their names. In the east is Preston Tower, in the west Meldrum Tower, in the centre of the south front Seton Tower, in the north Gordon Tower and in the north-west the Leith Tower. However, the word "Fyvie" does not derive from the English word "five" but from the Gaelic word for "stag's hill". Scottish monarchs stayed here at the beginning of the 12th c. when it was only a wooden fort, but it was reinforced in the 14th c. by stone walls and corner towers. At that time it belonged to Sir Henry Preston but it passed by marriage to the Meldrum family in the 15th c. In 1596 Alexander Seton bought the estate and set about converting it into the Scottish baronial style by adding tiny corner towers, oriel windows, conical roofs and stepped mouldings. About 1683 Robert White from Edinburgh finished the ceilings with some marvellous plasterwork, but this has only survived in the Morning Room. By the middle of the 18th c. the castle was in the hands of William Gordon who

★★ Fyvie Castle

Open:
Apr.–June, Sept.
daily
1.30–5.30pm;
July, Aug. daily
11am–5.30pm;
Oct., Sat., Sun.
1.30–5.30pm

drained the marshy terrain outside the east wing and built an artificial lake in the parkland. Pompeo Batonis' impressive portrait study of the young laird posing romantically in front of the Colosseum in Rome was painted during Gordon's journey to Italy in 1766. Financial distress forced the sale of Fyvie to Alexander Leith, an American steel magnate, who originated from near Fyvie. He assembled many expensive paintings – thirteen works by Raeburn – Brussels tapestries and a collection of weapons. The superb gallery on the second floor of Leith Tower must, however, be the castle's showpiece.

Loanhead Stone Circle
Brandsbutt Stone

Near Daviot about 8 miles/12.8km to the south-west stand the prehistoric Loanhead Stone Circles (HS) and at the north-western end of Inverurie is Brandsbutt Stone, a Pictish stone retaining symbols and inscriptions.

★Haddo House

Open:
Easter, May–Sept.
daily, 1.30–
5.30pm;
Oct. Sat., Sun.
1.30–5.30pm

This mansion (10 miles/16km south-east of Fyvie) was designed in 1731 for the 2nd Earl of Aberdeen by William Adam, father of the talented Adam brothers. In 1880 Wright and Mansfield renovated the furnishings in "Adam Revival" style. The elegant stucco and delicate pastel shades are typical of Robert Adam's interiors. The valuable paintings include Batonis' portrait of Lord Haddo (on the staircase), two van Dycks (in the Saloon) and several watercolours of Aberdeenshire castles (in the Giles Room), painted by James Giles for the 4th earl as book illustrations. The Pre-Raphaelite Edward Burne-Jones was responsible for the east window in the chapel. Every year the Haddo House Choral Society stages excellent concerts and opera evenings in the Community Hall (for further information: tel. (01651) 851440).

Tolquhon Castle

As indicated by an inscription near the gatehouse, William Forbes extended the 14th c. medieval tower house (3 miles/5km south of Haddo House) into a mansion between 1584 and 1589. Two huge round towers flank the tower house with its portal and heraldic panels. The inner courtyard and living accommodation lie ahead beyond the entrance hall (HS; open: Apr.–Sept. Mon.–Sat. 9.30am–6pm, Sun. 2–6pm; Oct.–Mar. Mon.–Sat. 9.30am–4pm, Sun. 2–4pm).

★Pitmedden Garden

Open:
May–Sept.
daily, 10am–6pm

The foundation stone for these colourful gardens was laid on May 2nd 1675 by Sir Alexander Seton. The gardens came under the administration of the National Trust for Scotland in 1952 and are situated 14 miles/22.4km north-west of Aberdeen. The floral designs, clipped box hedges and shrubs laid out around the central fountain follow a strict geometrical pattern and are a showpiece of Baroque garden landscaping. Holyrood Palace in Edinburgh (see entry) was the model for three of the four flowerbeds. "Tempus Fugit" is the subject of the south-east parterre, centred on a sundial, while the north-west parterre displays the heraldic emblem of Sir Alexander Seton, flanked by Scotland's saltire and thistle. The history of the garden from 1675 is recounted in one of the pavilions and the Museum of Farming Life illustrates the development of agriculture in the region.

Clyde Valley   E/F 6

Region: Strathclyde

River Clyde

The Clyde rises in the heather-covered mountains not far from Wanlockhead, an area where prospectors have searched for lead and gold since the 13th c. The water flows downstream between narrow walls of rock, first slowly and then speeding up before reaching the Falls of Clyde, a dramatic and beauty spot which has inspired many painters and writers including Wordsworth, Scott, Coleridge and Turner. The power of the water also impressed some key figures during the Industrial Revolution such as Richard Arkwright, David Dale and the socially committed Robert Owen. New Lanark was chosen by Owen for the site of one of Britain's largest cotton spinning mills. The Clyde with its rich green woodland and orchards, its fauna and flora and its fertile fields is still a popular destination for locals and visitors alike.

A signposted tourist route leads along the Clyde valley. It starts near Abington on the busy M74/A74 where the A702 turns to the east and then follows the course of the river northwards from the idyllic little villages at the foot of Tinto Hill via Biggar, Lanark and Hamilton and on to Blantyre. Further north in Monklands District based on Coatbridge (see Glasgow, Surroundings), the industrial traditions of the valley become stronger. The Clyde then flows through Glasgow (see entry) where a stroll "doon the watter" is an essential part of any tour of the city. For pure nostalgia, there is no substitute for a trip on the river in the "Waverley" steamer. Further downstream docks and huge shipyards used to dominate the skyline, striking symbols of the Victorian era, but today the centres of Port Glasgow and Greenock are now having to adapt to a post-industrial age. The Victorian resorts of Rothesay, Dunoon, Gourock, Millport and Largs along the Firth of Clyde continue to be popular destinations for the inhabitants of Scotland's major conurbations.

The tiny village of Wanlockhead is the highest village in Scotland. For more than 300 years lead ore was mined in the Lowther Hills. The lead it yielded sometimes met 80% of Britain's annual requirements. A tour round the museum begins in the Visitor Centre, an old village smithy where photos, models and a collection of minerals illustrate the history of mining in the region. Anyone intending to visit Lochnell Mine must obtained a helmet here. The gallery extends for close on 2650ft/800m into the mountain and the guides explain how mining techniques have changed over the centuries. Straitsteps Cottages are faithfully restored miners' homes built between 1740 and 1890 and they vividly demonstrate how difficult life was in those days. Every miner was an "independent contractor" who sold the lead he dug directly to the mining company. Everything that he needed for

Wanlockhead

★Lead Mining Museum

Miner's cottage c. 1740 . . .   *. . . and c. 1890: Wanlockhead Museum*

digging and meeting the needs of his family had to be purchased in the company shop who granted him credit for the first year. Even if he dug enough lead to pay the outstanding bill, there would hardly be any money left over to pay for the following year's requirements so he had to borrow again. This so-called "Truck System" meant that the miners remained indebted to the company for all their working lives. It was 1871 before a co-operative was formed which enabled the workers to survive independently of their bosses. A 19th c. winding engine can be seen near the cottages (open: Easter–mid-Oct. daily, 11am–4.30pm).

Biggar

★Gladstone
Court Museum

The little town of Biggar (pop. 1950; 22 miles/35km to the north-east) can offer four museums and a puppet theatre. Gladstone Court Museum in a Victorian covered lane north of High Street shows clearly how the ironmongers, photographers, tailors, cobblers and other skilled tradesmen of the town used to live (open: Easter–Oct. Mon.–Sat. 10am–12.30pm, 2–5pm, Sun. 2–5pm).

Albion Archive

The Albion building behind the museum houses the Albion Archive. The company started manufacturing cars in 1899 and developed quickly into one of Britain's leading producers of goods vehicles (now part of Leyland Daf).

★Gasworks
Museum

In 1812 after the London Gas Light and Coke Company – the world's first gas company – was entrusted with the task of supplying gas lights to streets and private houses, gas works enjoyed a period of rapid growth. By 1839 even a rural community such as Biggar had its own gas works. When it finally closed in 1973 it was converted into a museum, the only preserved coal-gas works in Scotland (HS; open: daily, June–mid-Sept. noon/2pm–5pm).

Victorian chemist shop: Gladstone Court Museum, Biggar

The Heritage Centre in Moat Park was opened in 1988 and documents 6000 years of history between the Tweed and Clyde valley, including a geological collection, models showing earlier types of settlement and a section on local fauna and flora (open: Easter–Oct. Mon.–Sat. 10am–5pm, Sun. 2–5pm).

Moat Park Heritage Centre

Greenhill farmhouse originally stood near Wiston on Tinto Hill but was faithfully rebuilt here. On display are documents and furniture belonging to the Covenanters from the second half of the 17th c. (open: Easter–mid-Oct. daily, 2–5pm).

Greenhill Covenanter's House

The miniature Victorian theatre regularly stages puppet plays and can accommodate 100 spectators (to the east on the B7016; open: Mon.–Sat. 11am–5pm, Sun. 2–5pm).

Puppet Theatre

See entry

New Lanark

Craignethan Castle (HS) is situated about 5 miles/8km north-west of Lanark. The locals still call it "Tillietudlum" after a novel by Sir Walter Scott. The huge tower house was built by Sir James Hamilton of Finnart in the 16th c. (open: Apr.–Sept. Mon.–Sat. 9.30am–7pm, Sun. 2–7pm; Oct.–Mar. Mon.–Sat. 9.30am–4pm, Sun. 2–4pm).

Craignethan Castle

The dukes of Hamilton's hunting lodge stands among the spreading trees of an extensive park near Ferniegair (1 mile/1.6km south of Hamilton). After renovation work lasting years, it is now back to its former glory. The design for the extravagant edifice was provided by William Adam in 1732 and the work was completed by 1744 (open: daily, 11am–4pm).

★ Chatelherault Castle

A fun swimming pool with white water rapids, jacuzzis, ice skating rink and fitness room are all part of Motherwell's Aquatec centre (open: daily, 10am–10pm).

Motherwell Aquatec

Blantyre's Livingstone Museum in Shuttle Row tells the life story of the African explorer David Livingstone (see Famous People) who was born in this house. The exhibition follows the tracks of Livingstone across the dark continent, explains his work as a missionary and describes his African friends such as Susi, Chuma and Jacob Wainwright who brought his coffin back to England in 1873. The dangers and difficulties of travelling in those days (Livingstone suffered badly from malaria), his struggle against slavery, his journeys along the Zambesi and to Lake Tanganyika and the discovery on November 17th 1855 of the spectacular Victoria Falls are also well documented. The Africa Room describes recent developments in the African continent (open: Mon.–Sat. 10am–6pm, Sun. 2–6pm).

Blantyre ★ David Livingstone Centre

High above the banks of the River Clyde stand the vast ruins of Bothwell Castle (HS) with its towers and curtain walls. This 13th c. stronghold serves as a monument to the skills of Scottish fortress builders. The sandstone walls which came under fierce attack during the Wars of Independence are 16ft/5m thick in places (open: Apr.–Sept. Mon.–Sat. 11am–5pm, Sun. 2–5pm).

★ Bothwell Castle

See Glasgow, Surroundings

Monklands District

See entry

Glasgow

Glasgow, Surroundings

Firth of Clyde

Region: Strathclyde

Cowal

Situation and Access

The Cowal peninsula to the north-west of Glasgow (see entry) has recently seen an upsurge in popularity. The scenery is magnificent and there are plenty of opportunities for sailing. Long narrow lochs extend from the Firth of Clyde far into the peninsula which enjoys a favourable climate. Glacial action has created a shape which on a map looks like a hand. If coming from Glasgow, cross the Firth of Clyde by ferry to Dunoon (see Practical Information, Ferries). It is possible to take a trip around the peninsula starting at Arrochar at the northern end of Loch Long.

Dunoon

The lively resort of Dunoon (pop. 9300) is the main town on the island. It boasts an attractive promenade, an eighteen-hole golf course and the Royal Clyde Yacht Club, which is well known among amateur sailors, particularly for the two-week regatta which is held every year in July. Dunoon is also noted for its Highland Gathering that takes place at the end of August in the sports stadium. The marina is full of brightly-coloured yachts and the busy harbour is used by pleasure boats from Rothesay (Bute), the "Waverley" steamer and ferries from Gourock.

Kilmun Arboretum

The Kilmun Arboretum with a host of rare shrubs and trees is situated on the northern bank of Holy Loch (7 miles/11.2km). Several members of the Campbell family are buried in the medieval church (15th c.), including Archibald Campbell the 1st Marquess of Argyll who was executed by Charles II in Edinburgh in 1661 for high treason.

★★ Younger Botanic Garden
★ Loch Eck

Take the A815 northwards past Holy Loch and on to Benmore and the Younger Botanic Garden (7 miles/11.2km). These gardens at the southern end of Loch Eck are an outstation of Edinburgh's Royal Botanic Garden (see Edinburgh). More than 250 different species of rhododendron and azaleas flourish here. The avenue of giant Californian redwoods makes a splendid sight (open: mid-Mar.–Oct. daily 10am–6pm).

★ Argyll Forest Park

Established in 1935 Argyll Forest Park was the first of its kind in Great Britain and with its network of footpaths covering 186 miles/300km, it offers nature-lovers plenty of beautiful countryside to explore.

Strone House Gardens

Strone Garden at the northern end of Loch Fyne near Cairndow claims to have the tallest tree in the country, the 190ft/58m "Grand Fir". In spring the displays of primroses and narcissi attract many visitors.

Rest and be Thankful, Loch Long

"Rest and be Thankful" is the name given to the highest point on the A83 (803ft/245m) between the northern end of Loch Fyne and Loch Long. Further east, as the road passes through pretty Glen Croe, the full beauty of the Cobbler or "Ben Arthur" (2891ft/882m) can be appreciated. A plaque by the A83 commemorates the soldiers who repaired the road in the 17th c.

Arrochar
★ Arrochar Alps

The scenic A83 finally reaches Arrochar (pop. 600) at the north end of Loch Long only 2 miles/3.2km from Loch Lomond (see entry). The tiny village makes a good base for climbing the "Arrochar Alps" north of Glen Croe, with Ben Ime at 3318ft/1009m the greatest challenge. For hill walkers aiming to complete the "Monros" (see Baedeker Special, "How to become a Munroist"), those summits in Scotland higher than 3280ft/1000m, this range has three other peaks in that category, plus the already mentioned Cobbler.

★ Loch Fyne
Castle Lachlan

The ruins of Castle Lachlan stand to the south-west of Cairndow by the banks of Loch Fyne. The medieval castle was begun in the 12th c. Loch Fyne is noted for its oyster beds.

Old stone bridge near Arrochar

South of the junction between the A866 and the A8003 the sailing centre of Tighnabruaich occupies a picturesque location by the waters of the Kyles of Bute. On the east side of the inlet at the end of the A866 lies the little village of Colintrave, where a ferry operates from the jetty to Rhubodach on the island of Bute (see Practical Information, Ferries).

★ **Kyles of Bute**
Tighnabruaich

Bute

Rothesay, Bute's main town, can also be reached directly from Wemyss Bay on the mainland (see Practical Information, Ferries). Built during the 1920s, the theatre by the pier on Victoria Street has been faithfully restored. It is a popular venue for films and other cultural events and its restaurant offers a fine sea view.

★ **Rothesay**

The castle at Rothesay was first mentioned in documents in 1228 when the Normans invaded. From the 14th c. it was used as a base by Scottish kings in their struggles with the "Lords of the Isles". In 1685 the English burnt the castle down and, although an attempt was made to restore it in the 19th c. it is still mainly a ruin. It is the only fortress in Scotland with four round towers overlooking a circular inner courtyard. The Great Hall on the first floor of the main tower is currently undergoing restoration. In order to escape an arranged marriage, the daughter of a High Stewart is said to have stabbed herself in the courtyard behind the chapel (open: Apr.–Sept. Mon.–Sat. 9.30am–6pm, Sun. 2–6pm; Oct.–Mar. Mon.–Thur., Sat. 9.30am–4pm, closed Wed. am, Sun. 2–4pm).

Castle

Amateur gardeners will enjoy a visit to the colourful Ardencraig Gardens, which specialises in cacti, pot plants, fuchsias and aquatic plants (open: May–Sept. Mon.–Fri. 9.30am–4.30pm, Sat. Sun. 1–4pm).

Ardencraig
Gardens

The small chapel on the west coast of the island was founded by St Ninian and his scholars at the end of the 6th c.

St Ninian's Chapel

127

Moorings at Rothesay, gateway to the Kyles of Bute

Culloden   E 4

Region: Highland

Situation

About 6 miles/9.6km east of Inverness (see entry) by the B5006 lies a flat, marshy tract of land ringed by alders and buffeted by the wind. It was here in the north-eastern corner of Drumossie Moor on April 16th 1746 that the last great battle was fought on Scottish soil. The fate of the "Stuarts" was determined once and for all and the incorporation of Scotland into England was cast in stone.

Visitor Centre

Donations and sales at a nominal sum enabled The National Trust for Scotland to acquire this battlefield site between 1937 and 1959. Bit by bit it has been restored to the state it was in during the 18th c. The Visitor Centre has been extended more than once in order to meet the requirements of the many tourists who visit this historic site. The audio-visual presentation portrays "Bonnie Prince Charlie" as an irresponsible adventurer rather than as a romantic hero (open: Feb., Mar., Nov., Dec. daily, 10am–4pm; Apr.–mid-May, mid-Sept.–Oct. daily 9am–5pm; mid-May–mid-Sept. 9.30am–6pm).

★Memorials

On both sides of the old road (laid out in Victorian times and widened by the NTS) lie the gravestones of the Scottish clans which Duncan Forbes, the owner of Culloden House, erected in 1881. He was also responsible for the 20ft/6m high memorial stone which commemorates the Battle of Culloden. On the nearest Saturday to the date of the battle, the Gaelic Society in Inverness holds a service beside this memorial to remember the battle and those who died in it.

Old Leanach Cottage, the last farmer's cottage from the days of the battle has been faithfully restored and the melancholic sound of the Gaelic folk

Old Leanach Cottage – the last on Culloden's battlefield

song "Mo run gealog" (My beautiful young darling) drifts from its rooms. Cumberland Stone marks the spot at the eastern edge of the battlefield where the Duke of Cumberland is said to have issued the orders to his troops. The whole field is strewn with stones which bear witness to the dead. For example, the Keppoch Stone (accessible from the northern footpath) indicates the spot where Alastair MacDonell the head of the Keppoch clan fell, and another recalls the Irish Wild Geese (mercenaries in the service of the French crown who fought on the side of the Highlanders). The "English Stone" (west of Old Leanach Cottage) commemorates the dead who fought alongside Cumberland.

Clava Cairns on the south side of the River Nairn have nothing to do with the battle. The mounds of stone surrounded by stone rings probably date from *c.* 1800–1500 B.C. and are among the best preserved of their kind in Scotland.

★Clava Cairns

On April 16th 1746 the troops of Prince Charles Edward Stuart ("Bonnie Prince Charlie") lined up to face the Duke of Cumberland in what turned out to be a bloody but decisive battle. The Jacobites, supporters of the Scottish king James II, had laid claim to the British throne and faced the army of George II, the Hanoverians. In the previous year the 25-year-old "Bonnie Prince Charlie" had returned from exile in France to the Hebrides (see entry). He had gathered the clansmen around him and marched south in order to assert the claims of his father against the Hanoverians. By the time he had reached Derby, fear of the impending attack was already widespread throughout London, but stricken with melancholy and indecision, fearing there was little support for him in England, he turned back. Furthermore, many of the clansmen had deserted him; homesickness and the wish to be back home in Scotland for the harvest proved to be a stronger emotion than the prospect of military success. Near Inverness the prince and his troops set up their winter camp and waited for the soldiers of the

The Battle of
Culloden

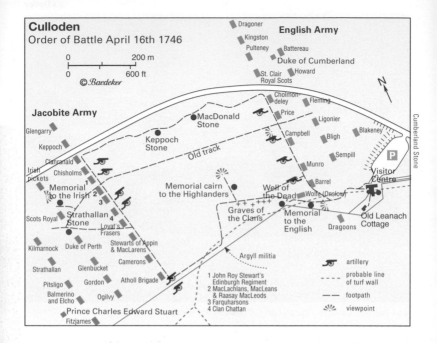

Culloden
Order of Battle April 16th 1746

English Army

0 — 200 m
0 — 600 ft
© *Baedeker*

N

Cumberland Stone

Dragoner
Kingston
Pulteney Battereau
Duke of Cumberland
St. Clair Howard
Royal Scots
Cholmon-
deley Fleming

Jacobite Army

MacDonald
Stone
Price
Glengarry
Keppoch
Stone
Campbell Ligonier
Keppoch
Blakeney
Bligh
Old track
Clanranald
Chisholms
Sempill
Irish
pickets
Munro
Memorial cairn
Memorial to the Highlanders
to the Irish 1
2 Well of
the Dead Barrel
3 Wolfe (Onslow)
Graves of
Scots Royal the Clans Visitor
Strathallan 4 Centre
Stone Memorial
Lovat's to the Old Leanach
Frasers English Dragoons Cottage
Kilmarnock Duke of Perth Stewarts of Appin
& MacLarens
Camerons
Strathallan Glenbucket Argyll militia
Pitsligo Gordon Atholl Brigade 1 John Roy Stewart's
Balmerino Edinburgh Regiment artillery
and Elcho Ogilvy 2 MacLachlans, MacLeans probable line
& Raasay MacLeods of turf wall
Prince Charles Edward Stuart 3 Farquharsons
4 Clan Chattan footpath
Fitzjames viewpoint

P

Duke of Cumberland as they headed northwards. On April 15th the duke celebrated his 25th birthday with a feast. When the Jacobite troops heard about this they set off through the night to surprise the enemy camp established by the River Nairn. But as they approached the camp, the sun rose, so they turned round and many fell asleep by the roadside exhausted – until the duke's Redcoats found them and slit their throats. By choosing the level surface at Culloden for the battle, the result was already clear. The Highlanders, experienced in mountain warfare, knew only one tactic: advancing by surprise attack – the rest was close man-to-man combat. Culloden, however, was tailor-made for the rested, disciplined and organised army of Lord Cumberland (including three Scottish regiments) and their artillery. About 5000 clansmen opposed 9000 Redcoats. Battle commenced at around noon when Cumberland's musketeers let loose a hail of shots from three-pounders and hand mortars. Charles hesitated about sending in his feared Highlanders armed with claymores. The element of surprise, noise and fear were supposed to put the enemy on the defensive, but the attack was slow and badly co-ordinated and many men were quickly lost. In less than an hour the Scottish army weary from their night-time march were soundly beaten. Some 1200 Scots died to only 350 of Cumberland's army. No prisoners were taken. Fleeing soldiers and the wounded were massacred. Even bystanders, farmers in their fields, women and children were not spared. The victorious Cumberland was nicknamed "The Butcher". The killing went on for days, all the easier for the English soldiers as they perceived their victims as "different" in both what they wore and how they spoke.

Anti-Scottish sentiments manifested themselves with a ban on kilts, tartan, Gaelic and the bagpipe. A piper in York was sentenced to death for playing a "forbidden weapon of war". In 1747 the Union Treaty was broken: a change in the law destroyed the power of the clan chiefs.

Prince Charles was able to escape the persecution that followed. With the assistance of Flora MacDonald he fled to the Hebrides (see entry) and then to France and Rome where he later died a sad alcoholic, "the last prince of a lost cause". His fourteen months in Scotland from the landing on the Hebrides, the abortive march on London, the bloody dénouement on the marshy fields of Culloden and the romantic escape all contributed towards the creation of a mystique surrounding "Bonnie Prince Charlie". Countless songs, ballads and tales immortalised in print, even in film at Hollywood, have created a nostalgic legend that pervaded Scotland in the 19th and 20th centuries.

Dee Valley   F/G 4

Region: Grampian

Overlooked by mountains on both sides, the A93 follows the pretty Dee valley from Aberdeen (see entry) to Braemar where it turns to the south and crosses the Cairnwell Pass north of Glen Shee before linking up with the roads from Dundee (see entry) and Perth (see entry).

Royal Deeside between Aberdeen and Braemar

Drum Castle, the third oldest tower house in Scotland, lies some 10 miles/ 16km west of Aberdeen (see entry). The huge granite structure was commissioned in 1286 by the first mayor of Aberdeen Richard Cementarius. In 1386 Robert the Bruce (see Famous People) granted his standard bearer William de Irwyn rights to the royal wood at Drum – the land is now planted with a marvellous rose garden and an arboretum containing a number of rare trees. The castle stayed within the de Irwyn family until 1976 when it was adopted by the National Trust for Scotland. The fortified tower – for defensive reasons the walls reach a thickness of 13ft/4m at ground

★Drum Castle

Open: Easter, May–Sept. daily, 1.30– 5.30pm; Oct, Sat., Sun. 1.30–5.30pm

Drum Castle: Renaissance-style splendour

level and 10ft/3m higher up – has changed very little over the centuries. Only in 1619 after the Reformation did the 9th laird, Alexander Irvine, request the Aberdeen mason Bell to convert the keep into a Renaissance style mansion. This part is still largely untouched. In the oak-panelled Saloon, it is the portraits – by Raeburn, Reynolds and Graham Gilbert – and the view of "Castlegate in Aberdeen" by the Scot Hugh Irvine which deserve most attention. In the Dining Room, look out for a magnificent Chinese porcelain tray (18th c.).

★★ Crathes Castle

Open:
daily,
11am–5.30pm

Follow the A93 westward and after 3 miles/4.8km the home of the Burnett family will come into view. It is now run by the National Trust for Scotland. Crathes Castle is a classic example of Scottish baronial style. The tower house with its small oriel windows, pretty corner towers and windows of varying sizes and surrounding ledges was begun in 1553 by Alexander Burnard (later Burnett) and his wife Janet Hamilton. Their initials can be made out above the original entrance door on the east front. The plans for the L-shaped complex, which was completed in 1596, were once again supplied by the local Bell family, who are also linked with Midmar, Craigievar and Castle Fraser (see Castle Trail). While issues of defence preoccupied earlier owners, the 16th c. building clearly reflects the residents' aesthetic concerns and issues of prestige. In the 18th c. the need for greater comfort led to the construction of an extension. This was burnt down in 1966 but has been rebuilt and restored to its original condition. The entrance to the castle is in the restored Queen Anne wing. The castle's upper storeys are worth a tour, if only for a glimpse of the beautifully painted wooden ceilings (1600). They were painted by local artists after the panels had been fitted. The figures depicted in the Room of the Nine Nobles – typical of the decorative work of the time – are the ancient heroes (Hector, Julius Caesar and Alexander the Great), three Old Testament characters (David, Jesse and Judas Maccabaeus) and three famous rulers (King Arthur, Charlemagne and Godfrey de Bouillon). The legendary ghost of Crathes is said to haunt the Green Lady's Room, where the ceiling is also painted decoratively. Nine muses dancing and playing music are depicted in the old Music Room, together with the Five Virtues. In the same room the great Gobelin-style tapestry on the wall was the work of William Morris c. 1868, while the Muses Room contains a Thompson chair, complete with the tiny wooden mouse which is found on all pieces from the Yorkshire furniture designers. Unique to Scotland is the Long Gallery (c. 1620) which runs the full width of the top floor. The oak panels with royal coats-of-arms plus those belonging to the family are the only ones of their kind in Scotland.

★ Crathes Garden

The parkland was first laid out in 1702 but at the beginning of the 20th c. landscape gardeners William Robinson and Gertrude Jekyll gave it a new look. The neatly trimmed yew hedge (18th c.) attracts a lot of attention, not to mention the magnolias, oleander and rose garden (open: daily, 9.30am until dusk).

Banchory
Museum

The local history museum in Bridge Street, Banchory (pop. 6200), was opened in 1993. Displays cover the production of perfume, Highland costumes, fiddler Scott Skinner and natural environment (open: June–Sept. daily, 10am–1pm, 2–5.30pm; Oct.–May Sat., Sun. 11am–1pm, 2–5pm).

Peel Ring
of Lumphanan

Although the surrounding stone wall was built in the 18th c., Peel Ring itself (HS; 11 miles/17.6km north-west of Banchory; A980) dates from the early Middle Ages. It was in this valley between the Dee and the Don that Macbeth met his death at the hands of Malcolm Canmore. Macbeth's Cairn indicates the site of the fateful encounter.

Ballater
MacEwan Gallery

Return to the Dee valley and continue west along the A93 as far as Ballater (pop. 1300). The village art gallery opened by the Swiss artist Rudolphe Christen in 1902 displays works by local artists was (open: daily, 10am–6pm).

Queen Elizabeth II's summer residence in Scotland (7 miles/11.2km from Braemar) has come to embody the Neo-baronial style of the Victorian era. The estate which was first mentioned in documents in 1484 and, after Queen Victoria bought it in 1852, she commissioned the Aberdeen architect William Smith to implement plans drawn up by her husband Prince Albert. Inside the castle, the Ballroom with its paintings and other objets d'art and also a collection of coaches are open to the public, but only when the royal family are not in residence (usually May–July, Mon.–Sat. 10am–5pm). The extensive parkland is ideal for a relaxing stroll.

★ Balmoral Castle

The highest point in the Balmoral forest is Lochnagar (3786ft/1154m), a peak that belongs to the royal family and Balmoral Castle. In 1845 John Begg named a whisky distillery after the mountain, as it was the source of the water he used in the distilling process. When Queen Victoria and her husband visited the distillery in 1848, they were so impressed with the sample they were offered that they granted Begg the right to supply the royal household – a privilege that the company still enjoys. The Special Reserve Single Malt is available for sampling in the Visitor Centre after a guided tour.

★ **Royal Lochnagar Distillery**

Open: Mon.–Fri. 10am–5pm; Easter–Oct. also Sat. 11am–4pm

The foundation stone for the parish church at Crathie was laid by Queen Victoria in 1893 and the chapel contains many reminders of the queen's connections with the region. Services here are attended by the royal family when they are in residence at Balmoral and they attract many onlookers.

Crathie Church

Braemar (pop. 800; 1100ft/335m) is one of the most popular centres in the Grampian region and many visitors are drawn here on the first Saturday in September for the Royal Highland Gathering (see Highland Games, Festivals and Folk Music). Members of the royal family often attend the grand occasion and have been known to take part. Many of the 20,000 or more spectators turn out in traditional Scottish costume – the women wear

Braemar
★★ Braemar Gathering

Whisky barrels at the Royal Lochnagar distillery

tartan dresses and the men a kilt and plaid (see Baedeker Special, "Tartan, Plaid and Kilt"). "Tossing the caber", a sport unique to Scotland, is one of the spectacular events at the gathering. While the bagpipes play, the trunks of young fir trees are tossed from a vertical position. The history of this Scottish equivalent of the Olympic Games is documented in the Braemar Highland Heritage Centre in Mar Road (open: daily, 10am–6pm).

Braemar Castle

Work on the crenellated Braemar Castle was started in 1628 by the Earl of Mar but by the end of the 17th c. the building was burnt down by the Jacobite Farquharsons of Inverey (see entry). After the defeat at Culloden (see entry), the L–shaped fortress fell into English hands and was used as a base for the Hanoverian troops. A star-shaped curtain wall was added for extra protection. Although the castle is still in use as the residence of the Farquharsons of Invercauld, visitors can view, among other things, the barrel vaulting in the lower storeys, the underground dungeon and the great iron gate (open: Easter–Oct. Sat.–Thur. 10am–6pm; tel. (01339) 741219).

Dumfries and Galloway   D–F 6/7

Situation and characteristics

The south-western part of the Scottish Lowlands between Dumfries and Stranraer has much to entice visitors: the scenic charm of the hills around the spa town of Moffat, the wilderness of Galloway Forest Park, the long sandy beaches and the breathtakingly beautiful rocky coast along the Solway Firth. The region can also boast many splendid gardens, which flourish in the favourable climate, romantic castles and ruined abbeys and not least Dumfries, the last place on the Robert Burns literary trail (see Famous People). The route starts in Ayr (see entry) to the north and winds its way south to the regional centre of Dumfries where Burns wrote the last of his immortal verses. His local pub the Globe Inn still possesses his favourite chair and he provided a window pane inscribed with an affec-

Dumfries and Galloway

© Baedeker

tionate verse to one of the waitresses. Walkers can follow the waymarked Southern Uplands Way, a journey of over 212 miles/339.2km. It starts in Portpatrick on the west coast and crosses to Cockburnspath on the east.

★ Dumfries

The administrative centre for the region, Dumfries (pop. 33,000) lies on the River Nith which flows into the Solway Firth a little further south. The town can look back over an eventful history. It obtained its charter as a "Royal Burgh" from Robert II in 1395. The old town hall in the middle of the market place was built in 1708 and the bridge, now reserved for pedestrians, dates from 1208.

Dumfries Museum

Although the Dumfries Museum on Corbelly Hill specialises in local history, it also possesses an observatory with a Camera Obscura that was installed in 1836 (open: Mon.–Sat. 10am–1pm, 2–5pm, Sun. 2–5pm; Oct.–Mar. closed Sun., Mon.).

★Burns' House

The house in Burns Street (formerly Mill Vennel) where the celebrated poet spent the last four years of his life and where his wife Jean Armour lived

Cistercian abbeys in the 12th c.   *Robert Burns's house, Dumfries*

until her death in 1834 is now a museum displaying Burns memorabilia (open: Mon.–Sat. 10am–1pm, 2–5pm, Sun. 2–5pm; Oct.–Mar. closed).

The poet's last resting place is to be found a short distance away in St Michael's churchyard. The mausoleum was erected in 1815.　**Burns' Mausoleum**

An 18th c. mill in Mill Road on the west bank of the River Nith documents the last few years of the poet's life and also recreates something of the atmosphere in Dumfries during the 1790s.　**Burns Centre**

East of Dumfries

The resort of Lochmaben (9 miles/14.4km to the north-east) is surrounded by five lakes so that it resembles an island. The lakes are of course popular with anglers, while the abandoned castle (HS) is claimed, alongside Turnberry Castle, as the birthplace of Robert the Bruce (see Famous People) whose statue stands in front of the town hall.　**Lochmaben**
Castle

The Victorian writer Thomas Carlyle was born in Ecclefechan and the house where he grew up maintains a collection of manuscripts and other memorabilia (open: May–Sept. daily; Oct.–Apr. Sat.–Sun. 1–5pm). Carlyle is buried in the graveyard.　**Ecclefechan**
Thomas Carlyle's birthplace

More than 1000 dolls, a large number of dolls' houses and other toys dating from 1830 can be seen in Alice's Wonderland Museum in Gretna just north of the border with England (open: Mon., Wed.–Sat. 10am–5pm, Sun. 11am–5pm).　**Gretna**
Alice's Wonderland

The Old Blacksmith's Shop where the wedding ceremony for runaway lovers used to be held has some romantic tales to tell (open: Apr.–Oct. daily, 9am–5pm).　**Gretna Green**
★ **Old Blacksmith's Shop**

135

Gretna Green – a Runaways' Hideout

The border village of Gretna Green was at one time the world's most famous refuge for young lovers. Nowhere else was it so simple to receive a priest's blessing for marriage without parental permission as in this village just off the A1 a few miles north of the English town of Carlisle.

After union with England in 1707 Scotland retained a legal system which had evolved in its own way over the centuries. Under Scottish law only two witnesses to the wedding ceremony were required. These "mock marriages" acquired notoriety throughout the world, especially as the village blacksmith's shop was usually the place where the knot was tied. In Scotland, once a youngster reached the age of sixteen, parents were not able to stand in their way if they wished to marry, whereas in England parental consent was needed for minors, i.e. those under the age of 21. In 1846 the law was amended and it became necessary for one of the partners to the marriage to reside in Scotland for at least 21 days before the ceremony, a change which helped to boost the hotel trade in the vicinity if nothing else. The practice continued with tales of parents chasing children across the border – and happy and tragic endings. The so-called "Anvil Marriages" were finally declared illegal in 1940.

The legends surrounding Gretna have had an enduring effect on young couples – every year throughout the last decade over 1000 marriages have taken place here. For many young lovers Gretna is still a romantic setting for a wedding. In the meantime, outlets for tartan and tweed have sprung up alongside handicraft centres and a coach museum.

Gretna Green: smithy where runaway couples used to wed

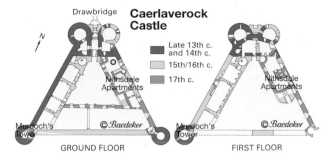

Caerlaverock Castle

Drawbridge

Late 13th c. and 14th c.
15th/16th c.
17th c.

Nithsdale Apartments

Nithsdale Apartments

Murdoch's Tower

Murdoch's Tower

© Baedeker

© Baedeker

GROUND FLOOR

FIRST FLOOR

Ruthwell and its early Christian cross are well worth a visit before returning to Dumfries. A niche in the purpose-built church houses one of the two most famous Christian crosses of Anglo-Saxon times. Carved out of sandstone probably in the 8th c., it reaches a height of 17ft/5.2m. It is possible to make out some Latin inscriptions as well as several biblical figures and leaf patterns (HS).

★Ruthwell Cross

The B735 leads past the imposing ruins of Caerlaverock Castle (HS; 8 miles/13km to the south-west) which was once the home of the Maxwell family. The castle dates from 1270 when the English established a bridgehead here in order to mount an invasion of the rest of Scotland. The triangular fortress plus drawbridge and water-filled moat was altered in the 15th c. and a double-tower gate house was added. The Nithsdale Apartments and ornate Renaissance façade on the east side of the castle originated in the 17th c. when, after the Union of Crowns in 1603, the castle became more a residence and less a fortification. The 1st Earl of Nithsdale improved the appearance of his home by adding heraldic symbols and pointed or round window and door pediments. A few years later, however, the interior was abandoned after an attack by the Covenanters. It is thought that "Ellangowan" in Scott's "Guy Mannering" is modelled on this moated castle.

★★Caerlaverock Castle

Open:
Apr.–Sept.
Mon.–Sat. 9.30am–
6pm, Sun. 2–6pm;
Oct.–Mar.
Mon.–Sat. 9.30am–
4pm, Sun. 2–4pm

The nearby marshland is a haven for swans, ducks and wading birds and in the winter thousands of Brent geese come here to breed.

North of Dumfries

The ruins of Lincluden Abbey lie about 1½ miles/2.4km north of Dumfries. This Benedictine monastery founded in the 12th c. was elevated to collegiate church by Archibald "the Grim". All that remains are the chancel, sacristy and parts of the small 15th c. sandstone chapel. Princess Margaret (d. 1430), daughter of Robert III, is buried in the chancel where the Late Gothic window tracery still survives (HS).

Lincluden Abbey

In 1788 at Ellisland Farm (6½ miles/10.4km north-west of Dumfries) Robert Burns began to employ new agricultural methods but with such little success that the land had to be sold off in 1791. The famous ballad about his friend "Tam o'Shanter" and "Auld Lang Syne" were written while he lived here (museum open: daily, 10am–1pm, 2–5pm).

Ellisland Farm
Burns Museum

Stephen Laurie bought 14th c. Glencairn Castle in 1611, changed the name to Maxwelton House and had the tower house extended. His granddaughter, the subject of a very popular ballad by Lady Scott, was born there in 1682. In 1968 the Stenhouse family bought the estate and started work on restoration which took a total of three years. Now the chambers, chapels and gardens are back to their former grandeur (13 miles/20.8km north-west of Dumfries).

★Maxwelton House

Open:
Easter–Sept.
daily, 10.30am–
5.30pm

Drumlanrig Castle, built by the first Duke of Queensbury

Glenkiln
★ Sculpture Park

Just 3 miles/4.8km further north-west near Moniave a special experience awaits art lovers. Just a mile or two south of the village on a lonely moor near Glenkiln estate, about halfway up the hillside, stand Henry Moore's life-size bronze sculptures entitled "King and Queen". The owner Sir William Keswick has gathered together an appreciable outdoor collection, including works by Rodin, Einstein and Renoir.

★★ Drumlanrig Castle

Open:
Castle: May–Aug.
Mon.–Wed., Fri.,
Sat. 11am–5pm
Sun. 1–5pm;
Garden: daily,
11am or
noon–6pm

Drumlanrig Castle is situated about 10 miles/16km north of Moniave. It was the seat of the Douglas family, later to become the dukes of Buccleuch and Queensberry. An avenue of beech trees leads up to this picture-book castle of red sandstone crowned with numerous small towers.

James Smith and his father-in-law Robert Mylne were commissioned by the first Duke of Queensberry to design the castle and work started in 1679 and was completed in 1689. When the duke was presented with the bill for the castle of his dreams, he is said to have been so taken aback that he only stayed there one more night. This four-winged Renaissance palace with its decorative façade possesses a unique collection of French furniture from the 17th and 18th c. Highlights include fine chests of drawers, cupboards and inlaid tables by Charles Cressent, Pierre II Migeon, Jacques Denizot and Adrien Delorme. Carvings by Grinling Gibbons are highlights of the Lounge and Dining Room and the collection of paintings with portraits by Kneller, van Dyck, Ramsay, Reynolds and Gainsborough deserve attention but the three masterpieces by Leonardo da Vinci, Hans Holbein the Younger and Rembrandt are the castle's most prized possessions. Some 17th c. Brussels tapestries, Chelsea, Derby and Meissen porcelain are also of interest. "Bonnie Prince Charlie" is said to have stayed the night here on December 22nd 1745 and a portrait and a gold casket belonging to the unfortunate Pretender are on display.

The post office in Sanquhar High Street (11 miles/17.6km to the north-west) has been in business without a break since 1763 and is said to be the oldest in Britain.

Sanquhar
Post Office

In the middle of the 17th c. the discovery of sulphur springs transformed the quiet village of Moffat (pop. 2000; 20 miles/32km north of Dumfries) into a popular spa town. Of more importance for the local economy, however, was sheep farming. A bronze ram on the Colvin fountain in High Street symbolises the prosperity that wool and textiles have brought to the region. The local woollen mill can offer a wide selection of high-quality woollen products from both the Southern Uplands and northern Scotland.

★Moffat

To the north-east of Moffat just before the boundary with the Borders region, the A708 passes a 200ft/61m high waterfall that cascades from the southern end of Loch Skene (NTS).

★Grey Mare's Tail

The Solway Firth from Dumfries to Stranraer

Follow the A710 south out of Dumfries. Before reaching the coast and the fine views over the Solway Firth, stop off at New Abbey and pay a visit to the delightful ruins of Sweetheart Abbey (HS). The Cistercian Abbey here was founded in 1273 by Devorgilla, who also played a part in the creation of Balliol College, Oxford. She always carried the embalmed heart of her beloved husband John Balliol with her in an ivory box and after her death it was buried alongside her – hence the origins of the name. A pretty mill dating from the late 18th c. grinds corn in the traditional style (HS; open: Apr.–Sept. Mon.–Sat. 9.30am–6pm, Sun. 2–6pm; Oct.–Mar. Mon.–Sat. 9.30am–4pm, Sun. 2–4pm).

New Abbey
★Sweetheart Abbey

★Corn Mill

The carefully prepared collection at the costume museum in Shambellie House brings to life the elegance of the Victorian and Edwardian eras. The premises were built by David Bryce c. 1856 for the Stewart family.

Shambellie House

Solway Firth and the English Lake District beyond are visible from points to the south-west of Criffell (1866ft/569m).

Criffell

The splendid gardens at Arbigland House near Kirkbean were laid out c. 1700. During the 18th c. John Paul Jones, the "Father" of the US navy, worked here. He was the son of the head gardener (open: May–Sept. Tues.–Sun. 2–6pm).

Arbigland Gardens

Medieval Threave Castle sits on a small island in the Dee. It lies barely 3 miles/5km south-west of the small town of Castle Douglas (pop. 3900). The four-storey keep was built by Archibald "the Grim", Lord Galloway, between 1339 and 1390. Three corner towers were then added c. 1450. However, as the last of the Douglas fortresses, in 1455 it had to be handed over to King James II. By the middle of the 17th c. it had been dismantled (HS; open: Apr.–Sept. Mon.–Sat. 9.30am–6pm, Sun. 2–6pm). Threave Gardens lie about 1 mile/1.6km further south, were laid out in the last century and in spring over 200 varieties of narcissi make a beautiful show (open: daily, 9.30am until dusk).

Castle Douglas
Threave Castle

★Threave Gardens

The A712 between New Galloway (to the north-west of Castle Stewart) and Newton Stewart passes through the magnificent woodland of Galloway Forest Park (152sq. miles/400sq.km). On the banks of Chatteringshaws Loch (6 miles/10km west of New Galloway) a granite stone commemorates the victory of Robert the Bruce (see Famous People) over the English in March 1307.

★Galloway Forest Park

Bruce's Stone

The pretty town of Kirkcudbright (pop. 2500; 10 miles/16km south-west of Castle Douglas) is situated further west along the Solway Firth. Attractively located where the River Dee flows into Kirkcudbright Bay, the town centre

Kirkcudbright

Dumfries and Galloway

Stewartry Museum — has several interesting sights including the 16th/17th c. Tolbooth, where John Paul Jones, founder of the American marines, was once a prisoner. Jones' life story is documented in the Stewartry Museum in St Mary Street, together with further information on the town's place in history (open: Mar.–Oct. Mon.–Sat. 11am–4pm; Nov.–Easter Sat. 11am–4pm).

Broughton House

MacLellan's Castle — Broughton House (18th c.) in High Street was presented to the town by the painter E. A. Hornel. Complete with original furnishings, the building contains Hornel's works and memorabilia. The imposing ruins of MacLellan's Castle (HS; late 16th c.) dominate the town's harbour.

★ Dundrennan Abbey — Dundrennan Abbey (6 miles/10km south-east) a 12th c. Cistercian monastery, still retains some of its earlier splendour. The transepts and the chancel in Late Norman Transitional style are well preserved and the gravestones are of interest. May 15th 1586 is said to have been the last night Mary Stuart spent in Scotland, before seeking refuge in England (HS; open: Apr.–Sept. Mon.–Sat. 9.30am–6pm, Sun. 2–6pm).

Orchardton Tower — The only existing round tower house on Scottish soil is the medieval Orchardton Tower (HS; 15 miles/24km east of Kirkcudbright near Palnackie). It was built in the 15th c. at the behest of John Cairns of Orchardton.

Gatehouse of Fleet — The history and development of the region is illustrated in an old mill by the River Fleet (open: daily, 10am–5.30pm), while the oldest house in the town the "Gait House" is a must for model railway enthuslasts (open: daily, 10am–5.30pm).

Cardoness Castle — Follow the A75 coast road from Newton Stewart eastward. The ruined Cardoness Castle with a 15th c. tower house is situated about 18 miles/30km away at the north end of Fleet Bay. It was formerly the seat of the McCullochs of Galloway (HS; open: Apr.–Sept. Mon.–Sat. 9.30am–6pm, Sun. 2–6pm; Oct.–Mar. Sat. 9.30am–4pm, Sun. 2–4pm).

Newton Stewart — About 10 miles/16km to the west lies the pleasant little town of Newton Stewart (pop. 4000). It is a popular spot with anglers and also boasts a good golf course.

★ Loch Trool

Bruce's Stone
★ Merrick — A detour via Bargrennan (7 miles/11.2km to the north) to Glentrool and loch of the same name is well worth the time. Nestling high up in the hills, it offers a splendid panoramic view. A granite memorial stone marks Robert I's first victory over the English in 1304. Merrick (2764ft/843m), clearly visible to the north, is the highest peak in the Southern Uplands.

The Machars — Scattered over the farmland of the Machars peninsula to the south of Newton Stewart are a number of prehistoric sites. The standing stones at Drumtrodden and the remains of an Iron Age fort at Barsalloch are particularly impressive.

Galloway House Gardens — Lord Garlies the oldest son of the 6th Earl of Galloway laid out this beautiful garden on the banks of Wigtown Bay in 1740. In early spring a carpet of snowdrops and narcissi bloom between the old trees. Later on, rhododendrons and azaleas provide a splash of colour (open: Mar.–Oct. daily, 9am–5pm).

Whithorn
★ Priory and Museum — At the end of the 4th c. St Ninian built a small chapel in Whithorn and named it "Candida Casa" on account of the white stone. The holy site was consecrated in the name of Martin of Tours, a teacher and friend of St Ninian who, as the historian Bede reported 300 years later, dispatched stonemasons to help with the construction. Soon Whithorn became an important early Christian abbey and the shrine of St Ninian developed into a popular place of pilgrimage. Whithorn was later elevated to a Celtic bishopric and c. 1160 a monastery for the Premonstratensian order was founded here. After the Reformation, a Protestant bishop resided in the abbey, but from 1689 the sacred site became the parish church. Little

Ruins of Glenluce Cistercian Abbey   *Medieval Whithorn Priory*

remains of what is often described as the "cradle" of Christianity in Scotland. St Ninian's "White House" lay to the east of the chancel but only the foundations remain and they are hard to identify. The medieval main nave, now minus roof, underwent a number of changes in the 17th and 18th c., however, the tombs and Norman west portal deserve close attention. The grave of St Ninian once occupied the crypt (c. 1200) and the Latinus or Barrovadus headstone in the museum is regarded as one of the earliest Christian monuments in Scotland (HS; open: Easter–Oct. daily 10.30am–5pm, last guided tour 4.30pm).

The remains of a small chapel can be seen on the offshore island of Whithorn at the south-eastern tip of the peninsula. It was built c. 1300 probably for pilgrims who arrived by boat.

St Ninian's Chapel

The A75 from Newton Stewart to Stranraer runs close to Glenluce and the picturesque ruins of Roland of Galloway's monastery (1192). It was the sixth Cistercian abbey on Scottish soil and was later taken over by the monks of Dundrennan Abbey. In the 13th c. the wizard Michael Scott is said to have attempted to rid the abbey of the plague by imprisoning it in a dungeon and leaving it to starve to death. Part of the southern transept of the abbey remains, as does the ribbed vaulting in the chapterhouse (1470). Entry to the chapterhouse is via a decorative round arch, which was probably renovated during the early 16th c. (HS; Apr.–Sept. Mon.–Sat. 9.30am–6pm, Sun. 2–6pm; Oct.–Mar. Sat. 9.30am–4pm, Sun. 2–4pm).

Glenluce
★Abbey

Exhibits at Glenluce Motor Museum include almost 40 two-wheel and four-wheel veteran and vintage vehicles (open: Mar.–Oct. daily, 10am–5pm; Nov.–Feb. Wed.–Sun. 11am–4pm).

Motor Museum

Pretty Glenwhan Garden near Dunragit was opened in 1979. Species cultivated here include hollies, eucalyptus, hydrangeas, rhododendron and other subtropical plants (open: Apr.–Sept. daily, 10am–5pm).

★Glenwhan
Garden

Lovely flowering gorse on the south coast of Dumfries and Galloway

Ferry from Stranraer to Northern Ireland and Isle of Man

About 3 miles/5km from the harbour at Stranraer take a detour off the A75 to the bewitching Castle Kennedy Garden. It is well known for its collection of old trees and colourful rhododendrons, magnolias and azaleas (open: Apr.–Sept. daily, 10am–5pm).

★Castle Kennedy Garden

Even the Romans appreciated the protected position of Loch Ryan and anchored their ships in the bay off Stranraer (pop. 11,300). The harbour is now used by ferries for Northern Ireland and, in the summer, for the Isle of Man (see Practical Information, Ferries).

Stranraer

The tower house at Castle St John (c. 1500) was once the home of the infamous persecutor of Covenanters, John Graham of Claverhouse, and later served as a prison. The small museum focuses on the history of justice from the Middle Ages to the present day (open: Easter–mid-Sept, Mon.–Sat. 10am–1pm, 2–5pm).

Castle St John

Although the 18th c. country house itself is not open to the public, visitors are welcome to wander through the beautiful park with rhododendrons, camellias, azaleas, roses, three small lakes and a fine view of Luce Bay (open: mid-Mar.–Oct. daily, 10am–6pm).

★Ardwell House Gardens

The 24 acre/10ha Botanic Garden is an outstation of the Royal Botanic Garden in Edinburgh (see entry). A favourable climate aids the growth of subtropical plants, including some rare palms and ferns from all over the world, eucalyptus, magnolias, various water lilies and other colourful flowers (open: mid-Mar.–Oct. daily, 10am–6pm).

★★Logan Botanic Gardens

Dundee
G 5

Region: Tayside. Population: 175,000

The fourth-largest city in Scotland spreads along the north bank of the Firth of Tay at the foot of Balgary Hill (480ft/145m) and Law (571ft/174m). Jute, jam and journalism were the three trades that for many years brought prosperity to the town. The jute factories and weaving mills have now closed (and also many of the shipyards), most of the printing presses have disappeared and production of the highly-prized jam has declined. Their places have been taken by service industries. Modern technology parks and a host of small and medium-sized companies working in synthetic fibres, biotechnology, precision engineering and instrument making are testimony to how Dundee has adapted to a new post-industrial economic structure. One aspect of the publishing industry does remain: "Oor Wullie", "Desperate Dan", the "Beano" and "Lord Snooty" are just some of the legendary Scottish comic heroes who are still very much alive and the artwork that accompanies these stories comes from the pens of Dundee designers. From the architectural point of view Dundee has undergone a period of renewal in recent years. The "Waterfront" has been renovated and new office blocks and leisure facilities have been built, with the Discovery Museum complex and Captain Scott's "Discovery", a new symbol for Dundee, as the focal points.

Position and characteristics

Domestic flights for Manchester and Aberdeen (see entry) leave daily from the airport in Riverside Drive. Edinburgh (see entry), Aberdeen (see entry) and Glasgow (see entry) are served both by buses from Seagate Bus Station and trains from Taybridge Station, South Union Street (contact Scotrail for times).

Communications

Sights

The famous iron bridge over the Tay was built between 1872 and 1878 by Thomas Bouch and it carried the railway line from Dundee to Edinburgh. With a span of 2 miles/3km it was then the longest bridge in the world.

Tay Bridges

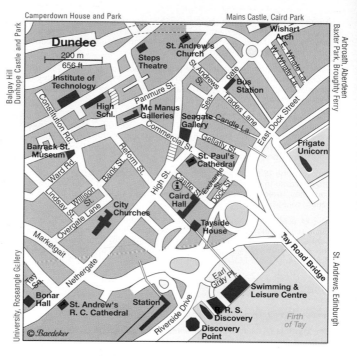

However, in 1879 after a storm it collapsed and a train plunged into the water drowning the 75 passengers. It took nine years for the present Tay Rail Bridge to be constructed. The Tay Road Bridge and footpath – completed in 1966 – is also 2 miles/3km in length. Two viewing platforms on the bridge afford fine views over the town and Firth of Tay.

★Discovery Point
★★R.R.S.
"Discovery"

Open:
Apr.–Oct.
daily, 10am–5pm;
Nov.–Mar. daily,
10am–4pm

To the west of the Tay Road Bridge on Riverside Drive lies the Royal Research Ship "Discovery", a vessel built in Dundee to take Robert F. Scott on his expedition to the Antarctic between 1901 and 1904.

This lovingly restored research ship which carried a crew of 30 into the polar ice has become a new symbol for the town. With the aid of special effects and audio-visual presentations, the new Discovery Point Visitor Centre (1993) documents the history of the sailing ship and also vividly illustrates the natural wilderness and awe-inspiring beauty of the polar regions.

★H.M. Frigate
"Unicorn"

This frigate is moored to the east of the Tay Bridge in Victoria Dock. Equipped with 46 cannons, it was launched in 1824 in Chatham and as the oldest seaworthy warship in the British Isles, it is well worth a closer look (open: Jan.–Easter Mon.–Fri. 10am–4pm; Easter–Oct. daily, 10am–5pm). Carved from Canadian pine, the splendid figurehead, a white unicorn with the royal coat-of-arms, was designed in Hampshire by Trevor Ellis.

St Mary's Tower

With Dundee the centre of many conflicts, few historic buildings have survived. The only witness to the city's medieval past is the 155ft/47m high St Mary's Tower (15th c.). It was rebuilt after suffering damage during the Second World War.

Scott's expedition ship "Discovery" . . .   *. . .stove in the officers' mess*

The 46-gun frigate "Unicorn" moored in Victoria Dock

Dundee

Mercat Cross	On the south side of the church (1630) stands a replica of the medieval market cross, formerly in Seagate.
Barrack Street Museum	To the north in Barrack Street, the museum of the same name houses the city's natural history collection, including the skeleton of a humpback whale which swam up the Dee to Dundee in 1883 (open: Mon.–Sat. 10am–5pm).
The Howff	Situated opposite, Dundee's 300-year-old graveyard used to be a garden in Greyfriars monastery, which was a gift to the town by Mary Stuart. Up until 1778 the Howff was the meeting place for the town's nine craft guilds and the tradesmen's marks and symbols can be seen on many of the gravestones.
★McManus Galleries Open: Mon.–Sat. 10am–5pm	Just a few yards further east lies Albert Square which is dominated by a grand Victorian building designed by Sir George Gilbert Scott in 1867. Inside, the McManus Galleries keep a collection of works by 19th and 20th c. European masters and local painters (including art nouveau by George Dutch Davidson) and also local history exhibits from prehistoric times to the present day. The archaeological department contains some particularly interesting artefacts from ancient Egypt.
St Andrew's Church	Follow busy pedestrianised Panmure Street eastward to King Street. On the left stands St Andrew's Church. Designed by Samuel Bell in 1772, much of the finance for it came from the guilds and their coats-of-arms appear in the stained glass windows (open: Tues., Thur. Sat. 10am–noon).
St Paul's Cathedral	The tall tower (213ft/65m) of the Neo-Gothic St Paul's Cathedral stands proudly over the city and is visible from many miles away. The cathedral, to the south-west of St Andrew's in Castlehill, was designed by Sir George Gilbert Scott and was completed in 1853. A retable by the Venetian Salviati adorns the altar (open: Mon.–Fri. 10am–4pm, Sat. 11am–3pm, Sun. 12.15–12.45pm).
Seagate Gallery	The temporary exhibitions held in the gallery opposite (36–40 Seagate) are usually devoted to the work of modern European artists (open: Tues.–Sat. 10am–5pm).
City Square	High Street leads on to City Square (pedestrianised zone), the busy heart of the city. It is overlooked by the town hall, Caird Hall, a concert and conference hall with seating for 2500 (1923), and the tourist information office. City Square is a good place to start a tour of the shops. The main stores are located in High Street, Commercial Street and Panmure Street.
Verdant Works	The museum in this renovated jute factory situated to the west of the city by West Henderson's Wynd documents the heyday of Dundee's textile industry during the 19th c. (open: daily, 10am–5pm; until 4pm Nov.–Mar.).
Dudhope Park	Dudhope Park with a 16th c. castle (not open to the public) is situated 1 mile/1.6km north-west of the city centre. It was originally the seat of the Scrymgeor family but in 1683 it passed to the Graham family. In the mid-18th c. the castle became a wool factory and later a barracks. It has been fully restored and is used by the city council for official functions.
Mills Observatory	The Mills Observatory (1935) stands on Balgary Hill about 2 miles/3km west of the city centre with the chance of viewing the night sky (open: Apr.–Sept. Mon.–Fri. 10am–5pm, Sat. 2–5pm; Oct.–Mar. Mon.–Fri. 3–10pm, Sat. 2–5pm).
Botanic Gardens	Follow Riverside Drive west from the Tay Road Bridge for about 3 miles/5km. The Botanic Gardens of Dundee University were laid out in 1971 and are noted for their varied species of conifers, aquatic plants and herbs

(open: Mar.–Oct. Mon.–Sat. 10am–4.30pm, Sun. 11am–4pm; Nov.–Feb. Mon.–Sat. 10am–3pm, Sun. 11am–3pm).

Camperdown Country Park, 4 miles/6km north-west of the city centre, is devoted to preserving wildlife. Visitors to the park can observe red deer, brown bears, wolves, lynx, pine martens, polar foxes, pheasants and golden eagles (open: Mar.–Sept. daily, 10am–4.30pm; Oct.–Feb. daily, 10am–3.30pm).

★Camperdown
Wildlife Centre

The A92 passes through the residential district at the east end of the city before the rambling towers of Claypotts Castle (HS) come into view. This grand Z-plan tower house was built for the Strachan family between 1569 and 1588 (open: Apr.–Sept. Mon.–Sat. 9.30am–6.30pm, Sun. 2–6.30pm; closed at present).

★Claypotts
Castle

Surroundings

The castle at Broughty Ferry (3 miles/4.8km to the east) on the banks of the Tay was built in the 15th c., but was destroyed more than once by the English in the 16th and 17th c. The museum here documents the history of whaling, an important industry for Dundonians in the second half of the 18th c. (open: Mon.–Thur. and Sat. 10am–1pm, 2–5pm, Sun. 2–5pm Jul.–Sept. only).

Broughty Ferry
Castle

Glamis Castle (12 miles/19.2km north of Dundee) is probably one of Scotland's finest sights. This fairy-tale castle is surrounded by parkland designed by Lancelot "Capability" Brown c. 1770. The L-shaped castle, most of which dates from the 17th c. and was built in baronial style, lies at the end of a long avenue of oaks. A castle is said to have stood on this site 1000 years ago and most of the time since then it has been the seat of the earls of Strathmore, ancestors of the Queen Mother. According to

★★**Glamis Castle**

Open:
Easter–Oct. daily,
10.30am–5.30pm
(from 10am Jul.
and Aug.)

Glamis Castle – steeped in history and legend

Shakespeare, Macbeth, king of Scotland from 1040 to 1057 and laird of Glamis castle was murdered here by his rival Duncan. Up until the 19th c. visitors to the castle were shown the bed in Duncan's Hall where the deed was done, but in fact the crime took place near Elgin (see entry).

The entrance to the castle grounds is situated to the north, but the main entrance to the castle itself is to be found opposite the drive in a corner tower that was begun by the 1st Earl of Kinghorn (Earl Patrick) in the 17th c. and completed by the third earl. His bust adorns a round niche above the entrance portal with the king's coat-of-arms beneath it. The castle contains a wealth of fine objets d'art including furniture, tapestries, Chinese porcelain, old weapons and paintings, including portraits of Elizabeth I and the Queen Mother when she was the Duchess of York (a copy of a portrait by de Laszlo). Probably the most striking feature in the Victorian Dining Room which dates from the mid-19th c. is a magnificent fireplace with a heraldic centrepiece in oak bearing the coat-of-arms of the 12th Earl of Strathmore. The plasterwork ceiling is decorated with Scottish thistles, English roses and lions of the Lyon family. Swords, pistols and armour are displayed in the medieval hall where the earl's retinue used to eat. In the Drawing Room – overflowing with family portraits – monograms of the second earl can be made out on the old plasterwork in the vaulting. Paintings by Jakob de Wet (1688) decorate the richly-ornamented wall and ceiling panelling in the Chapel. Recent research indicates that the biblical scenes on the ceiling are based on engravings by Boetius a Bolwert (1622). The painting above the Gillow dresser in the Billiard Room is the "Fruit Market" believed to be the work of Frans Snyders, while the fine English Gobelin tapestries (c. 1650) show scenes from the life of Nebuchadnezzar. The Queen Mother's chambers are open to the public. Princess Margaret, Elizabeth II's sister, was born in the bedroom in 1930. She was the first royal princess to be born on Scottish soil for 300 years. The Dining Room and 16th c. Kitchen may be booked for lunch and dinner parties (tel. (01307) 840242, fax. 840257).

Angus Folk Museum	The Angus Folk Museum in Kirkwynd Cottages (19th c.) at Glamis illustrates the history of rural life in the region (NTS; open: Easter, May–Sept. daily, 11am–5pm; Oct. Sat. and Sun. 11am–5pm).
★Meigle Museum	The 25 early Christian stones (10 miles/16km to the west) are thought to date from the Celtic period between the 7th and 10th c. and were found in or near the graveyard at Meigle (HS; open: Apr.–Sept. Mon.–Sat. 9.30am–6pm, Sun. 2–6pm).
Kirriemuir Barrie's Birthplace	Some 5 miles/8km north of Glamis lies Kirriemuir (pop. 6500), whose most famous son is Sir James Barrie. The author of "Peter Pan" was born at no. 9 Brechin Road and a museum there keeps many of his manuscripts and memorabilia (open: Easter, May–Sept. Mon.–Sat. 11am–5.30pm, Sun. 1.30–5.30pm).
Forfar	The historic town of Forfar (pop. 10,300) in the Strathmore valley 12 miles/19.2km north of Dundee was once an important centre for the jute industry.
Restenneth Priory	The Pictish king Nechtan is said to have laid the foundation stone to the little church of St Peter (HS; 1½ miles/2.4km north-east of Forfar). It is, after St Ninian in Whithorn (see Dumfries and Galloway), the oldest stone church in Scotland. King David I ordered the church to be rebuilt in 1153 for the Augustinians, but the spire for the Norman tower was not added until the 15th c. The abandoned monastery buildings and other parts date from later years.
Aberlemno Sculptured stones	The best of the four Pictish stones of Aberlemno (HS; 6 miles/9.6km north-east of Forfar) stands in the graveyard and dates from the 8th c. As well as a Celtic cross, battle scenes and several animal symbols can be identified. Of the roadside stones in the village, the biggest shows a Celtic cross flanked by angels as well as hunting scenes, a double discus and a half-moon.

Dunfermline   F 5

Region: Fife. Population: 43,000

Dunfermline, about 25 miles/40km north of Edinburgh (see entry) on the
Fife peninsula, is famous as the historic capital of the Scottish kingdom. In
later years it derived its prosperity from coal-mining and also as a world
centre for trade in damask linen. Steel magnate and philanthropist Andrew
Carnegie (see Famous People) has helped to enrich his home town by the
donation of several social and cultural facilities.

Situation and
characteristics

Sights

Situated in the west of the town and a good starting point for a tour of the
town is Malcolm Canmore's (Malcolm III) Tower in Pittencrieff Gardens.
The foundation walls of this fortress date from the second half of the 11th c.
when Malcolm built his royal residence in the town. During his 35-year
reign he and his wife Margaret tried to create a united and civilised nation,
however, he fell victim to an ambush at Alnwick in 1093.

★ **Pittencrieff Park**
Malcolm
Canmore's
Tower

The 76 acre/31ha park with pretty flower beds, nature trails, rockeries and
lakes was commissioned by Andrew Carnegie in 1902 and he is remembered by a statue at the northern end of the park. An elegant 17th c. country
house accommodates Pittencrieff Museum and its displays illustrate the
development of the park (open: Apr.–Oct. Wed.–Mon. 11am–5pm).

Carnegie
Memorial

About 1070 Queen Margaret helped to establish a priory for Benedictine
monks in the town. Her son David I elevated the priory to an abbey and by
1128 it had been extended in Norman style. It now forms the west side of

★ **Abbey**

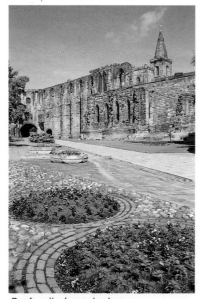

Dunfermline's royal palace . . .

. . . and Benedictine abbey

the church. Between 1818 and 1821 the east side above the destroyed chancel was rebuilt in Neo-Gothic style by William Burn. The words "Robert the Bruce" can be read on the balustrade of the rectangular tower.

Grave of Robert the Bruce

The grave of Robert I (see Famous People), victor at Bannockburn (see entry) and Scottish hero, was rediscovered by accident in 1818. His last remains now lie under the pulpit, with a brass plate marking the spot. The main nave is supported externally by stepped piers (16th c.). It is thought that the builders of Durham Cathedral influenced the style of the interior. The six-arched arcade with cylindrical pillars is one dominant feature, but many visitors are also impressed by Sir Noel Paton's stained-glass window (19th c.) on the west portal. Both the medieval refectory and Robert Pitcairns's Abbot's House (16th c) are sections of the old monastery buildings that have been well preserved. The latter was adapted to accommodate a Heritage Centre in 1994 and it details the history of Dunfermline and the abbey (open: Apr.–Sept. Mon.–Sat. 9.30am–4pm, Sun. 2–6pm; Oct.–Mar. Mon.–Thur. Sat. 9.30am–4pm, Sun. 2–4pm).

St Margaret's Church

Queen Margaret died three days after her husband and was canonised in 1250. Shortly after, a chapel was built at the west end of the abbey in her memory. The marble shrine of St Margaret and most of the superstructure were destroyed in the chaos which followed the Reformation (1560), but the chapel foundations are still a place of pilgrimage.

Royal Palace

Facing the abbey to the south lie the ruins of the Royal Palace which James VI (from 1603 James I of England) rebuilt in 1590. In 1600 his wife Anne of Denmark bore a son (later Charles I) here, but three years later the royal court moved to London after the "Union of Crowns" (for opening times, see Abbey).

★ Carnegie Birthplace Museum

Open:
Apr.–Oct. Mon.–
Sat. 11am–5pm,
Sun. 2–5pm;
Nov.–Mar.
daily, 2–4pm

"The child who is granted the opportunity to grow up in an area like Dunfermline draws in with every breath poetry and romance, with every look he absorbs the environment, the history and traditions of his home town. These first impressions will remain locked in his memory until death; they may disappear for a short time but they will always return and fill his thoughts, giving light and colour to his life. No intelligent child from Dunfermline can erase the memories of the monastery, the palace and the gorge. They touch his soul, they fan the spark within into a flame, they make something different, something greater out of him, than would have been the case if he had been less fortunate in the place where he was born." These were the words that Andrew Carnegie (see Famous People) the steel magnate and philanthropist used to describe the town of his birth in his memoirs of 1920. In fact, few inhabitants of Dunfermline at that time would have waxed quite so lyrical about life in the "Hungry 1840s", but this warmth reflected the long-lasting affection that Carnegie, like many other emigrants, felt for his home town.

The small cottage in Moodie Street where Carnegie was born in 1835 is now part of a museum devoted to his life. A comprehensive collection of pictures and documents describes how a poor weaver's son became one of the richest industrialists and greatest benefactors of his time, the man who was the embodiment of the "American dream". On the ground floor of the museum stands the Jacquard loom that his father William Carnegie used to earn the paltry sum of 42 pence a day.

Dunfermline can thank the town's favourite son for the nearby Carnegie Hall, the Carnegie Clinic, the Carnegie Leisure Centre in Pilmuir Street (dating from 1877 it was probably the first public swimming pool in Scotland), the Central Library, the first of almost 300 free lending libraries, and also Pittencrieff Park mentioned earlier.

Dunfermline Museum

Dunfermline Museum in Viewfield Terrace has a notable collection of damask. It is also a venue for temporary exhibitions (open: Mon.–Sat. 11am–5pm).

The Andrew Carnegie Birthplace Museum

Surroundings

See entry   Fife

Edinburgh   F 6

Region: Lothian. Population: 435,000

Of all the cities in the world, Edinburgh, the capital and cultural centre of
Scotland for over 500 years, occupies one of the most beautiful locations.
Sometimes described as the "Athens of the North", the famous festival city
boasts Doric columns on Calton Hill, a wide choice of museums and art
galleries as well as a host of other historical gems. Edinburgh actually
consists of two cities. The castle, set on high basalt rock, dominates the
densely-populated old town, a labyrinth of narrow alleys, rows of houses
and back yards. The famous "Royal Mile" links the castle with the Palace of
Holyroodhouse. The Georgian new town, itself a masterpiece of town
planning from the 18th c., is characterised by grand squares, wide avenues
and elegant facades. Edinburgh is now home to many prosperous service
industries and the area around George Street is one of Europe's largest
investment centres.

★★ Scotland's
capital in a
magnificent
location

During the 14th c., Edinburgh, like other royal cities, would almost certainly
have had a coat-of-arms, but it only gained official recognition in 1732
when one was granted by Lord Lyon. A new version of the coat-of-arms for
the City of Edinburgh was introduced after the administrative reforms of
1975. A shield showing a castle on a rock of black basalt and towers with red
flags is topped by the Scottish crown and the Admiralty anchor. The motto
"Nisi Dominus Frustra" meaning "Nothing of lasting value can be done
without God's help" comes from Psalm 127. The shield is supported on the

*Nisi Dominus
Frustra*

151

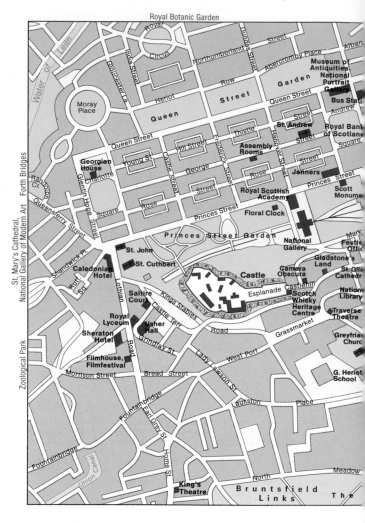

left by a girl – in the Middle Ages the castle was known as "Castrum Puellarum" (The Maidens' Castle) as according to legend it was a safe refuge for princesses – and on the right by a hind, the symbol of St Egidius, the patron saint of Scotland's capital.

Festivals

The Edinburgh Festival which begins on the second Sunday in August and lasts for three weeks has taken place every year since 1947. It was the brainchild of the Englishman Rudolf Bing who first sought the support of the authorities in Oxford and Cambridge, but they showed little interest, so he chose Edinburgh. The events include drama, opera, music and art exhibitions. (Edinburgh International Festival, 21 Market Street; tel. (0131)

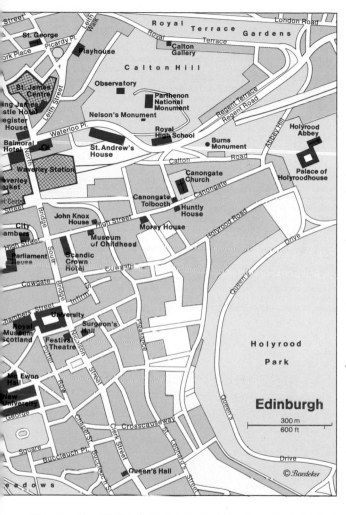

Edinburgh

300 m
600 ft

© Baedeker

226 4001, fax. 225 1173.) The Edinburgh Fringe Festival has become an important sideshow for the main event. Unknown theatre groups, amateurs and new talent present anything from avant-garde drama, impromptu street theatre and cabaret to rock, pop and classical music. (Fringe Festival, 180 High Street; tel. (0131) 226 5257, fax. 220 4205.) In the evenings a few days before the festival begins, a Military Tattoo takes place on the Esplanade in front of the castle. Regiments from all over the world parade up and down with their drums and pipes. (Tattoo Office, 32 Market Street; tel. (0131) 225 1188, fax. 225 8627.) Running in tandem with the main festival are the International Jazz and Blues Festival (116 Canongate; tel. (0131) 668 2019), the Drambuie Edinburgh Film Festival (Filmhouse,

88 Lothian Road; tel. (0131) 228 4051, fax. 229 5501) and the Book Festival (Scottish Book Centre, 137 Dundee Street; tel. (0131) 228 5444, fax. 228 4333). For full listings of day-to-day events see "The Scotsman".

Theatres and concert halls

The city of art and culture possesses a number of famous venues. The repertory theatre in the Royal Lyceum is a Victorian gem (Grindlay Street; tel. (0131) 229 7942, fax. 220 0112) and the grand Edwardian King's Theatre (Leven Street; tel. (0131) 220 4349) is the usual stage for touring productions including opera and ballet. The recently renovated Playhouse is often used for musicals and rock concerts (18–22 Greenside Place; tel. (0131) 557 2590, fax. 557 6520), while the Traverse (Cambridge Street; tel. (0131) 228 1404, fax. 229 8443) has a reputation for staging innovative productions. The biggest theatre is Usher Hall which has space for 2500 people (Lothian Road; tel. (0131) 228 8616, fax. 228 8848) and the Festival Theatre was re-opened in 1994 after a major modernisation programme. Both are available for opera and concert tours (see page 168).

Communications

The M8 motorway links Edinburgh with Glasgow (see entry), while the A90 heads north to Perth (see entry). A small airport is situated 7 miles/11km to the west of the city centre. Waverley Station, the main railway station, lies in the heart of the city between Princes Street and the Royal Mile. The bus station is by St Andrew Square. Edinburgh is a city for pedestrians. Park the car and tour the sights on foot.

History

Little is known about Edinburgh during the time of the Roman occupation or before. According to legend, in the 5th c. the Picts built a fortress on the volcanic castle rock which they called in Gaelic "Din Eidyn". But the settlement became strategically important when the Angles from Northumbria overran Lothian and most people assume that the name originates from Edwin, king of Northumbria (617–633). When the Scottish Picts pushed south in the middle of the 10th c., the town was probably reconquered.

View from Salisbury Crags over Holyrood to the Forth

Malcolm III (Canmore) built a castle on Castle Hill and his wife Margaret, who was later canonised, built a chapel. By the time Robert I, the Bruce, had granted Edinburgh a number of special rights in 1329 and had handed over the port of Leith, the eastern slope of Castle Hill had become quite densely populated. When Berwick was lost (1482), Edinburgh, which had now become an important centre for traders and craftsmen, was declared the capital and the first ramparts were constructed, although the king often stayed elsewhere. The defeat at Flodden Field aroused concerns about an English invasion and a second protective wall was built around the city centre. Despite the upheavals of the Reformation, the invasion by Henry VII and the unfortunate reign of Mary Stuart, during the 16th c. the city enjoyed a period of great prosperity. Union with England in 1707 left the city without a parliament, but it retained its importance as a regional capital and also as a cultural centre. The university which had been founded in 1582 developed into a respected centre for research. While Peter the Great was Tsar of Russia, for example, nearly all his doctors trained in Edinburgh. From about 1750 this creative spark which influenced the arts and the sciences attracted intellectuals, writers and artists from all over Europe. During the Victorian era, some cultural influence ebbed away to London, but Edinburgh remained a dominant force in the world of medicine. James Young Simpson discovered chloroform and Joseph Lister demonstrated the value of antiseptics. At the same time, banking houses, insurance companies, publishing companies, breweries, docks and the railway brought with them economic success. At the beginning of the 19th c. the area around Nor' Loch (now Princes Street Gardens) was drained and three bridges (North Bridge, George IV Bridge and Waverley Bridge) were built to connect the old and new towns.

The old town

★★Castle

Dominating the inner city is the most popular national monument in Scotland. Edinburgh Castle (HS) is situated on a black basalt rock and affords a magnificent view of the city. A drawbridge leads over a dried out moat from the broad Esplanade where the famous Military Tattoo is held every August. The main entrance to the castle is flanked by bronze statues of William Wallace (c. 1270–1305), who led the Scottish resistance against Edward I and was later executed in London, and of Robert the Bruce (see Famous People), Scotland's national hero, who defeated the English under Edward II at Bannockburn (see entry).

Open:
Apr–Sept. daily 9.30am–6pm,
Oct.–Mar. daily 9.30am–5pm

The portcullis gate is situated beneath the state prison, better known as Argyll's Tower as the Marquis of Argyll was imprisoned there. The highest point on Castle Rock (443ft/135m above sea level) is called the citadel or King's Bastion.

Argyll's Tower

St Margaret's Chapel was built around 1090 and is probably the oldest building in Edinburgh. Despite its size – only 17ft/5.2m long and 11ft/3.4m wide – it is an interesting example of early Norman architecture. It was used as the royal chapel until the reign of Mary Stuart, when it became an ammunition store. It was restored in 1853 at the request of Queen Victoria and underwent further renovation work in 1934.

St Margaret's Chapel

A time cannon is situated near the Half Moon Battery. It is fired at 1pm every weekday. At the same time, a time ball drops at the Nelson Monument on Calton Hill. This tradition dates from a time when the sailing ships on the Firth of Forth checked their chronometers by training a telescope on the castle. The 18-pound cannons on the battery were all made in Falkirk at the end of the 18th c.

The One O'Clock Salute

Few visitors will fail to be impressed by the Scottish National War Memorial which is situated on the north side of Crown Square. Robert Lorimer was responsible for designing the Hall of Honour in memory of Scottish sol-

Crown Square
Scottish National War Memorial

Edinburgh Castle

1 Esplanade	9 Foog's Gate	16 Vaults, Mons Meg
2 Statue of Robert I, the Bruce	10 Scottish National	(cannon)
3 Statue of William Wallace	War Memorial	17 Military jail
4 Gatehouse	11 Royal Palace	18 New Barracks
5 Former stables	12 Half Moon Battery	19 Former Governor's House
6 Portcullis Gate	13 Casemates	(now the Officers' Mess)
(with Argyll's Tower above)	14 Great Hall	20 Butts Battery
7 St Margaret's Chapel	15 Scottish United Services	21 Hospital
8 Water tank	Museum	22 Restaurant

diers who died in World War I. Every regiment has its own memorial and even the animals that worked alongside the soldiers are remembered. A silver shrine holds the roll of honour with the names of the 150,000 dead. Many well-known artists were invited to help with the final decorations of the memorial which was consecrated in 1927.

Among the rooms within the Royal Palace is the chamber where Mary Stuart (see Famous People) gave birth to her son James VI, later to become James I of England. For centuries the palace was the repository for state documents and the crown jewels, but they were removed on two occasions. In 1291 Edward I sent all papers and jewels to London and then about 400 years later just before Oliver Cromwell captured the castle, the regalia were taken to Dunnottar Castle for safekeeping. When the Union Treaty was signed in 1707 the regalia were returned to Edinburgh, but were locked away in the vaults in order that the Scottish public should not be roused to anger by the sight of them. The oak chest in which they were stored was finally opened in 1818 at the request of Sir Walter Scott. The contents have been displayed in the Crown Chamber ever since. The coronation insignia includes a sceptre (1494) which was a present from Pope Alexander IV to

Palace

◀ *Enjoying the sunshine in Princes Street Gardens, Edinburgh*

Bust of Mary Queen of Scots . . .   *. . . and knights in armour*

Great Hall

James VI, a sword (1501) presented to James IV by Pope Julius II and a crown (1540) made from Scottish-mined gold with 94 pearls and 40 jewels. Built at the beginning of the 16th c., the Great Hall at the south side of Crown Square was the meeting place for the Scottish parliament until 1640. Later it was used as a barracks and a military hospital, before being restored at the end of the 19th c. It now houses a comprehensive collection of arms and armour.

French prisons

During the Napoleonic wars, French prisoners were interned under the Great Hall. Although boring, the captives' lives seem to have been reasonably tolerable as they were allowed to while away their time making toys and jewellery boxes which they were able to sell. Others became so successful at making counterfeit money, that in 1812 the banks put a notice in the "Edinburgh Gazette" offering a reward of £100 to anyone who could provide information about the forgers.

Mons Meg cannon

Despite a whole range of other cannons, it is "Mons Meg" which attracts most attention. Manufactured in Mons, Flanders, in 1449, it was presented to James II by the Duke of Burgundy. Some 110lb/50kg of gunpowder could propel a 550lb/250kg cannonball about 2 miles/3km, while a 1000lb/500kg iron cannonball would travel about 1500yd/1400m.

Scottish United
Services Museum

On the west side of the square, a military museum founded in 1931 displays uniforms, weapons and other memorabilia from the Scottish regiments.

★★Royal Mile

Royal Mile

The streets which link Edinburgh Castle and the Palace of Holyroodhouse are known in local parlance as the "Royal Mile". This historic thoroughfare is lined with elegant town houses and living quarters, but it is the shops which draw the crowds. Kiltmakers such as Hector Russel, Ragamuffin, Geoffrey or the Scottish Experience vie with well-known outlets for woollen goods, designer boutiques, pubs, museums and numerous restaurants.

The tall six- to fifteen-storey blocks are known as "lands", the little alleys as "wynds" and the hidden backyards as "closes".

At the upper end of the Royal Mile, or Castle Hill, stands Sir Patrick Geddes' Outlook Tower (1853) and Camera Obscura.

Castle Hill

On display inside are a series of old photographs of Victorian Edinburgh and some examples of holography, three-dimensional designs produced with laser technology. Handicrafts and holograms are sold in the Obscura shop (open: Apr.–Sept. Mon.–Sat. 10am–5.30pm, Sun. 10am–6pm; Oct.–Mar. Mon.–Sat. 10am–4pm, Sun. 10am–4pm). The magnificent panoramic view from the top of the building should not be missed.

The Scottish Whisky Heritage Centre which lies diagonally opposite unveils some of the mysteries surrounding "uisge beatha", the Celtic word for whisky. An electric car takes the visitor on a journey into the past. The social and industrial history of the famous drink is represented in an informative way, and the main events from the years when smugglers traded whisky and the years of prohibition are also included. The processes used to make single malt and blended whisky are explained (see also Baedeker Special, "Scotch Whisky") and displays trace the history of several major distilleries (open: Mon.–Sat. 10am–6pm, Sun. 10am–5.30pm).

★ Scottish Whisky
Heritage Centre

The Tolbooth-St John's Highland Church was completed in 1844 and it boasts the tallest church tower in the city.

Tolbooth-
St John's

Set back a little on the left-hand side of Lawnmarket stand James' Court, the former residence of the philosopher David Hume c. 1760 (see Famous People), and also Gladstone's Land, which was built in 1631 by Thomas Gladstone. The six-storey merchant's house has been restored by the National Trust for Scotland. One floor with its pretty ceiling paintings and original furniture accurately reflects life for the gentry during the Middle Ages (open: Apr.–Oct. Mon.–Sat. 10am–5pm, Sun. 2–5pm).

Lawnmarket
★ Gladstone's
Land

The small Writers' Museum (open: June–Sept. Mon.–Sat. 10am–6pm, Sun. 2–5pm during the Edinburgh Festival only; Oct.–May Mon.–Sat. 10am–5pm) in the adjoining Lady Stair's Close (1622) displays manuscripts, portraits and memorabilia of the poet Robert Burns and the writers Sir Walter Scott and Robert Louis Stevenson (see Famous People for all three).

Writers' Museum

★ Lady Stair's
Close

Riddle's Court (16th c.) with a remarkable stair tower and Brodie's Close named after the artisan Francis Brodie face the museum. Both are well worth a visit. The double life of Brodie's son Deacon William Brodie inspired Robert Louis Stevenson to write the novel "Dr Jekyll and Mr Hyde" although the author did move the story to London. Brodie's crimes resulted in him meeting his death on the same gallows that he had designed for the city.

Riddle's Court,
Brodie's Close

The patron saint of Edinburgh gave his name to Edinburgh's High Kirk of St Giles. St Egidius or St Gilles du Gar was born in Athens in 640 and later lived as a hermit in Provence. His links with Scotland go back to the old ties between Scotland and France.

★ **St Giles
Cathedral**
Open:
Mon.–Sat.
9am–7pm
(5pm in winter),
Sun. 1–9pm

Consecrated in 1243, the cathedral is Edinburgh's principal church. Although it is often described as a cathedral, it has only functioned as such since the 17th c. A church stood on the same spot in the middle of the 9th c., but it was replaced by a Norman-style chapel in 1120. Work started on the Gothic church at the end of the 14th c. after its Norman predecessor was burnt down by Richard II. Only an entrance portal and part of the choir remain. About 1460 the church was extended to the east, before St Giles received a charter from James II which placed the cathedral directly under

Deacon Brodie – "Dr Jekyll and Mr Hyde" *St Giles: Thistle Chapel*

St Giles Cathedral on Edinburgh's Royal Mile

St. Giles' Cathedral

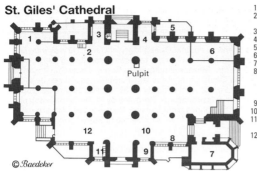

Pulpit

© *Baedeker*

1 Albany Aisle
2 John Knox
  Statue
3 St Eloi's Chapel
4 Chambers Aisle
5 Shop
6 Holy Cross Aisle
7 Thistle Chapel
8 Royal Pew
  (H.M. the Queen
  and the Duke of
  Edinburgh)
9 Chapman Aisle
10 Preston Aisle
11 Tomb of the
   Regent Moray
12 Moray Aisle
   (Memorial
   plaques to
   Stevenson and
   Livingstone)

the authority of the Pope. The "Crown Steeple", a Late Gothic central tower (161ft/49m high) with eight arched buttresses forming a huge crown, has become a symbol for the church. The four octagonal pillars which support the tower are said to be parts of the original Norman construction. When in the first half of the 16th c. the reformer John Knox (see Famous People) returned to Edinburgh from exile and took over as minister of the parish, the Scottish church was withdrawn from papal control, the 44 altars of St Giles were removoved, the statue of St Egidius sunk in Nor' Loch and the pulpit raised to a prominent central position. After the Reformation the building was partitioned. Parliamentary sittings were held in the western section and other parts served as a school, court and prison. Between 1750 and 1830 the cathedral housed up to four parish churches. During the 19th and 20th c. large-scale restoration work was undertaken, many stained glass windows were installed and the old internal partitions removed.

Tour

The nave and choir are equal in length but are separated by a short transept. To the left of the main entrance lies the side aisle which was endowed by the Duke of Albany in 1409. It contains memorials to the dead of the First World War. Of particular note here are the stained-glass windows designed by the Pre-Raphaelites Burne-Jones and William Morris. Just in front of the Albany Aisle stands a statue of John Knox by Pittendrigh MacGillivray. The adjoining St Eloi's Chapel contains the splendid marble tomb of the Marquis of Argyll who was executed in 1661 for high treason. The carved figures from Caen stone which adorn the pulpit represent the six Acts of Grace from the New Testament. The Chambers Aisle slightly further north is dedicated to the 19th c. church restorer William Chambers. The most impressive features in the choir are the fan vaulting and the medieval capitals bearing the coats-of-arms of James II, Mary of Gueldres and the Duke of Rothesay, later to become James II. The fleur de lys adjacent symbolises the "Auld Alliance" between France and Scotland.

★★Thistle Chapel

The "Chapel of the Most Ancient and Most Noble Order of the Thistle" with its marvellous oak carving, heraldic emblems and the seals of the "Knights of the Thistle" was designed in 1911 by Sir Robert Lorimer and is a superb example of modern Gothic style. Founded in 1470 by James III the Order of the Thistle is Scotland's oldest order of knights. Apart from the monarch, it was allowed to have no more than sixteen members. Choir stalls reserved for the royal household and the Duke of Edinburgh are situated to the left in front of the chapel. While the Queen is head of the Church of England, she is not the head of the Church of Scotland which elects its chief representative every year. The Preston Aisle is named after Sir William Preston who bequeathed to the church a precious reliquary, a diamond-studded ring around a bone from the arm of St Egidius. The southern Chapman Aisle was endowed by Walter Chapman who together with Andrew Myllar brought the art of printing to Scotland *c.* 1507. Under a monumental tomb lies the body of the Marquis of Montrose (1612–50), initially a Covenanter but then an opponent of the Marquis of Argyll who had him executed at the Mercat Cross. Another tomb provides a reminder of the regent Moray who in 1559 led the reformers against Queen Mary of Guise. He was married in St Giles in 1552 by John Knox who later read the peroration at his graveside after he was murdered. Memorial plaques to Robert Louis Stevenson and the African explorer David Livingstone (see Famous People) can be seen in the Moray Aisle. The great west window (1985) is dedicated to the popular poet Robert Burns. It was prepared in Germany by W. Derix following plans drawn up by Leifur Breidfjord from Iceland. Represented here are nature, brotherhood and the power of love, a reference to Burns' poem "My luve's like a Red, Red Rose".

High Street
Heart of
Midlothian

A heart-shaped mosaic of granite stones on the pavement in front of the main portal of St Giles marks the spot where the Old Tolbooth, immortalised by Scott in his "Heart of Midlothian", stood for over 400 years. According to Scottish custom, it brings good luck to spit into the heart.

Parliament
Square

What was previously the cemetery opposite St Giles is now Parliament Square. The militant reformer John Knox was probably buried here in 1572. The equestrian statue of Charles II in the middle of the square is one of the oldest lead statues in Great Britain.

Parliament House

The Parliament building was constructed between 1632 and 1640, but underwent a number of major alterations in 1808. Until union with England in 1707 it was the meeting place for the Scottish parliament. The 122ft/37m long hall is decorated with a beautiful Neo-Gothic hammerbeam roof and a series of Raeburn portraits. One of the statues in the room represents Sir Walter Scott who was the senior court official from 1806 to 1830. This hall and the adjoining rooms are used partly by the Scotland's highest court. The Seal Library is also situated here and its Upper Library (1822) designed by William Stark is regarded as an architectural masterpiece.

Museum of Childhood in the High Street

John Knox's House

Tartans galore: kiltmakers window on the Royal Mile

During the Middle Ages, heralds read out royal proclamations here. It was also the site of public executions.

Mercat Cross

The City Chambers on the other side of the High Street have been the seat of the city council since 1811. Outside the chambers stands the cenotaph, built as a memorial to the dead from the two world wars.

City Chambers

The Scot Ian Begg designed the Scandic Crown Hotel which was opened in 1990. Its façade is broken up with various roof levels and different building materials – blocks of sandstone, red and beige plaster – so that it fits in well with the nearby historic buildings.

Scandic Crown Hotel

Patrick Murray opened the Museum of Childhood over 30 years ago. Old toys including model railways, fruit machines, dolls and games from all over the world are displayed over five floors (open: June–Sept. Mon.–Sat. 10am–6pm, Sun. 2–5pm during the Edinburgh Festival only; Oct.–May Mon.–Sat. 10am–5pm).

★Museum of Childhood

Opposite in Chalmers Close the restored section of the old Trinity College (1460) houses a comprehensive collection of brass replicas. Brass signs can be made to order (open: June–Sept. Mon.–Sat. 10am–6pm, Sun. noon–5pm during the Edinburgh Festival only; Oct.–May Mon.–Sat. 10am–5pm).

Brass Rubbing Centre

The town house at no. 45 was built in 1490 but has been extended. During his term as the parish priest of St Giles, John Knox (see Famous People) lived here and in two other houses. A museum in this building recalls the life of the great reformer and a facsimile of his principal work "History of the Reformation in Scotland" and as well as his tirade against "The Monstrous Regiment of Women" are on display. Contemporary prints and writings provide background information on the reformation in Scotland (open: Mon.–Sat. 10am–4pm).

★John Knox House

The Royal Mile becomes Canongate as it enters the elegant district of the same name. The name refers to the Augustine canons who were granted their own parish by David I in the 12th c.

Canongate

Moray House	The German novelist and travel writer Theodor Fontane regarded Moray House as the jewel of the Royal Mile, but it has since acquired fame for its marvellous garden. Cromwell established his headquarters in the house during 1648 and the Union Treaty was signed here in 1707.
★Huntly House	The city's official museum is housed in Huntly House or Hammermen's House, a half-timbered structure which was commissioned by Countess Gordon c. 1570. Exhibits include Edinburgh silver and glassware, Scottish pottery and shop signs (open: June–Sept. Mon.–Sat. 10am–6pm, Sun. 2–5pm during the Edinburgh Festival only; Oct.–May Mon.–Sat. 10am–5pm).
Canongate Tolbooth ★People's Story	On the other side of the road stands the delightful Canongate Tolbooth (1591). Formerly the town hall and prison, the building has dainty turrets around the steeple which are worth a closer look. The building is now a museum which tells "The People's Story" of life and work in Edinburgh since the 18th c. Models, photographs and everyday objects show how industry, commerce and trade developed. The recreated interiors of old shops, workshops, kitchens and private homes plus costumes from yesterday and today complete the picture (open: June–Sept. Mon.–Sat. 10am–6pm, Sun. 2–5pm during the Edinburgh Festival only; Oct.–May Mon.–Sat. 10am–5pm).
Canongate Church	The cemetery at Canongate Church (1688) is the last resting place of the economist Adam Smith (see Famous People), the poet Robert Fergusson (1753–1828) and Agnes MacLehose, or "Clarinda", of whom Robert Burns was so fond.
★White Horse Close	At the end of Canongate take a stroll along this old lane to see the 300-year-old White Horse Inn, an old coaching house with stables for over 100 horses.

★★Palace of Holyroodhouse

Open:
Apr.–Oct.
Mon.–Sat.
9.30am–5.15pm,
Sun.
9.30am–4.30pm;
Nov.–Mar.
daily
9.30am–3.45pm

The Royal Mile ends proudly outside the wrought-iron gates of Holyroodhouse Palace, which stands out against the backdrop of Salisbury Crags. The climb is steep but is rewarded with a magnificent view of the city and Holyroodhouse. The palace has frequently been at centre stage as Scottish history has unfolded. James II and James IV were both married here, Mary Stuart wed Lord Darnley, James V and Charles I were crowned and "Bonnie Prince Charlie" held court at the palace for a short time in 1745. After the visits of Queen Victoria in the middle of the 19th c., Holyrood was promoted as the official residence of the British monarch in Scotland and for that reason, during the summer months, at times it may not be open to the public.

Holyrood Abbey

The history of the palace and abbey began with a small chapel on the rock. Queen Margaret, canonised in 1251 and named as Scotland's patron saint, died here in 1093. She possessed a sacred crucifix ("holy rood") that was said to have been made of wood from Jesus' cross and the Augustine abbey that her son David I founded here in 1128 was probably named after this relic. About 1220 the monastery church underwent considerable extension and was further added to during the 13th and 14th c. Badly damaged on more than one occasion, it deteriorated towards the end of the 18th c. and the central nave is now all that remains of the medieval abbey. David II, James II and his wife, James V and Lord Darnley are all buried in the church.

Holyroodhouse

Delighted with the location, Scotland's monarchs decided to build a house for guests at a spot to the west of the abbey. This eventually became a royal residence and James IV and his son James V extended the building into a palace at the beginning of the 16th c. In 1544 the greater part of the palace was burnt down and Cromwell's troops further devastated the rebuilt structure with another fire in 1650. Following the death of Elizabeth I, Mary Stuart's son James VI became James I of England and he moved his court

Palace of Holyroodhouse

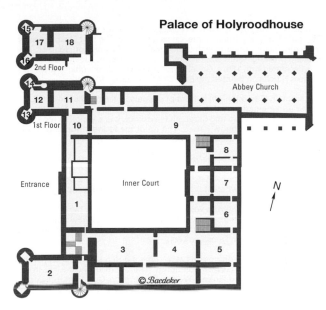

1 Dining Room	7 King's Bedchamber	13 South Closet
2 West Drawing Room	8 King's Closet	14 North Closet
3 Throne Room	9 Gallery	15 North Privy Room
4 Evening Room	10 Queen's Lobby	16 South Privy Room
5 Morning Room	11 Queen's Antechamber	17 Mary, Queen of Scots Inner Chamber
6 King's Antechamber	12 Queen's Bedchamber	18 Mary, Queen of Scots Outer Chamber

to London. Holyrood lost its importance and only rarely hosted royal guests. On the occasion of Charles I's coronation, castle and abbey were renovated. Work on the present building took place between 1671 and 1679 following the Classical style of the Renaissance and according to plans by Sir William Bruce of Kinless. The royal master builder Robert Mylne was responsible for its completion. A low central section with a charming façade was interposed between the old north-west and new south-west tower, and Doric columns and the coat-of-arms of the Scottish royal king were added to the main portal. The painter Jakob de Witt was commissioned to carry out the interior decorations, with Jan van Santvoort responsible for the woodcarving and John Hulbert, George Dunsterfield and Thomas Alborn the stucco plastering. Expensive tapestries were ordered from Flanders and Paris.

Charles II's royal chamber with its elegant furnishings is now used by the Queen when she stays in Edinburgh. The north wing which escaped the worst of the 1544 fire houses 89 portraits of Scottish monarchs – from Fergus, the founder of the dynasty, to James VII. These were the work of the Dutchman Jakob de Witt who at the request of Charles II completed them all between 1684 and 1686. The chambers of Mary Stuart form part of the north-west tower, which dates from the time of James IV. On March 9th 1566 in the queen's ante-room on the second floor, David Rizzio was murdered. He fell victim to some 50 stab wounds at the upper end of the main staircase. A brass plaque marks the probable spot where he met his death. In the queen's boudoir and bedroom, the original oak coffered ceilings may still be seen. They bear the initials of her parents: IR and ER. J. Michael Wright's 17th c. painting of a clan chief – probably Sir John

Interior

165

Campbell of Glenorchy, Earl of Breadalbane – adorns the Dining Room. This painting is of particular interest as it is one of the first illustrations of the highlanders' costume with girded plaid and Restoration doublet. The Evening Drawing Room was restored at the request of Queen Victoria and was decorated with 18th c. Gobelin tapestries from Buckingham Palace. Sir William Hutchison painted the portrait of the Queen Mother.

Fountain

The fountain (20ft/6m high) in front of the palace is embellished with Late Gothic ornamentation and stylish Renaissance figures such as Mary Stuart, the flute-playing Rizzio and Elizabeth I (reading). It is a Victorian replica of the fountain at Linlithgow Palace. The tip of the fountain forms a crown with a globe bearing the Scottish lion.

Holyrood Park

Features within the 642-acre/260ha park on the north side of the palace include a sundial, the two artificial lakes of St Margaret's and Dunsapie Loch and, at the foot of Abbeyhill, a small building with a pyramid roof, Queen Mary's bath, where it is said the queen bathed in wine to preserve her beauty.

★Arthur's Seat

Arthur's Seat (820ft/250m), a volcanic outcrop named after the 6th c. Arthur of Strathclyde, is the highest point in Holyrood Park. The view from the top encompasses the city of Edinburgh and the mouth of the Forth. The easiest way to the top is from Dunsapie Loch.

Duddingston

Duddingston near Duddingston Loch – now a bird reserve – Is one of the prettiest historic villages near Edinburgh. Raeburn recorded the lake in the evocative "Reverend Robert Walker Skating on Duddingston Loch" (National Gallery). The village's Sheep's Heid Inn is the ideal place for a break. The skittle alley in this 14th c. pub is said to be the oldest in the country.

★Grassmarket and Greyfriars

★**Grassmarket**

The picturesque Grassmarket has been an important market place since the Middle Ages and is mentioned in documents as early as 1477. Public executions were held here from 1660. On the north side of the market place stands The White Hart Inn where the poets Robert Burns and William Wordsworth are said to have been guests. In 1791 Burns penned the poem "Ae Fond Kiss" to his beloved "Clarinda". There

are now a number of cosy pubs and little shops around this historic square.

★National
Library
of Scotland

Only a few yards away on George IV Bridge stands one of the four largest libraries in the country. It grew out of the Advocate's Library that was founded in 1689 and now receives a copy of every book published in the United Kingdom. The seven figures in the entrance symbolise different teaching methods. As well as its permanent exhibition on Scottish history, the library also houses touring exhibitions on historical themes (exhibitions open: Mon.–Sat. 10am–5pm, Sun. 2–5pm).

**Greyfriars
Church**

To find the 17th c. Greyfriars Church follow Candlemakers Row to the south. The graveyard here, the oldest in Edinburgh, is the last resting place for a number of celebrated Scots including the architects William Adam (1689–1748) and James Craig (1740–95), the poet Allan Ramsay (1686–1758) and the humanist George Buchanan (1506–82). The first "National Covenant", directed against Charles I's attempt to impose the constitution of the Anglican church on Scotland, was signed here in 1638. Under this framework, the church would be subjected to the power of the state. The

Foyer of the Royal Museum of Scotland   *Greyfriars Bobby*

Covenanters, on the other hand, wished to promote Presbyterian beliefs, in particular the freedom and independence of the church (open: church Apr.–Oct. Mon.–Fri. 10.30am–4.30pm, Sat. 10.30am–2.30pm; churchyard all year daily 10am–6pm).

Outside the churchyard stands the famous dog memorial known as Grey-friars Bobby. In 1858 this Skye terrier loyally followed the coffin of his master, John Gray, to the graveyard. Up until his death fourteen years later, the dog refused to leave the graveyard and a kennel had to be built for him there. The story moved Baroness Burdett Coutts so much that in 1873 she had a memorial erected in his honour.

Greyfriars Bobby

The founder of this square, Gothic-Palladian complex was James IV's court jeweller George Heriot. William Wallace began work on the boys' school in 1627 and the task was finished by William Ayton in 1650. The clearly articulated façade with decorative gables is typical of the Renaissance period, while the corner towers are rather reminiscent of medieval fortifications.

George Heriot's School

Not far to the east along Chambers Street lies the Royal Museum of Scotland, currently housed in a Victorian-style building that was built between 1861 and 1888, although it is hoped that a new extension will be completed by the end of the 1990s. The airy entrance hall with fountains playing between Asiatic sculptures and Mediterranean-style palm trees is ringed by gallery arches. It must rank as one of the most successful cast iron constructions on Scottish soil. The plans were drawn up by Captain Francis Fowke of the Royal Engineers along the lines of London's Crystal Palace. The museum is divided into archaeological, ethnographic, natural history, geological and technological departments and exhibits range from primitive art to the space age. On the ground floor the Hall of Power offers visitors the opportunity to generate energy, while other exhibitions cover the evolution of man, insects, birds and mammals, the achievements of the

★Royal
Museum
of Scotland

Open:
Mon. and
Wed.-Sat.
10am–5pm,
Tues. 10am–8pm,
Sun. noon–5.30pm

Industrial Revolution (steam engines, locomotives, lighthouses, bridge construction, etc.) and the early days of photography. The library is situated on the first floor together with displays of European art from the 15th to the 19th c., ancient Egypt, costume, timepieces and the work of modern goldsmiths. The second floor concentrates on Chinese and Islamic art, minerals, fossils and the development of scientific instruments.

University

Edinburgh University, one of the largest seats of learning in the country, can look back over a long tradition. It was founded in 1583 although the buildings largely date from the end of the 18th c. and beginning of the 19th c. Old College with some tastefully furnished rooms in the Upper Library was designed by Robert Adam in Classical style and the huge dome was added in 1883 by Sir Rowand Anderson. Outside stands a memorial to the inventor James Watt (see Famous People). During the 20th c. other buildings elsewhere in Edinburgh have become part of the university campus, such as King's Buildings in West Main (1928), Heriot-Watt University (1966) and the university building with library on George Square, to

George Square

which James Brown lent Classical character from 1766 onwards. In the years that followed, well-heeled advocates moved into these desirable properties, including the family of Sir Walter Scott in 1772 (no. 25). The south side of the elegant square was demolished during the 1960s to make way for modern university premises.

★Festival Theatre

Edward Moss built the Empire Palace Theatre in 1892. It was the first theatre on Nicholson Street and architect Frank Matcham designed it to accommodate an audience of 3000. No expense was spared on the decorations which include elephants, Nubian riders, nymphs and cherubs. Some very distinguished artists, such as Vesta Tilley, Anna Pavlova, Charlie Chaplin and Charles Laughton have performed in the Empire. After conversion by the Milburn brothers, the theatre was used from 1928 to 1963 for variety performances, musicals, operas and ice spectaculars, before being converted back into a theatre. Almost 30 years passed before Colin Ross was commissioned to give the building a new face, ushering in a new era of dramatic performances. Since June 1994 theatre-goers have appreciated the bright glass-fronted foyer with café and bar. Matcham's auditorium has been restored and only partly altered to meet modern demands (13/29 Nicholson Street; tel. (0131) 529 6000, fax. 662 1199).

Masterpiece of town planning

The new town between Princes Street and the Firth of Forth is still regarded as a masterpiece of Georgian town planning. The plans were proposed in 1767 by the 26-year-old James Craig. His chequerboard street pattern with Classical, three-storey buildings arranged around grand crescents and squares was later realised by architects Robert Reid, Archibald Elliot, William Playfair and James Gillespie Graham.

★Shopping **Princes Street**

Busy Princes Street is the new town's main thoroughfare. It extends for almost a mile and is lined with colourful gardens and elegant shops, including the tradition-conscious Jenners built by William Hamilton Beattie in 1895. This shop claims to be the oldest independent department store in the world. Frasers at the western end is not quite so grand, while Waverley Market, opened in 1985, with its small shops set among fountains and cafés offers goods of varying quality. Bargain hunters should head for the shops in the St James Centre situated at the eastern end on the corner of Leith Street. The shops form part of a huge complex which was built during the 1970s and is regarded by many as an example of the architectural excesses of that era. The main tourist information office is situated in Waverley Market. As well as the temples to consumerism and the designer boutiques, Princes Street can boast several reputable hotels and restaurants to suit all pockets – from fast food to gourmet bistros.

Waverley Station North Bridge ★Balmoral House

Beyond Waverley Station old and new Edinburgh are linked by the North Bridge, the site of Hamilton Beattie's Balmoral Hotel – built in 1902 in the style of the expansion era. Even before its extensive renovation, it was the top hotel on the square.

The Scottish national archives, some of which date from the 13th c., are kept in Register House, a building designed by Robert Adam. In front of the elegant mansion stands a memorial to the Duke of Wellington (by Sir John Steel).

Register House

Wellington
Memorial

This Neo-Gothic monument (200ft/61m high) to Sir Walter Scott (see Famous People) on East Princes Street was unveiled in 1844 and was built according to the plans of George Meikle Kemp. A winding staircase of 287 steps leads up to the top. Restored in 1992, the marble statue of the poet with his favourite dog Maida at his feet was also the work of Sir John Steel. The 64 figures on the monument are either characters from Scott's novels or from Scottish history.

★Scott Monument

A few yards further on by Waverley Bridge stands a memorial to the missionary and African explorer David Livingstone (see Famous People).

Livingstone
Memorial

The City Art Centre in Market Street (1–4) which runs parallel to Princes Street is an important municipal art gallery. As well as a permanent exhibition of about 3000 paintings, drawings, prints and sculptures, mainly by Scottish artists from the 17th to the 20th c. such as Hornel, Lorimer, Fergusson, Peploe and Elizabeth Blackadder, it is also a venue for major touring exhibitions (open: June–Sept. Mon.–Sat. 10am–6pm, Sun. 2–5pm during the Edinburgh Festival only; Oct.–May Mon.–Sat. 10am–5pm).

★City Art Centre

To the west and about halfway along Princes Street The Mound cuts through to the old town. At the foot of The Mound stands a Classical building which houses the Royal Scottish Academy. Designed by William Henry Playfair (1789–1867), it is used for touring exhibitions (open: Mon.–Sat. 10am–5pm; Sun. 2–5pm).

The Mound
Royal Scottish
Academy

The highlight of Princes Street Gardens is a floral clock (1903) for which the plants are renewed throughout the year. It is said to be the oldest such clock

★Princes Street
Gardens

National Gallery of Scotland (see page 170)

in the world. At the western end of the garden lie the churches of St John and St Cuthbert and the Ross Open Theatre where bagpipe music and Scottish dancing are performed during the summer.

★★ National Gallery of Scotland

Open:
Mon.–Sat.
10am–5pm,
Sun. 2–5pm
(extended hours
during the
Edinburgh Festival)

The National Gallery (2 The Mound), also the work of Playfair, contains Scotland's biggest collection of European paintings and sculptures, from the Renaissance to Post-Impressionism. Prince Albert laid the foundation stone for the building in 1850 and it was opened in 1859. Galleries 1 and 2 on the ground floor display work by Venetian artists of the 16th c. including Jacopo Bassano's "The Adoration of the Kings" as well as Titian's "The Three Ages of Man" and "Diana and Acteaon". The highlights of galleries 3 and 4 (16th/17th c.) are El Greco's "Saviour of the World", a portrait of a woman by the nineteen-year-old Velázquez and Claude Lorraine's "Apollo and the Muse". Gallery 5 contains Nicholas Poussin's "Seven Sacraments". Dutch and Flemish art of the 17th c. occupy galleries 6, 7 and 9 with portraits by Frans Hals and Rembrandt, Rubens' "Reconciliation between Jacob and Esau", a landscape by Ruesdael, Elsheimer's "Stoning of St Stephen", Vermeer's "Christ in the House of Martha and Mary" and van Dyck's "Martyrdom of St Sebastian". Gallery 8 is reserved for touring exhibitions, but every January there is a display of watercolours by William Turner. Because of their sensitivity to light, they can only be displayed in the winter. Galleries 10 to 12 (18th/19th c.) house portraits by Gainsborough, the Anglo-American Benjamin West and Raeburn (including his portrait of "Reverend Robert Walker" skating on Duddingston Loch), a still life by Chardin, Watteau's "Feast in Venice", Delacroix's "Chess Player", landscapes by Constable and the "Medicus" by Goya. Masterpieces on the first floor include some Renaissance altar paintings and Raphael's "Madonna", in addition to some works by European masters from the 18th and 19th c., such as van Gogh's "Olive Trees" and "Dutch Peasant Girl", impressions of the South Seas by Gauguin, Degas' "Diego Martinelli", sculptures by Rodin ("Young Mother") and Degas' "Grand Arabesque" and "The Bath Tub". Impressionists such as Monet ("Haystacks"), Seurat, Sisley, Pisarro, Renoir ("Mother and Child") and Cézanne ("Mont Ste-Victoire") are also represented. The New Wing, opened in 1978, is devoted to Scottish painting and displays works by the landscape painter Sir William McTaggart ("The Storm"), portraits by Sir James Guthrie and by Allan Ramsay the Younger (1713–84) who enjoyed a successful career at the court of George III in London.

Processional frieze by William Hole

Paintings of some of the leading figures in Scottish history from the 16th c. to the present day can be seen in the Scottish National Portrait Gallery at no. 12 Queen Street to the north-east of Princes Street.

★ **Scottish National Portrait Gallery**

Open:
Mon.–Sat.
10am–5pm,
Sun. 2–5pm
(extended hours
during the
Edinburgh Festival)

The highlight here is certainly the huge processional frieze (William Hole, 1898) showing Scotland's most famous personalities. Among the celebrities recorded in oil are Robert Burns (Nasmyth), Sir Walter Scott (Raeburn), David Hume (Ramsay), Sean Connery (John Bellany), Robert Louis Stevenson, James Watt and Mary Stuart (for all seven see Famous People), Bonnie Prince Charlie and Flora MacDonald (see Baedeker Special, "The Prince and the Hebridean Girl"), Lord Byron, Winston Churchill, Thomas Carlyle, Hugh McDiarmid, Muriel Spark and the Queen Mother. Portrait artists whose works are displayed here include Reynolds, Epstein, Tischbein, Kokoschka, Gainsborough, Moffat, Robert Heriot Westwater and James Guthrie. Historical landscapes such as studies of Falkland Palace (see Fife), Seton Palace and Peter Tilleman's "Battle of Glenshiels" are also on show.

The Museum of Antiquities owes its existence to the eccentric 11th Earl of Buchan (1749–1829). However, since 1891 the collection has shared the Portrait Gallery's premises. With three floors of exhibits, interest will probably focus on the Neolithic tools (4000–2500 B.C.), a reconstruction of Skara Brae, a Late Neolithic village (see Orkney Islands), early Pictish sculptures (10th–7th c. B.C., the Pictish silver hoard from St Ninian's Isle (see Shetland Islands), the Hunterston Brooch, an 8th c. Celtic ornament, Roman finds including parts of the Antonine Wall (see entry) and the Treasure of Traprain 5th c. B.C. which was discovered in 1919, Scottish costumes and an extensive collection of early Scottish silver and gold.

★★ **National Museum of Antiquities of Scotland**

Open:
Mon.–Sat.
10am–5pm,
Sun. 2–5pm

The Classical façade on the north side of Charlotte Square – near the west end of Queen Street – was completed in 1791 by Robert Adam and many people regard it as his finest work. The Georgian House at no. 7, now in the hands of the National Trust for Scotland, provides an insight into the everyday life of a middle-class family at the end of the 18th c. (open: Apr.–Oct. Mon.–Sat. 10am–5pm, Sun. 2–5pm). Alexander Graham Bell, inventor of the telephone, (see Famous People) was born at no. 16 and Joseph Lister, who first discovered the importance of antiseptics in medicine, lived at no. 9.

★ **Charlotte Square**
★ Georgian House

From Charlotte Square follow George Street eastward. At no. 67 stands the Malcolm Innes Gallery which specialises in displaying works by Scottish artists from the 19th and 20th c. including Elisabeth Cameron, Brian Rawling and Louise Wood (open: Mon.–Fri. 9.30am–6pm). Sir Walter Scott lodged at no. 107 from 1797 before moving into Castle Street and then Abbotsford House.

George Street
Malcolm Innes
Gallery

The imposing Royal Bank of Scotland on the east side of the square was built in 1772 by William Chambers as a home for Sir Lawrence Dundas, the first Viscount of Melville. A memorial to the Viscount of Melville stands on the square as well as an equestrian statue of the Earl of Hopetoun.

St Andrew Square

An image of idyllic village life is created by Dean Village, north-west of Princes Street (Queensferry Street–Belford Road–Bells Brae). This picturesque little spot lies in a wooded gorge carved by the meandering waters of the Water of Leith, which during the Middle Ages supplied the water power for Edinburgh's flour mills. Weavers, tanners and breweries soon followed. Inscriptions and house signs from the 17th c. recall the bakers' guild, while St Bernard's Wall by Leith Walkway is an attractive example of Classical landscaping. The round temple with a statue of Hygieia was erected in 1789 by Alexander Nasmyth.

★ Dean Village

To the south-west on Belford Road, the Neo-classical Scottish National Gallery of Modern Art, which was opened in 1984, displays 20th c. masterpieces including paintings by Henry Matisse, Georges Braque, Paul Klee,

★ **Scottish National Gallery of Modern Art**

Edinburgh

Open:
Mon.–Sat.
10am–5pm,
Sun. 2–5pm
(extended hours
during the
Edinburgh
Festival)

Otto Dix and Pablo Picasso ("Mother and Child" from the "Blue Period"), surrealist works by René Magritte, Joan Miró, Max Ernst and Giacometti, contemporary Scottish paintings by Bruce MacLean, Callum Innes, John Bellany, Kate Whiteford and Gwen Hardie and sculptures by Barlach, Epstein, Henry Moore, Barbara Hepworth, Matthew Smith, George Rickey and David Hockney. The "Scottish Colourists", such as Peploe, Cadell, Hunter and Fergusson, are also represented.

★ Zoological Park

Edinburgh's zoo was founded in 1913. It extends for an area of about 80 acres/32ha in Corstorphine Road. Entrance at 134 Corstorphine Road. This, the largest zoo in Scotland, can boast a collection of over 1000 animals including lions, tigers, leopards, Scottish wildcats, Highland cattle, brown bears, polar bears, gorillas, Californian sea lions, antelopes, hippopotamuses, camels, guanacos, kangaroos, reptiles, flamingoes and a very wide collection of birds. The penguin colony is thought to be the largest in the world (open: Apr.–Sept. Mon.–Sat. 9am–6pm, Sun. 9.30am–6pm; Oct.–Mar. daily 9am–4.30pm, Sun. 9.30am–4.30pm).

★★ **Royal Botanic Garden**

Open:
daily from 10am (to
6pm Mar./Apr. and
Sept./Oct.; to 8pm
May–Aug.; to 4pm
Nov.–Feb.)

The Royal Botanic Garden, situated to the north of the city centre, is the second oldest botanical garden in the British Isles. Within the magnificent 70 acre/28ha site, there is an herbarium and Great Britain's biggest palm house, a tropical house with exotic orchids, a collection of cacti and succulents, an alpine house, a terraced moorland garden, a heather garden with all the calluna vulgaris species that grow in the Highlands, an extensive arboretum with some rare giant trees (from the Himalayas, North America and China), a woodland garden with colourful azaleas, hydrangeas, camellias, saxifrage and rhododendrons, an aquatic house with tropical water plants such as the pink water lily from India and the huge South American water lily (*Victoria Regis*), a rock garden and the Exhibition Hall which has regular temporary exhibitions.

Royal Botanic Garden: Palm House . . .   *. . . and South American Victoria regis*

172

View from Calton Hill

Calton Hill provides a panoramic view of the city that should not be missed. The hill itself is of volcanic origin. To the west lie Princes Street and the castle, to the south the old town is silhouetted against Arthur's Seat, while in the east and north the Firth of Forth and the docks at Leith are clearly visible. At the foot of the hill stands the Royal High School (13th c.) where Sir Walter Scott was once a pupil.

★Calton Hill
Royal High
School

Opposite in Regent Road stands a memorial to the Scottish poet Robert Burns (see Famous People), who even during his lifetime endeared himself to Edinburgh society.

Burns' Monument

The impressive National Monument on Calton Hill was erected to remember the dead from the Napoleonic Wars. Henry Playfair designed the memorial using the Parthenon in Athens as his inspiration and work began in 1822 but the project had to be abandoned due to lack of money. The Nelson Monument, a few yards away, was unveiled in 1816 after Horatio Nelson's victory at the Battle of Trafalgar (1806). The time ball which works in conjunction with the One O'Clock Salute at Edinburgh Castle (see above) is situated here.

National
Monument

Nelson's
Monument

Visitors to James Craig and William Playfair's observatory (1774–1818) are supplied with 3-D glasses for a 20-minute slide show on Scotland's captivating capital city (open: Apr.–June and Oct. Mon.–Fri. 2–5pm, Sat., Sun. 10.30am–5pm; July–Sept. daily 10.30am–5pm). Other sights located on the hill include memorials to the philosopher Dugald Stewart (1753–1828) and the mathematician John Playfair (1748–1819).

Edinburgh
Experience

Memorials to
Stewart and
Playfair

The Royal Observatory stands on Blackford Hill to the south of the city and the amazing world of the universe is revealed to visitors with the aid of telescopes, models, videos and computer games (open: Apr.–Sept. daily noon–5.30pm; Oct.–Mar. daily 1–5pm, to 9pm Fri.). The commanding position of the observatory offers another fine panoramic view of the city.

Blackford Hill
Royal
Observatory

Edinburgh

★Leith

Situated at the mouth of the Water of Leith in the Firth of Forth, Leith is Edinburgh's main port. Until 1920, it was an independent town which had grown considerably in importance during the Industrial Revolution mainly through shipbuilding. Four new docks alone were built during the second half of the 19th c., but with the decline of the port after the Second World War, the town's economic fortunes waned. However, in the last decade, redevelopment has brought new hope to the fragile local economy. The houses around the Shore, Constitution Street and Bernhard Street have been brightened up, including the old Customs House and Andrew Lamb's House in Burgess Street which was built in the 17th c. by a prosperous merchant. A good example of modern architecture is the King's Landing housing estate. The name derives from the visit of George IV to the town in 1822. He was the first monarch to set foot on Scottish soil for more than a 100 years.

Clan Tartan Centre

Computer technology is used at this centre in Bangor Road to provide genealogical histories of the various clans and also information about tartan patterns. The adjoining shop supplies the full Scottish costume (open: daily 9am–5.30pm).

Scottish Malt Whisky Society

This club for wealthy whisky drinkers buys the precious spirit direct from the distillery and fills numbered bottles for its members. The distinguished club rooms in Giles Street (no. 87) can be opened at the request of guests (tel. (0131) 554 3451).

Kinloch Anderson

The Heritage Room in Kinloch Anderson's premises (founded in 1868) with its various tartans and the uniforms of Scottish regiments illustrates the long history of the kiltmaker. The shop next door sells woollen goods and all the other accoutrements for kilt wearers (open: Mon.–Sat. 9am–5.30pm, to 5pm in winter).

Ratho Canal Centre

To the west of the city centre the Bridge Inn in Baird Road, Ratho (8 miles/12.8km) owns two small, luxurious canalboat restaurants. An exhibition in the inn documents the history of canalboats (open: Sun.–Thur. 10am–11pm, Fri. and Sat. to midnight).

Surroundings

Scottish Agricultural Museum

The history of rural life in the Edinburgh region is the subject for this agricultural museum near the airport in Ingliston (open: daily 10am–5pm; Oct.–Mar. Mon.–Fri. only).

Niddry Castle

A tour of this 15th c. castle (10 miles/16km west of the city) passes through the Great Hall, guardroom and dungeon as well as the chamber where Mary Stuart once sought refuge. Tea is served in the Laird's Hall (open: May–Sept. Sun. 2–4pm).

Malleny Gardens

The 17th c. house (8 miles/12.8km south of the city) is not open to the public, but the magnificent gardens with their splendid bush roses and the National Bonsai Collection is open daily from 10am to dusk.

★Craigmillar Castle

Begun in the 14th c. Craigmillar Castle (HS; 2 miles/3km east of the city) was a favourite with Mary Stuart who withdrew here after Rizzio was murdered in 1556. The death of her husband Lord Darnley was, so it is said, planned here. The L-shaped tower house dating from 1374 was extended c. 1427 with a curtain wall and small towers. The three-storey east wing was added in the middle of the 16th c. As well as the 17th c. living quarters, the kitchen and dungeon are of particular interest (open: Apr.–Sept. Mon.–Sat. 9.30am–6.30pm, Sun. 2–6pm; Oct.–Mar. Mon.–Wed. and Sat. 9.30am–4.30pm, Thur. 9.30am–12.30pm, Sun. 2–4.30pm).

Butterfly and Insect World

Hundreds of colourful butterflies from all over the world flutter freely through an exotic rainforest of tropical plants. Leaf-cutting ants, stick

Craigmillar Castle: a favourite with Mary Queen of Scots

insects and scorpions are among the more unusual insects on view (Dobbies Garden Centre, at Lasswade on the A7 5 miles/8km south of the city; open: Mar.–Oct. daily 10am–5.30pm; Nov.–Jan. daily 10am–4.30pm).

The two mines of Prestongrange and Lady Victoria (see below) document the history of the Scottish mining industry.

Prestongrange lies on the B1348 near Prestonpans to the west of Edinburgh. The museum's underground gallery gives the visitor an insight into the tough working environment of the miner. Particularly impressive are the huge plane, scraper and coal cutter (open: Apr.–Oct. daily, 11am–4pm).

Prestongrange Industrial Heritage Museum

Prestongrange

A visit to the Lady Victoria Colliery near Newtongrange 10 miles/16km southeast of Edinburgh is a rewarding experience. A working mine from 1890 and a showpiece for the Scottish coalfields, it closed in 1981 but then the old plant and coal seams were converted into a museum. Of greatest historical interest is the "Grant-Richie" winding engine which was used to lift the coal from a depth of almost 1640ft/500m. The mine was named after the wife of the former mine owner Lord Lothian (open: Mar.–Sept. daily, 10am–4pm).

★**Scottish Mining Museum** (Lady Victoria Colliery)

Newtongrange

The mining village of Roslin (pop. 1600) about 5 miles/8km south of the city was a popular spot around 1800 because of a poem by Scott entitled "The Lay of the Last Minstrel". What attracts most visitors to the village today is William Sinclair's 15th c. chapel with its ornate stone carvings and allegorical sculptures such as the "Dance of Death". According to legend, a richly decorated Late Gothic column known as the "Prentice Pilar" was produced by an apprentice.

Roslin ★Rosslyn Chapel

To learn something of the mysteries of glass blowing and crystal cutting, take a 30-minute tour through the glass factory in Eastfield/Penicuik 10 miles/16km south of Edinburgh (open: Mon.–Sat. 9am–5pm, Sun.

Penicuik Edinburgh Crystal Visitor Centre

Winding machinery at the Lady Victoria Colliery Museum

The Forth Railway Bridge

11am–5pm; tours Mon.–Fri. 9.15am–3.30pm, Sat. and Sun. 11am–2.30pm Apr.–Sept. only).

On a hill by the banks of Tyne Water stands Crichton Castle (HS; 12 miles/ 19.2km east of Edinburgh). Praised by Scott in his "Marmion", the original 14th c. tower house had three wings added in the 15th c. and in the second half of the 16th c. the 5th Earl of Bothwell gave it an Italianate elegance by supplementing the north wing with Florentine arcades and enhancing the façade and brickwork with diamond bosses. It is thought that Mary Stuart and Lord Darnley stayed here during their honeymoon – at least the stone over the two central pillars on the east side of the courtyard bear the initials MSD (open: Apr.–Sept. Mon.–Sat. 9.30am–6.30pm, Sun. 2–6.30pm).

★ Crichton Castle

The official sign outside the fantastic gardens belonging to the Scottish artist Ian Hamilton Finlay refers to them as "Stonypath". However, "Little Sparta" is the name chosen by Finlay for this 4 acre/1.6ha cultural oasis near Dunsyre in the thinly-populated Pentland Hills about 24 miles/39km south-west of Edinburgh. The artist gardener and his wife Sue started work here in 1966 and out of an abandoned farmhouse they have created a world of fairy tales, myths and history. Sundials, Classical chapels and stones engraved with mottoes catch visitors unawares among the broom, lilies and lupins. Hidden away in a labyrinth of allusions to form and sense are paving slabs adorned with the motto "The order of the present is the disorder of the future", a memorial pyramid to the Romantic Caspar David Friedrich, a bust in shimmering gold of the French revolutionary St Just with the words "Apollon Terroriste" on his forehead, aircraft carrier sculptures in miniature parodying military action and the Classical façade of an ancient temple to Philemon and Baucis. Finlay is now well-established internationally in the world of art.

Dunsyre
★ Stonypath

See Haddington

East Lothian

See entry

Fife

Along the south bank of the Firth of Forth

Several places of interest are within easy reach of the western side of Edinburgh to the south of the Firth of Forth. Cramond is a popular suburb with whitewashed houses which overlook the River Almond as it opens into the Firth of Forth. Excavations have provided evidence that a Roman camp was based here as early as 142. A Roman bath has been uncovered near Cramond Inn.

Cramond

This Edwardian country mansion (in Cramond Road South, 4 miles/6.4km north-west of the town centre) was originally built by Sir Archibald Napier, the father of the mathematician and discoverer of logarithms John Napier. In 1827 it was bought by the banker and newspaper publisher Thomas Allan who commissioned William Burn to make considerable extensions. Around 1903 William Reid, the owner of Morrison joiners in Edinburgh, provided furniture for the mansion's interior and he also acquired the valuable 18th c. English and Italian works, the Blue John vases from Derbyshire and the Crossley wool mosaic (open: Apr.–Oct. Sat. to Thur. 11am–1pm and 2–5pm; Nov.–Mar. Sat. Sun. 2–4pm; grounds daily 9am–dusk).

★ Lauriston Castle

Just outside Dalmeny (8 miles/12.8km north-west of Edinburgh), a road branches off to the right to Dalmeny House, which occupies a commanding position overlooking the Firth of Forth. This residence of the earls of Rosebery was designed in 1815 by William Wilkins in Tudor Gothic style. Of greatest interest from an architectural point of view are the dragon beam hall and the fan vaulting in the corridors. It is, however, the valuable art treasures that probably attract most visitors. In 1878 the 5th Earl of Rosebery married a Rothschild heiress and as a result the collection was

Dalmeny
★★House

considerably extended. The French furniture dates mainly from the time of Louis XV and Louis XVI, including a Jean-François Oeben bureau which belonged to the dauphin. Sèvres and Vincennes porcelain, Beauvais tapestries by François Boucher and silk curtains said to have been embroidered by Marie Antoinette and her court ladies form another part of the Rothschild collection. Portraits by Reynolds, Raeburn, Gainsborough and Nasmyth and tapestries designed by Goya (1800) are also on display. The Napoleon Room contains paintings and personal effects belonging to the emperor and also a seat used by the Duke of Wellington (open: May–early Sept. Mon., Tues. noon–5.30pm; Sun. 1–5.30pm). Dalmeny also boasts one of the finest Norman churches in Scotland. St Cuthbert's, which dates from the middle of the 12th c., has a richly decorated south portal – two relief arches with signs of the zodiac, masks and the lamb of God – and some fine wood carving. It also retains the original cross vaulting.

★Church

Queensferry
★★ Forth Bridges

South Queensferry (pop. 7,500) lies 2 miles/3.2km to the west of Dalmeny. The village is dominated by two famous bridges. The vast Forth Railway Bridge stands 150ft/45m above the water and extends for 2756yd/2529m. The engineer Sir John Fowler and Sir Benjamin Baker collaborated on its design and it was completed in the 1880s. The more delicately engineered Forth Road Bridge was opened in 1964. With a span width of 1977yd/1814m it is one of the longest suspensions bridge in Europe. Historic Hawes Inn by the pier of the same name is mentioned in Robert Louis Stevenson's "Kidnapped" and Scott's "The Antiquary".

Hawes Inn

★ Deep Sea World

This new underwater experience opened in 1993. Situated opposite North Queensferry, it provides an opportunity to watch and admire sharks, squid, lobsters, eels and colourful coral reefs from a 122yd/112m tunnel (open: Apr.–early Nov. 10am–6pm; early Nov.–Mar. Mon.–Fri. 10am–4pm, Sat. and Sun. 10am–6pm).

Hopetoun House – the epitome of Baroque elegance

Hopetoun House

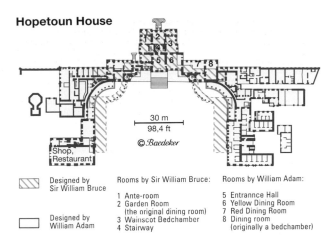

Scale:
30 m
98,4 ft
© Baedeker

Shop, Restaurant

Designed by Sir William Bruce

Designed by William Adam

Rooms by Sir William Bruce:

1 Ante-room
2 Garden Room (the original dining room)
3 Wainscot Bedchamber
4 Stairway

Rooms by William Adam:

5 Entrannce Hall
6 Yellow Dining Room
7 Red Dining Room
8 Dining room (originally a bedchamber)

Generations of the Hope family, later the Marquess of Linlithgow, have resided in the impressive Hopetoun House. Lying some 3 miles/4.8km to the west of South Queensferry, it was begun in 1699 by Sir William Bruce, who also built the Palace of Holyroodhouse in Edinburgh. By 1703 he had completed the rectangular central section. His pupil William Adam and sons John and Robert Adam extended the house between 1721 and 1754. It was Adam who provided the Baroque mansion with a finely ornamented two-storey façade adding semi-circular colonnades and pavilions to both

★★ Hopetoun House

Open: Easter–early Oct. daily, 10am–5.30pm

sides. The original entrance hall was converted into a garden room – the oak panelling and gilded capitals are original. The splendid rooms of the mansion are decorated with damask wallpaper, tapestries from Antwerp and Aubusson (17th c.), delightful stucco ceilings and furniture from the 18th and 19th c. In the Red Drawing room hangs Canaletto's "The Doge's Palace and Campanile by the Grand Canal in Venice". Portraits by Raeburn, Ramsay and Gainsborough decorate the Dining Hall. Also represented are Rembrandt, Titian and works from the Rubens School ("The Adoration of the Shepherds" in the Yellow Room). Early 19th c. Meissen and Derby dinner services and vases take place of honour in the porcelain collection.

Blackness Castle

Viewed from the east Blackness Castle (3 miles/4.8km to the west) resembles the hull of a ship with its bow and stern marked by two towers. The fort was built in the 15th c. above a harbour that has since disappeared. It was used as a prison for Covenanters, from 1870 as a weapons store and more recently as a Youth Hostel. In 1990 a version of "Hamlet" starring Mel Gibson was filmed against the backdrop of the castle (HS; open: Apr.–Sept. Mon.–Sat. 9.30am–6.30pm, Sun. 2–6.30pm; Oct–Mar. Mon.–Wed. 9.30am–4.30pm, Thur. 9.30am–noon, Sat. 9.30–4.30pm, Sun. 2–4.30pm).

★House of the Binns

Open:
May–Sept.
Sat.–Thur.
1.30–5.30pm;
Park:
Apr.–Oct.
daily 9.30am–7pm,
Nov.–Mar.
daily 9.30am–4pm

Although this country house has been under the administration of the National Trust for Scotland since 1944, the Dalyell family still live in one of the wings of the "Binns". Situated 2 miles/3.2km to the south, the house has been fully restored and was re-opened in 1993. Little remains of the medieval fort (15th c.) with most of the building work taking place between 1615 and 1630. Tam Dalyell was a wealthy businessman who led a turbulent life fighting as a Royalist against the Covenanters. When Charles II was deposed, he served the Russian tsar and it is said that he even escaped from the Tower of London. Of particular interest are the stone chimneys and the stucco ceilings (mid-17th c.) in the High Hall and the King's Room where the heraldic emblems of England and Scotland are joined in a decorative manner.

Linlithgow

★Palace
(see plan
page 181)

The town of Linlithgow (pop. 4300) lies 4 miles/6.4km further west and it possesses a fine row of well-preserved 16th c. houses. However, the town can also boast two important historic sites. One is Linlithgow Palace, a castle set in an attractive lakeside location and birthplace of Mary Stuart (see Famous People) in 1542. Begun in 1424, it was almost 200 years before the castle with its tower defences was completed. A few months after "Bonnie Prince Charlie" stayed here, the four-winged building fell victim to a major fire. James V belonged to four knightly orders and their emblems can be seen above the external castle gate: the English garter, the Scottish thistle, the golden fleece of Burgundy and the royal lily of France. The gatehouse on the east front, the main entrance under James I, bears the royal coat-of-arms. An octagonal fountain built by James V in 1530 adorns the middle of the inner courtyard and a replica can be seen in front of Holyroodhouse in Edinburgh (see entry). The 100ft/30.5m long Great Hall by Lyon Chalmer gives some idea of the palace's splendour. It has a 23ft/7m wide three-part mantelpiece, which was added during the reign of James I at the beginning of the 15th c. The frieze and tapestries in Mary Stuarts's chamber in Holyroodhouse give a clear impression of how the royal bedchamber here might once have looked (HS; open: Apr.–Sept. 9.30am–6pm, Sun. 2–6pm; Oct.–Mar. Mon.–Sat. 9.30am–4pm, Sun. 2–4.30pm).

★St Michael

The second historic site near Linlithgow is St Michael, a large burgh church dating from pre-Reformation times. Consecrated in the 13th c. work was restarted after 1424 and finally completed in the middle of the 16th c. The nave (1497) and the choir (1531) are particularly impressive and the tracery on the windows in the Catherine side aisle is worth noting. The late Gothic window in the south chapel is regarded as one of the finest of its kind in Scotland (open: June–Sept. daily, except Sat. and Sun. Oct.–May, 10am–noon and 1.30–3.30pm).

Linlithgow Palace

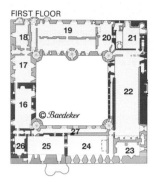

FIRST FLOOR

GROUND FLOOR

1 South Porch (entrance)
2 Fountain
3–5 Cellars
6,7 Kitchens
8,9 Brewery
10 Barbican
11 Former main entrance
(time of James I)
12 Guard Room
13 Dungeon
14 Stables
15 Guard Room
16 King's Room
17 Audience Chamber
18 Bedchamber
19 Dining Room
20 Larder
21 Kitchen
22 Great Hall
23 Private Apartment
24 Royal Chapel
25 Ante-room
26 South-west Tower
27 Gallery

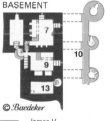

BASEMENT

Phases of construction		
James I. 1424-1437	James III. 1460-1488	James V. 1513-1542
	James IV. 1488-1513	James VI. 1618-1624

About 4 miles/6.4km south of Linlithgow lie the stones of Cairnpapple Hill. This prehistoric sacred site probably dates from the Neolithic Era about 3000 B.C., although the stone circles and burial chamber were probably added during the early Bronze Age by the Beaker people (open: Apr.–Sept. Mon.–Sat. 9.30am–6.30pm, Sun. 2–6.30pm).

Cairnpapple Hill

Nature trails and pretty picnic sites attract many visitors to Almondell and Calderwood Country Park which is located south-east of the M8 near Livingston. Guided tours of the park are available on request. The Visitor Centre can supply information on fauna and flora and also local history (access via the A89 from Broxburn. The park is open all the year round; Visitor Centre: Apr.–Sept. Mon.–Wed. 9am–noon and 1–5pm, Thur. 9am–noon and 1–4pm, Sun. 10.30am–noon and 1–6pm; Oct.–Mar. Mon.–Thur. 9am–noon and 1–4pm, Sun. 10am–noon and 1–4.30pm).

Almondell and Calderwood Country Park

The railway museum at Bo'ness (full name: Borrowstounness; pop. 14,400) by the Firth of Forth has a fine collection of steam locomotives. It is possible to take a short train ride towards Grangemouth. In Kinneil House (16th/17th c.) James Watt (see Famous People) worked on the first steam engine.

Bo'ness Railway

Grangemouth, Kincardine- on-Forth	Take the M9 or the A905 to the west past the oil refineries of Grangemouth (pop. 19,000). Now Scotland's main centre for petro-chemicals, Grangemouth is supplied with North Sea oil via a pipeline from Cruden Bay. A bridge near Bowtrees carries the A876 across to Kincardine-on-Forth where the A985 leads east along the north bank of the Firth of Forth through the industrial belt to Dunfermline (see entry) and the Fife peninsula (see entry).
Antonine Wall	See entry

Elgin   F 4

Region: Grampian. Population: 20,000

Situation	The administrative centre for Moray District is Elgin, close on 40 miles/64km east of Inverness (see entry). The impressive remains of the old episcopal palace, Spynie Palace, and the ruins of one of Scotland's finest cathedrals are proof that the town was an important centre in the Middle Ages.

Sights

High Street Museum	The front of Duff o'Bracco's House (1694) with its pretty arcade is among the several 17th. and 18th c. preserved town houses which line the High Street. The town museum (no. 1) has notable archaeological and geological sections relating to the Moray region (open: Apr.–Sept. Mon., Tues., Thur., Fri. 10am–5pm, Sat. 11am–4pm, Sun. 2–5pm).
★ Cathedral	The first cathedral (13th c.) was proudly described by the then bishop as "the glory of the kingdom, the delight of foreigners", but in 1390 the town was destroyed by Alexander Stewart "the Wolf of Badenoch" in an act of revenge for his excommunication. More damage was inflicted later on by the plundering supporters of John Knox (see Famous People) and the troops of Oliver Cromwell. Now only the remains of the cathedral tower show the one-time splendour of the 314ft/96m long "Lantern of the North" as the church in King Street used to be known. The west façade designed in French style, the choir with its Early Gothic lancet windows (c. 1270), the great east rose window ("Omega Window") and the octagonal chapter-house with its fine stonework (c. 1390) are the most striking features of what remains (HS; open: Apr.–Sept. Mon.–Sat. 9.30am–6pm, Sun. 2–6pm; Oct.–Mar. Mon.–Thur. Sat. 9.30am–4pm, Sun. 2–4pm).
Gordon & MacPhail	Many people regard Elgin as the capital of malt whisky, particularly as large bottling plants such as Gordon & MacPhail are based here. Anyone looking for a special scotch or a rare malt would do well to start their search at Gordon & MacPhail in South Street (nos. 58–60) as their range of whiskies is beyond compare.

Surroundings

Linkwood Distillery	No fewer than eight distilleries are located in the region to the south of Elgin. Linkwood Distillery, as the name suggests, is surrounded by woodland on the banks of the Lossie. The company was founded in 1821 and the premises have subsequently been altered on several occasions (guided tours by arrangement).
Birnie Church	Before the diocese chose Elgin as its centre, the bishop's seat was in Birnie (3 miles/4.8km to the south). A Norman church was built on the site of a

6th c. Celtic chapel c. 1140 and the church is thus able to claim to be the oldest surviving church on Scottish soil.

Pluscarden Abbey stands in the shadow of several ancient trees (6 miles/ 9.6km south-west). It was founded in 1230 for members of the Valliscaulian Order. Like the cathedral in Elgin, it was destroyed by the "Wolf of Badenoch" in 1390. Benedictine monks settled here until 1560. Followers of the Benedictine Order returned in 1943 and restored the ruins (open: daily, 5am–8.30pm).

Pluscarden Abbey

At the end of the 15th c. the episcopal seat at Spynie (2 miles/3km to the north) was one of the finest sacred buildings in Scotland. In the 17th c. an Italianate terraced garden was added. The massive David's Tower was built between 1470 and 1480 by Bishop David Stewart as a defence against attacks by the Gordon Clan (HS; open: Apr.–Sept. Mon.–Sat. 9.30am–6.30pm, Sun. 2–6.30pm; Oct.–Mar. Sat. 9.30am–4.30pm, Sun. 2–4.30pm).

★ Spynie Palace

Duffus Castle (5 miles/8km north-west), once the seat of the Murray family, is a fine example of a Norman motte and bailey castle and it dominates the flat farmland between Elgin and the coast. Surrounded by a water-filled moat, the wooden palisades were replaced by a stone tower house with stout walls.

★ Duffus Castle

Prince Philip, Prince Charles and his brother Andrew were educated at Gordonstoun boarding school. It was founded in 1934 by the German educationalist Kurt Hahn.

Gordonstoun

The town museum in Lossiemouth (pop. 7400; 6 miles/9.6km to the north) concentrates on the role of the fishing industry locally, but it is also a place of pilgrimage for British socialists as the study of Ramsay MacDonald, Britain's first Labour prime minister and a son of Lossiemouth, has been recreated here (Pitgaveny St; open: Easter–Sept. Mon.–Sat. 10am–5pm).

Lossiemouth Fisheries Museum

Little is known of the origin and age of Burghead Well (HS; 7½ miles/12km to the north-west). It is a man-made cave which was probably carved out of the rock as part of an Iron Age fort. The 3ft/1m deep water-hole may well have been used as a baptismal font.

Burghead Well

Forres (pop. 9000) has won prominence in recent years for its colourful floral displays in the "Britain in Bloom" competition. William Shakespeare chose Forres as the setting for the opening of "Macbeth" In the play Macbeth, under pressure from his wife, murders King Duncan, who, it has now been historically proven, lived in Forres at the beginning of the 11th c. A huge 22ft/7m high finely decorated stone stands at the eastern end of the town. On one side of Sueno's Stone (HS) a Christian wheel cross is depicted, while the other side shows battle scenes.

Forres

★ Sueno's Stone

Hugh and Alexander Falconer's museum (1870) focuses on social history and geology in the region (Tolbooth Street; open: May, June, Sept. Mon.–Sat. 9.30am–6.30pm, Sun. 2–6.30pm; Oct.–Apr. Mon.–Fri. 10am–12.30pm, 1.30–4.30pm).

Falconer Museum

This magnificent estate has been the seat of the Brodie family since 1160 when the land was loaned by Malcolm IV. The castle (3 miles/4.8km to the west of Forres) was built c. 1567 by Alexander, the 12th Brodie of Brodie and the west wing was added in the early 17th c. Troops of Lord Lewis set fire to the castle in 1645 after the laird signed the "National Covenant". Reconstruction followed in 1730. In the 19th c. the Z-shaped sandstone tower was extended by William Burn and since 1980 the castle has been in the possession of the National Trust for Scotland. Fine French furniture from the 18th and 19th c., Chinese porcelain and objets d'art, Meissen and English tableware and a notable collection of paintings including the work

★ **Brodie Castle and Country Park**

Open:
Apr.–Sept. Mon.–Sat. 11am–5.30pm
Sun. 1.30–5.30pm

of French Impressionists and English and Dutch artists from the 17th–19th c. are among the items on display in the elegant interior. A tour around the extensive grounds should include a visit to the 6ft/2m high Pictish Rodney Stone, carved with Celtic animal symbols and inscriptions.

★Dallas Dhu
Distillery

This small, picturesquely-situated whisky distillery (2 miles/3.2km south of Forres) was founded in 1898 by Wright and Greig, a blending company based in Glasgow. At the time, the softer malts of Moray and Banffshire were gaining in popularity at the expense of the peaty Highland and Island malts. The location of Dallas Dhu ("dhu" = black) turned out to be ideal. The nearby Laigh of Moray supplied the barley and the water came from Altyre Burn. "Roderick Dhu" became perhaps the best known of the blended whiskies produced here. It was named after one of the protagonists in Scott's "The Lady of the Lake". Dallas Dhu remained in business until 1983, but then the distillery was taken over by Historic Scotland and converted into a working whisky museum (open: Apr.–Sept. 9.30am–6pm, Sun. 2–6pm; Oct.–Mar. Mon.–Sat. 9.30am–4pm, Sun. 2–3pm; see Baedeker Special "Scotch Whisky").

Darnaway Farm

Darnaway Farm (3 miles/4.8km south-west of Forres) is a working farm where visitors are welcome. Children will enjoy the animal enclosure (open: May–mid-Sept. daily, 10am–5pm).

Randolph's Leap

The River Findhorn winds its way through a narrow sandstone gorge about 8 miles/12.8km south of Forres. From a footpath above the ravine near Randolph's Leap, there is a beautiful view over the babbling waters of the Findhorn.

Grampian

See entry

Malt Whisky Trail

See entry

Fife   F/G 5

Regions: Fife, Tayside

Peninsula
between Forth
and Tay

The Fife peninsula extends from the broad Forth estuary in the south to the Firth of Tay in the north. Where once the Picts held sway and where trade with the Friesians, Flemings and Normans flourished in the Middle Ages, now tourism and young, ambitioùs service and electronics companies centred on Glenrothes in the so-called "Silicon Glen" provide employment for the local people. The region is administered from the town of Cupar.

West Fife

Dunfermline

See entry

★★Culross

Much of the picture-book burgh of Culross (6 miles/9.6km west of Dunfermline) is now in the hands of the National Trust for Scotland. It is a popular spot with tourists as it is probably Scotland's best surviving example of how the middle classes lived between 1600 and 1800. At that time the settlement was a busy centre where the inhabitants earned their living from coal, salt and the manufacture of cast-iron plates on which the famous Scottish scones were baked. Work on restoring the village started in the 1950s. Distinctive features include the cobbled alleys, whitewashed houses, red pantile roofs, stepped gables and outside stairways leading to first-floor entrances.

Tour

Leave the car on the car park at the west end of the village. On the left side of Sandhaven stands "Bessie's Bar" named after a 17th c. maltster. Behind it lies the recently restored "Palace". This Dutch-style mansion was built in

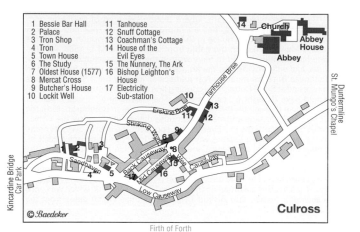

1 Bessie Bar Hall	11 Tanhouse
2 Palace	12 Snuff Cottage
3 Tron Shop	13 Coachman's Cottage
4 Tron	14 House of the
5 Town House	Evil Eyes
6 The Study	15 The Nunnery, The Ark
7 Oldest House (1577)	16 Bishop Leighton's
8 Mercat Cross	House
9 Butcher's House	17 Electricity
10 Lockit Well	Sub-station

© *Baedeker*

Culross

Kincardine Bridge Car Park

Dunfermline St. Mungo's Chapel

Firth of Forth

1597 for the wealthy businessman Sir George Bruce. Note the elegant double staircase and the beautifully painted ceiling beams. The inscription "SGB 1611" is thought to refer to the year of completion and the year in which Sir Bruce was knighted. The square at the end of Sandhaven is dominated by the Town House (1626) which was crowned with a belfry in 1783. The municipal scales, known as the tron, stood on the stone plinth opposite. A row of delightfully restored 17th c. houses line Back Causeway. Note the stepped gables and roofs of Dutch hollow tiles. The "Study"

Back Causeway . . .

. . . and Culross Town House

185

(1633) on the market square, where Bishop Leighton of Dunblane conducted theology lessons, has an impressive gabled roof and look-out tower, while the oldest house in Culross bears the inscription "1577"; the replica Mercat Cross on the gable front was completed in 1588. An educated sea captain is said to have written the Greek inscription "God provides and will provide" on the adjacent house. A few yards further on in Tanhouse Brae the meat cleaver and scales identify the 17th c. Butcher's House and at Snuff Cottage the opening line of an old Scottish saying "Who would have thought it" can be read. The second line "it was made for noses" can be seen on the house of a snuff-maker in Edinburgh. Both the Coachman's Cottage and the old Tanhouse date from the end of the 17th c., while the House of the Evil Eyes (16th c.) opposite the church owes its name to the gable's weird-looking windows. The local parish church (1633) includes the chancel and central tower of a Cistercian abbey (1217). On the road to Dunfermline stands the Chapel of St Mungo (1503), which is now just a ruin. It is said that St Mungo – the patron saint of Glasgow (see entry) – was born here. The road back to the car park passes the Nunnery – look for the veiled head of a woman on the stepped gable – the Ark, which was once a seamen's hostel, and Bishop Leighton's House which dates from the second half of the 17th c.

Limekilns

The narrow streets of this old port (pop. 1100) were once used as hunting grounds for the feared "Pressgang", shipowners' agents who went in search of "volunteers" to man the ships that exported coal and chalk worldwide. Robert Stevenson (see Famous People) immortalised the town's "Ship Inn" in Limekilns in his "Adventure of David Balfour". The hero sought a boat in the inn to carry him safely across the Forth.

Inverkeithing

The little market town of Inverkeithing (pop. 2600; 5 miles/8km to the south-east) was founded in the 12th c. and ranks as one of the oldest "burghs" in Scotland. The Church of St Peter is the town's dominant feature, while the old monastery now serves as the town museum (open: Wed.–Sun. 11am–5pm).

★ Inchcolm Abbey

Boat trips leave North Queensferry for the well-preserved Augustinian monastery on the island of Inchcolm. Alexander I founded it in 1123 for monks from Scone but it is now in the hands of Historic Scotland. An example of Early Gothic ribbed vaulting can be seen in the octagonal chapterhouse, while 13th c. frescos in the chancel depict a funeral. The island is popular with nature lovers, not just for the bird sanctuary but also for the colony of seals.

East Fife

Aberdour
Castle

The harbour at Aberdour (pop. 1200; 4 miles/6km east of the Forth bridges), where the beaches are justifiably described as "silver sands", is overlooked by Aberdour Castle. Started in the 14th c. by the Douglas family and then extended in the 16th/17th c., the castle boasts some fine paintings on its walls and staircases (HS; open: Apr.–Sept. Mon.–Sat. 9.30am–6pm, Sun. 2–6.30pm; Oct.–Mar. Mon.–Sat. 9.30am–4.30pm, Sun. 2–4.30pm).

Kirkcaldy

Some fine 17th c. houses line Sailor's Walk near the harbour in the linoleum and mining town of Kirkcaldy (pop. 52,500). One of the town's most celebrated sons is the architect Robert Adam (1728–92). Together with his brother, they created the Classical "Adam style". Another native of Kirkcaldy was the economist Adam Smith, (see Famous People). He wrote his celebrated "Wealth of Nations" while working as a senior customs officer in 1776.

Art Gallery
and Museum

The Art Gallery and Museum on the Esplanade contains work by Scottish painters and some interesting exhibits documenting the history of linoleum production (open: Mon.–Sat. 11am–5pm, Sun. 2–5pm).

Ravenscraig
Castle

The imposing ruins of Ravenscraig Castle stand on a rocky projection by Dysart Road. Defended by two huge round towers built by James II, the castle dates from the mid-15th c. (HS; open: daily).

The A955 leaves Kirkcaldy and follows the east coast of the Fife peninsula to the pleasant resort of Wemyss. It continues east through Coaltown, Buckhaven and Leven before reaching the idyllic East Neuk Villages on Largo Bay.

Wemyss

Time seems to have forgotten these picturesque villages with their crooked fishermen's cottages and pretty gabled houses. It often seems that the artists, watersports enthusiasts and golfers have the place to themselves. In the main street at Lower Largo (pop. 800) a bronze statue reminds passers-by of Alexander Selkirk whose fate inspired Daniel Defoe to write "Robinson Crusoe"; however Defoe's literary hero was English. Selkirk, who was born in Lower Largo in 1676, set off on board the "Cinque Ports" on a voyage across the Pacific. After a series of disputes with the captain, he was deposited on the island of Juan Fernandez 400 nautical miles off the Chilean coast. It was 52 months before he sighted a ship which took him back to England.

★ East Neuk Villages

Lower Largo Statue of Selkirk

The nearby resort of Elie (pop. 900) can boast a pretty harbour with gabled houses and a pleasant beach.

Elie

Among the pretty little villages on the south-eastern corner of the peninsula are St Monance (pop. 1300) with its interesting Gothic parish church and a number of charming little cottages (now very popular with artists) and Pittenweem (pop. 900) where rows of attractive houses encircle the old harbour and the parish church possesses a huge tower (1592).

★ St Monance

Pittenween

The estate at Balaskie was acquired by Sir William Bruce in 1665 and he promptly set about converting the medieval tower into a grand country house (open June–Aug. Sat. Sun. 2–6pm).

Balaskie House

The Isle of May a few miles off the peninsula's south-west coast is a nature reserve with the second oldest bird-watching station in Great Britain. It has been run since 1934 by the Scottish universities. With such species as puffins, razorbills, guillemots and kittiwakes to observe, ornithologists are always keen to visit the island.

★ Isle of May

The oldest part of Kellie Castle (3 miles/5km north of Pittenweem) probably dates from c. 1350. The castle, as it is today, belonged to the Earls of Mar and Kellie and was built during the 16th c. and early 17th c. James and Robert Lorimer carried out a major restoration of the T-shaped castle c. 1878, but the site is now administered by the National Trust for Scotland. The 17th c. panelling in the Lounge, the landscape pictures on the panelling in the Dining Room and Jakob de Witt's ceiling paintings in the Vine Room showing the Greek gods and the rich plasterwork on the ceiling deserve special attention. The Late Victorian garden is noted for its display of roses.

★ Kellie Castle

Open Easter, May–Sept. daily, 1.30–5.30pm; Oct. Sat., Sun. 1.30–5.30pm

Up until the 1940s the pretty port at Anstruther (pop. 3300) was the centre of the Scottish herring industry and the story of its rise and fall is told in the Scottish Fisheries Museum by the harbour (open: Apr.–Oct. Mon.–Sat. 10am–5.30pm, Sun. 11am–5pm; Nov.–Mar. Mon.–Sat. 10am–4.30pm, Sun. 2–4.30pm). In the harbour a fishing boat used at the turn of the century and the North Carr lightship (1933–75) are both open to the public. "The Manse", the oldest surviving parsonage in Scotland, bears the date 1590. The parish church of St Andrew a few yards further on was consecrated in 1634.

★ Anstruther

Scottish Fisheries Museum

In a fit of anger the devil is said to have thrown a piece of the Isle of May at the church in Crail but fortunately he missed. What other explanation could there be for the huge stone in the graveyard? Crail (pop. 1300) may well be at the centre of many legends, but there is always a pleasant atmosphere in the village, especially when the fishing boats land their catches of prawns and lobsters and the fishermen prepare them on the quayside. The white-washed houses with stepped gables and red pantile roofs are favourite subjects for painters and photographers. Crail Museum and Heritage Centre housed in an 18th c. cottage documents the full story of Crail's past (open: June–mid-Sept. Mon.–Sat. 10am–12.30pm, 2.30–5.30pm).

★ Crail

Museum and Heritage Centre

The fishing harbour at Anstruther, Fife

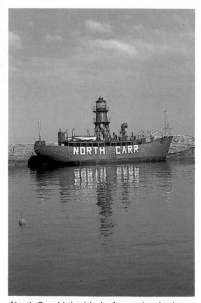

North Carr Lightship in Anstruther harbour

Memorial to Alexander Selkirk

Loch Leven (10 miles/16km north of Aberdour on the M90) is best known for the pink-fleshed trout that swim in its waters. Lochleven Castle and its 14th c. tower house (HS) stands on one of the islands in the lake. It owes its place in history to Mary Stuart (see Famous People) who after a year's incarceration escaped from the island with the help of the young Lord George Douglas and her page William. This night-time escapade is recorded in Scott's "The Abbot" (1820). The ruins of the monastery church of St Serf (HS) are situated on the other island.

Loch Leven
Lochleven Castle

St Serf's Church

On a stay in France the court architect Sir William Bruce visited Vaux-le-Vicomte, a castle near Paris built by Le Vau. Its parkland was designed by Le Nôtre and was regarded as a masterpiece of landscape design. Undoubtedly what Bruce saw in France inspired him when he came to design his own house and garden at Kinross. In the two-storey Palladian structure, which Daniel Defoe described as the "finest and most perfectly balanced piece of architecture in Scotland", perfect symmetry combines with the restrained design of Ionic columns, Corinthian pilasters, angular gables and small chimney stacks.

★ Kinross House

Garden open:
Mon.–Sat. 2–7pm

Balgonie Castle (2 miles/3.5km east of Glenrothes) dates from the 14th c. when the huge keep with its 10ft/3m thick walls and chapel were built. Little remains of the extensions that were completed c. 1702. The castle fell into disrepair from the middle of the 19th c. but in 1985 Raymond Morris the 30th laird of Balgonie started work on its restoration. Now the medieval tower is used for banquets and weddings are frequently solemnised in the chapel (open: daily, from 10am).

Balgonie Castle

Falkland Palace in the pretty town of Falkland (pop. 1200; 11 miles/18km north of Glenrothes) used to be a hunting lodge for the Stuarts and now belongs to the Queen, although it is administered by the National Trust for Scotland. It is first mentioned in documents in 1160 when the estate was the seat of the MacDuffs. In 1371 it became the property of the Albany family but in 1425 it fell to the Crown and James II laid plans to convert it into a palace, although it was between 1501 and 1541 that today's palace took shape. James V died here in 1542 a week after the birth of his daughter Mary Stuart (see Famous People) who in later life became a frequent visitor to the palace.

★★ Falkland Palace

Open:
Apr.–Oct. Mon.–Sat.
11am–5.30pm,
Sun. 1.30–5.30pm

Of the three original wings that Cromwell's army set fire to in 1654, only the east wing and the south wing (restored in 1887) with royal chambers remain. The Early Renaissance courtyard façade is reminiscent of the French Loire valley châteaux. This was certainly no coincidence as the "Auld Alliance" between Scotland and France was re-affirmed by the marriage of James V and Mary of Guise here in 1538. The façades overlooking the inner court are decorated with busts of figures from antiquity, while the external façade of the south wing retains its Late Gothic features. Two huge circular towers flank the gatehouse at the entrance. Flemish Gobelin tapestries from the 17th c. and 19th c. oak panelling are of particular note in the south wing Gallery; however, the Royal Chapel with a frieze around the walls, screen and 16th c. oak panelling is probably the highlight of the palace. The wooden ceiling, painted with the heraldic emblems of Scotland, France and England – the thistle, fleur de lys and the rose – date from the 17th c. like the Flemish tapestries, while the magnificent bed (17th c.) in the east wing's Royal Chamber is probably where James V died. The rest of the furniture was made during the 19th c. but followed the style of the original fittings. In the beautiful gardens to the rear lies Britain's first tennis court. Laid out at the behest of James V in 1539, it is still in use.

Abernethy (pop. 900; 8 miles/13km to the north-west) was once the capital of the Pictish kingdom and in the 9th c. a stronghold of the Scottish church. The only relic of a glorious past is the 78ft/24m high tapering Round Tower (HS), one of two such round towers on the mainland (the other is in Brechin; see Aberdeen, Brechin). The base of the tower dates from the 9th c., while the upper section dates from the 11th or 12th c. A Pictish stone with religious motifs sits at the foot of the tower.

Abernethy
Round Tower

Falkland Palace...   *... and Bruce Fountain*

The narrow alleys in the attractive town of Cupar (pop. 7700) demonstrate the architectural style of the 18th c. The parish church was first consecrated at the beginning of the 15th c. and was altered in the 18th c.

Cupar

The mansion at Tarvit (2½ miles/4km to the south) has been faithfully restored by the National Trust for Scotland. Sir Robert Lorimer designed the property for the wealthy railway executive and art collector Frederick Sharp. The original building, the work of Sir William Bruce (1696), did not meet the needs of the new owner who required more room for his collection of fine furniture, tapestries, Chinese porcelain, Dutch masters and paintings by Raeburn and Ramsay. The Edwardian south side of the country house overlooks Lorimer's terraced gardens. Flemish tapestries (17th c.) and Scottish and English oak furniture (17th/18th c.) adorn the wood-panelled hall. French furniture in the Lounge displays hints of Rococo, while the Georgian Dining Room has a distinctly Palladian atmosphere. Scotstarvit Tower on the estate dates from 1579.

★★ Hill of Tarvit

Open
Easter, May–Sept.
daily, 1.30–5.30pm
Oct. Sat., Sun.
1.30–5.30pm

Destroyed during the Reformation the abbey itself was founded by Cistercian monks in 1229. It is said that Queen Ermingade the second wife of William "the Lion" laid the foundation stone.

Balmerino Abbey

Leuchars (pop. 2500) lies 10 miles/16km to the east beside St Andrew's Bay. The Norman Church of St Athernase was started at the beginning of the 13th c. by Sair de Quinci and the chancel and apse have not been altered since. The main nave and tower date from the 17th c.

Leuchars

This fortress with turreted walls up to 5ft/1.5m thick was erected in the 16th c. and the barons of Earlshall have lived there ever since. The fine, painted ceiling and the panelling in the Long Gallery are of particular note (open: Apr.–Oct. daily, 1–6pm).

★Earlshall
Castle

See entry

St Andrews

◀ *Kinross House, Loch Leven, designed by Sir William Bruce*

Fort William   D 5

Region: Highland
Population: 9300

Situation

The busy resort of Fort William lies at the south end of Caledonian Canal (see entry). It makes an excellent starting point for excursions into the unspoilt North-West Highlands (see entry) and also for ascents of Ben Nevis.

The fort referred to in the town name was built by William of Orange in the middle of the 17th c. but it was demolished in 1890 to make way for the new railway line. Local people find employment in the aluminium works, a paper factory, the Ben Nevis distillery (founded in 1825 by John MacDonald – from whom "Long John" whisky gets its name – but now owned by the Japanese firm, Nikka Distillers) and, increasingly, tourism.

★West Highland Museum

Open:
July, Aug. Mon.–Fri. 9.30am–6pm, Sun. 2–5pm;
Sept.–June Mon.–Sat. 10am–1pm, 2–5pm

The West Highland Museum is situated opposite the tourist office in Cameron Square. Furniture, paintings and tools used in the production of whisky during the 19th c. are on display including "quaichs", special bowls for drinking the spirit, and also old bottles (see Baedeker Special "Scotch Whisky"), plus weapons, everyday objects and Highland costumes.

Also look out for the documents relating to the opening of the West Highland Railway in 1894 and the celebrated conquests of Ben Nevis, notably that by Henry Alexander who in 1911 drove a Ford Model T to the summit.

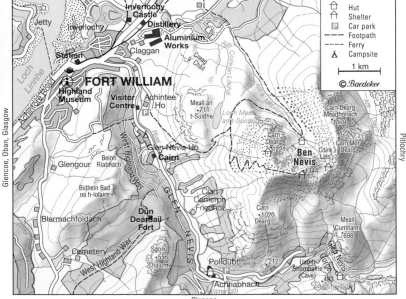

★★Ben Nevis

Fort William's main attraction is undoubtedly Ben Nevis, at 4406ft/1343m Britain's highest mountain. The origin of the name is subject to one or two interpretations, but the most likely meaning is "shrouded in fog" – and on most days of the year it is! However, on a clear day the bare, reddish shades of granite and porphyrite gleaming in the sunset make an unforgettable sight. Attempting to climb Ben Nevis is something that should not be underestimated, but a relatively easy ascent is possible by following the route from Aichintee House (2½ miles/4km; car park). This route requires about 3½ to 4 hours. Every year in September a race to the summit starts here with a time of 87 minutes as the current record. A longer route to the summit via Allta a'Mhuillin and the neighbouring peak of Carn Mor Dearg provides some breathtaking views. The summit itself is a stony desert, apart from the ruined weather station – abandoned in 1894 – and a hotel that closed in 1915. The flattish area around the summit falls gently to the south, but then very steeply down to Glen Nevis. Aonach Mor (4060ft/1237m) to the east can be reached by a cable car from Torlundy.

On a clear day the view from Ben Nevis extends for about 150 miles/ 240km and takes in the Scottish Highlands and Islands as far as the Hebrides (see entry) and the Irish coast. Many walkers choose to start their ascent in the evening and then bed down in a sleeping bag at nightfall so as to be able to savour a Ben Nevis sunrise, another unforgettable experience – as long as the fog does not intervene. Despite the relatively easy climb, the dangers posed by rapid changes in the weather should not be underestimated and walkers should take all the necessary precautions. The long north-east face presents the biggest challenge and it should only be undertaken by experienced climbers. The tourist office in Fort William and the Scottish Mountaineering Club can provide detailed route maps.

Mountain tours

★Carn Mor Dearg

Aonach Mor

★★Panorama

Ben Nevis (right): Britain's highest mountain

Glasgow

Region: Strathclyde. Population: 689,000

Glasgow sits astride the Clyde about 19 miles/30km from where the river opens into the Firth of Clyde. It is Scotland's largest city and in 1990 was fêted as European City of Culture. In comparison to its arch-rival Edinburgh (see entry) Glasgow has an image problem: it is seen as a grey, sprawling industrial city whose inhabitants are reserved and unfriendly; however, in recent years Glasgow has undergone something of a transformation. Since the disastrous decline of the commercial fleet and the dockyards, the pace of life has speeded up as the successful post-industrial restructuring has brought a new culture and new service industries, even though many districts of the city continue to suffer from urban blight.

★★City of Industry and Culture

In the mid-80s the Exhibition and Conference Centre opened its doors, derelict buildings by the banks of the Clyde were cleared to create plenty of green, open spaces and the old dockland sites on the opposite bank of the river were converted into residential quarters. Sandblasters cleaned up the sooty façades of the Victorian buildings in the heart of the city and shopping arcades, the glass-covered St Enoch shopping and entertainment centre and the elegant Prince's Square were opened. Many new opportunities were created for cultural events, so that now this working-class metropolis seems to have successfully and in its own way met the two requirements of enlightened tourism, "real life" and "culture"

With one or two exceptions Glasgow's architectural heritage does not go back much further than 200 years. The urban beauty of Glasgow lies in the commonplace, as the architects of Victorian and Edwardian times have left their mark on department stores, banks, the offices of insurance companies, hotels, pubs and stations. A comprehensive programme of building and redevelopment leading up to the turn of the century, combining imagination and practicality, helped earn Glasgow the title of "UK City of Architecture and Design 1999".

UK City of Architecture and Design 1999

An important element in Glasgow's architectural development has been the expansion of the Clyde as a port accessible to all ocean-going vessels – 200 years ago it was possible to cross the river on foot at low tide. Now eleven bridges and a road tunnel link the two sides of the city.

The full wording of Glasgow's motto is "Lord, let Glasgow flourish through the preaching of Thy word and praising Thy name", a message that was recorded on the bell at Tron Church in 1631. The coat-of-arms shows St Mungo together with symbols representing the four legends associated with Glasgow's patron saint. The fish with a ring in its mouth derives from a traditional tale about Queen Langoureth who gave her wedding ring to one of her husband's entourage. In a jealous rage King Hydderch Hael took the ring and on a hunting trip threw it into the Clyde. On his return he asked his wife to show him the ring or face the sternest consequences. In panic the queen turned to St Mungo who sent one of his monks down to the river. He caught a salmon and, believe it or not, the ring was in its mouth. The bird in the shield represents the revival of a dead robin, the oak tree a frozen hazelnut branch with which St Mungo rekindled the monastery fire and the bell on the tree is said to have been presented to the Pope in Rome.

Let Glasgow Flourish

The name Glasgow originates from the Gaelic words "Glas ghu" meaning a "lovely green place", a description that is confirmed by the city's 70 or so parks and open spaces. As for art and culture, some of Glasgow's museums and galleries are of world class, the city has a lively music scene and avant-garde film and play producers are active. Glasgow would not be Glasgow were it not for the two footballing rivals of Glasgow Rangers and

Art and culture

◀ *Glasgow Museum and Art Gallery*

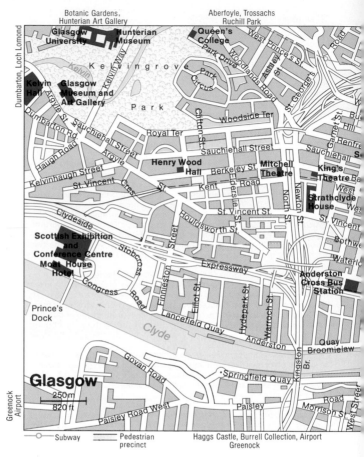

1 McLellan Galleries	3 Savoy Centre	6 St. George's
2 Glasgow Film Theatre	4 Pavilion Theatre	Tron Church
	5 Old Athenaeum Theatre	7 Stock Exchange

Glasgow Celtic. Perhaps the best-known of Glasgow's museums are the Burrell Collection in Pollock Park, the Glasgow Museum and Art Gallery which houses one of the finest municipal art collections in Britain, the respected McLellan Galleries where top-class temporary exhibitions of contemporary art take place and the Museum of Religion near St Mungo's Cathedral (1993), thought to be the only one of its kind. Glasgow's Citizens Theatre was founded in 1942 by James Bridie and enjoys an excellent reputation. Other eminent theatres include the King's, the Tron and the Tramway, not to mention the Theatre Royal, home of the Scottish Opera, and the new Concert Hall for the Royal Scottish Orchestra. The Pavilion Theatre is used for musicals, pop and rock concerts. Other important cultural events range from the colourful Mayfest, the Celtic Festival, the Gourock International Games and Streetbiz to the international jazz and

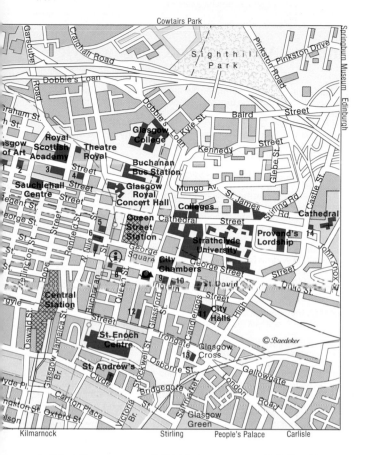

8 Stirling's Library
9 Italian Centre
10 Hutchesons' Hall

11 Ticket Centre
12 Virginia Galleries
13 Tron Theatre

14 St. Mungo Museum
    and Cathedral
    Visitor Centre

folk festivals (for further information contact the Ticket Centre, Candlerigg; tel. (0141) 227 5511).

Glasgow airport is situated 8 miles/13km to the west of the city with access via the M8 motorway. It is served by buses from the railway and bus stations. Central Station serves the south and west and Queen Street Station the north and east, including Edinburgh (see entry). InterCity trains leave every hour for London (5hrs) and the "Roundabout Glasgow Ticket" gives unlimited travel for a day on the rail and underground network within the Greater Glasgow Region.   Communications

The circular underground line within the city stops at fifteen stations, with Buchanan Street and St Enoch Centre the main interchanges.

Mackintosh – Art Nouveau Glasgow-style

The most significant British contribution to the European Art Nouveau movement was made at around the turn of the century in Glasgow and it had a unique Scottish flavour. Although the most successful Glasgow architect in the so-called Free Style was Sir John James Burnet and other Art Nouveau designers such as James Salmon II left their mark on the city by the Clyde, one man became synonymous with this artistic movement, the architect and designer Charles Rennie Mackintosh.

Mackintosh, the son of a police officer, was born in 1868 the second of eleven children. The talented young man undertook his artistic training at Glasgow Academy of Art. Apart from learning his profession in the offices of architect John Hutchison, he went to night classes. Together with the woman who was later to become his wife Margaret MacDonald, her sister Frances and a student friend called Herbert MacNair, he formed the "Four" who developed their own interpretation of Art Nouveau and then received international acclaim when their work was displayed. Inspired by the Pre-Raphaelites, Aubrey Beardsley's line drawings, the two-dimensional work of William Morris, Celtic motifs and Japanese prints, the "Four" created bold, original graphics, furniture and metalwork that displayed a clever contrast between functional simplicity and poetic detail. Having taken a new approach to proportion which permitted experimentation in the use of form based on geometric patterns, they developed clear, angular figures linked by long but soft lines using predominantly white, matt olive, pale violet and pink.

The 28-year-old Mackintosh became famous almost overnight when his design for the Glasgow School of Art in Renfrew Street was made public. Walter Gropius of Bauhaus fame praised the synthesis of the rational and the functional with the original and the fanciful as "the beginning of a break-through". The building which was not completed until 1909 and therefore took up most of Mackintosh's creative career was seen even at the time as a milestone in the development of architectural style.

In the meantime the brilliant avant-garde artist was revered more in international circles than in his own home town. His reputation was enhanced greatly in 1900 by an exhibition at the Secession in Vienna. During 1902 the "Scottish Pavilion" in Turin also aroused considerable interest and this was followed by successes in Moscow and Munich. Mackintosh's main client in Glasgow was Miss Catherine Cranston who entrusted him with the interior design of a chain of tea-rooms in Buchanan Street, Argyll Street, Ingram Street and Sauchiehall Street – only the Willow Tea Room has survived. Mackintosh designed everything for her from the furniture to the cutlery and menus. Simplicity and charm characterised these exotic establishments that catered for that section of Glasgow's business community looking at ways of escaping from the puritanism of the Victorian era into something more stylish. At the same time Mackintosh was working on residences and country houses, including publisher Walter W. Blackie's Hill House, which is now owned by the Royal Institute of British Architects. In Germany the gifted designer won plaudits for his "Haus eines Kunstfreundes" (Art Lover's House) which won second prize in a Darmstadt competition in 1901. Despite some strong opposition at home Mackintosh produced the Herald

Building (1895) in Mitchell Street, Queen's Cross Church (1897), now headquarters of the Charles Rennie Mackintosh Society (870 Garscube Road; tel. (0141) 946 6600), the Daily Record Building (1901) in Renfield Lane and the Scotland Street School Museum of Education (1904–06) south of the river in Kingston.

At the beginning of 1913 Mackintosh left the firm (Honeyman and Keppie) in which he had been a partner since 1904. Hostility and narrow-minded conservatism made life unbearable for him in Glasgow so he and his wife moved to London, but they found little work there either. During his years "in exile" all he did was to complete a conversion in Northampton. In 1920 Mackintosh moved to Port Vendres in France where he produced a series of memorable watercolours, but he died in 1928 in poverty and practically ignored.

Now "Toshie" is revered in Glasgow. Prints of his designs are to be found everywhere and the restored Willow Tea Room in Sauchiehall Street has become a popular meeting place for young trendsetters. Scotland Street School Museum of Education and Hill House in nearby Helensburgh are places of pilgrimage for students of architecture but it will be 1996 before Bellahouston Park is completed. This is a replica of the Art Lover's House (1901) which consolidated Mackintosh's reputation abroad.

The special fascination of these buildings rests on Mackintosh's obvious passion for harmony in colour, the well-balanced contrasts between high and low, light and shade, and on his extraordinary sensitivity in combining gently arching curves with horizontal and vertical lines in both an original and decorative way.

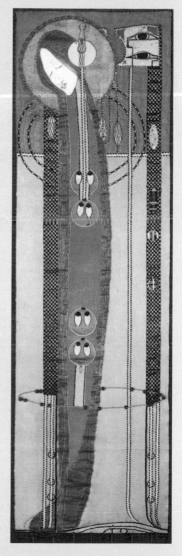

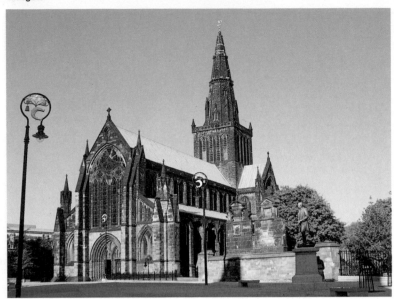

St Mungo's Cathedral

Cruises on the Clyde	In summer the paddle steamer "Waverley" makes round tours of the Clyde from Anderston Quay near Kingston Bridge (tel. (0141) 221 8152). Caledonian MacBrayne (tel. (01475) 650100) and Clyde Marine (tel. (01475) 21281) also run trips downstream into the Firth of Clyde.
History	In 543 St Kentigern, who was baptised by his teacher St Mungo, built a chapel over his grave on the edge of Glasgow. Work on a cathedral at the same site started in 1136 and a medieval settlement grew up around it. After the Reformation the city centre shifted to Glasgow Cross and in 1451 Bishop William Turnbull founded the country's second university nearby.

Trade with North America blossomed after the 1707 union with England. The clippers belonging to the Glasgow tobacco barons were the fastest ships on the route to Virginia and, until the American War of Independence in 1776, Glasgow was Britain's premier tobacco port. In the same year the economist Adam Smith (see Famous People) who had taught at Glasgow University between 1751 and 1763 published his seminal work entitled "An enquiry into the nature and causes of the wealth of nations" which defined the nature of classical economics. The mid-18th c. saw the rise of the textile industry and in 1769 the engineer James Watt (see Famous People) invented the steam engine which revolutionised production methods. At nearby Paisley in 1792 the first mechanical looms were installed. Watt became the leading engineer responsible for improving the navigability of the Clyde and a 19 mile/30km stretch of the waterway was deepened so that ships could sail up the river as far as Glasgow where docks and industrial sites sprang up. In 1812 Henry Bell's "Comet" the first seaworthy steamship sailed from here and by the mid-19th c. 80% of all British steamers were made in Glasgow shipyards. World-famous Glasgow-based shipping lines such as Clan, Cunard and Donaldson sailed the high seas. Until well into the 20th c. luxury Atlantic liners, including the "Queen Elizabeth II", were built on Clydeside. The construction of ships and steam locomotives brought immense prosperity, with Glasgow enjoying its heyday towards the end of the 19th c. Churches and public buildings were funded by wealthy merchants, shipowners and textile magnates although few now remain. The other side of Glasgow's success story was the massive population increase within a small period of time and with that came impoverishment. The many opportunities for employment had attracted immigrants from far afield. Glasgow became a melting pot of different nationalities but was unable to offer the workers decent housing. Although many of the newcomers came from abroad, famine in Ireland and the clearances in the Highlands brought thousands of Irish and Scots to the city. A safety valve for the religious and social rivalry between the two communities was often the football pitch where Rangers (1888; Scottish Protestant) faced Celtic (1873; Irish Catholic). The notorious slum quarters in the east end and the Gorbals south of the Clyde were demolished at the end of the 19th c. only to be replaced by Victorian tenement blocks which soon became overcrowded. When these were torn down after the Second World War, large sections of the population moved out into the satellite towns.

With the decline of heavy industry in the Clyde region, the population fell. The burgeoning oil industry centred on Aberdeen attracted many Glaswegians and the inner-city areas started to decay once more. Even in the 1970s the image of Glasgow was tainted by football hooliganism, unemployment, alcoholism, violence, poverty, dirty factories, run down housing estates and vast areas of derelict land. In the early 1980s a huge renovation programme was started on Clydeside. The massive GEAR (Glasgow Eastern Area Renewal) project covering some 4000 acres/1600 hectares was one of the most ambitious attempts ever undertaken to solve the problems of a decaying inner city. More recently status-building campaigns, such as Glasgow's role as European City of Culture, have helped to improve the city's self-image and have encouraged investment.

Sights

At the heart of the Victorian city centre stands the flower-bedecked George Square where twelve statues of famous men and women survey the bustling scene. They include Robert Burns, Sir Walter Scott (on the Doric column at the centre) and James Watt (see Famous People), Queen Victoria and Prince Albert, Thomas Campbell, William Gladstone, Sir John Moore and Sir Robert Peel (1788–1850), prime minister and rector of the university.

★**George Square**

The east end of the square is dominated by the town hall and its 230ft/70m high tower. It was designed by William Young following the Italian Renaissance style and was completed in 1888. The most impressive features are the loggia, the staircase finished with Breccia and Carrara marble and a banqueting room with some marvellous barrel vaulting (guided tours: Mon.–Fri. 10.30am and 2.30pm).

★City Chambers

The Merchants' House (1877) on George Square is the headquarters for the oldest Chamber of Commerce in Great Britain (founded 1605). Note the model of a tobacco ship. Other buildings around the square include the General Post Office and the Bank of Scotland, both of which display typical late 19th c. façades.

Merchants' House

A group of mid-19th c. warehouses to the south of City Chambers were given a face-lift in 1990 by the architects Page and Park. The Italian Centre with its open inner courtyard, café, restaurant and ten designer boutiques can offer Glaswegians continental-style shopping.

Italian Centre

Facing the Italian Centre, the elegant Hutcheson's Hall owned by the National Trust for Scotland was designed in 1802 by David Hamilton but its frontage includes statues from an earlier building of 1641 (open: Mon.–Fri. 10am–5pm).

Hutcheson's Hall (NTS)

Flowering borders in Bellahouston Park

Glasgow City Chambers in George Square

High Street, Saltmarket, Gallowgate and Trongate all meet at Glasgow Cross, a busy road junction. The only evidence remaining of the square's original function as the heart of the old inner city is the 111ft/34m high Tolbooth Steeple (17th c.). The Mercat Cross was erected in 1929. Robert Adam's only contribution to Glasgow's heritage stands on one side of the square. This merchants' guildhall is fronted by double Ionic columns and a fine gable. A monument to Robert Adam by sculptor Sandy Stoddart is due to be completed soon and this will add to the splendour of the square.

Trades' House

The huge Barras street market begins a few hundred yards further east. At the weekends as many as 1000 traders congregate here to sell food, antiques, bric-à-brac, household goods and clothing. With luck it is possible to pick up a designer outfit at a very reasonable price (open: Sat., Sun. 9am–5pm).

★ Barras Market

To the west of George Square at the corner of Queen St and Ingram St can be seen a Corinthian-columned building (1832) by David Hamilton. Formerly the Stirling Library, in 1996 it became the city's new Gallery of Modern Art.

Stirling Library (Gallery of Modern Art)

Just a short distance to the north, Glasgow's Stock Exchange is housed in a Venetian Gothic edifice designed by William Burdett and built between 1875 and 1877 on the corner of Nelson Mandela Place and Buchanan Street.

Stock Exchange

The elegant, glass-roofed Prince's Square shopping arcade runs to the south of Buchanan Street's pedestrianised zone. Continue through Argyle Arcade, the address of Sloan's, one of Glasgow's oldest restaurants (19th c.), towards Howard Street and passing the stylish shop windows beneath the futuristic glass roof of the vast St Enoch Shopping Centre.

Buchanan Street
Prince's Square
★ Argyle Arcade
St Enoch's
Shopping Centre

Slater Menswear, a men's outfitter at 165 Howard Street, has been certified by the Guinness Book of Records as the biggest menswear shop in the world. It stocks over 18,000 suits ranging from Cacherel to St Laurent.

Slater Menswear

The north end of Buchanan Street joins the bustling shopping mecca of Sauchiehall Street, now almost entirely given over to pedestrians. It offers the largest range of shops in the city.

Sauchiehall Street

Sir Leslie Martin provided the design for Glasgow's new concert hall (completed in 1990). An audience of almost 2500 can listen to the Royal Scottish National Orchestra in its new home (tel. (0141) 332 6633). On the south side, shops line the circular concourse.

Royal Concert Hall

Hope Street branches northward off Sauchiehall Street to the Theatre Royal, Scotland's only opera house. It is also a venue for ballet (tel. (0141) 332 9000).

Theatre Royal

When in 1902 Catherine Cranston opened her café on the first floor of 217 Sauchiehall Street Charles Rennie Mackintosh and his wife designed everything for her, right down to the menu. Extensive restoration work was carried out in the early 80s and the café was re-opened in 1983. A wide choice of teas is available served in a stylish ambience.

★ Willow Tea Room

The McLellan Galleries (no. 270), a little to the west, were re-opened in 1990. They specialise in exhibitions of modern Scottish art (open: Mon.–Sat. 10am–5pm, Sun. 11am–5pm).

★ McLellan Galleries

Two studio theatres, an art gallery and a café form part of the Third Eye cultural centre. It has become a forum for young actors and an exhibition centre for contemporary art (tel. (0141) 332 7521).

Third Eye Centre

The building at no. 518 houses the Regimental Museum of the Royal Highland Fusiliers. Displays cover uniforms, arms and paintings illustrating the regiment's history (open: Mon.–Fri. 8.30am–4pm).

Regimental Museum

Mackintosh's art academy (1876) at 167 Renfrew Street, running parallel to Sauchiehall Street further north, is essential viewing for lovers of fine architecture. Completed in 1909, this Art Nouveau building confirmed the

★★ **Glasgow School of Art**

Burns Monument

Façade: Glasgow School of Art

Guided tours
Oct.–May, Mon.–Fri.
11am, 2pm, Sat.
10.30am;
June–Sept.
Mon.–Sat.
11am, 12 noon,
2pm, 5pm,
Sun. 2pm, 3pm

★Tenement
House

28-year-old designer's reputation not just as a master of the exterior – while the grand west façade is dominated by three 65ft/20m high oriel windows, the smaller windows on the east front are reminiscent of Scottish castles – but also as a superb interior designer. Of special interest are the principal's room, one of the first of Mackintosh's "White Rooms", the so-called Mackintosh Room for meetings of the Academy of Art and the unique Library with gallery (for information, tel. (0141) 353 4526).

To the north-west at 145 Buccleuch Street, the Victorian Tenement House offers an insight into how the middle-classes lived in the early part of the 20th c. (NTS; open: Mar.–Oct. daily, 2–5pm).

King's Theatre

In 1904 Frank Matcham equipped the King's Theatre in Bath Street with a splendid auditorium. It is used mainly for plays, light entertainment and musicals (tel. (0141) 227 5571).

Mitchell Library

The Mitchell Library is housed in a striking building in North Street (1874). It is Europe's largest reference library with over 1.3 million books including the world's most comprehensive collection of works by Robert Burns (open: Mon.–Fri. 9am–9pm, Sat. 9am–5pm).

★ Cathedral of
St Mungo

The most significant historic building in Glasgow is the cathedral and its length of 295ft/90m makes it the largest church in Scotland after St Andrews. In line with the presbyterian constitution of the Church of Scotland, there is no bishop but the building, situated to the east of George Square, is still referred to as "Glasgow Cathedral".

David I commissioned the first chapel on this site in 1136, but it was destroyed by fire a few years later. At the end of the 12th c. Bishop Jocelin ordained that the chapel be rebuilt. The Lower church, chancel and tower had been rebuilt by the mid-13th c. and the chapterhouse and sacristy were completed in 1447. In 1480 the nave was finally consecrated. The window

Glasgow Cathedral

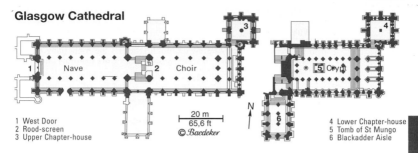

1 West Door
2 Rood-screen
3 Upper Chapter-house

20 m
65,6 ft
© Baedeker

4 Lower Chapter-house
5 Tomb of St Mungo
6 Blackadder Aisle

on the west front showing Adam and Eve in Paradise also dates from about this period. Seen from both inside and out, the cathedral looks as if it has come out of a mould. The lines are clear and there is no superfluous ornamentation. In the well-proportioned nave, it is worth having a look at the screen – a rare feature in Scotland. The figures around the altars represent the seven deadly sins. Projecting from the south transept is the Blacader Aisle named after the first bishop of Glasgow. Note the richly decorated ribbed pillars and fine bosses. The grandest room in the cathedral, the crypt or lower church, houses the tomb of St Mungo, who founded the bishopric in the 6th c. and was buried here in 603. Pre-Reformation Gothic fan vaulting, ribbed pillars and capitals embellished with flowers are the most distinctive features (open: Apr.–Sept. Mon. Sat. 9.30am–6.30pm, Sun. 2–6.30pm; Oct.–Mar. Mon.–Sat. 9.30am–4.30pm, Sun. 2–4.30pm).

★★Crypt

During the late 1980s Page and Park redesigned the memorial to David Livingstone (see Famous People) which adorns the concourse.

Livingstone Memorial

Glasgow's largest cemetery on Fir Park Hill was laid out in the 18th c. In most cases, the grand tombstones recall the lives of wealthy merchants who made their fortune during Glasgow's heyday in the last century. A monument erected on a Doric column (1825) commemorates the reformer John Knox (see Famous People).

Necropolis

Opened in 1992, this unique museum (2 Castle Street) examines the world religions, their rites and how their doctrines deal with the issues of life and death. Exhibits range from Egyptian mummies, Hindu statues of Shiva and African fetishes to Salvador Dali's "Christ of Saint John of the Cross" (1951). A Zen Buddhist garden flourishes in the courtyard (open: Mon. and Wed.–Sat. 10am–5pm, Sun. 11am–5pm).

★St Mungo Museum of Religious Life and Art

Facing the museum stands Provand's Lordship, Glasgow's oldest house, a three-storey building with a stepped gable. It was built c. 1471 for the head of St Nicholas Hospital. James II and James IV are said to have stayed there and Mary Stuart (see Famous People) spent the winter of 1566 in the house while she visited her sick husband Lord Darnley who was murdered soon after. The Curate's Room (16th c.) and a fine collection of furniture (17th/18th c.) are the most interesting exhibits in the museum (open: Mon. and Wed.–Sat. 10am–5pm, Sun. 11am–5pm).

Provand's Lordship

Springburn Museum a little further north in Ayr Street documents the changing social and industrial history of Glasgow with an emphasis on the days of locomotive building (open: Mon.–Fri. 10.30am–5pm, Sat. 10am–4.30pm, Sun. 2–5pm).

Springburn Museum

Glasgow's oldest park (1662) runs alongside the banks of the Clyde. A museum in the People's Palace illustrates the development of trade and industry, the trade unions, the women's movement, entertainment and sport. Tropical and sub-tropical plants flourish in the large winter garden (open: Mon. and Wed.–Sat. 10am–5pm, Sun. 11am–5pm).

**Glasgow Green
★People's Palace**

Glasgow

Nelson's Monument

The 144ft/44m high Nelson's Monument, a few yards further on, was erected in 1806 to the memory of Lord Nelson, victor of the Battle of Trafalgar (1805).

St Andrew

In the Classical-style St Andrew's Church (18th c.) the mahogany choir stalls, which were provided by wealthy benefactors, are the most interesting features.

Citizens Theatre

Gorbals Street on the south side of the Clyde leads to the Citizens Theatre, and Glasgow's most innovative repertory stage (tel. (0141) 429 0022).

★Scotland Street School Museum of Education

A short distance to the west in Scotland Street stands a school building with 21 classrooms and a kitchen. It was used as a school until 1979 but was later converted into a museum. The furniture, educational equipment and textbooks used in local schools document the history of education in Glasgow from Victorian times to the present day (open: Mon.–Sat. 10am–5pm, Sun. 2–5pm).

Scottish Exhibition and Conference Centre

In 1985 to the south-east of the city centre but north of the Clyde, the Scottish Exhibition and Conference Centre was opened in the old dockland district. The centre has a total of five halls and there is seating for 10,000 visitors. The Moat House Hotel with award-winning restaurant is situated alongside.

Moat House Hotel

Kelvingrove Park

Kelvingrove Park to the west of the city centre lies in the Kelvin valley with the university, municipal museum and Kelvin Hall close by.

★★Glasgow Art Gallery and Museum

Time should be set aside to visit the Glasgow Art Gallery and Museum. Opened in 1901 it probably has the finest municipal collection of British and continental paintings in the United Kingdom. Among the artists whose works can be seen are van Gogh ("Portrait of Alexander Reid", 1886 – Reid

Domestic science room: Scotland Street School Museum

FIRST FLOOR

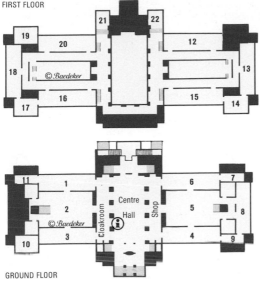

Glasgow Art Gallery and Museum

FIRST FLOOR

12 Scottish Gallery
13 Glasgow c. 1900
14 Temporary exhibitions
15 Modern art
16 Classical tradition
17 Church treasures
18 Realism
19 The Victorian Age
20 Modern artists
21 Pottery
22 Silver

GROUND FLOOR

1 Archaeology
2 Weapons and armour
3 Temporary exhibitions
4 Geology
5 Natural History of Scotland
6 Ethnology
7 Conference Room
8 Café
9 Mammals
10 Temporary exhibitions
11 History

GROUND FLOOR

was a well-known Glasgow art collector), Bellini ("Madonna with Child", c. 1475), Botticelli ("The Annunciation", c. 1490), Guardi ("San Giorgio Maggiore by the Canale Grande in Venice", c. 1755), Rembrandt ("The Carcase of an Ox", c. 1630, "A Man in Armour", 1655), Picasso ("Flower Seller", 1901), Camille Corot ("Mademoiselle de Foudras", 1872), Matisse ("Study of a Young Woman", c. 1919), Juan Gris ("The Glass", 1918) and Georges Braque ("Still Life with Fruit", 1926). French Impressionists are also well represented with Degas ("Dancers", c. 1898), Signac (Sunset in Herblay, 1884), Seurat ("Riverbank", c. 1883), Cézanne ("Fruit Basket", c. 1877), Monet ("Vetheuil", c. 1880), Sisley ("Boatyard in Saint-Mammes", c. 1886) and Pissarro ("The Tuilerie Gardens", 1900). William Aikman and Henry Raeburn ("Mr and Mrs Campbell of Kailzie") represent British portrait artists but others include William Turner ("Stirling", 1831), the Anglo-American Whistler ("Portrait of Thomas Carlyle", 1872), Graham Sutherland, Ben Nicholson and Ben Johnson ("The Gatekeeper", 1977).

Among the Scottish artists with work on display here are the portraitist Allan Ramsay, Alexander Nasmyth ("Rocky Landscape", 1817), Horatio McCulloch ("Glencoe", 1864), Robert Herdman ("Execution of Mary Queen of Scots", 1867), the Glasgow Pre-Raphaelite Burne-Jones, Thomas Faed ("The Last of the Clans", 1865), the Aberdonian William Dyce, James Guthrie ("Old Willie", 1886), George Henry ("Landscape in Galloway", 1889), Edward A. Hornel ("The Fish Pond", 1894), John Q. Pringle ("Two Figures by the Fence", 1904), Leslie Hunter ("Old Mill in Fifeshire"), William McTaggart ("Paps of Jura", 1902), Peploe and Cadell ("Interior", 1928 – probably the lounge in Cadell's Georgian town house in Edinburgh), Stanley Spencer ("Port Glasgow", 1952), William Gillies from Edinburgh ("Still Life in Blue and Brown", 1952), Mackintosh (La Lagonne, 1924), William Gear ("Summer Garden", 1951) and Glasgow's Bruce McLean ("Acrylic and Chalk Collage", 1984).

Elsewhere in the museum are sculptures, Egyptian mummies and Scottish archaeological finds, including Bronze Age tools and jewellery from Arran, Kintyre and Glenluce. The ethnography department displays Ashanti figures from Ghana, bronze heads from Benin, masks from Zaire,

Open
Mon.–Sat.
10am–5pm,
Sun. 2–5pm

"The Execution of Mary Queen of Scots" by Robert Herdman

Maori figures from New Zealand and a model of a Samurai warrior from Japan. Other exhibits of interest include weapons and armour, such as helmets, crossbows and swords from the 15th/16th c., Flemish tapestries, Glasgow-made jewellery, silverware, glassware and pottery from various periods. The natural history section also merits a visit. It documents the history of shipbuilding and maritime travel on the Clyde.

★Hunterian Museum and Art Gallery

Open: Mon.–Sat. 9.30am–5pm

Opened in 1807, the Hunterian is the oldest museum in Glasgow. It is named after William Hunter, a Glaswegian doctor who lived in the 18th c. and bequeathed not only his own collection of anatomical parts, objets d'art and items from many disciplines of science but also large sums of money. The museum has now expanded and possesses departments of ethnography, zoology, geology and archaeology, including many finds from Roman sites. Hunter also owned a fine collection of coins and these are exhibited in a purpose-built gallery (1980). Prints and paintings belonging to the university were also transferred here and works by Rubens, Rembrandt, Chardin, Reynolds, Pissarro, Sisley and Koninck are on display. The Whistler Collection, one of the Art Gallery's highlights, merits special attention. Integrated into the gallery is Mackintosh's terraced house in Southpark Avenue where he lived with his wife from 1906 to 1914. On show are the couple's original furniture and the biggest collection of the celebrated Glaswegian's paintings. His versatility in interior design is reflected in the emphasis on colour and pattern. The "White Room", for example, is finished in light, discreet tones, while the small bedroom is decorated with blue and white patterns.

★University

The main University of Glasgow building was designed by Sir Gilbert Scott stands at the northern edge of Kelvingrove Park. This seat of learning dates from 1451 and is the second-oldest school of higher education in Scotland. Classes were first held in the cathedral and then in the Old College on High Street, before the present Neo-Gothic buildings were opened in 1871. The university can boast some illustrious teachers including James Watt, Adam Smith (see Famous People) and the "father of antiseptic surgery", Joseph Lister. A permanent exhibition at the Visitor Centre in University Avenue goes into more detail about the important discoveries made by these three scholars and other famous scientists associated with the university (open: Mon.–Sat. 9.30am–5pm, Sun. May–Sept. only 2–5pm). Strathclyde University, founded in 1795, is situated to the north-east of George Square.

The recently extended Transport Museum is located in Kelvin Hall. Exhibits include ship models, locomotives, trams, vintage cars, horse-drawn carriages and a reconstruction of a 1938 Glasgow street (open: Mon. and Wed.–Sat. 10am–5pm, Sun. 11am–5pm). Facilities for athletics, tennis, football and other activities are available in the nearby sports centre.

Kelvin Hall
★ Museum of Transport

Kibble Palace in the Botanic Gardens on Great Western Road is one of the finest glasshouses in the country and its collection of orchids almost certainly the highlight. Afterwards it is relaxing to take a walk through the extensive parkland. The eccentric engineer John Kibble built his steel construction by Loch Long in 1863. Ten years later he decided to take it with him to Glasgow and he had a special raft made so that it could be shipped safely up the Clyde (open: Garden, daily, 7am until dusk; Kibble Palace, daily, 10am–4.45pm; Glasshouses, daily, 1–4.45pm).

Botanic Gardens

Close on 4 miles/6km south-west of the city centre stands Pollock House in grounds covering an area of 355 acres/144 hectares. This mansion, the home of the Maxwell family, was designed c. 1752 by William Adam and his sons. Inside, the collection of Spanish paintings by El Greco, Goya, Murillo, Velazques and others is particularly interesting. Also on view are several significant works by William Blake and numerous antiques, including a splendid snooker table (open: Mon. and Wed.–Sat. 10am–5pm, Sun. 2–5pm).

Pollock Country Park
★ Pollock House

Portrait of Alexander Reid by Van Gogh

Japanese block print: Burrell Collection

1 Entrance
2 Cloakroom
3 Information stall
4 Dining room from Hutton Castle
5 The Warwick Vase
6 Doorway from Hornby Castle
7 Ancient Civilisations (sculpture, vases and bronze-work from Egypt, Greece, Italy, Iran, Iraq and Turkey)
8 Drawing room from Hutton Castle
9 Chinese ceramics, Islamic prayer-rugs, Coptic textiles
10 Japanese prints
11 Hall from Hutton Castle
12 Chinese jade and bronze-work
13 Tapestry gallery
14 Medieval European stained glass
15 Medieval European embroideries
16 Medieval European carvings and bronze-work
17 Medieval European altar furniture, tombs, etc.
18 European Medieval and Early Renaissance ceramics, sculptures, suits of armour, silver and glass
19 Altar panels and paintings (15th/16th c., Cranach the Elder, Memling, Bellini)
20 Elizabethan Room
21 17th/18th c. paintings (Rembrandt, Hals, Hogarth, Raeburn)

22 French paintings (Géricault, Delacroix, Courbet)
23 Impressionists (Manet, Degas, Cézanne, Renoir, Sisley)
24 Water-colours, drawings (Ingres, Corot, Manet, Millet, Crawhall)
25 Hague School (Mauve, Maris)
26 Gothic Room
27 Bronze sculptures (Rodin, Meunier, Epstein)
28 European painted glass (13th–16th c.)

29 Islamic metalwork and ceramics (9th–17th c.); carpets (Caucasian, Indian and Persian, 16th–19th c.)
30 Temporary exhibitions
31 Ancient Civilisations (ceramics, votive statues)
32 Chinese porcelain
33 Medieval European (English) drinking vessels, brassware, sculptures
34 Embroidery, embroidered panels, lace

Burrell Collection

★★ Burrell Collection

Open:
Mon. and
Wed.–Sat.
10am–5pm,
Sun. 11am–5pm

Shipping magnate Sir William Burrell (1861–1958) bequeathed his marvellous art collection to the city of Glasgow in 1944. Barr Gasson, John Meunier and Brit Anderson were responsible for the design of the modern gallery which was opened by the Queen in 1983. Objets d'art from the Neolithic era right up to the 20th c. are among the more than 8000 artefacts on display.

Prized exhibits, however, include bronzes and pottery from Greek and Roman times such as the Warwick Vase (2nd c.), paintings by Lucas Cranach the Elder, Hans Memling, Cézanne, Delacroix, Manet, Degas and Joseph Crawhall, an artist who received encouragement from Burrell, medieval church furnishings (choir stalls, sacramental objects, stained-glass windows), Chinese jade, Japanese wood prints, Indian and Persian carpets, Flemish tapestries, statues by Rodin, richly ornamented oak panelling (1500) from Hutton Castle, a portal from Hornby Castle (16th c.), illuminated manuscripts, English embroidery (16th/17th c.), arms, silver and glass.

Haggs Castle
Children's
Museum

A museum devoted to children is housed east of Pollock Park in John Maxwell's Haggs House (1585–87; 100 St Andrews Drive). Exhibits include a pretty Victorian children's room, a 16th c. kitchen range and a little house from the 18th c. (open: Mon.–Sat. 10am–5pm, Sun. 11am–5pm).

★ Bellahouston Park

Dumbreck Road cuts through to the extensive Bellahouston Park which is noted for its colourful flower beds. The World Pipe Band Championship is held here every August and the world's best bagpipe player is selected from scores of entrants. Mackintosh's plans for his Art Lover's House were drawn up in 1901, but work did not start until 1989 and the ambitious project is not expected to finish until 1996 (for information tel. 427 6884).

Glasgow Zoo lies in some 60 acres/25ha of Calder Park (6 miles/9.6km south-east of the city centre; entrance in Hamilton Road). Lions, leopards, reptiles, elephants, polar bears, monkeys and camels are the main attractions but young children will find plenty to entertain them (open: 9.30am–6pm, in winter 4pm).

Glasgow is well known for its wealth of open spaces, but there are three which are worth a special mention: part of Rouken Glen Park (Giffnock) is given over to Eastwood Butterfly Kingdom (open: Late Mar.–Sept. daily, 10am–5pm), Victoria Park (Victoria Park Drive) contains the remains of trees that grew here over 330 million years ago (discovered in 1887), while in Greenbank Garden (Old Mearns Road, Clarkston; NTS), there are some fine woodland paths, a walled garden and an advice centre for gardeners (open: daily, 10am–5pm).

Surroundings

In the industrial area of Port Glasgow (pop. 19,000; 25 miles/40km west of the city centre) stands a well-maintained 16th c. mansion with gatehouse and tower house, once the seat of the Maxwell family. The oldest sections of the building date from the 15th c. A small museum traces the development of Glasgow's harbour (open: Apr.–Sept. Mon.–Sat. 9.30am–6.30pm, Sun. 2–6.30pm).

Greenock (pop. 50,000) was the birthplace of the engineer James Watt, the man who made the Clyde navigable. The town was famous for its shipyards but most of them have now closed and the name Greenock has become synonymous with computers. The body of "Highland Mary", immortalised by Robert Burns (see Famous People), is buried in the town's central cemetery.

By the coast at Gourock (pop. 11,700; 34 miles/55km west of Glasgow) stands a 6ft/2m high slate monolith that was probably a meeting place for druids. Later, fishermen came here and made small offerings in return for fine weather and good catches. It is still the custom for newly-weds to circle the stone after the wedding ceremony in the hope that Granny Kempock will bring good luck to their marriage.

Dumbarton Castle perches on a basalt rock on the north bank of the Clyde, facing Port Glasgow. This strategically important stronghold was started in the 6th c. and remained in the hands of Britons until the 11th c. In the 13th c. it was taken over by the royal family. Only the dungeon and 12th c. gateway remain from the medieval edifice. Mary Stuart (see Famous People) embarked for France here at the age of five (open: Apr.–Sept. Mon.–Sat. 9.30am–6pm, Sun. 2–6pm; Oct.–Mar. Mon.–Thur. 9.30am–4pm, Sun. 2–4pm).

Lovers of Art Nouveau will not be disappointed by a visit to Hill House in Helensburgh's Upper Colquhoun Street. After Charles Rennie Mackintosh had designed Windyhill in Kilmacolm on the other side of the Clyde for his friend William Davidson (1901) and in the same year had produced the plans for his Art Lover's House, he began work on a third private residence, this time for publisher Walter Blackie. Hill House, set on a hill with views over the Firth of Clyde, is surrounded by a delightful garden. Viewed as a whole there are similarities with a Scottish castle, while the figural elements, rounded edges, oriel windows and small chimney stacks bear all the hallmarks of the gifted designer. Internally, Mackintosh left his imprint too. Nearly all the furniture was designed by him. In the wide hall, the dark wooden panels contrast with the light wallpaper, supplemented with abstract patterns and delicate pastel shades. The L-shaped lounge fur-

FIRST FLOOR © Baedeker ATTIC

GROUND FLOOR

Hill House
in Helensburgh

1 Entrance
2 Cloakroom
3 Library
4 Fireplace
5–7 Storehouse
8 Coalhouse
9 Dressing room
10–19 Bedrooms

© Baedeker

nished simply but stylishly seems bright and airy despite the black ceiling. Art Nouveau patterns in pink and light green soften the effect of the walls, windows and lamps. The bedroom on the first floor above the lounge is regarded as the most successful of Mackintosh's "White Rooms". The carefully placed pink and green flower ornamentations show a masterful touch as do the two black chairs with their severe geometric design. The building is now run by the National Trust for Scotland (open: Apr.–Dec. daily, 1–5pm).

Glengoyne Distillery

The traditional methods of whisky production are revealed at the Glengoyne Distillery in Dumgoyne near Killearn (18 miles/28.8km north of Glasgow; open: Mon.–Sat. 10am–4pm, Sun. noon–4pm Apr.–Nov. only; nosings Wed. 7.30pm Apr.–Nov. only).

Strathkelvin District
Forth and Clyde Canal

The Forth and Clyde Canal (1790) winds its way through the Strathkelvin District to the north of Glasgow. The pleasure boat "Ferry Queen" plies up and down the canal during the summer.

Kirkintilloch

The Barony Chambers of Kirkintilloch is a museum which documents the social and economic development of the region (open: Tues., Thur., Fri. 2–5pm, Sat. 10am–1pm, 2–5pm).

Monkland District
Drumpellier Country Park

Drumpellier Country Park lies to the west of Coatbridge in Monkland District. Broad expanses of heathers, a butterfly farm and a golf course are among the attractions (open: park at all times; visitor centre summer, 10.30am–7.45pm, winter, noon–4pm; butterfly house Apr.–Oct.).

★Coatbridge
Summerlee Heritage Park

Summerlee Heritage Park in West Canal Street, Coatbridge (pop. 49,000) looks at the region's industrial history. Exhibits include Victorian steam engines, an exhibition on coal mining c. 1840 and Scotland's only working electric tram (open: daily, 10am–5pm, Sat., Sun. from noon in winter).

Art Nouveau bedroom in the Mackintosh designed Hill House (see page 211)

18th century loom in Kilbarchan Weaver's Cottage

A "fun" swimming pool and an ice-skating rink are just some of the facilities available at the Time Capsule Leisure Centre in Buchanan Street.

Renfrew District

Renfrew District with Paisley (pop. 75,700) as its administrative centre lies on the western edge of the Glasgow conurbation.

Paisley
Museum and Art Gallery

The development of the textile industry and the story of the distinctive "drip" on the world-famous Paisley pattern is told in the Paisley Museum (High Street). Exhibits include the old looms on which the best-selling designs were produced (open: Mon.–Sat. 10am–5pm)

★Abbey

Some surviving parts of Paisley Abbey (1193) date from the 12th c. St Mirin chapel (1499), the chancel and the windows are worth closer inspection (open: Mon.–Sat. 10am–12.30pm, 1.30–3.30pm)

Sma Shot Cottages

Looms and other everyday objects of the Victorian era are on display in the two faithfully restored cottages in George Place (nos. 11/17; open: Sat. and 1st Wed. in the month, 1–5pm).

Kilbarchan
★Weaver's Cottage

The Weaver's Cottage in Kilbarchan (pop. 3800) dates from 1783. The exhibits on display inside offer an insight into the techniques used by Clydeside weavers (Shuttle Street; NTS; open: Easter, May–Sept. daily and Oct. Sat., Sun. 1.30–5.30pm).

Glencoe
D 5/6

Region: Strathclyde

Situation and characteristics

Translated from Gaelic, Glencoe means "The Valley of the Dogs". It is situated on the west coast about 15 miles/24km south of Fort William (see entry). The valley of Glencoe stretches for about 10 miles/16km from Buachaille Etive Mǿr in the east, the "Great Herdsman" (3345ft/1022m), as far as Loch Leven, a saltwater arm of Loch Linnhe. The valley road is famed for its breathtaking scenery, winter sports, walking and mountain climbing, but to the Scots the valley also recalls a tragedy of epic proportions. It is still referred to as the "Valley of Tears" after the MacDonalds were massacred by the Campbells on February 13th 1692. Most of the valley is administered by the National Trust for Scotland (14,195 acres/5747ha).

The first road through the glen was laid in 1785 and it was almost certainly the unfortunate soldiers involved in the backbreaking work who gave the pass through to Fort William the name "Devil's Staircase". Since 1644 slate has been mined near the village of Ballachulish and during the 18th c. that mine provided work for up to 2000 men. A monument to the south of Ballachulish remembers James of the Glens who was falsely hanged for the murder of Colin Roy Campbell or "The Red Fox" – the inspiration for Robert Louis Stevenson's "Kidnapped" (1886; see Famous People), part of which is set in Glencoe. About 50 years later Alfred Hitchcock used the valley as a backdrop for the classic thriller by John Buchan "The Thirty Nine Steps".

Visitor Centre
Folk Museum

In 1976 a visitor centre was opened in Clachaig and the fascinating multi-media exposition of the Glencoe Massacre certainly attracts most attention, but other displays include mountaineering in the region and also aspects of the glen's history (open: Apr.–mid-May, mid–Sept.–mid-Oct. daily, 10am–5pm; mid-May–mid-Sept. daily 9.30am–6pm). The Leishman mountain research centre at Achnacon Farm was opened in 1976 on land acquired by the National Trust a few years earlier. The Folk Museum in Glencoe welcomes visitors (open: mid-May–Sept. daily, 10am–5.30pm).

History and Legends

Many legends surround Glencoe. Fingal (Fionn McCumhail) the mythical Scottish giant who defeated the Vikings is said to have lived here. His son Ossian provided James Macpherson with the opportunity to advance the cause of Gaelic history. During the 18th c. Macpherson produced a trans-

Glencoe

1 Altnafeadh	4 Ossian's Cave	6 Glencoe Visitor Centre	9 Achnacon
2 Allt-na-reigh	5 Achnambeithach	7 Clachaig Hotel	(Mountain-Rescue Post)
3 Achtriochtan	(Mountain-Rescue Post)	8 Signal Rock	10 Youth hostel

lation of Ossian's writings but they were later found to be fakes. Witches and fairies are also associated with Glencoe. Bean Nighe, for example, is a woman who washes clothes in the River Coe and death comes quickly to anyone who catches sight of her. Hardly surprising then that she was glimpsed by many on the eve of the massacre. In about 600, St Mundus, a pupil of the Irish saint Columba, came to the valley and stayed for a while on Eilean Munde, the small island in Loch Leven which remained a religious centre for centuries. The remains of the small chapel can still be seen. From the 11th c. the valley was part of the McDougall clan's territory and was ruled from Dunstaffnage Castle near Oban (see entry). In 1308 the McDougalls joined forces with the English to fight Robert the Bruce (see Famous People). The Campbells and the MacDonalds fought side by side for Bruce and defeated the McDougalls on the Brander Pass, about 20 miles/32km south of Glencoe. As a gesture of thanks Bruce gave the valley to Angus Og MacDonald thus establishing that clan's dominance over the region for the next 500 years. The population in the relatively fertile valley rarely exceeded 500. Living in small stone cottages, the inhabitants shared the land with tough mountain sheep, who provided them with meat, milk and wool, and also the prized black Highland cattle. Herring was plentiful in Loch Leven so they were able to supplement their diet with smoked fish.

After about 1500 the tension started to mount. The gap between the prosperity of the Lowlanders and the poverty of the Highlanders became more marked. Cattle rustling became common and the dispute between the loyal Campbells, the earls and later dukes of Argyll and the "wild" McGregors, McLeans and MacDonalds of Glencoe came to a head. It first came to a head in the Atholl Raid (1685) when the MacDonalds seized stock from the weakened Campbells. Two ways of life collided – the old and the new, the free and independent Highlanders clashed with a sober and insensitive central government. On the one hand, the Massacre of Glencoe was just one particularly brutal chapter in the history of clan rivalry but, on the other hand, it was also a manifestation of how the governments in London and Edinburgh were seeking to win control over the "lawless" Highlanders.

The Massacre
of Glencoe

After William of Orange had defeated his Scottish rivals in Ireland in 1690, on August 27th 1691 he offered a pardon to those clans that had either fought against him or were ill-disposed towards him. These former foes were obliged to take an oath of allegiance by January 1st 1692 and Alastair MacDonald arrived in Fort William in good time to take the oath but was sent to the Campbell stronghold of Inveraray and missed the deadline by five days, a delay which was to prove costly within a matter of weeks. On February 1st Robert Campbell of Glenlyon, then aged 60, and 120 men met Alastair MacDonald, requested hospitality and the two groups lived alongside each other in peace for several days. But Campbell was awaiting the order from Edinburgh to kill all the inhabitants of the valley below the age of 70. On February 12th the order came and at 5 o'clock the following morning the slaughter commenced. The instructions to the Campbell party were "root out the old fox and his cubs" although in the end "only" 38 of the MacDonalds succumbed. The rest, about ten times that number, escaped, but many died as they tried to cross the mountains in winter. Thanks to the investigations of an Irish journalist called Charles Leslie, the news of the Massacre of Glencoe led to a political scandal which at least temporarily brought an end to the career of the Scottish minister Sir John Dalrymple. The final demise of the MacDonald clan did not occur until the Battle of Culloden (see entry) half a century later on. Alastair the 14th chief of Glencoe who as a small child had survived the massacre fought alongside Bonnie Prince Charlie. After this defeat the homes of the MacDonalds were burnt down, their cattle driven away and the clan chief arrested.

★★ Mountain
tours

Some of the peaks in Glen Coe exceed 3275ft/1000m such as Buachaille Etive Mór in the east (3345ft/1022m), Stob Coire nan Lochan (3657ft/1115m) in the west – a very popular spot for winter sports enthusiasts – and Bidean nam Bian (3742ft/1141m). However, it ought to be borne in mind that these slopes are more suitable for mountaineering than mountain walking and should only be tackled by accomplished climbers appropriately equipped. Nevertheless some routes in the more remote areas are safe and inexperienced walkers can enjoy the true beauty of the valley. The weather is an important factor. Too often Macauley's description of the glen as the "Valley of the Shadows" or even the gloomy "Valley of Tears" seem more apt. But when the sun is shining brightly the splendour of this mountain range is more likely to match the words "oblivious of humanity" used by Henry V. Morton. Signal Rock, Devil's Staircase and Loch Achtriochtan are possible destinations for walkers or tourers.

Grampian   F/G 4/5

Grampian Region
and the Grampian
Mountains

Grampian Region was created by the local government reforms of 1975. It incorporates the old counties of Aberdeenshire, Kincardine, Banff and a large part of Moray. The administrative centre of this green and fairly flat corner of north-east Scotland is Aberdeen (see entry) at the mouth of the Dee. There are a number of other smaller towns with Peterhead ranking as the second biggest, but it is only a tenth of the size of Aberdeen in population terms. The region is named after the highest mountain range in the region, the Grampian Mountains, but the hillside heathers and moors also overlap into the adjoining regions of Tayside, Strathclyde, Central and Highland. Formed as a result of glaciation, the Grampian Mountains which are separated from the North-West Highlands (see entry) by the Caledonian Canal (see entry) include many of Britain's highest peaks such as Ben Nevis (4397ft/1343m; see Fort William) and Ben Machdui (4265ft/1309m). The Cairngorm Mountains (see entry), the largest highland plateau in the

Grampian

Aberdeen

© Baedeker

British Isles, are also a principal feature in the Grampian region. Covering an area of about 60sq. miles/155sq.km the Cairngorms lie at average height of 914ft/279m with four of the summits exceeding 4000ft/1220m. Heathers and bracken, birch and mountain ash predominate, although in recent years pine forests have been planted widely. Red deer proliferate and the region is a haven for many rare bird species.

The region is well-known for its Angus cattle, but sheep farming is also common. In the Moray Firth which enjoys a relatively mild climate animal fattening is a profitable business. About a third of all Scottish oats and barley is grown in this region, with a large proportion of the latter going to the distillation of whisky. Over half of the 130 distilleries in Scotland are located in Grampian. Salmon and trout are plentiful in the rivers Dee, Don, Ythan, Ugie, Deveron and Spey and these pretty valleys attract not just anglers but also commercial fish farmers.

Economy

The discovery of oil in the North Sea about 130 miles/200km east of Aberdeen (see entry) has contributed greatly to the industrialisation and prosperity of the region and this has taken place without damaging the natural beauty of the landscape. Oil and related industries have not only halved unemployment in Grampian but have also raised wage levels and property prices, and that has not always been to the advantage of the long-established local firms or the low-wage fishing industry of north-west Scotland. Grampian is, nevertheless, one of the fastest-growing regions in the country.

See entry

Aberdeen

See entry

Castle Trail

See entry

Dee Valley

See entry

Malt Whisky Trail

★The North Coast · From Peterhead to Elgin

Scotland's most easterly town the busy port of Peterhead (pop. 18000) was founded in 1593 by the 5th Earl Marischal George Keith. Now the countless oil tanks by the harbour are proof that the town receives an important share of the work supplying the oil rigs out at sea. In addition Peterhead's fishing port is the largest in the country. Early birds can see for themselves the bustling activity around the fish auctions on workday mornings. Arbuthnot Museum in St Peter Street documents the history of the town's herring and whaling industry (open: Mon.–Sat. 10am–5pm). The oldest salmon smokehouse in Scotland (1585) is situated by the River Ugie opposite the golf course. Both fresh and smoked salmon are available here (open: Mon.–Fri. 9am–noon, 2–5pm, Sat. 9am–noon).

Peterhead

Fish market
Arbuthnot
Museum
Salmon Fish
House

Bullers of Buchan is a rocky chasm 230ft/70m deep (7 miles/12.6km to the south of Peterhead). Thought to be a cave that collapsed, this open-air

★Bullers of
Buchan

Scotland's oldest salmon smokehouse, Peterhead

bubbling cauldron makes a spectacular sight particularly when the sea is rough (cliff footpath from the car park).

Cruden Bay

The nearby resort of Cruden Bay (pop. 490) is noted for its 2 mile/3km long sandy beach and an excellent golf course, frequently a venue for international competitions.

Slains Castle

The writer Samuel Johnson wrote that Slains Castle – built in the 16th c. and extended in the 19th c. – was the most beautiful castle that he had ever seen. Now sadly it is just a ruin perched on a steep rock. Another writer Bram Stoker visited the castle when it was still intact and the home of the 19th Earl of Errol. It provided him with the inspiration for his legendary Count Dracula story.

Aden Country Park

Nature trails and well-tended gardens are to be found at Aden Country Park about 10 miles/16km west of Peterhead. Films, models and tapes in the Agricultural Heritage Centre bring 200 years of rural history to life (open: May–Sept. daily, 11am–5pm; Apr., Oct. Sat., Sun. noon–5pm).

Deer Abbey

The remains of a Cistercian abbey founded in 1218 by William Comayn are located 1 mile/1.6km further west. Since the 17th c. the red sandstone from the Early English style church has been taken by local builders (HS).

Fraserburgh

First the A952 and then the A92 link Peterhead with the fishing port of Fraserburgh (pop. 12,000) at the north-eastern tip of Scotland. In 1570 Alexander Fraser the 8th laird of Philorth built a fortress at the edge of the town but by the 18th c. it had been converted into Scotland's first lighthouse. The nearby haunted Wine Tower, however, is Fraserburgh's oldest building (early 16th c.). Close on 4 miles/6km to the south stands a burial mound that is thought to date from the Bronze Age.

Memsie Cairn

★North East Coastal Trail

"Local Hero"

The North East Coastal Trail is signposted with a blue anchor and runs along the coast between Fraserburgh and Portgorden passing through the idyllic fishing village of Pennan – known to filmgoers as the setting for Bill Forsyth's popular film "Local Hero" starring Burt Lancaster – followed by

Mary Stuart slept here: Delgatie Castle

Crovie, Gardenstown, MacDuff, Banff, Portsoy, Cullen, Portknockie and Findochty, all villages that owe their livelihood to the North Sea and its fish. White and grey-washed houses occupy the narrow coastal strip huddling together around tiny harbours. Again and again, it seems as though time has passed a little more slowly around these parts than elsewhere in Scotland.

Inland about 11 miles/17.6km south of MacDuff stands the tower house known as the Hays of Delgatie. While parts of the castle go back to the 11th c. most of it was built during the 16th and 17th c. The portrait of Mary Stuart in one of the bedrooms relates to the fact that she stayed here in 1562 after the Battle of Corrichie. The superb ceiling paintings (1590) merit closer inspection, while in the park the Shetland ponies will appeal to all ages (open: Apr.–Oct. 2–5pm).

★Delgatie Castle

Some 3km/2 miles north of Delgatie Castle John Urquhart built a castle *c.* 1602 and the property remains within the family to this day. The 16th c. wood panelling and the old library are the highlights of the interior (tours by prior arrangement; tel. (01888) 5228).

Craigston Castle

The picturesque ports of Banff and Macduff at the mouth of the River Deveron are connected by a seven-arched bridge which makes it difficult to separate the two towns. As early as the 12th c. Banff was a busy trading centre in the "northern Hanse", but it did not have its own harbour until 1775. A number of Georgian houses which belonged to the Scottish gentry during the 17th and 18th c. line the steep lanes and most of them are now protected by a preservation order. An elegant mansion designed by John Adam was built on the foundations of a medieval castle in the 18th c. A small museum in High Street has a collection of silverware, old weapons and a display about James Ferguson, a local astronomer, who lived during the 18th c. (open: June–Sept. Fri.–Mon. 2–5.15pm).

★Banff and Macduff

Haddington

★Duff House
Even though the money ran out and it was never finished Duff House is a jewel of Georgian architecture by William Adam. Built in the style of the Roman Villa Borghese it was commissioned by William Duff the 1st Earl of Fife, but in 1741, after six years, the work had to stop. The two-storey building is decorated with Corinthian pilasters, ornate gables and four corner towers. During the 19th c. some of the bedrooms were fitted out in Victorian style. Historic Scotland runs the estate and in 1995 converted the house into an art gallery. (Information: Janet Mclaren, tel. (0044) 224 522943.)

Portsoy
★Fordyce
Portsoy is noted for its marble some of which was used in the Palace of Versailles. Some 2 miles/3km to the south-west, the picturesque village of Fordyce was voted Scottish village of the year in 1990. The highlight of the main street is an L-shaped castle in Scottish baronial style (16th c.) with small corner towers and pretty stepped gables. Craftsmen and women can be seen at work in the Visitor Centre.

Cullen House
Sir Walter Ogilvie of Deskford whose tombstone stands in the old church nearby had the L-shaped Cullen House built in 1660. A little later Robert Adam and then David Bryce (1861) extended the property quite considerably. Robert Adam and Grinling Gibbons designed the elegant interior. Once the seat of the earls of Seafield, the house has been closed since 1975.

Buckie
★Maritime
Museum
Buckie's Maritime Museum examines the arduous life of the herring fishermen and the development of boat design and fishing nets (open: mid-June–Oct. Mon.–Sat. 10am–6pm, Sun. 11am–5pm).

Tugnet Ice House
Further west in an old ice store (1830) at the mouth of the River Spey, a museum explains the background to the Spey salmon grounds and also details some aspects of the local fauna and flora (open: May–Sept. daily, 10am–4pm).

Elgin
See entry

Haddington   G 6

Region: Lothian. Population: 8500

Situation
Popular destinations for the city-dwellers of Edinburgh (see entry) are Haddington and the Lammermuir Hills in East Lothian, a contrast to the heavy industrialised old counties of Mid- and West Lothian. Haddington, the administrative centre for East Lothian, lies in a pretty spot on the banks of the River Tyne, crossed here by the 16th c. Nungate bridge. David I founded the town in the 12th c. and John Knox is said to have received divine inspiration here in 1515 (see Famous People). A memorial to the controversial reformer stands in front of the Knox Memorial Institute.

Sights

★Townscape
Haddington consists of many faithfully restored streets and boasts more than 100 buildings of architectural interest from the 17th, 18th and 19th c. with most of them in High Street. The Classical town hall was designed by William Adam in 1748 and the 170ft/52m tower by Gillespie Graham was added in 1831. The 206ft/63m long St Mary's Parish Church which is known as the "Lamp of Lothian" was begun in the 14th c; it retains the original central tower, while the nave and west front were restored in the 20th c.

St Mary's

Haddington House
Three houses dating from the 17th c. are worth seeking out: Haddington House (now the town museum) and its magnificent rose garden in nearby St Mary's Pleasance, Boswell Castle and the Moat House. The stepped gable and pantile roofs in Mitchell's Close have been faithfully restored.

Surroundings · East Lothian

Stevenson House is situated about 2 miles/3.2km east of the town centre. It dates from the 16th c. and became the property of the Sinclairs of Longformacus in 1624. The 3rd baronet had the building extended and also gave the interior its early Georgian character. When the 9th baronet died without issue in 1931, the estate went to the Dunlop family who initially showed little interest in maintaining it. The careful restoration work was undertaken fairly recently by John Dunlop.

★Stevenson House

Open:
June–mid-Aug.
Thur., Sat., Sun.
2–5.30pm

Medieval Lethington Tower which belonged to the Maitlands from the 13th c. was converted into a grand country house in the 17th c. (1 mile/1.6km south of Haddington). The estate name derives from the Duchess of Lennox or "La Belle Stewart", a beautiful court companion to the wife of Charles II, who resisted the favours of the king and remained faithful to the Duke of Richmond and Lennox. The house was later named Lennoxlove in memory of her husband. It has been the seat of the dukes of Hamilton since 1947. Of interest are the expensive presents that the king gave to the duchess in his attempts to win her heart, family portraits by Raeburn, van Dyck and Lely and a piano that Chopin is supposed to have played. Note also the portrait of the reformer John Knox (see Famous People), the porcelain collection (Derby, Dresden and Worcester) and some memorabilia belonging to Mary Stuart (see Famous People): her death mask and the small jewellery box where the forged letter purporting to show her complicity in the murder of Lord Darnley and foreshadowing the end of her regency. Colourful flowerbeds and old trees are the main features of the surrounding parkland.

★★Lennoxlove House

Open:
May–Sept.daily
2–6pm;
Oct. Sat., Sun.
2–5pm

The Lammermuir Hills which rise to a height of 1750ft/533m are visible to the south of Haddington. The rivers that rise in these hills are famous among anglers for their trout stocks. The small town of Gifford makes a

Lammermuir Hills, Gifford

Delightful garden at Lennoxlove House

good starting point for excursions into the hills. Yester Castle, now a ruin, was immortalised in Scott's "Marmion" and the hillside castle at Nunraw (17th c.), now a Cistercian abbey, was the setting for Scott's "The Bride of Lammermoor".

Pencaitland
Glenkinchie
Distillery

Production of malt whisky at the Glenkinchie distillery started in 1835. The distillery is situated amid cornfields near Pencaitland (6 miles/9.6km west of Gifford). Its malting floors (closed in 1968) on which the sprouted barley was spread have been converted into a whisky museum (open: Mon.–Fri. 9.30am–4.30pm; see Baedeker Special, "Scotch Whisky").

Winton House

Fine stepped gables, unusual chimneys and pretty roof towers are the distinguishing external features of Winton House, a Renaissance-style mansion converted c. 1620 by William Wallace. Situated at the eastern end of Pencaitland, the house boasts magnificent plasterwork ceilings, a painting by Canaletto, period furniture and ornate fireplaces (tours by prior arrangement; tel. (01875) 340357).

Gosford House

Situated on the banks of the Firth of Forth near Longniddry (6 miles/9.6km north of Haddington) stands another of Robert Adam's Classical-style mansions. Work started c. 1790 but the north and south pavilions were replaced by larger wings from designs by William Young in 1890. Ornithologists will be interested in the parkland as wild geese have been breeding here since 1983 (open: June, July Wed., Sat., Sun. 2–5pm).

Aberlady
Luffness Castle

The nearby coastal village of Aberlady (pop. 700) is noted for its fine sandy beaches and the sea bird reserve in Aberlady Bay. The 16th c. Luffness Castle is an extension of a medieval keep (13th c.).

Gullane
★★Golf courses

Muirfield, a traditional eighteen-hole course, is Gullane's best known golf course but there are four other courses in the vicinity. Muirfield itself, several times the venue for the British Open, is owned by the "Honourable

The harbour, North Berwick   *Dirleton Castle – Norman origins*

Company of British Golfers", an organisation that grew out of the "Gentle-men Golfers of Leith" (1744), the world's first golf club and ten years older than the Royal Ancient Golf Club in St Andrews (see entry). A small museum near the clubhouse on West Links Road in Gullane traces the history of the small white ball from the 15th c. to the present day (visits by prior arrangement; tel. (018757) 870277).

★ Heritage of Golf

The remains of one of Scotland's first sandstone castles with its curtain wall and moat are to be found in the little village of Dirleton. The origins of this Norman fortress date from 1225. It was rebuilt in the 15th c. but destroyed by Cromwell in 1650. Beneath the castle lie fine Victorian flower beds and a magnificent 16th c. garden which was laid out by the earls of Gowrie (HS; open: Apr.–Sept. Mon.–Sat. 9.30am–6pm, Sun. 2–6pm; Oct.–Mar. Mon.–Sat. 9.30am–4pm, Sun. 2–4pm).

Dirleton Castle

The refined resort of North Berwick (pop. 5100) can boast a number of golf courses. It is also where Robert Louis Stevenson (see Famous People) spent many summers as a child.

★ **North Berwick**

Bass Rock rises 350ft/107m out of the sea a mile or so off the coast. Boat trips sail out to this island of dark grey volcanic basalt. The island is a favourite breeding ground for solan geese which used to be caught for their down – 230 such birds were required for one bedcover.

★ Bass Rock

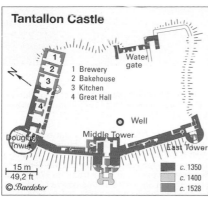

Tantallon Castle

1 Brewery
2 Bakehouse
3 Kitchen
4 Great Hall

Water gate

Well

Middle Tower

Douglas Tower

East Tower

15 m
49,2 ft

© Baedeker

c. 1350
c. 1400
c. 1528

★ Tantallon Castle

Some 3 miles/4.8km to the east and perched on a 100ft/30m rock lie the red sandstone ruins of Tantallon Castle. The fortress was built in 1374 for the Douglas clan. Both James IV and James V failed in their attempts to capture the stronghold which was equipped with ramparts, ditches, corner towers and a central gatehouse. Cromwell's troops under the command of General Monk did succeed in capturing and destroying it in 1651 (HS; open: Apr.–Sept. Mon.–Sat. 9.30am–6pm, Sun. 2–6pm; Oct.–Mar. Mon.–Sat. 9.30am–4pm, Sun. 2–4pm).

Head inland through Whitekirk to East Linton (pop. 850), a pleasant little town on the Tyne which flows through a gorge here and is crossed by a 16th c. bridge.

East Linton

This 18th c. mill in a picturesque spot on the banks of the Tyne is the only working mill of its kind in Scotland. The nearby dovecot once accommodated more than 500 birds. (NTS; open: Apr.–Sept. Mon.–Sat. 11am–1pm, 2–5pm, Sun. 2–5pm; Oct. Sat. 11am–1pm, 2–4.30pm, Sun. 2–4pm).

Preston Mill and Phantassie Dovecot

To the north-west near East Fortune a former RAF airbase houses a museum of over 30 old aeroplanes, including a De Havilland Puss Moth (1930), a Weir W-2 (1934), a Supermarine Spitfire and a Sea Hawk (open: Apr.–Sept. daily, 10.30am–4.30pm).

★ Museum of Flight

Hailes Castle is situated about 2 miles/3km south-west of East Linton. It was built in the 13th c. but destroyed by Cromwell in 1650. The narrow dungeons below both towers are particularly interesting.

Hailes Castle

Old biplane in the Museum of Flight

Traprain Law	To the rear rises Traprain Law (724ft/221m) where a hoard of 4th c. Roman silver coins was found in 1919. They are now kept in Edinburgh's Museum of Antiquities (see entry).
Dunbar	Remains of another medieval castle (15th c.) stand at the entrance to Dunbar's harbour (12 miles/19.2km to the east). The pretty resort's name derives from the Gaelic words "dun" meaning fort and "barr" meaning mound. Mary Stuart (see Famous People) fled here after the murder of her trusted ally Rizzio. The Renaissance town hall dates from the 17th c. and Lauderdale House at the end of High Street has an impressive façade and
John Muir House	two wings which were designed by Robert Adam (1790–92). In 1836 John Muir was born at 126 High Street. He is famous in the United States as the founder of the National Parks such as Yosemite and the Sequioa National Park in California. The upper floor of the house was converted into a museum in 1981 (open: June–Sept.).
Muir Country Park	Situated by the coast to the west of Dunbar, this country park (1976) with nature trails was named after John Muir.

Hebrides   B/C 3–C/D 6

	Regions: Western Isles Area, Highland and Strathclyde Region
Situation	More than 500 islands off the north-west coast of Scotland make up the
Map see page 233	Hebrides (2812sq. miles/7285sq.km in total) and about 80 of them are inhabited. The islands are broken up into those lying close to the mainland, the Inner Hebrides with Skye, Mull, Islay, Jura, Rhum, Eigg, Coll and Colonsay the biggest and best known, and the 130-mile/210km long outer arc, known as the Outer Hebrides or Western Isles (Nah Eileanan Siar) with

View across Portree harbour (Skye) to the Isle of Raasay

Lewis and Harris ("Long Island"), North Uist, Benbecula, South Uist and Barra as the main islands. The North Minch, Little Minch and Sea of the Hebrides separate the Inner and Outer Hebrides. The former islands are part of the Highland and Strathclyde regions, while the Outer Hebrides form the Western Isles region and are administered from Stornaway.

The Hebrides are formed from Pre-Cambrian gneiss, metamorphic schist and volcanic rocks. Heathers and moorland predominate in the cool, windy, and wet climate. As well as cattle rearing and the cultivation of small plots of land, woollen products, such as tweeds, fishing and tourism provide the main employment opportunities for the islanders.

Topography

Since 1995 a bridge (toll payable) crossing the Kyle Akin from Kyleakin on Skye has replaced the former ferry which used to ply between the Kyle of Lochalsh on the Scottish mainland and Kyleakin. In the summer months there are also ferries between Mallaig and Armadale (Skye) and the Kyle of Lochalsh (thus linking two Scottish railway termini). From Mallaig (and in the summer months from Arisaig) passenger boats run to the smaller islands of Eigg, Muck, Rhum and Canna. In summer there are also ferry links between Gleneig and Kylerhea (Skye). Iona can be reached by ferry from Fionnphort (Mull), Staffa by boat trips from Mull or Oban (see entry). Scalasaig (Colonsay) is also accessible from Oban. Car ferries operate between Kennacraig/Kintyre and Port Ellen and Port Askaig (Islay) with connections from Port Askaig to Feolin Ferry (Jura) and Scalasaig (Colonsay). Car ferries to the Outer Hebrides leave from Uig (Skye) for Tarbert (Harris) and Lochmaddy (Uist). In addition there are boats from Oban (see entry) via Tobermory (Mull) to Castlebay (Barra), Lochboisdale (South Uist), to the island of Coll and Scarinish (Tiree). Ferries to Stornoway (Lewis) leave from Ullapool. Within the Outer Hebrides, services exist between Castlebay and Lochboisdale and between Lochmaddy and Tarbert.

Communications
Ferry links

See also Practical Information, Ferries.

Airfields

It is possible to fly to the Inner Hebrides islands of Skye, Islay, Coll and Tiree, and Lewis, Benbecula and Barra on the Outer Hebrides. The runway at Barra is the beach at Tràigh Mhór so planes can only land and take off at low tide.

Inner Hebrides

Isle of Skye

★★Topography

The largest of the inner isles, Skye, was known to the Vikings as "Skúyo" (= "cloud island"), while in Gaelic it became known as "Eilean Sgiathanach" ("winged island") because of the irregular coastline. Thanks to the prevailing weather conditions it was also termed "Eilean a Cheo" ("misty island"). The attractions of Skye are its unspoilt natural environment, the wild, romantic mountain scenery and the green valleys, caves and attractive glens, magnificent waterfalls and sandy beaches. It measures about 50 miles/ 80km in length and between 4 and 15 miles/6.4–24km in width with many inlets reaching deep inland. To the south of the island lie the remains of primeval oak forests interspersed with birch, mountain ash, holly and hazel.

The wildlife includes otters, seals, salmon and trout and well over 200 different species of birds such as red-throated divers, corncrake, solan geese and a few pairs of golden eagles.

Bridge

Kyleakin
Castle Moil

Today Skye can be reached from Kyle of Lochalsh either by the new toll bridge (opened 1995) or by ferry. Both cross the Kyle Akin narrows to Kyleakin (pop. 250), the main tourist arrival point, with the remains of Castle Moil. For details of ferry services see p. 324.

On the way to the Old Man of Storr   *Illicit whisky still*

Only half a mile away on Loch Alsh is Kyle House, with an enchanting garden laid out more than 30 years ago by Colin Mackenzie (open: May–Aug.).

Kyle House

Broadford (pop. 1250) 8 miles/12.8km to the west is the second-largest settlement on the island and a good base for tours.

Broadford

Domain of the "Lords of the Isles"

Armadale at the south end of the island is often a starting point for touring the island as ferries arrive here from the mainland port of Mallaig, but it can also be reached via the A851 from Broadford. The castle that was built between 1815 and 1819 by Gillespie Graham and the Clan Donald Centre are well worth a visit. A museum illustrates thrilling tales of the "Lords of the Isles" who during the 15th c. dominated the region between the Outer Hebrides, the northern coast of Antrim in what is now Northern Ireland and Easter Ross. An attractive garden is laid out in the castle grounds.

Armadale Castle
★ Clan Donald Centre

Open:
Apr.–Oct. daily,
9.30am–5.30pm

One of the most interesting excursions from Broadford starts with a visit to Loch Scavaig (15 miles/24km) which affords a splendid view of the Blaven (3042ft/927m) followed by Loch Slapin and finally Elgol, a tiny village with a steep descent to the coast. The breathtaking view from Elgol encompasses numerous offshore islands. "Bonnie Prince Charlie" is said to have hidden from the English in one of the nearby caves.

Loch Scavaig,
Blaven,
Elgol

Set in an idyllic rocky landscape Loch Coruisk is best viewed from a boat. It is linked to Loch Scavaig by a river and lies at the foot of the black Cuillin Hills or Coolins. This range of hills is formed from gabbro, a rock of volcanic origin, and it attracts hundreds of enthusiasts from all over Britain as there are climbs here to suit all abilities. The highest of the 20 peaks above 3000ft/900m is Sgurr Alasdair (3251ft/991m). Only experienced climbers should venture on to these higher peaks since the steep scree slopes can prove very hazardous. The high iron content of the rock can often distort compass readings so walkers need to exercise great care.

★★ **Cuillin Hills**
★ Loch Coruisk

The best known mountain is called Sgurr nan Gillean. Glen Sligachan mountain climbers' hotel and pony trekking centre attracts many tourists to this part of the island. Glenbrittle is another base for mountaineers and courses in climbing are organised. There are good opportunities for bathing in Loch Brittle and boats cross to Rhum, Canna and Eigg.

Sgurr nan
Gillean,
Glen Brittle

The A850 from Broadford to Portree passes the Old Skye Crofter's House. This dwelling offers an insight into the arduous life of Skye's peasant farmers at the beginning of the 20th c. (open: daily, 9am–6pm).

Crofter's House

For Robert Louis Stevenson (see Famous People) the strong, peaty Talisker whisky was the "king o'drinks". This excellent malt whisky has been produced on the banks of Loch Harport since 1831 when the MacAskill brothers opened what is now the only distillery on the island (open: Mon.–Fri. 9am–4.30pm; see also Baedeker Special "Scotch Whisky").

★ Talisker
Distillery

The Prince and the Hebridean Girl

The Hebrides were the scene for an episode in Scottish history which combined both drama and romance. It revolved around the "Young Pretender" Charles Edward Stuart, also affectionately known to Scots as "Bonnie Prince Charlie". As a descendant of Mary Stuart he sought to reclaim the throne that his grandfather James II had lost.

The handsome, Italian-educated prince, described by his contemporaries as warm-hearted and bold, resolved to do battle for the Stuarts and win back the lost throne. After repeated setbacks Charles Edward Stuart finally disembarked from the French frigate "Du Tellay" on to the stony shores of the Hebridean island of Eriskay on July 23rd 1745. Within a few weeks the blond-haired, charismatic pretender had mobilised the Scottish clans into an army which was to challenge and defeat the English at Prestonpans on September 21st 1745. A little later "Bonnie Prince Charlie", who was proclaimed by his father as James VIII the king of Scotland, triumphantly entered Edinburgh wearing a kilt, white cockade and star of St Andrew. To the jubilation of the Highlanders, Scotland was back under Jacobite rule. In November of the same year the Prince Regent set off with his supporters to march on London. But shortly before reaching his destination his luck ran out. Desertions, home-sickness and the desire of many clansmen to be at home for the harvest depleted the Jacobite army and they were obliged to return to Scotland. The escapade ended in disaster on the marshy soil of Drumossie Moors near Culloden on April 16th 1746.

Charles Edward, now with a price of £30,000 on his head, was forced to flee and wandered for months through the tough terrain of the Scottish Highlands. The popular hero only survived this period thanks to the loyalty of his supporters and many legends have sprung up surrounding their acts of bravery. He eventually reached South Uist, an island in the Outer Hebrides. He would almost certainly have been captured there had it not been for a 24-year-old farmer's daughter by the name of Flora MacDonald. She disguised him as Betty Burke her servant girl and managed to smuggle him through the English lines and on to a French boat at Skye. Whether this was done out of love or compassion is not clear. The end of the adventure took place in Portree on July 1st 1746 and the event was marked by the gift of a lock of hair to his saviour, to whom he uttered these oft-quoted parting words: "For all that has happened, I hope, Madam, we shall meet at St James' (Palace in London). I will reward you there for what you have done." Sadly the prince was not able to fulfil his promise and in the same year was forced to seek exile in Rome where he died with his ambitions unfulfilled.

In the meantime Flora MacDonald was imprisoned for eight months in the Tower of London for high treason. After her release she returned to Skye but in 1773 emigrated to North Carolina with her husband Alan MacDonald and their seven children. She returned to Skye five years before her death. Wrapped in the sheet on which the fleeing pretender had once rested, Flora was buried in the graveyard at Kilmuir on March 4th 1790. Her much-visited gravestone bears the words of Dr Samuel Johnson: "Her name will be mentioned in history and, if courage and loyalty are virtues, held in high esteem."

This romantic but sad tale lives on in Scotland – mainly on the island of Skye where part of the tale was enacted – in songs and ballads, and those places where the famous events took place are assured of a lasting place in the history books. The same is true of South Uist where Flora MacDonald was born, the

The Prince bids farewell to Flora MacDonald (1746, G. W. Joy)

small island of Eriskay a little further south where Bonnie Prince Charlie first set foot on Scottish soil and Loch nan Uamh Bay near Arisaig where the defeated prince escaped to France on the inappropriately named "L'Heureux" on September 20th 1746.

Portree, "capital" of Skye

Portree

Portree (pop. 2000) is the largest town on Skye. It has an idyllic harbour with views across the Sound of Raasay. It is said that in 1746 "Bonnie Prince Charlie" and Flora MacDonald parted company in the Royal Hotel. The Heritage Centre in Viewfield Road documents life on the island from 1700 to the present day (open: Mar.–June, Oct.–Dec. daily, 9am–6pm; July–Sept. daily, 9am–9pm).

Skye Heritage Centre

Trotternish Peninsula

The A855 follows the coastline of the Trotternish peninsula northwards affording fine views across to Raasay in the east. It is worth making a detour to Prince Charlie's Cave, another hideaway used by the "Young Pretender" before heading for Loch Fada and Loch Leathan to see the Old Man of Storr rock, a 164ft/50m high black basalt monolith surrounded by smaller pinnacles known as The Old Man's Wife, Castle and Dog. Kilt Rock is so named because of the strange tartan-like pattern on the brownish basalt rock. Further north stand the Quiraing Needles, a collection of bizarrely-shaped basalt rocks with needles, jagged peaks and steps.

★**Old Man of Storr**

Kilt Rock

★**Quiraing Needles**

★**Skye Museum of Island Life**

The A855 cuts off the northern tip of the peninsula before reaching the seven cottages which make up the Skye Museum of Island Life. The thatched huts give an insight into the rural life of crofters in the mid-19th c. (open: Apr.–Oct. Mon.–Sat. 9am–5.30pm).

Flora MacDonald's tomb

The Hebridean heroine Flora MacDonald is buried in Kilmuir cemetery.

Uig

Before returning to Portree stop off in Uig, departure point for the ferries to Lewis and North Uist. See Practical Information, Ferries

★**Dunvegan Castle**

Open:
Mar.–Oct. daily,
10am–5.30pm

Dunvegan (pop. 250) lies by the loch of the same name to the west of the island. It is noted mainly for its castle, one of the last inhabited seats of a Scottish clan, namely the MacLeods, who for centuries fought bloody battles against the MacDonalds of Armadale for supremacy of the island. The original building dates from the 13th c., but the keep was added in the 14th c. and the Fairy Tower at the south-east corner of the rock was built

c. 1500. Norman, the 23rd clan chief, converted the building into a comfortable Victorian-style residence in the 19th c. Legends about fairies and crusaders surround the Fairy Flag (Am Bratach Sith), a piece of silk that originated in Rhodes or Syria and is said to date from between the 4th and 7th c. This ancient banner became a talisman for the MacLeods in battle and, according to legend, twice saved the clan from disaster. Of special interest in the castle are the family portraits which include work by Ramsay and Raeburn, letters from Sir Walter Scott and Dr Samuel Johnson who stopped off here on his Hebridean journey with companion James Boswell in 1773, an exhibition about the music and poetry of the MacCrimmons, old bagpipes, works by the Gaelic poetess MacLeod of Rodel (d. 1710) and the harp-playing bard Ruaraidh Dall Morrison.

About 3 miles/4.8km to the west of Dunvegan the harsh semi-tropical rural Skye in the mid-19th c. is brought to life in the straw-roofed Black House of Colbost (open: daily, 10am–6pm).

Duirinish Peninsula
Colbost Folk Museum

The first school for pipers is said to have been founded c. 1500 by the Mac-Crimmons the legendary pipers for the MacLeod clan in Boreraig and to have survived until 1800. Opposite the ruins of the old piping school, the Skye Piping Centre traces the history of the bagpipe and the traditions of the old clans right up to the present day (open: Apr., May Tues.–Sun. 2–5.30pm; June–Aug. daily, 11am–5.30pm; Sept. Tues.–Sun. 11am–5.30pm; see Baedeker Special "Bagpipes").

★Skye Piping Centre

Old Highland bagpipes c. 1700, with only two borduns drones)

Isle of Mull

The largely treeless island of Mull (pop. 2400) is the third-biggest of the Hebridean islands. As a holiday destination it offers impressive scenery, footpaths for walkers and sport and leisure facilities including golf, pony trekking and watersports. The south and east of the island are mountainous; Ben More reaches 3169ft/966m, making it the only "Munro" (see Baedeker Special "How to become a Munroist") in the Hebrides apart from the Isle of Skye. On the other hand the hills in the north are lower and the vegetation and wildlife are similar to those found on Skye. See Practical Information, Ferries.

★★Topography

An old cow shed near Dervaig is home to Britain's smallest theatre (43 seats). There are performances throughout the year.

Little Theatre

Tobermory (pop. 650) is the main town on the island. Colourful houses overlook the ferry terminal and fishing harbour in this busy tourist centre. The settlement was founded in 1788 and its name derives from "Mary's spring" near the chapel ruins to the west of the town. In 1588 the "Florencia" a fully-laden ship belonging to the Spanish Armada sank off the coast, but only a few coins have been found from the treasure that was thought to have been on board.

Tobermory

Scotch drinkers will enjoy sampling the fine Ledaig malt produced in the Tobermory Distillery at the end of High Street (open: Apr.–Oct. Mon.–Fri. 10am–4pm).

Tobermory Distillery

The main road on the island (A848, A849) follows the Sound of Mull from Tobermory to Craignure in the south-east. Between April and October a miniature railway runs from Craignure's old pier to the early Victorian Torosay Castle that David Bryce designed in 1858. The interior is Edwardian in style while the beautiful terraced garden, laid out by Sir John Lorimer, is

Craignure
Isle of Mull Railway, Torosay Castle

Waterfront at Tobermory, Isle of Mull

decorated with Italian marble statues, rhododendron and eucalyptus trees (open: mid-Apr.–mid-Oct. daily, 10.30am–5.30pm; garden 9am–7pm).

Duart Castle

Duart Castle stands in a prominent position on the eastern tip of Duart Bay. Dating from the 13th c., this seat of the MacLean family was left to decay in the 17th c. Restoration took place in 1911 under Sir Fitzroy MacLean. The keep (c. 1360) houses an exhibition on the history of the clan (open: May–Sept. daily, 10.30am–6pm).

★Carsaig Arches

The scenery along the southern coast of Mull to the west of Carsaig is particularly impressive. At low tide a footpath about 3 miles/4.8km long leads to the huge arches and tunnels known as Carsaig Arches which have been forged out of the black basalt by the waves.

The Burg

A 5 mile/8km long footpath, in parts rather treacherous, runs along the northern shores of Loch Scridain from Tiroran (car park) to a fossilised tree that was encased in lava about 50 million years ago.

Iona

History

Boats cross from Fionnphort at the south-west tip of Mull to the offshore island of Iona (see Practical Information, Ferries). Day trips to Iona are also possible from Oban (see entry). Now under the administration of the National Trust for Scotland (1979), the island was a druid shrine long before St Columba landed there in 563. Known originally as "Hy", then "Iona insula", the monastery that St Columba and his twelve companions founded on Iona served as their base as they sought to convert Scotland to Christianity.

About 100 people live on Iona and most of these inhabit the village of
Baile-Mor which means "large town". On a clear day the view from Dun-I a
332ft/101m high hill behind the cathedral encompasses over 30 islands.

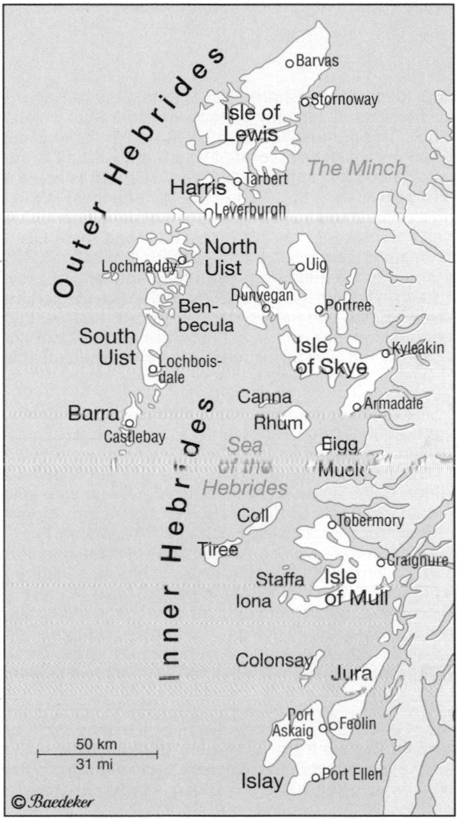

Baile-Mor

The monastery
on Iona was de-
stroyed on more
than one occa-
sion by Vikings,
but it was always
rebuilt. About
1200 Reginald
MacDonald
founded a Bene-
dictine monas-
tery on the site of
the old abbey.
The chancel and
parts of the 13th
c. Norman chapel
are still intact.

★Abbey

The "Street of the
Dead" runs west-
ward to St Oran's
Cemetery, Scot-
land's oldest
Christian grave
yard, where
many Scottish
kings are buried,
and then on to
MacLean's Cross,
a richly deco-
rated 11ft/3.35m
stone cross (15th
c.). Among the
graves of proba-
bly more than 60
Scottish kings are
those of Kenneth
MacAlpin, who
unified Scotland,
Macbeth and his
victim Duncan;
all the tomb-

St Oran's
Cemetery
(Reilig Odhrain)
and MacLean's
Cross

stones, however, were thrown into the sea at the time of the Reformation.

The St Oran Chapel in the graveyard is the oldest building on the island. It
was probably built in the late 11th c. at the behest of Margaret, the wife of
Malcolm Canmore, on the site of St Columba's church.

St Oran Chapel

Opposite the west portal of the cathedral stands the imposing St Martin's
Cross (10th c.). This 14ft/4.27m Celtic cross was built as a memorial to St
Martin of Tours. The much-admired sculpture shows figures, animals and
the holy family.

★St Martin's
Cross

This red granite building which was started in the 12th c. is predominantly
Norman in style, but it has been enlarged on several occasions and so
displays a number of different styles. The oldest part of the cathedral is the
northern transept. The square tower (70ft/21.34m) rises up at the intersec-
tion of the nave and transept and is supported by four Norman arches. The

St Mary

Map of the Hebrides showing the Outer Hebrides (Isle of Lewis, Barvas, Stornoway, Harris, Tarbert, Leverburgh, North Uist, Lochmaddy, Benbecula, South Uist, Lochboisdale, Barra, Castlebay) across The Minch, and the Inner Hebrides (Isle of Skye, Uig, Dunvegan, Portree, Kyleakin, Armadale, Canna, Rhum, Eigg, Muck, Coll, Tiree, Tobermory, Staffa, Iona, Isle of Mull, Craignure, Colonsay, Jura, Port Askaig, Feolin, Islay, Port Ellen) in the Sea of the Hebrides. Scale 50 km / 31 mi. © Baedeker

233

ornately decorated column capitals in the chancel show demonic figures, floral ornamentation and biblical motifs. The adjoining convent and other buildings which were formerly part of the cathedral have been restored by the Iona community, a charitable organisation embracing many faiths, whose members live and work on the island during the summer.

Staffa

★ Basalt
rock formations

The tiny island of Staffa (6 miles/9.6km north-east of Iona) now belongs to the National Trust for Scotland. It can only be reached from Mull or Iona when the weather is fine. This uninhabited island is famed for its unusual black basalt rock formations which were formed by a huge volcanic eruption during the Tertiary Era about 70 million years ago. Theodor Fontane a German writer who visited the island in 1860 described Staffa thus: "When the god Vulcan's work was done and he had brought the tens and hundreds of thousands of basalt columns into the world, Staffa stood there like a tightly-bound bundle of stone pine trees, but the ocean, that has reigned with absolute power and washed these parts from the beginning of time, was angered by the new arrival from the underworld and began to exercise its superior might. Whole pieces and halves were torn down and washed away, and so emerged, depending on the extent and nature of the destruction, the embankments and cave formations which are peculiar to this island".

★★ Fingal's Cave

The vast Fingal's Cave is certainly the highlight of an excursion to Staffa. Discovered by the explorer Sir Joseph Banks in 1772, this geological marvel extends for 227ft/69m. It resembles a cathedral with bizarre basalt pillars and vast ribbed columns in magnificent colours. The name derives from Fingal, the mythical Celtic figure and the father of Ossian who was popularised by James Macpherson of Kingussie (see Cairngorm Mountains, Kingussie) in his epic poem. Its Celtic name is "An Uaimh Binn" meaning "musical cave", a reference to the droning echo of the waves that crash against the dark cavern walls. This dramatic scene has inspired poets, painters and composers with William Wordsworth, Lord Tennyson, Sir Walter Scott, William Blake, Herder and Brahms among the most celebrated artists to come under its spell. Felix Mendelssohn-Bartholdy visited Staffa in August 1829 and went on to write his Hebrides Overture. Three years later William Turner was moved to express the clash of the elements on canvas.

Coll and Tiree

On the treeless islands of Coll and Tiree, accessible by plane or by car ferry (see Practical Information, Ferries) from Tobermory (Mull), Gaelic is the principal language of the inhabitants. The breakers that roll in from the Atlantic attract surfers who often have the broad sandy beaches to themselves.

Islay

Access

The islands of Islay and Jura formed from schist and Torridon sandstone are separated by the ½ mile/0.8km wide Sound of Islay (car ferry) and often seem like one island. They can be reached from Oban (see entry) via the island of Colonsay or, more quickly and more easily, from West Tarbert on the Kintyre peninsula (car ferries to Port Askaig and Port Ellen; see Practical Information, Ferries).

Islay (pop. 4000) lies at the southern end of the Inner Hebrides and is characterised by unspoilt scenery, picturesque rocky reefs, bays and sandy beaches. Historic monuments include a number of Celtic crosses and two abandoned castles – Finlaggan Castle the former seat of the "Lord of the Isles" near Port Askaig in the north and Dunyvaig Castle on the coast near Ardbeg in the south. Bathing and angling are popular pursuits with visitors and the Machrie golf course near Port Ellen is used for tournaments.

The 18th c. round church at Bowmore, Islay

Laphroaig Distillery, Port Ellen

Pot still at Bowmore Distillery

The Paps of Jura from Islay's Port Askaig

Bowmore
Round Church

The island's main town is Bowmore (pop. 800). Its most interesting feature is the Kilarrow parish church built in 1769 by Thomas Spalding. The Campbells of Shawfield commissioned it as part of a planned settlement and it is the only round church from this period. According to legend the round walls prevented the devil from hiding away in a corner.

★Distillery

The renovated distillery at the north end of Bowmore dates back over 200 years. Self-malting barley and the peaty water of the River Loggan combine to give the whisky produced here a distinctive character (open: Mon.–Fri. from 10am; see Baedeker Special "Scotch Whisky").

★Kildalton Cross

Dating from the 9th or 10th c. the Kildalton Cross 2 miles/3km north-east of Port Ellen is one of the best preserved crosses in Scotland.

★Other whisky distilleries

Islay is home to a number of famous distilleries where distinctive malt whiskies are produced. Bruichladdich, the westernmost distillery in Scotland, was founded in 1881 and produces a lighter spirit imbued with the scent of the sea, as does Bunnahabhain near Port Askaig at the northeastern tip of the island where the River Margadale flows into the sea. The Caol Ila distillery is also situated here and is noted for a very peaty single malt with a hint of seaweed. At Stillhouse there is a magnificent view over the Sound of Islay to Jura. Around Port Ellen at the southern tip of the island are some of the top distilleries in Scotland: Ardbeg which was reopened in 1989, Lagavulin, producer of one of the six "Classic Malts" and Laphroaig, noted for its smoky, peaty malt with a touch of sherry (see Baedeker Special "Scotch Whisky").

Jura

Some 30 miles/48km long and 7 miles/11.2km wide, this almost treeless island has until recently attracted few tourists. The word "Jura" means "stag island" a reference to the large red deer population. Jura's highest

★The Paps

point on the island is the double peak known as "The Paps" (a vulgar

Scottish word meaning "breasts"; 2571ft/784m). The best place to start an ascent of The Paps is from Feolin where the ferry arrives. In Barnhill at the north end of the island Eric Blair, alias George Orwell, wrote "1984", his satire of a totalitarian state (published in 1949). The "Isle of Jura" distillery near Craighouse began producing black malt in the 16th c. but in 1963 the new plant started making a lighter variety.

A narrow channel separates the two Hebridean islands of Colonsay and Oronsay, which were named after St Columba and St Oran (car ferry from Oban or Port Askaig/Islay, see Practical Information, Ferries). Wildlife on Colonsay include otters, seals and sea birds, while at Kiloran Gardens rhododendrons, mimosas, eucalyptus and magnolia thrive in the mild climate (open daily).

Colonsay
Kiloran Gardens

At low tide it is possible to walk across to Oronsay in about two hours. On the island look out for the ruins of a 14th c. priory with an unusual 16th c. cross and the finds from a Viking grave in which a man was buried in his boat with his horse beside him.

Oronsay

Eigg, Muck, Rhum and Canna (see Practical Information, Ferries) form a little group of islands to the south of Skye but few people live there today. The small volcanic island of Canna probably ranks as the prettiest. Compass Hill in the north-east was regarded with suspicion by mariners as the high iron content in the rock distorted compass readings and ships unwittingly took a wrong course.

Small islands

Canna

A geological curiosity is the main attraction on Eigg: the Sguir or Sgurr consists of pitchstone pillars which soar 1300ft/400m out of the solid rock. In view of the island's range of rare fauna such as red deer, Manx shearwaters and sea eagles, Rhum was declared a protected area by UNESCO in the 1980s. Kinloch Castle is a grand hotel that was built at the turn of the century for Sir George Bullough.

Eigg

★Rhum

Outer Hebrides · Western Isles (Nah-Eileanan Siar)

The gneiss and granite of the windy and weatherbeaten islands of the Outer Hebrides are, in geological terms, an extension of the mainland. These hilly and mainly treeless islands display a rugged beauty with the layer of peat above the barren topsoil a prominent feature. The landscape to the east is typified by expanses of moorland and heather, while the western coasts which are exposed to the Atlantic winds can boast unspoilt white, sandy beaches. The characteristic sand-blown machair pastures that have been used for centuries by crofters not only as grazing land but also for cultivating oats and potatoes are mainly found on the western side of the islands. The Hebrides are popular chiefly with nature-lovers, anglers and archaeologists who have uncovered some unique pre-historic remains here.

★★Topography

Altogether there are 12 inhabited islands: Lewis and Harris, Bernera, Scalpay, Berneray, North Uist, Baleshare, Grimsay, Benbecula, South Uist, Eriskay, Barra and Vatersay. Together they support a population of about 31,000. Since 1974 the islands have been administered by the Comhairle nan Eilean in Stornoway. The people of the Western Isles, most of whom speak both English and Gaelic, are descended from the Celts. In the 9th c. the Vikings occupied the islands and retained them until 1280 when Norway handed them back to the Scottish kings under the Treaty of Perth. Cultural traditions have been passed down through the generations via the music played for celebrations such as the feisans, mods and ceilidhs. Fishing, agriculture, salmon farming, tourism and Harris tweed provide the inhabitants with their livelihood.

Population

Up until 1885 the farmers, shepherds and fishermen on the Western Isles were given practically no rights by their landlords. Anyone who did not fit

Crofters

in would be driven from his land by the so-called inspectors. Many of the wealthy lords and merchants who discovered the islands for themselves in the 19th c. and bought out the clan chiefs showed little concern for the native crofters. Famine followed and in some parts of the islands emigration left whole villages deserted. The "Small Crofters (Scotland) Act" of 1885 protected the islanders from eviction.

Warning

Although most road signs show English and Gaelic place names, since the renaissance of the Gaelic language on the Western Isles it is not uncommon to find signs written in Gaelic only and a detailed bilingual map will prove invaluable.

Lewis (Leodhais)

Stornaway (Steornabhagh)

There is only one town on Lewis the northernmost of the Western Isles. Stornaway (pop. 7500) dates from the 17th c. when it was established by the Clan MacKenzie of Seaforth. Its natural harbour is an important centre for the fishing industry. Rigs for the offshore oil industry are fabricated at Arnish Point. Regular flights link Stornaway Airport with Glasgow (see entry). Loganair run services onward to Benbecula and Barra. Buses serve the outlying villages on the island. See Practical Information, Ferries.

Castle

Stornaway Castle dates from the middle of the 19th c. and was once the home of Lord Leverhulme the founder of one of Britain's biggest soap manufacturers (now Unilever). He acquired the islands of Lewis and Harris from Duncan Matheson in 1918 with the aim of setting up a modern fishing fleet. The idea was to transport fresh fish by road and rail to Harris where it could be processed for sale in the main Scottish centres of population. However, Lord Leverhulme's innovative project was not welcomed by the locals and in 1923 he was forced to abandon the scheme. He then set up a

Stornaway Castle, once owned by Lord Leverhulme

Callanish Stone Circle, Lewis

trust fund for Stornaway and sold the rest of the islands. The castle is now used as a technical college.

A museum in Francis Street displays archaeological finds and documents the history of the fishing industry and the traditional way of life on Lewis (open: June–Aug. Tues.–Sat. 10am–12.30pm, 2–5.30pm; Sept.–May, Tues.–Sat. 2–5pm).

Museum nan Eilean

The mystery of the Standing Stones of Callanish (HS) has yet to be resolved. Probably the finest stone circle in Scotland, it lies about 12 miles/24km west of Stornaway. The site has been dated at between 3000 and 1500 B.C. during the Late Bronze Age or Early Iron Age. The monument consists of 47 stones arranged in a circle and also in lines radiating from the centre thereby creating a Celtic cross. The northward line (268ft/82m) consists of nineteen monoliths up to a height of 12ft/3.6m, the eastward line (75ft/23m) has five, the westward line (42ft/13m) four and the southward line (91ft/27.8m) five. In the centre stands a 15ft/4.75m high megalith weighing about 5 tons surrounded by a ring of thirteen stones (diameter 36–43ft/11–13m). The stone circle is thought to have the same function as Stonehenge in England and Carnac in Brittany: as a focal point for sun worship and to calculate the time of year. At the equinoxes, for example, the sun goes down directly behind the westward line. A burial chamber has been discovered near the central stone.

★★ Standing Stones of Callanish

By the west coast stands Dun Carloway Broch (16 miles/25.6km north-west of Stornaway). This Pictish fortified farm dates from the 4th c. B.C. It stands at a height of about 164ft/50m above sea level and measures 52ft/16m in diameter. The double walls are 10ft/3m thick in places and on one side they reach a height of 33ft/10m. Several steps form a link inside the mortar-free double walls and four chambers can be made out within the inner wall (HS).

★ Dun Carloway Broch

Traditional Black House, Arnol, Lewis

Shawbost Folk Museum	The A858 follows the coast northwards to Shawbost Museum which documents the islanders' traditional way of life (open: Apr.–Nov. Mon.–Sat. 10am–6pm).
★Black House	The term "Black House" (Gaelic = "tigh dubh") was first used *c.* 1850 when the whitewashed exterior common on the mainland gained a foothold on the islands. This style contrasted sharply with the dark, dry-stone double-walled Hebridean houses roofed with thatch, where man and beast sought protection from the elements together. The Black House near Arnol dates from the mid-19th c. and was inhabited until 1979. It has been faithfully restored and now serves as a tearoom and craft centre.
Steinacleit Cairn	Further north a group of stones arranged in an oval can be seen near Ballantrushal. These standing stones are thought to date from the 3rd or 2nd millennium B.C.
★Butt of Lewis	The black rocks at the exposed northern tip of the Western Isles are formed from Pre-Cambrian gneiss.
Harris (Na Hearadh) Tarbert, Clisham	The A859 heads south-west from Stornaway to Tarbert, Harris' main town (pop. 500). Ferries arrive here from Uig (Skye) and also from the Western Isles further south. On a clear day it is possible to see the Scottish mainland from Clisham, the Outer Hebrides' highest mountain (2622ft/800m). It is within easy reach of Tarbert and presents few difficulties for walkers.
★Sound of Taransay	The A859 continues south before returning to the wild western coast and passing the idyllic sandy beaches which overlook the Sound of Taransay. Scarp, an island off Hushinish Point, was the scene of a bizarre experiment in 1934. A German by the name of Zucker attempted to convey the island's post to Harris in a home-made rocket. The prototype exploded on landing and further experiments were abandoned.

Lonely beach, Sound of Taransay, Harris

The island sheep – usually a cross-breed of Blackface and Cheviot – graze outside throughout the year. Coloured brands on the fleece or cuts in the ear indicate the owner. Ewes and castrated rams are allowed to roam free, but other rams are not allowed to mingle with the ewes until the second half of November so that the lambs are born after the winter storms. Shearing begins in the middle of summer and the shearers must follow the guidelines of the wool board. All fleeces that are not sold to buyers from the mainland are kept on the island for the production of the famous Harris Tweed (from the French "toile" meaning "cloth").

★Harris Tweed
(Clo Mhor)

Until the mid-19th c. tweed (or "clo mhor" meaning "large cloth") as the Gaelic-speaking Hebrideans call it) was produced in sufficient quantities to meet the needs of the local people but, during the famine of 1840, Lady Dunmore who owned large parts of Harris succeeded in interesting the Victorian gentry in tweed and it soon became the fashion among sporting men and women. The first tweed mill opened on Harris in 1900. Some 20 years later the wooden loom was replaced by the iron Hattersley model which is still widely used today.

The co-ordination of colours (created mainly by plant dyes made from mosses), carding and spinning are all under the control of the Harris Tweed Authority which has held the marketing right since 1930. Almost 75% of the hard-wearing material is exported. For a garment to show the coveted Harris tweed symbol of a globe and Maltese Cross, wool from Scottish sheep must be used and the material must be hand-woven by islanders.

The hamlet of Rodel lies at the southernmost point of Harris and the tiny St Clement chapel which was built *c.* 1500 and restored in the 18th c. is certainly worth a visit. The remains of Alasdair Crotach, one of the famous MacLeods, lie beneath a splendid black slate stone. He commissioned the gravestone in 1528, nineteen years before his death (HS).

Rodel
St Clement

North Uist – Benbecula – South Uist

North Uist
Uibhist a Tuath

★ Topography

To the south of the Sound of Harris lies North Uist (pop. 2200) which is linked to Benbecula and South Uist by causeways. The rugged landscape is dotted with countless lakes, some saltwater and some fresh. With so many bays and inlets, the coastline extends for just under 360 miles/580km. Birdwatchers make up a large proportion of the island's visitors as diving birds, teal and shovelers are among the species that breed by the lochs. North Uist can also boast red deer, otters and seals and anglers will find the rivers and lakes well stocked. The inhabitants of North Uist live off the land and produce woollen goods to supplement their earnings. Seaweed is plentiful on the sandy beaches and some residents collect it to use as a fertiliser.

Lochmaddy
(Loch nam Madadh)

The main town on North Uist is Lochmaddy (pop. 1800). Ferries from Uig (Skye) arrive here and it is an important centre for the southern isles. A road runs from Lochmaddy to Carinish in the south-west of the island and then crosses a causeway (1960) through the North Ford to Benbecula.

Benbecula
(Beinn na Faoghla)

Benbecula (pop. 2000) lies between North and South Uist. Planes from Balivanich Airport serve Glasgow (see entry), Stornaway (Lewis) and Barra. Culla Bay has probably the finest beach on the island.

South Uist
(Uibhist a Deas)
Lochboisdale
(Loch Baghasdail)

South Uist (pop. 3000) is the second-largest island in the Outer Hebrides and the main town is Lochboisdale (pop. 300) where in the summer the harbour receives ferries from Oban.

Our Lady of the Isles

A good road runs from north to south. One of the first landmarks is Reuval Hill with its 33ft/10m high Madonna, designed by Hew Lorimer in 1930.

Loch Druidibeg Reserve

Loch Druidibeg Bird Reserve lies at the foot of the hill. It is one of the few places where greylag geese breed.

Flora MacDonald's birthplace

A popular destination is the house near Askernish where Flora MacDonald was born. She is best known for her bravery in helping "Bonnie Prince Charlie" to escape from the English in 1746. A memorial to the courageous heroine stands in the ruined cottage (see Baedeker Special "The Prince and the Hebridean Girl").

Eriskay

It was at Eriskay on June 23rd 1745 that "Bonnie Prince Charlie" first set foot on Scottish soil. The tiny island off the southern tip of South Uist can be reached by passenger ferry from Ludag (see Practical Information, Ferries). In 1941 the "SS Politician" sank with a cargo of 20,000 crates of whisky which the inhabitants rapidly concealed. The full story was told in the film "Whisky Galore".

Gaelic Emigrants' Song

Tìr a'mhurain, tìr an eòrna,
Tìr's am pailt a h'uile seòrsa,
Far am bi na gillean òga
Gabhail òran 's 'gòl an leanna . . .

Nam biodh agam fhìn do stòras,
Dà dheis aodaich, paidhir bhrògan.
Agus m'fharadh bhith 'nam phòca,
'S ann air Uibhist dheannainn seòladh.

Land of bent grass,
    Land of barley,
Land, where everything is abundant,
Where young men sing songs
And drink ale . . .

If only I had two suits,
A pair of shoes
And the money in my pocket
    for the fare
I would set sail for Uist forthwith.

Barra
(Barraigh)

Car ferries sail from Oban (see entry) and Lochboisdale (South Uist). There is also a passenger ferry from Ludag (South Uist). During low tide planes land at the airport on Cockle Beach (Tràigh Mhór). Anglers head for the trout-rich lochs that lie at the foot of Ben Heaval (1260ft/384m). The main town of Castlebay (pop. 1300) was once a flourishing herring port, but the fishermen now go in search of lobsters and prawns.

Castlebay
(Bagh a Chaisteil)

The medieval Kisimul Castle perches on a rock in the middle of the bay. The clan McNeil of Barra, who made a name for themselves as skilled seafarers and feared pirates, lived here from 1314, but the building was ruined by fire at the end of the 18th c. In 1938 the 45th clan chief, an American architect, returned it to its original condition (open: May–Sept. Wed., Sat. afternoon).

Kisimul Castle

Although the scenery is similar to Barra, deserted beaches and bizarre rock formations characterise the coastlines of the small islands that lie to the south: Vatersay (Bhatarsaigh), Sandray (Sanndraigh), Pabbay (Pataigh), Mingulay (Miu' Laigh) and Berneray (Bearnaraigh) with Barra Head (Ceann Barraigh) marking the southern tip.

Vatersay.
Sandray, Pabbay,
Mingulay,
Berneray

Inverness

E 4

Region: Highland. Population: 42,000

Inverness is the administrative centre for the Highland region, which consists of the old counties of Inverness, Nairn, Ross and Cromarty, Sutherland and Caithness. The town has benefited from its sheltered position at the mouth of the Moray Firth and at the north-eastern end of the Caledonian Canal. In the 6th c. Inverness was the residence of Pictish kings and in 565 St Columba visited the town to pay his respects to Brude, king of the Picts. Given the town's favourable location at the gateway to the North-West Highlands (see entry), Inverness has become a busy tourist centre and it makes a good starting point for excursions.

Situation and
characteristics

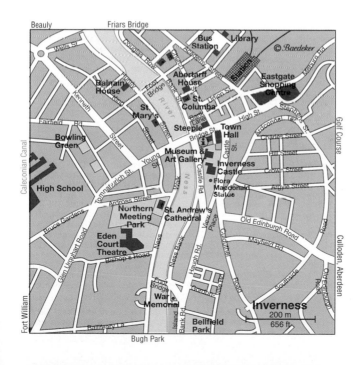

Sights

Castle

It is said that Duncan was killed by Macbeth in the old fortress which lay to the east of the present castle, but Cawdor Castle (see Surroundings) or Glamis Castle north of Dundee (see entry) may have witnessed the cruel deed that Shakespeare immortalised. The first castle was built by David I in the middle of the 12th c. but some 500 years later Cromwell ordered his men to build a stone castle on the same site. In 1715 James Francis Edward was proclaimed king there and the last time it was under Jacobite control was during the short reign of "Bonnie Prince Charlie" in 1745. After the Battle of Culloden (see entry) when the "Young Pretender" was defeated, the Duke of Cumberland ordered it to be burnt to the ground. The present Victorian castle was erected during the first half of the 19th c. and the premises are now used as offices.

Flora MacDonald Statue

★Museum and Art Gallery

A statue on the Esplanade recalls the part Flora MacDonald played in helping "Bonnie Prince Charlie" to escape through enemy lines after the disaster at Culloden (see Baedeker Special, "The Prince and the Hebridean Girl"). The nearby museum on Castle Wynd illustrates the town's rich cultural heritage and also the history of the Highlands (open: Mon.–Sat. 9am–5pm; July, Aug. also Sun. 2–5pm).

St Andrew's Cathedral

The Neo-Gothic St Andrew's Cathedral (1866–69), designed by Alexander Ross, stands opposite Castle Hill on the banks of the Ness.

★Abertarff House

Church Street can boast the town's oldest building, Abertarff House, which was built as a town residence for the Lovat family in 1592. Note the remarkable outside staircase. It was restored by the National Trust for Scotland in 1966 and it now serves as their Highlands region head office. The Highland Association, an organisation whose aim is to advance the Gaelic culture and language, is also based at the house.

★Balnain House Home of Highland Music

At No. 40 Huntly Street the musical tradition of the Highlands is comprehensively documented from the earliest days right up to the present. Visitors are encouraged to try their hand at playing the bagpipes, the fiddle or the harp, as well as sampling the whole range of traditional Scottish fare from the much-vaunted haggis to oatcakes (open: Tues.–Sun. 10am–5pm, July and Aug. also Mon.).

Surroundings

North-West Highlands

See entry

Culloden

See entry

★★Cawdor Castle

Open:
May–1st Sun.
in Oct. daily,
10am–5.30pm

Cawdor Castle is situated almost 10 miles/16km north-east of the Culloden battlefield (see entry) by the B9090. It was here, according to Shakespeare, that in 1040 Macbeth, the "Thane of Cawdor", murdered Duncan but this contradicts the fact that Cawdor Castle was not built until the mid-14th to 15th c. and that Duncan was murdered by Macbeth in the Battle of Elgin. The theory that the murder was committed at Glamis Castle near Dundee (see entry) does not stand up to close scrutiny either. In the 16th and 17th c. the medieval central tower (1372) was extended and altered. A large collection of Shakespearean literature and some fine period furniture such as the Venetian four-poster bed in the bedchamber form part of this fairy-tale castle that is now owned by the Campbell family. A hawthorn tree dated at 1370 acted, according to legend, as a sign to the first thane to build a castle here. In the grounds a garden with colourful flower-beds is well worth a visit. There are also nature trails and a nine-hole golf course.

Royal Brackla Distillery

The nearby whisky distillery (founded in 1812) is one of only three distilleries in Scotland which has the prefix "Royal". It was William IV who granted the company this much-prized title in 1835.

Cawdor Castle, immortalised by Shakespeare in "Macbeth"

The pretty resort of Nairn (pop. 10,200; 14 miles/22.4km north-east of Inverness) lies at the mouth of the River Nairn and overlooks the Moray Firth. Several golf courses are within easy reach of the town which also boasts a long sandy beach. Fishertown Museum in King Street documents the rise and fall of the herring industry using models and old photographs (open: May–Sept. Mon.–Sat. 2.30 4.30pm, Mon., Wed., Fri. also 6.30–8.30pm)

★Nairn
Fishertown
Museum

After the Battle of Culloden (1746) a huge artillery fortress was built on a headland west of Nairn in order to keep the defeated Highlanders in check. As well as extensive military installations, the fort also houses the regimental museum of the Queen's Own Highlanders (HS; open: Apr.–Sept. Mon.–Sat. 9.30am–6pm, Sun. 2–6pm; Oct.–Mar. Mon.–Sat. 9.30am–4pm, Sun. 2–4pm).

★Fort George

Kintyre

D 6

Region: Strathclyde

To the west of the island of Arran (see entry) lies the beautiful Kintyre peninsula. It can be reached by car from the north via the A83 or by ferry from Lochranza/Arran to Claonaig/Kintyre and from Portavadie/Cowal to Tarbert/Kintyre (see Practical Information, Ferries)

Situation and access

★Tour

Skipness Castle stands just north of Claonaig Bay where the ferries from Arran arrive. This 13th c. border fortress built for the Campbell clan offers a fine view over the Kilbrannan Sound.

Skipness Castle

Unspoilt Kintyre, looking towards Arran

Carradale Garden	The B842 follows the largely unspoilt east coast south to the fishing village of Carradale (25 miles/40km). There are some fine walks in the area and Carradale Garden is noted for its rhododendrons and azaleas.
Saddell Abbey	Saddell Abbey was founded *c.* 1160 by Somerled Lord of the Isles. Parts of the walls remain and a number of finely decorated gravestones are worth a closer look.
Campbeltown	Campbeltown, Kintyre's main town (pop. 6200), was once the seat of the Campbells of Argyle. During the 18th/19th c. the town flourished thanks to the coal, whisky production and fishing industries. The local Springbank Distillery still produces a fine malt whisky. Sir William MacKinnon (1823–93) is one of Campbeltown's most famous sons. He was the founder of the British East Africa Company. Another famous Campbeltowner was William McTaggart (1855–1910) the Impressionist landscape painter.
★Machrihanish Golf Course	The golf course at Machrihanish (5 miles/8km to the west) enjoys a magnificent location.
Southend Columba's Footsteps	A footprint said to have been made by St Columba when she first set foot on Scottish soil can be seen in Carskey Bay near Southend (10 miles/16km south of Campbeltown).
★Mull of Kintyre	The southern tip of the peninsula immortalised in Paul McCartney's song is marked by a lighthouse. It lies 7 miles/11km west of Southend and on a clear day it is possible to see the coast of Antrim in Northern Ireland. The Gaelic word "mull" means "foothills".
★MacAlister Clan Centre	The A83 follows the west coast past the home of Laird and Lady Glenbarr (Mr and Mrs MacAlister) who personally show visitors round the fine 18th/19th c. mansion and recount the full history of the MacAlister clan.

Campeltown Loch . . .   *. . . and the MacAlister Clan Centre*

Kilts, plaids, old toys, Sèvres porcelain, the laird's valuable collection of thimbles, family memorabilia and gloves belonging to Mary Stuart are among the exhibits (open: Easter–mid-Oct. Wed.–Mon. 10am–6pm).

Ferries leave Tayinloan for Ardminish on the small green island of Gigha (see Practical Information, Ferries). Achamore House Gardens and their collection of sub-tropical plants are the principal attraction on the island (open: daily, from 10am).

Gigha Island
★Achamore
Gardens

The watersport centre of Tarbert situated beyond Kennacraig and between West Loch Tarbert and Loch Fyne is the departure point for ferries to Islay (see Hebrides). It was once an important herring port.

Tarbert

Loch Lomond, Loch Katrine and the Trossachs

E 5

The idyllic Loch Lomond north-west of Glasgow (see entry) is Britain's largest lake and according to Walter Scott "The Queen of Scottish Lakes". While the plentiful stocks of trout, salmon and whitefish attract anglers from far afield, the many day-trippers, not to mention the watersports enthusiasts, walkers and those in search of rest and relaxation are drawn by the wonderful scenery around the lake. Boat trips on the "Maid of the Loch" give visitors a chance to admire the beauty of the lake and its surroundings. It is possible to climb Ben Lomond (3192ft/973m) from Rowardennen and appreciate the waters from a different angle as well as admire the views to the east. Loch Lomond is often the first stop for tourists heading north along the Western Highland Way which runs from Glasgow through the beautiful Argyll countryside to Fort William (see entry). Cameron House at the south end of Loch Lomond is an excellent place to savour the romance of a Scottish castle, breathe in the lakeside air and

★★Loch Lomond

Loch Lomond, Loch Katrine and the Trossachs

The "bonnie banks" of Loch Lomond

enjoy a wide range of outdoor activities (see Practical Information from A to Z, Castles and country hotels).

On the bonnie, bonnie banks o' Loch Lomond

An old folk song about Loch Lomond which is sung the world over is one reason why the lake attracts so many sightseers. The verses tell of two Scottish soldiers after the Jacobite uprising of 1745. One is said to have been executed in Carlisle, but the other was free to roam the "bonnie, bonnie banks o' Loch Lomond". This "national anthem" came to symbolise the melancholy of homesick Scottish emigrants.

Balloch Castle

The parklands of Balloch Castle are situated on the east bank of the lake and on the ground floor a museum documents the development of the region (open: Easter–Sept. daily, 10am–6pm).

★Queen Elizabeth Forest Park

A large area of land between Loch Lomond and the Trossachs has been in the hands of the Forestry Commission since 1928. Footpaths, cycleways, nature trails and shelters are just some of the facilities available for those wishing to explore the beautiful countryside (Information centre 1 mile/ 1.6km north of Aberfoyle; tel. (018772) 258). The splendid woodland areas of Ardgartan, Benmore and Glenbranter encompass about 60,000 acres/24,000 ha.

★★Trossachs

To the north-east of Loch Lomond lie the Trossachs, another recreational area that is popular with Glaswegians. This picturesque valley that nestles between Loch Katrine and Loch Achray and the peaks of Ben An and Ben Venue is only an hour's drive from Scotland's most densely populated region. "Trossachs" means something like "bristly area". At the beginning of the 19th c. the English poets Taylor Coleridge and William Wordsworth and his sister Dorothy visited the valley and found inspiration for their romantic verse. In 1803 Dorothy Wordsworth wrote in her diary: "Here we were completely alone and everything that we saw was loveliness and beauty in perfection". Seven years later the historic novelist Sir Walter Scott (see Famous People) was bewitched by the beauty of the Trossachs. The densely wooded gorges and the history of the MacGregors provided him with the setting for the "Lady of the Lake". The lady in question was Ellen Douglas who while fleeing from the king's sheriffs with her father seeks refuge with Roderick, the MacGregor clan chief, on an island in Loch Katrine. While out on a hunting expedition King James loses his way and finds shelter with Ellen who is not aware of his identity. A bitter struggle between the king and Roderick ensues but, despite all the intrigues, the story has a happy ending. The romance became a bestseller for Scott and Queen Victoria's visit to the valley has ensured that the Trossachs and Lake Katrine would remain universally popular.

"Lady of the Lake"

This lake's name is probably derived from the lawless "Catterin" family who once brought fear to the lakeside's inhabitants. The tiny island at the eastern end is known as Ellen's Island after the heroine in Scott's "Lady of the Lake". "Sir Walter Scott", a steamer that made its maiden voyage in 1900, offers trips on the loch, leaving the Trossachs Pier three times a day (twice on Sat.). The pier is also a popular base for walks up into the hills from which there are spectacular views.

★★ **Loch Katrine**

Greater Glasgow's drinking water is supplied by this lake and consequently windsurfing, swimming, fishing and boating are not permitted. Some rare breeds of waterfowl have taken advantage of the peace and quiet along the banks and they should not be disturbed.

Rob Roy is another historical figure who is closely linked with the Trossachs. Thanks to Scott's novel, the red-haired outlaw by the name of Robert MacGregor, or Rob Roy, became a sort of Scottish Robin Hood who like his English counterpart stole from the rich and gave to the poor. MacGregor was actually a cattle dealer but as he owed money to the Duke of Montrose, the latter seized MacGregor's house and evicted the family. Rob Roy was forced to flee into the mountains and was initially despised by the people, but he

won respect as he roamed the countryside symbolically avenging the dispossessed. In 1995 Hollywood produced a film based on his exploits, with Liam Neeson in the title role. Contrary to most assumptions, Rob Roy died peacefully in his bed in 1734 and he is buried in the cemetery at Balquhidder by Loch Voil a few miles north of the Trossachs.

The Rob Roy and Trossachs Visitor Centre is situated at Ancaster Square in Callander to the east of Loch Venachar. Displays in the centre provide a detailed explanation of the background to the Rob Roy legend and also the history of the Trossachs (open: Mar.–May, Oct.–Dec. daily, 10am–5pm; June and Sept. daily, 9.30am–6pm; July–Aug. daily, 9am–10pm).

Callander
★ Rob Roy and Trossachs Visitor Centre

Malt Whisky Trail

F 4

Region: Grampian

The justification for the 1994 celebration of 500 years of Scottish whisky was provided by the "Scottish Exchequer Roll" of 1494. At the behest of James IV, a monk by the name of John Cor was supplied with eight "bolls" of malted barley for the production of aqua vitae. Initially administered as a medicine, this powerful "water of life" soon developed into the Highlanders' everyday drink.

Liquid Gold

Pot stills at the Glenfarclas Distillery

According to the "Chronicles of England, Scotland, Ireland" published in 1578, the spirit will "if consumed in moderate quantities lengthen old age and retain youth, drive away melancholy and bring relief to heart and mind". Now the highly-taxed beverage brings in well over one billion pounds to the British exchequer and, after Scotland's other liquid gold, North Sea oil, it is the country's most valuable export.

Speyside Whisky

For many serious whisky drinkers, Speyside is almost synonymous with "Scotch". The "Golden Triangle" formed by Grantown-on-Spey, Elgin and Dufftown/Keith contains the highest concentrations of malt whisky distilleries in the world. Cardhu, Glenfiddich, Glenlivet, Glen Grant and Glenfarclas are just some of the famous names associated with the Spey valley region.

Devotees of the "uisge beatha" would do well to follow the signposted Malt Whisky Trail (68 miles/110km). Many of the distilleries on this circuit are still family concerns. Each of the old distilleries has a different way of welcoming guests, but all allow them to sample a "wee dram" of the precious drink.

★★A selection of distilleries on the Malt Whisky Trail

Grantown-on-Spey

The pleasant town of Grantown-on-Spey on the A95 is a good base for a tour of the Spey valley. It is also noted for its eighteen-hole golf course.

Livet Valley

★The Glenlivet Distillery

In the Livet valley (10 miles/16km to the east) lies the Glenlivet distillery, housed in an early Victorian building topped with the traditional "pagodas", demonstrating the long history of this distinctive malt whisky. The finely equipped Visitor Centre recounts the "Ballad of Glenlivet". A young Highlander by the name of Thomas Smith settled here at the time of the

Some famous names: Speyside whisky labels

Jacobite uprising in 1715 and set up a small "black" distillery alongside his smallholding. In 1824 his grandson George Smith was one of the first Scots to acquire a distiller's licence and he started legally producing whisky on a farm in Upper Drumin – a decision that won him few friends among the smuggling fraternity. With the assistance of the Duke of Gordon, Smith built the Glenlivet distillery and it soon gained a reputation for producing fine whisky. Before long the farm premises proved incapable of meeting the demand so in 1858 George and his son John Gordon opened a new distillery on the present Minmore Farm site. That distillery now produces one of the leading brands of malt whisky, although in 1978 it was sold to the Canadian Seagram company (open: mid-Mar.–June, Sept., Oct. Mon.–Sat. 10am–4pm; July–Aug. Mon.–Sat. 10am–7pm).

Tamnavulin Distillery is also situated on the banks of the Livet and its six stills produce a slightly smoky flavoured single malt. A visitor centre in the picturesque old wool mill gives the distillery its name (the Gaelic "tamnavulin" means "mill on the hill"; open: Mar.–Oct. Mon.–Fri. 9.30am–4.30pm; Apr.–Sept. also Sat. 9.30am–4.30pm).

Tamnavulin Distillery

In 1869 John Smith built the small Cragganmore distillery in Ballindaloch at the confluence of the Spey and Avon. Now owned by United Distillers, Cragganmore is one of the top "classic malts" (open: Mon.–Fri. 10am–12.30pm, 1–4pm). The castle is worth a visit.

Cragganmore Distillery
Ballindaloch Castle

Glenfarclas Distillery has been in the Grant family for five generations. It is situated just south of the A95 and boasts the biggest still on Speyside. The founder of the plant in the "glen of green grassland" at the foot of Ben Rinnes was Robert Hay (1836), but in 1865 the factory was sold to John Grant. Maturation of this strong, full-bodied whisky takes ten years with the spirit stored in Spanish sherry barrels (open: Apr.–Oct. Mon.–Fri. 9am–4.30pm, June–Sept. also Sat. 10am–4pm; Nov.–Mar. Mon.–Fri. 10am–4pm).

★Glenfarclas Distillery

Cardhu Distillery was founded in 1824 by John Cumming but amalgamated with Johnnie Walker in 1893. When taken over by United Distillers in 1961, it became one of the leading brands of malt whisky. To produce the "black rock" as the word "cardhu" means in Gaelic, spring water from the Mannoch Hills is used (open: Mon.–Fri. 9.30am–4.30pm; May–Sept. also Sat. 9.30am–4.30pm).

Knockando
★Cardhu
Distillery

Tamdhu Distillery was re-opened in 1947 with Tamdhu Burn directly beneath the distillery the source for its water. The whole barley grains continue to be aired in large Saladin boxes. Tamdhu first became available as a single malt in 1976. The unusual Visitor Centre in an old station deserves a special mention (open: Apr.–Oct. Mon.–Fri. 10am–4pm; June–Sept. also Sat. 10am–4pm).

★Tamdhu
Distillery

Founded by James Duff, Dufftown (pop. 1700) was once an important centre for textiles, but with no fewer than nine distilleries it has now become Speyside's whisky capital.

Dufftown

Scotch Whisky

The origins of whisky distillation is a mystery to historians but there is some evidence that the skills were brought to Scotland by Irish monks. The earliest historical reference occurs in an order made for "eight bolls of malt" in 1494 by a monk called John Cor. The Gaelic word for the spirit is "uisge beatha" or "usque-baugh" meaning the water of life but during the 18th c. this was shortened to "usky" and later "whisk(e)y". Although a Royal Commission on the spirits industry written in 1909 always referred to "whiskey", the Oxford English Dictionary does differentiate between "Scotch whisky" and "Irish whiskey". American bourbon and Canadian rye also include an "e" in the final syllable.

The last 200 years of the whisky industry reflect something of the historical antagonism between Scotland and England. After the Act of Union in 1707, English customs officials tried to bring some sort of order to Scottish whisky production and dramatically increased the dues payable on the liquid gold, but illicit distilleries and smugglers continued to challenge the British tax authorities. Bloody altercations often occurred and in 1782 alone over 1000 "black" distillers were arrested; however, the public gave the "sma stills" moral support and every other dram of Scotch continued to come from an illegal source. The contempt for the law was brought to halt in 1823 when a fairer licensing system was introduced.

The whisky trade has always been susceptible to the economic cycle of boom and recession, but ironically the outbreak of phylloxera in the European vineyards at the end of the 19th c. helped to bring a degree of stability. One side-effect of the vine disease was the drastic reduction in the supply of brandy. The Scottish "whisky barons" such as Messrs. Walker, Dewar and Buchanan were quick to take advantage of the problems in continental Europe and made a fortune by marketing their product first in the rest of the United Kingdom and then worldwide. On the other hand, the First World War and the American Prohibition took their toll on the industry. The flat "hip flask" became popular during the Prohibition. It was an invention of the Scottish distillery workers who attached a "copper dog" or narrow tube to the barrel tap and drained off quantities of maturing whisky into special containers hidden underneath the waistband of their loose trousers. Later on, larger flasks were produced for carrying underneath a jacket and these became essential fashion items for "gentlemen" at the races or out hunting. Whisky is now "big business" and many of the whisky distillers are owned by multinational companies. The so-called "blended whiskies" have cornered the lion's share of the market, but the distinctive, pure malt whiskies have enjoyed a revival in recent years.

Although chemists are able to describe the distillation process in detail, how precisely the delicate aromas of the different spirits occur is less easy to explain and many mysteries still surround the "bottled sunlight" as George Bernard Shaw once described his favourite drink. The most important ingredient, apart from high-quality barley, is the water. Springs in the remote areas of the Highlands and Lowlands, where rainfall is high, yield water that carries a distinctly peaty flavour and even the casual whisky drinker will detect that earthy quality in the pure spirit. The first stage in malt whisky distillation is the malting when the barley grains are soaked in water and then spread out on the "malting floor" to germinate. To prevent the grains from becoming too warm they have to be turned, a task that was formerly carried out by hand with a wooden shovel but is now a mechanised process. The enzymes that form at this stage later help to convert the starch in the mash into sugar. The sprouted barley is then laid on the drying floor of the "kiln", the structure that resembles a pagoda and is now often the symbol for a whisky distillery.

Cheers!   *Slàinte mhath!*

Water content is reduced to about 3%, the germination process of the malted barley is brought to a halt and the malt dried by peat burners. The dried malt is then ground coarsely and mixed in the "mash tun" with hot water. When subjected to constant stirring the soluble starch changes into the sugar-rich "wort". This is cooled again and pumped into giant "wash backs". Yeast is added which converts the sugar into raw alcohol creating a liquid not unlike beer and with an alcohol content of 5–7%.

Now the distillation process can be started. For some unknown reason the shape of the stills and also the way in which they are heated influence the character of the single malt and every distillery retains its own traditional design. During distillation the alcohol vaporises and is then driven off through the neck of the still into what is usually a spiral cooling pipe where the vapour condenses. The end result of the first distillation are the "low wines" which have an alcohol content of almost 20%. The skill of the "stillman" lies in the second distillation as here he has to judge when to draw off the "middle cut" of about 68% alcohol content. The first and last "runnings" are returned to the "low wines" to be redistilled. The colourless spirit is poured into oak casks that have often been used previously for bourbon or sherry. It is in the old casks that the liquid acquires not just its unique aroma but also its yellowish, golden or chestnut-brown colour. However, some of the precious liquid is lost through evaporation at the sides of the casks, the so-called "angels' share". The law requires that Scotch whisky matures for at least three years in a bonded warehouse. At the bottling stage only water and alcohol caramel may be added. A good whisky will mature for eight, twelve or fourteen years.

Blended whiskies are a mixture of Scotch whisky distillates. The age given refers to the youngest constituent alcohol. To create the required a composition, the blender will take a special tulip-shaped "nosing glass" and smell whiskies from a range of Highland and Speyside malts, richly-flavoured and peaty Islay and Campbeltown malts or the softer Lowland malts. Then grain whiskies – Scottish whiskies which are produced from malted and unmalted cereals such as barley, wheat or maize – are added. De luxe blends often consist of old malt whiskies with matured grain whiskies, while vatted malts are made only from matured malt whiskies.

How to drink this highly-prized elixir has become almost an article of faith. Many people regard the addition of ice or soda as sacrilege, but in the end personal taste will determine how to sample a "wee dram" of the "water of life". If, after a good nosing, neat spirit is perhaps too much to take, then of course choose Scottish water as the best way of unlocking that unique aroma.

Glenfiddich Distillery, still a family firm

★Glenfiddich
Distillery

Since production started on Christmas Day 1887, the distillery which was founded by William Grant has remained within the family. After working for 20 years at the Mortlach Distillery, Grant purchased the land together with the Robbie Dubh spring and then with his seven sons set to work building the factory. Five generations later, the distillery continues to produce one of the best-known pure malts and it is the only company in the Highlands to bottle its whisky on the premises. The distinctive Glenfiddich bottle is triangular in shape and the label is adorned with a stag, representing the local "Valley of the Deer". As well as Glenfiddich which came to prominence in 1963 after an intensive marketing campaign that helped to revive the popularity of the Scottish single malt, William Grant & Sons Ltd also own the Balvenie Distillery opposite and Kininvie Distillery which opened in 1990. Its first single malt appeared in the shops in 1994. Visitors who tour the factory will also be treated to a film show on the production of Scotch whisky (open: Jan.–mid-Dec. Mon.–Fri. 9.30am–4.30am; Easter–mid-Oct., also Sat. 9.30am–4.30pm, Sun. noon–4.30pm).

Mortlach
Distillery

Mortlach is the oldest distillery in Dufftown. It first opened in 1823 but passed to George Cowie in 1854 and his name appears on the licence to this day. Updated several times since it opened, the distillery uses coal to heat the kilns and the traditional-style malting process is still employed (tours by prior arrangement).

Balvenie Castle

The picturesque ruins of Balvenie Castle, once the seat of the Comyns family, date from the 13th c. The fourth Earl of Atholl extended the tower house at the end of the 15th c. and added an ornate battlemented clock tower. Mary Stuart (see Famous People) is said to have stayed at the castle in 1562 and Cumberland's troops stopped off here on their way to Culloden (see entry) in 1746 (HS; open: Apr.–Sept. Mon.–Sat. 9.30am–6pm, Sun. 2–6pm).

★Auchindoun
Castle

On a lonely hill in the middle of an Iron Age fortress site about 3 miles/4.8km south-east of Dufftown stand the remains of Auchindoun Castle. A well-preserved curtain wall surrounds the L-shaped tower house which was built by Robert Cochrane in the 15th c. (HS).

Coopers can be seen at work in Craigellachie's Dufftown Road. Oak from the American states of Missouri, Kentucky and Tennessee is used in the production of wooden barrels that are expected to last for 40 years or more. Old barrels are often burnt as firewood in salmon smokehouses (open: Mon.–Fri. 9.30am–4.30pm; Easter until mid-October, also Sat. 9.30am–4.30pm).

Craigellachie
Speyside
Cooperage

The Macallan Distillery on the left bank of the Spey produces a whisky that is the colour of sherry and many regard it as the Rolls Royce of single malts. It is matured in oloroso barrels shipped from Spain and these are often used twice. Macallan is said to have acquired its first licence as early as 1824 shortly after whisky distillation became legal. The company's logo, the elegant mansion (now a guest house) on a hill overlooking the Spey, is shown in a special display box (visits by prior arrangement; tel. (01340) 871471).

Macallan
Distillery

This iron bridge (1814), the work of Thomas Telford, stands at the north end of the town. It is guarded by two stone towers and until 1973 when a new bridge was opened it was the main crossing point over the River Spey.

Telford Bridge

This handsome distillery in Charlestown of Aberlour which dates from 1826 produces a malt with a lingering, silky, flowery aftertaste. It has been owned by Pernod-Ricard since 1974. According to legend, St Dunstan once used the Aberlour springwater for baptisms (open: Mon.–Fri. 9.30am–4.30pm).

Aberlour
Distillery

The old-fashioned Strathisla Distillery in Keith (pop. 4900) still uses coal as its heat source. It was founded in 1746 under the name Milltown and along with Littlemille (Bowling/Dumbartonshire) and Glenturret (Crieff/Perthshire) is one of the oldest distilleries in the world (open: Mon.–Fri. Apr.–Sept. 9am–4pm).

Keith
★Strathisla
Distillery

Rothes (pop. 1400) can boast no fewer than five distilleries. Glen Grant malt is one of the most popular of all whiskies. The long-established distillery that was founded by James and John Grant in 1840 produces an excellent, light single malt that has held a considerable share of the international market since the beginning of this century (open: mid-Mar.–Sept. Mon.–Fri. 10am–4pm; July, Aug, also Sat. 10am–4pm).

Rothes
★Glen Grant
Distillery

New Lanark   F 6

Region: Strathclyde

The industrial village of New Lanark, now under a preservation order, lies about 35 miles/56km south-east of Glasgow (see entry) on the banks of the Clyde (see entry) which at this point has cut a broad path through the reddish sandstone. This famous settlement which was the brainchild of the social reformer Robert Owen attracted considerable attention in the early 19th c. from politicians and administrators who appreciated the effect of industrialisation on workers' living conditions.

★Model 19th c.
village

David Dale, Robert Owen's astute father-in-law, was the founder of the industrial village. Many people who met the textile merchant were impressed by both his sense of humour and inventiveness. He was born in Stewarton (Ayrshire) and later joined forces with Richard Arkwright, an English expert in mechanised weaving. In 1783 the two realised that the power of the Clyde as it descended into the Central Lowlands could be harnessed to operate Arkwright's new cotton weaving machinery. Two years later the factory was working. The children who made up almost 70% of the workforce had been brought by Dale from orphanages in Glasgow and Edinburgh and they were accommodated in what at that time were exemplary conditions.

David Dale and
Richard
Arkwright

Robert Owen

After marrying Dale's daughter Caroline, Robert Owen took over the running of the mills and by then the New Lanark cotton factory was one of the most famous in Britain. Owen was Welsh and came from a humble origins, but by the age of nineteen he was involved in the management of a textiles factory in Manchester, the citadel of early industrial capitalism. This reform-minded entrepreneur was convinced that it was in a company's interests to look after its workforce. In his opinion, good living and working conditions and a proper education boosted not only the worker's health and welfare but also the efficiency of the factory and this in turn improved the profitability of the company. For Owen social costs such as the construction of workers' homes and improvements to conditions in the workplace were an important element of investment. He saw the need for close monitoring of each worker's productivity as well as the importance of offering welfare provisions. Health insurance, free medical care and shops selling goods at cost price were just some of the innovative approaches that Owen provided for his workers. But education was as important. Owen set up a privately-financed school system known as the Institute for the Formation of Character. The premises were used both as a school and also as a cultural centre. By 1816 it employed fourteen teachers who cared for 300 children. Dancing, music and nature study were part of the broad curriculum and corporal punishment was banned. The working day was restricted by Owen to ten hours 30 minutes and he decreed that no child below the age of ten should work in the factory. Owen's commitment to worker welfare also included involvement in the movement to reform factory legislation and he played a vital part in the first British laws on protecting workers. His reformist ideas won support elsewhere and other model industrial villages were established. Success in New Lanark encouraged Owen to attempt a similar experiment with "New Harmony" in the American state of Indiana but political and religious disputes led to failure after four years. As a consequence Owen was obliged to sell his shares in the New Lanark venture.

★★Museum for
Industrial and
Social History

Open:
daily, 11am–5pm

Up to 2500 people once lived and worked in New Lanark's multi-storey homes and factories, sandstone structures with wood and cast iron supports. The production of yarn and textiles and later tent canvas, sails and fishing nets continued until 1968. The premises were then taken over by a metal processing company and began to decay but, in 1983, restoration work started and by 1990 the old industrial village was ready to be opened to the public, although the final stage is unlikely to be completed before 1996. However, New Lanark is not just a landmark in industrial and social history. About 100 flats have been renovated, weaving and dyeing continues and the old factory by the Visitor Centre in no. 3 spinning mill is to be converted into hotels, small business premises and exhibition and conference rooms.

North-West Highlands   D 5–F 3/4

Region: Highland

Situation

The term North-West Highlands usually refers to the northern third of Scotland that is separated from the rest of the country by the "Great Glen" or "Glen More". This fault line has been exploited by man to create the Caledonian Canal (see entry) which extends from the west coast to the east, from Loch Linnhe to the Moray Firth and which serves as the boundary between the North-West Highlands and the Grampian Mountains (see entry).

★★Topography

Although Great Britain's tallest peaks are found in the Caledonian range, the altitudes are low in relative terms. The movements that occurred during the Pleistocene Era resulted in the formation of low-lying land as well as the dissection of valleys. Many Ice Age fjords penetrate deep inland. The jagged coastline between Loch Shiel and Cape Wrath which receives a fierce battering from the elements is founded on the oldest layers of rock in Scotland, the crystalline Lewisian gneiss, which is between 1.4 million and 2.8 million years old. Suilven, Cul Mor, Cul Beag and Quinag are just some of the impressive rock islands of dark red or grey Torridon sandstone (800 million years old) which project out of the gneiss. Some of the peaks such as Beinn Eighe and Canisp are topped with light grey or white Cambrian quartzite. To the east of the gneiss lie expanses of Cambrian limestone (about 600–800 million years old) adjoined by a wide area of grey-black, micaceous moine schist (800–1000 million years old). The mountain ranges which generally follow a west–east line are

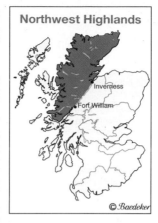

Northwest Highlands

important factors in creating the climatic differences which occur in the Highland region with its warm westerly Gulf Stream influences. Exposure to low-pressure areas from the north-west explains the high rainfall (about 80in./2000mm per year) in what is the wettest region in the country. Only the protected coastal plain around the Moray Firth, Caithness and a few wind and frost protected zones in the south-west can support intensive crop cultivation.

Environmental factors restrict the period when plants prosper. The podsolic and marshy land contains few nutrients and so only hardy plants such as the common heathers, bell heathers and also reindeer moss can survive while wild grasses grow on the upper slopes. The range of flora above limestone and moine schist is more varied. At Knockan Cliff, for example, purple foxglove, mountain avens and alpine lady's mantle thrive. Around Beinn Eighe old Scots Pine forests remain at lower altitudes, while above the tree line heather and moorland vegetation are plentiful.

Red deer, pine martens, badgers, wild cats, otters and white hare are all able to endure the harsh environment and birdwatchers come to observe willow grouse, golden plovers, whinchats, redwings, ring ouzels, corn crakes and golden eagles.

The celebrated Royal Dornach is one of a number of challenging golf courses in the Highland region, while experienced mountaineers and hillwalkers will appreciate the wild beauty of the majestic mountain landscapes – the choice ranges from coastal footpaths and woodland walks to much more demanding climbing expeditions. For many experienced fly fishermen, the Highlands is synonymous with salmon and brown trout, while the sheltered harbours, inland lakes, estuaries and inlets of the

Outdoor pursuits

My heart's in the Highlands, my Heart is not here;
My heart's in the Highlands, a-chasing the deer;
A-chasing the wild deer, and following the roe –
My heart's in the Highlands wherever I go.

Farewell to the Highlands, farewell to the North,
The birthplace of valour, the country of worth
Wherever I wander, wherever I rove,
The hills of the Highlands for ever I love.

Folk poem by Robert Burns

North-West Highlands offer amateur sailors plenty to explore. Yachts and motorboats are available for hire and there are a number of sailing schools for beginners. Other opportunities for watersport enthusiasts include skiing, windsurfing and canoeing. Sunken wrecks and a fascinating underwater world attract divers, while bathers are guaranteed crystal clear water.

Clans

See map page 23 and Baedeker Special, "Tartan, Plaid and Kilt".

Regional planning

Although for centuries emigration has plagued the Highlands region, more recently population movements have occurred within the region. In the urban areas along the Caledonian valley state-subsidised small industries have attracted workers, while communications have improved between Inverness (see entry) and Wick, encouraging population growth. In the peripheral areas, however, where there has been little investment and few opportunities for employment other than on the land, the population, particularly the younger people, has continued to drift away. Against a background of limited opportunities and the socio-economic consequences of the 19th c. Sutherland Clearances, the Highlands and Islands Development Board (HIDB) was set up in 1965 with the aim of strengthening the whole local economy. The introduction of new industries would, it was hoped, secure the long-term future of the region and stabilise the population. Initiatives have included improving the road network (with the aid of EU subsidies), helping crofters to adjust to a market economy by enabling them to buy plots of land (since 1976) and establishing competitive co-operatives to market the region's products. Inshore fishing has also received help while a forestation scheme has proved to be somewhat controversial. Tourism has been promoted especially in spring and autumn.

From Fort William to Mallaig

★Scenic route
(A830)

The A830 heads west out of Fort William (see entry) towards Mallaig (42 miles/67.2km) following a winding scenic route. Mallaig is a terminal for ferries to Skye, Rhum and Eigg (see Practical Information, Ferries). The Glenfinnan Monument at the north end of Loch Shiel (20 miles/32km) was erected in 1815 to commemorate Bonnie Prince Charlie's proclamation of August 1745. It was here that he met the clan chiefs and they agreed to back his struggle against English domination (see Baedeker Special, "The Prince and the Hebridean Girl"). A memorial stone by Loch Nan Uamh recalls the flight of the "Young Pretender" after the debacle at Culloden (see entry) and his month-long trek through the Highlands. He boarded a French ship nearby and escaped from his English pursuers.

Glenfinnan
Monument

Loch Nan
Uamh Cairn

From Fort William to Ullapool

Fort William

See entry

Caledonian Canal

See entry

★Road to the Isles
(A87)
Loch Duich
★Eilean Donan
Castle

The magnificent "Road to the Isles" branches off the A82 at Invergarry (22 miles/35.2km north-east of Fort William) and follows the romantic Glen Shiel past the "Five Sisters of Kintail" (NTS) to Kyle of Lochalsh and the new bridge over Loch Alsh to Skye (see The Hebrides). Eilean Donan Castle is one of the best known and most photogenic of

Scotland's castles. It sits on a small island in Loch Duich against the impressive background of Beinn a Chuirn. Reached by a stone causeway the castle dates from 1220 (Gaelic "eilean" 5 "island"). It was later taken over by the Mackenzies of Kintail and is now the seat of the McRae clan. During the Jacobite uprisings the major part of the structure was destroyed by the cannons of an English warship (1719). Restoration work did not start until 1912 and was completed in 1932. A small exhibition is devoted to the "Jacobite attempts" and the history of the clan (open: Easter-Sept, daily 10am–6pm). Two Iron Age brochs with walls up to 32ft/10m in height are located about 12 miles/19.2km west of Shiel Bridge (HS). The strenuous 7 mile/11.2km long climb to the superb Falls of Glomach (NTS) starts at the northern end of Loch Long and it will probably take at least 8 hours to complete the return journey. These falls are, however, probably the most impressive in Great Britain. Several nature reserves by the road to Ullapool are administered by the National Trust for Scotland but it also owns the Balmacara Estate by Loch Alsh at the western end of Loch Duich. Lochalsh Woodland Garden with its exotic plants from Tasmania, Chile, Japan and China forms a part of the 5620 acre/2275ha estate (open: daily, 9.30am until dusk). A well-known 19th c. geologist by the name of Donald Murchison is remembered in the memorial before Kyle of Lochalsh. The road continues beyond Kyle of Lochalsh to Loch Carron, which is noted for its attractive lakeside scenery, and Castle Strome which was destroyed in 1602 (NTS). For many years it belonged to the powerful Mackenzie barons of Kintail. The coat-of-arms bears a stag's antlers (caberfeidh), symbolically the payment rendered in return for the granting of royal estates.

Glenelg Brochs

★Falls of Glomach

★Lochalsh Garden

Murchison Memorial

Loch Carron Strome Castle

A trip off the beaten track will reap a worthwhile reward. At Kishorn branch off the A896 to the west. Climb a steep mountain road with several hairpin bends over the Belach na Ba pass, beyond which the road suddenly drops from 2000ft/600m down to a level plain and the fine, sandy beach of Applecross.

Detour to Applecross

The A896 now leaves Loch Carron, continues north to Loch Shieldaig (NTS), an inlet surrounded by fine woodland, and then on to the mountain region of Torridon dominated by the towering "Munros" (over 3000ft/1000m). The red sandstone (over 750 million years old) of Liathach (3456ft/1055m) and Beinn Alligin (3232ft/985m) on the north bank of Upper Loch Torridon are much admired by geologists. The National Trust for Scotland is responsible for the upkeep of this wild terrain and at the junction of the A896 and Diabaig Road it runs a visitor centre which goes into considerable detail about the region's fauna and flora (open: May–mid-Sept. Mon.–Sat. 10am–5pm, Sun. 2–5pm). The Stag Museum is of interest, while walkers ought not to miss the remarkable Auchnashellach Forest Walk along Loch Clair and Loch Coulin southward to Auchnashellach railway station.

Torridon ★★Mountain terrain

Park rangers lead guided tours into the Beinn Eighe Nature Reserve near Kinlochewe. (Visitor centre on the A832 1100yds/1km to the north). Opened in 1951, it was Britain's first nature reserve and in 1976 it was upgraded to a UNESCO biosphere reservation. Scots pines and birch woods dominate the landscape on the lower slopes, but at higher altitudes alpine flora such as alpine azaleas and fir club-moss can be found. Wildlife includes red deer, pine martens, wild cats, snow hares, red foxes and golden eagles.

★Beinn Eighe Nature Reserve

Loch Maree Nature Reserve lies along the south bank of Loch Maree, a deep Pleistocene valley with water low in nutrients but nevertheless a habitat favoured by otters and black-throated divers. Access to the nature reserve is through a birch wood about 1 mile/3km west of Kinlochewe. The nature trail through breathtaking mountain scenery

★Loch Maree

View across Upper Loch Torridon to Beinn Alligin

stays below the tree line. The more demanding mountain trail, a 4-mile/6.5km circular tour, begins at the car park. It rises to just under 1800ft/550m and offers an unforgettable view over Loch Maree.

Victoria Falls

The waterfall near Shatterdale – accessible via a signposted footpath – was named after Queen Victoria who visited Loch Maree in 1877.

Gairloch
Heritage Museum

The attractive village of Gairloch (pop. 1100) is the next stop on the tourist route northwards. It lies in a sheltered, sandy bay and boasts a nine-hole golf course. The Heritage Museum details the cultural and economic development of the western Highlands from the Stone Age to the present day. A reconstructed crofter's house and models of fishing boats are among the exhibits (open: Easter–Sept. Mon.–Sat. 10am–5pm). The road to Ullapool runs alongside, sandy beaches, majestic mountain ranges and fjord-like inlets. Campers find it hard to resist some of the secluded bays.

★★Inverewe
Gardens

Thanks to the extremely mild climate a lush, subtropical garden overlooks a sheltered bay by Loch Ewe near Poolewe (6 miles/9.7km north of Gairloch). Rhododendrons, azaleas and magnolias, eucalyptus from New Zealand, Japanese ferns, South American water-lilies, rock gardens, ponds, Scots pines and rare varieties of palms are just some of the unusual plants and features to be admired in the delightful Inverewe Gardens. Osgood Mackenzie was only 20 years old when in 1862 he proved that plants from distant lands could survive on the poor Torridon sandstone and acid peaty soil, if it is enriched by loam from the coast and the wet peat is drained; (NTS; open: Apri.–Oct. daily 9.30 am–9pm; Nov.–Mar. daily 9.30am–5pm).

Rhododendron blooms, Inverewe Gardens   *Boats at Ullapool, Loch Broom*

The scenic A832 winds round Gruinard Bay and then follows the south bank of Loch Broom to Braemore (38 miles/60.8km).

A suspension bridge over the Corrieshalloch Gorge offers the best view of the spectacular Measach waterfalls as it cascades over 150ft/46m into the valley.

Braemore
★Corrieshalloch Gorge
★Falls of Measach

The A835 links Braemore with one of the North-West Highland's most popular resorts. The fishing village of Ullapool (pop. 1100) was founded in 1788 by the British Fisheries Association. Its pretty whitewashed houses in the village nestle on the north bank of Loch Broom. The art world is familiar with this remote spot thanks to some evocative watercolours by the Austrian-born Expressionist painter Oskar Kokoschka (1886–1980) who visited the area on more than one occasion during the 1940s. Loch Broom Museum's collection of old photographs, paintings and traditional furniture tells the story of Wester Ross (Argyle Street; open: mid-Mar.–beginning Nov. Mon.–Fri. 10am–5pm, June–Sept. also 7–9pm). Car ferries leave Ullapool for Stornaway (see Practical Information, Ferries).

★**Ullapool**

Loch Broom

The Summer Isles lie to the north-west of Ullapool, just off the mainland. The largest island is called Tanara Mhor and like some of the smaller islands it can be visited by boat from Ullapool.

Summer Isles

The remote 41sq. miles/109sq.km Inverpolly Nature Reserve which lies about 20 miles/32km north of Ullapool was opened during the 1960s. It is characterised by open moorland, birch woods and lonely lochs.

★**Inverpolly** Nature Reserve

Knockan Cliff is of interest to geologists because the sequence of rock strata has become reversed by tectonic movement and the older moine schist lies above the younger Torridon sandstone. A nature trail (about 1 mile/2km from the car park) explains about the "moine thrust", a 125 mile/200km fault line between the Isle of Skye and Loch Eriboll.

★Knockan Cliff

Mountain and moor: the Inverpolly Nature Reserve

Evidence of glacial activity during the Ice Age are the rounded peaks and deep valleys. Instead of taking the direct route along the A835 to Ledmore, a more adventurous alternative winds its way below the constantly changing mountain backdrop and alongside the coast to Inverkirkaig where the Kirkaig waterfalls (2 miles/3.2km south of Lochinver) cascade into the valley. To the west of the A835, Ben More Coigach (2438ft/744m) and Cul Beag or Stac Polly (2009ft/613m) are the first peaks to come into view followed by Cul More (2787ft/850m) and Suilven (2399ft/732m), an impressive "sugarloaf" mountain. All the mountains in this range are popular with mountaineers.

From Lochinver to Thurso – Sutherland and Caithness

★★Loch Assynt
Ardvreck Castle

Almost 22 miles/35.2km north of Ullapool the A835 crosses the unforget-table picture-book landscape to the north of Loch Assynt. At the eastern end stand the ruins of Ardvreck Castle which was built c. 1590 for the MacLeods. The Seaforth MacKenzies took over the estate in 1691 but were obliged to sell it to the Earl of Sutherland in 1757 to meet their tax debts. Loch Assynt, well-known among the angling fraternity for its salmon and trout, is ringed by a majestic mountain panorama. Geologists are fasci-nated by the rock formations visible at the Inchnadamph Nature Reserve. The route along the north bank of Loch Assynt ranks very highly on the list of Scotland's finest panoramic routes.

★Inchnadamph
Nature Reserve

Lochinver

Numerous lochs surrounding the rural community of Lochinver (pop. 700) provide a wealth of opportunities for anglers. Lochinver was an important port for the herring industry during the 17th and 18th c. but now the catch is primarily white fish and crustaceans. Locally-produced ceramics are available from the Highland Stoneware Pottery.

Spectacular mountain scenery around Loch Assynt

It is possible to take a boat trip from Kylesku, north-east of Loch Assynt, along Loch Glencoul to see the seal colony. The Eas a Chual Aluinn Falls are Britain's highest waterfalls (658ft/200m) and lie at the head of Loch Glencoul (daily 11am and 2pm; tel. (01571) 844446).

Kylesku
★Eas a Chual Aluinn Falls

The bird reserve on Handa Island is run by the Scottish Wildlife Trust and lies almost 3 miles/4.8km north-west of the crofting community of Scourie. As one of the biggest seabird colonies in northern Europe, it gives bird-watchers a rare opportunity to see puffins, guillemots, razorbills, great skuas, fulmars, shags and kittiwakes at close quarters. Seals often bask on the rocks in the sun (Easter-Sept.: boat trips or ferry from Tarbert).

Scourie
★Handa Island

The tiny settlement of Kinlochbervie is an important port for white fish. Catches are auctioned every day in the new fish market (1988).

Kinlochbervie

To the north of Blairmore a 5 mile/8km long footpath leads to Sandwood Bay. It is not only one of the remotest but also one of the most beautiful beaches in Scotland. The spirit of a bearded sailor from a ship wrecked off the coast is said to haunt the beach and mermaids are also supposed to sit on the shore.

★Sandwood Bay

Durness (pop. 1400) consists of a series of scattered settlements. At the west end of the village look out for the picturesque remains of Balnakeil Church (c. 1619), a golf course and Balnakeil beach where the grave of a Viking warrior was recently discovered. Craftsmen and women can be seen at work in the nearby craft village. Faraid Head to the north is another popular spot with ornithologists.

Durness
Balnakeil Church

Faraid Head

Smoo Cave, which lies to the east of the village, is a vast limestone cavern with three chambers. The first one (220ft/67m long and 120ft/37m high) is reminiscent of the nave of a Gothic church. Continuing erosion has opened up a number of holes in the roof and daylight has led to the growth of some

★Smoo Cave

Suilven from Lochinver

Old cottage, Strathnaver Museum

unusual vegetation on the walls. The other two chambers are only accessible by boat.

★Cape Wrath

In summer a passenger ferry from near Cape Wrath Hotel operates across the Kyle of Durness and then a minibus service covers the final few miles on to Scotland's magnificent north-western tip ("hvarf" = "turning point"). On a clear day a fine view from the storm-battered rocks extends across to Lewis and Harris (see Hebrides) and in the east as far as the Orkneys

★★Clo Mor Cliffs

(see entry). The manned lighthouse built by Robert Stevenson in 1827 stands a little further to the east on the spectacular Clo Mor Cliffs (920ft/280m). The north coast road, in many places just single-track, passes

Loch Eriboll

through delightful scenery as it winds its way to Thurso. Loch Eriboll, a salmon farming centre, is a good place for a break. A walk to Whiten Head offers further splendid views. An Iron Age broch (HS) is situated about 10

Dun Dornaigil Broch

miles/16km to the south. The remaining walls reach a height of 22ft/6.7m.

Tongue
Bharraich Castle

Bharraich Castle near Tongue was once the seat of the MacKays. It is thought that the fortress dates from Viking times.

Bettyhill
★Strathnaver Museum

Like many other coastal settlements in Sutherland, Bettyhill owes its existence to the Highland Clearances. Strathnaver Museum in the old village church describes the devastating consequences of the land clearances. Also on display is a traditional Highland cottage, which gives some insight into the everyday life of the crofters before they were evicted, and clan memorabilia belonging to the MacKay family (open: Apr.–Oct. Mon.–Sat.

Invernaver Nature Reserve

10am–5pm). The nature reserve at nearby Torrisdale Bay is noted for its boreal vegetation.

Dounreay
Nuclear Power Station

The fast breeder reactor at Dounreay fisrt came into operation in 1959. An exhibition explains how nuclear energy is produced (open: mid-May–mid-Sept. Tues.–Sat. 10am–4pm; guided tours at 11.45am, 1pm, 2.15pm).

Abreast the nuclear power complex, about 330yd/300m offshore is an ocean swell powered renewable energy generating station (OSPREY), the first commercial station of its kind in the world. With an output of 2 megawatts it has been producing electricity since 1995.

★OSPREY
wave powered
generator

The remains of St Mary's Chapel are situated near Crosskirk, about 6 miles/9.6km outside Thurso. The holy site dates from the 12th c. (HS).

St Mary's Chapel

Thurso (pop. 8000; "Thors-a" = "by the river") has the northernmost railway station on the mainland. The medieval St Peter's Church (12/13th c.) is the oldest building in the small town. It is thought that the foundation stone was laid by Bishop Gilbert of Moravia. The Heritage Museum (High Street) documents the traditions and customs of the local people. It also displays a collection of minerals belonging to Robert Dick (1811–66), a well-known geologist, and a reconstruction of a typical Caithness cottage (open: June–Sept. Mon.–Sat. 10am–1pm, 2–5pm). Golf enthusiasts will appreciate the eighteen-hole Reay Golf Club.

Thurso

Car ferries to Stromness (see Orkney Islands) leave from the fishing port of Scrabster just to the west of Thurso (see Practical Information, Ferries).

Scrabster

The Heart of Sutherland

Situated in central Sutherland Loch Shin (15 miles/24km long and 2 miles/3.2km wide) is a popular watersports and fishing centre and also a source of hydro-electric power.

★Loch Shin

Lairg (pop. 1000) at the south end of the lake is the venue for the largest lamb market in the country. From mid-July until the end of summer it is possible to watch salmon jumping at the nearby Shin Falls.

Lairg,
Shin Falls

Loch Naver and the tiny village of Altnaharra (pop. 60) further north nestle in the centre of a splendid mountain region and a short distance south of the hamlet of Syre lies the abandoned Rosail Clearance Village which bears witness to the dramatic changes wrought by the Highland Clearances. The wild peat moor to the north-east of Altnaharra is impressive for its size alone. The "flows" are sometimes 16ft/5m wide and flanked by small lakes are a favourite breeding ground for curlews, black- and red-throated divers, golden plovers and greenshanks.

Altnaharra

Rosail Clearance
Village

★Flow Country

From Inverness to the Pentland Firth

See entry

Inverness

The delightful stretch of road from Inverness to John o'Groats at the north-eastern tip of Scotland by the Pentland Firth (110 miles/180km) closely follows the coast. Few opportunities exist to sample wine in Scotland so Moniack Castle just around Beauly Firth is something of an exception. In the hands of the Fraser clan since 1580, Philippa Fraser began to produce wines and liqueurs from the various wild berries and fruits in 1980 (winery open: Mon.–Sat. 10am–5pm).

Moniack Castle
(Winery)

Beauly (pop. 1500; 12 miles/19.2km west of Inverness) owes its title "beau lieu" to the magnificent location of a priory which was founded by French Valliscaulian monks c. 1230. The west portal and sections of the main nave (restored in the 16th c. by Bishop Robert Reid) have survived and the fine tracery on three windows of the south side dates from the 13th c. (HS).

Beauly
★Priory

The Black Isle, in contrast to its name, is a beautifully green and fertile peninsula between Beauly and Cromarty Firth, and certainly merits further exploration. The main town on the "isle" is the twin settlement of Fortrose-Rosemarkie (pop. 1900), formerly an important port and now a popular

★Black Isle

Fortrose-
Rosemarkie

The Sutherland Clearances

On a lonely hill by Ben a'Bhragaidh north-west of Golspie stands a huge statue of the first Duke of Sutherland. The statue was erected in 1833 initially to acknowledge his contribution to the kelp industry, fisheries, house and road building, but it quickly came to symbolise one of the bitterest episodes in Scottish history: the Highland Clearances.

The origins of these traumatic events can be traced back to the defeat of the Scottish clans. With the exception of Caithness, the traditional structure of Highland society rested for centuries on a system of almost 180 clans that lived independently of each other, cultivated the valleys to fulfil their own requirements and bred "Black Cattle". The land belonged to the clans, which were represented by a clan chief, and every individual had rights and duties arising from his or her membership of the clan. After the convincing defeat at Culloden in 1746, the clan system was banned and the clansmen's property became the property of the English administrators who showed little concern for the welfare of the crofters whose livelihood depended on that land. After 1780 the estates were returned to clan chiefs who vowed allegiance to the crown. These landowners were known as "lairds" and were able to grant feudal rights to the small-scale farmers.

Spurred on by the success of the southern Scottish estates where the "laird" system was well tried and also the burgeoning demands of the expanding English textile industry, these new Highland landlords saw opportunities for profitable exploitation of the vast expanses of land. Large-scale sheep farming was seen as an escape from low yields, poverty and famine that accompanied traditional, labour-intensive cultivation of the land. The numerous sheep breeders of the Lowlands were offering to pay three times as much to graze their Cheviot and Linton flocks but this meant that a large proportion of the farmers would have to be resettled in the coastal regions. The forced eviction of two thirds of the farming families, the "Highland Clearances" as they became known, started at the beginning of the 18th c. and continued until the 1870s. After a vain attempt by the crofters to stop the advance of sheep farming at Easter Ross in 1792, there was little organised resistance to the power of the lairds. The result was the almost entire removal of settlements from the Highland region and overcrowding in the coastal regions. Fishing and collecting seaweed as a fertiliser was an inadequate second source of income for the crofters who were given only small plots of land, so many of them, faced with little chance of a decent livelihood at home, were forced to emigrate south to the industrial regions of Scotland and England or else to go abroad. After the famines of 1836 and 1846 and incentives offered by overseas governments, the Highlands, before 1745 home to three fifths of the total Scottish population, were by 1870 almost deserted. One Canadian province, Nova Scotia, owes its existence to the disastrous Highland Clearances.

The county of Sutherland earned notoriety from the Highland Clearances as some 15,000 Highlanders were forced to leave their native soil. Those who did not leave voluntarily, faced the bailiff and anyone who stood up to him had to endure brutal violence. Homes were razed to the ground, families torn asunder and agitators were rounded up and sent to penal colonies in Australia. The initiator of the Sutherland Clearances was George Granville, at the time one of Europe's wealthiest businessmen. This Englishman, the Marquess of Stafford, had married the daughter of the Earl of Sutherland in 1785. When Queen Victoria visited the seat of the Sutherlands in 1832, she is said to have been aware that the simplicity of her own home, Balmoral Castle, contrasted with the splendour of Dunrobin Castle, which is even today one of Scotland's largest ancestral homes. Immediately after his wedding, the 27-year-old marquis set about resettling his crofters near the coast and handing over the agricultural land to sheep farmers from the Lowlands. He built new homes, schools, roads and even a railway line as part of the "land reform" and in 1833 was rewarded with a dukedom. Twenty years later, however, Karl Marx wrote in the "New York Herald Tribune" that he had committed an act of brutal despotism on a par with that of Genghis Khan.

Memories of the Clearances run deep in the psyche of the unfortunate victims and an objective assessment of the policy is impossible. Scottish emigrants in all parts of the former British Empire, some four or five generations on, are said to be able to put a name to the soldier – almost certainly a Highlander – who ejected their ancestors from their homes. Further information on the background to the mass evictions is available in the Timespan Heritage Centre (1987) in Helmsdale and the Strathnaver Museum where finds from the abandoned village of Rosail (7 miles/11.2km to the south) are also exhibited. A painting by the contemporary artist Thomas Faed (1826–1900) entitled "The Last of the Clan" (1865) shows the misery and desperation of the victims. It is now on display in the municipal art gallery in Glasgow

Highland Clearances: "The Last of the Clan" (1865) by Thomas Faed

resort with an eighteen-hole golf course. Little remains of Fortrose Cathedral (HS) which was started in the 12th c. and altered during the 13th/14th c. apart from the two-storey chapterhouse. The stones from the church were transported to Inverness (see entry) by Cromwell's men for use in the construction of the castle there. Rosemarkie is an even older settlement dating from the 6th c. In 1125 David I declared the town a bishopric but that was later moved to Fortrose.

Hugh Miller's Cottage

In Cromarty's Church Street stands the cottage where Hugh Miller (1802–56) was born. The house, which survives in its original condition, is now a museum with mementoes of the highly-regarded geologist and writer (NTS; open: Apr.–Sept. Mon.–Sat. 10am–1pm, 2–5pm, Sun. 2–5pm).

Cromarty Firth

Onshore installations, drilling rig docks and light industry zones around the Cromarty Firth have developed out of regional development programmes designed to support the North Sea oil industry.

Dingwall

Turn north when leaving the peninsula and the road leads to Dingwall (pop. 5000), a railway junction on the north bank of Cromarty. This small market town became a royal burgh in 1226 and its history is clearly documented in the old town hall.

★Strathpeffer Spa

As illustrated by an exhibition in the old well house, the elegant spa town of Strathpeffer with its smart villas, delightful gardens and eighteen-hole golf courses (4 miles/6.4km to the west) was one of Scotland's most fashionable resorts in Victorian times. In the village square it is still possible to sample the mineral-rich water and the woods around the village are ideal for relaxing walks. Craftsmen and women from around the region display their skills and products in the restored railway station.

Alness, Invergordon

The A9 passes through Alness, home of the Dalmore and Teaninich whisky distilleries and then follows the north bank of the Cromarty to Invergordon (pop. 4200). Its harbour was once an important military base but is now dominated by the oil industry. The town is one of the main repair and maintenance centres for the British sector of the oil drilling industry. In 1749, scarcely ten years after the last Jacobite uprising, Sir John Gordon devised a scheme to convert the town into a holiday resort with bathing machines and pleasure boats but the project was only partially completed.

Fearn Abbey

As the "Brahan Seer" a famous 17th c. Highland prophet predicted, the roof of the medieval Fearn Abbey (9 miles/14.4km further north) collapsed during a service in 1742 and 42 people were buried beneath the rubble. The north and south chapels of the restored Premonstratensian abbey remain roofless.

Tain

Locally-quarried red and yellow sandstone gives the houses in Tain (pop. 4100) an attractive appearance. This small royal market town by the Dornoch Firth has several sights of interest including the town hall in Scottish baronial style and the nearby Collegiate Church of St Duthus (14th c.). The ruined St Duthus Chapel (1246), a popular place of pilgrimage during the Middle Ages, is situated in the cemetery by the seashore.

St Duthus Chapel and Collegiate Church

Glenmorangie Distillery

Opened in 1843 and owned by MacDonald and Muir since 1918, the Glenmorangie Distillery produces one of Scotland's best-loved malts. It is distilled in Scotland's tallest "pot stills" and stored in bourbon or sherry barrels.

Beyond Tain, a tunnel near Ardjachie Point passes under the Dornoch Firth to the southern tip of Sutherland.

★**Dornoch** Cathedral

The coastal town of Dornoch (pop. 1100) is noted for its cathedral which was established in 1224 by Gilbert of Moravia. Fine arcades, original stone-masonry (13th c.) in the chancel and a splendid west window are among the cathedral's most interesting features. Little remains of the old castle – once an episcopal palace – apart from the tower which has since been incorporated into a hotel. The Whitch's Stone serves as a reminder of a cruel chapter in Scottish history. Janet Horne, a woman thought to be a witch, was burnt to death at the stone. She was the last of more than 4500 women who, following the Reformation, were accused of involvement in witchcraft, tortured and then executed. Today Dornoch is best known for its eighteen-hole golf course and its long sandy beach.

Whitch's Stone

Skibo Castle (5 miles/8km to the west on the A949) was built in 1898 for the philanthropist and steel magnate Andrew Carnegie (see Famous People). He frequently visited Scotland and wanted to spend his twilight years in the country of his birth. This handsome little castle is now used as an exclusive private club.

Skibo Castle

The main road north continues alongside the coast to Golspie (pop. 1300; 10 miles/16km to the north). It is the administrative centre for Sutherland and can boast a long sandy beach, a go-kart track and an eighteen-hole golf course overlooking the sea.

Golspie

Only a mile or so north-east of Golspie stands the imposing Dunrobin Castle, seat of the influential counts and dukes of Sutherland, who could once claim to own the whole of Sutherland. At the end of the 19th c. the 3rd duke owned more land than any other landowner in western Europe. The castle itself – a sight that should not be missed – was begun in 1275. Robert, when 2nd Earl of Sutherland, built a huge tower fortress. However, the major part of the structure designed by Sir Charles Barry dates from the mid-19th c. and is in Neo-Baronial style. The attractive corner towers with conical slate roofs lend a "fairy-tale" look to the castle which undoubtedly bears a strong resemblance to some of the famous Loire valley chateaux in France. A fire badly damaged the interior and Sir Robert Lorimer was given

★★ **Dunrobin Castle**

Open:
Easter, May, Oct.
Mon.–Sat.
10.30am–4.30pm,
Sun. 1–4.30pm;
June–Sept.
Mon.–Sat.
10.30am–5.30pm,
Sun. 1–5.30pm

Dunrobin Castle and its gardens

responsibility in 1915 for creating a new decor. Of the 189 rooms probably the Drawing Room stands out as the highlight. Louis XV-style furniture, the two studies of Venice by Canaletto above the fireplace and the Mortlake tapestries (18th c.) alongside showing scenes from the life of the Greek philosopher Diogenes are of special interest. The family portraits were painted by Reynolds and John Hoppner. The extensive Italian-style gardens are ideal for a stroll and also offer fine views over the Dornoch Firth. A display in the summer house belonging to William Earl of Sutherland sets out the full family history.

Brora

Brora (pop. 1100; 6 miles/9.6km to the north) lies at the mouth of the Brora, a river much acclaimed by anglers for its salmon. Other attractions include an eighteen-hole golf course and a long sandy beach. The village is home to Hunters Woollen Mill which produces fine tweeds.

Clynelish
Distillery

A whisky distillery was opened in Brora in 1819 at the behest of the then Duke of Sutherland and it survived until 1983. It was originally known as Clynelish but when new premises were opened in 1968 the latter's output was renamed Brora. The Clynelish name was retained exclusively for whiskies produced by the new distillery. The pale golden fourteen-year-old Clynelish (flora and fauna design) with its seaweed and peaty aroma is probably one of the finest Highland single malts (open: Mon.–Fri. 9.30am–4.30pm).

Helmsdale
★Timespan
Heritage Centre

The tiny port of Helmsdale (pop. 900; 11 miles/17.6km) owes its origins in the 19th c. to the herring industry. The award-winning "Timespan" centre in Dunrobin Street uses an audio-visual presentation and life-sized models to explain the history of the Highlands from the Picts and Vikings, to the dramatic Highland Clearances and the arrival of the oil rigs in the North Sea (open: Easter–Oct. Mon.–Sat. 10am–5pm, Sun. 2–5pm, July–Aug. 2–6pm).

Strath of
Kildonan

A short detour inland up the Strath of Kildonan is worthwhile. In 1869 gold prospectors moved into the region after particles of the precious metal were found in the river bed. It is still possible to find the occasional gold speck.

Berriedale

The A9 continues to wind its way through magnificent mountain scenery and deep gorges. Berriedale (10 miles/16km), where Langwell Water and Berriedale River flow into the sea, is the site of an abandoned castle, while Morven (2313ft/705m) and the lower peaks of the Scaraben can be seen to the west.

Dunbeath
Heritage Centre,
Lhaidhay Croft
Museum

The fishing village of Dunbeath (pop. 490; 10 miles/16km to the north) was the birthplace of the writer Neil M. Gunn (see Language and Literature). The Heritage Centre here is devoted to the cultural history of Caithness (open: Easter–Oct. Mon.–Sat. 10am–5pm, Sun. 11am–6pm), while in the Lhaidhay Croft Museum life in a traditional Caithness longhouse is recreated (open: Easter–Oct. daily, 10am–5pm).

Clan Gunn
Heritage Centre

The former parish church in Latheron documents the family history of the Gunns (open: June–Sept. Mon.–Sat. 11am–5pm; July, Aug. also Sun. 2–5pm).

**Prehistoric
Standing Stones**

★Grey Cairns of
Cambster

The road between Latheron and Wick (17 miles/27km) passes several prehistoric standing stones such as the oval-shaped Hill o'Many Stones (HS) by the A9 near Mid Clyth and the Cairn of Get near Ulbster. The two well-preserved burial chambers known as the Grey Cairns of Cambster (HS; 6 miles/9.6km north of Lybster) date from the 4th millennium B.C.

Wick
★Caithness Glass

The lively town of Wick (pop. 8000) whose name is derived from the Nordic word "vik" meaning "bay" earns its living from fishing and the oil industry. The Caithness glass factory by Harrow Hill is worth a visit as its hand-made glass products combine traditional manual skills and innovative design (open: Mon.–Sat. 9am–5pm, Sun. 11am–5pm).

Timespan Heritage Centre, Helmsdale   *Caithness glass: elaborate paper-weight*

Wick's Heritage Centre is situated in Bank Row and its displays focus on the tough life endured by the herring fishermen (open: June–Sept. Mon.–Sat. 10am–5pm).

Heritage Centre

The striking ruins of Old Wick Castle (HS) perch on coastal rocks to the south of the town. Brig o'Tram rock arch nearby is an interesting sight, while at the commanding viewpoint of Noss Head to the north of the town the remains of Girnigoe Sinclair Castle are visible.

Old Wick Castle
Noss Head,
Girnigoe
Sinclair Castle

The harbour at John o'Groats overlooks the Pentland Firth and marks the north-eastern tip of the Scottish mainland. The signpost outside the Victorian John o'Groats hotel must rank as one of the country's most-photographed landmarks.

Pentland Firth
★John o'Groats

Old photographs and other memorabilia testify to the harsh existence of the region's fishermen and the sunken wrecks in the Pentland Firth. The tale is also told of the Dutchman Jan de Grot (John o'Groats) who settled here in 1489 and is buried in Canisby church (open: June–Sept. Mon.–Sat. 11am–5pm, July, Aug. also Sun. 2–5pm); two souvenir shops beside the hotel await the countless visitors who descend on this otherwise lonely spot. It is possible to see the Orkney Islands (see entry) from the cliff tops. Between May and September Day trips to the Orkney Islands leave from the harbour at John o'Groats (see Practical Information, Ferries).

Last House
in Scotland

Strictly speaking the north-eastern tip of Scotland is Duncansby Head which lies a further 2 miles/3km to the east. The view from here is even more stunning.

★Duncansby
Head

The Queen Mother owns Castle Mey which is situated by Tang Head to the west of John o'Groats. At certain times during the summer the castle garden is open to the public.

Castle Mey

John o'Groats: at the north-east tip of mainland Scotland

★Dunnet Head   Some 10 miles/16km further on, Dunnet Head, with is lighthouse, juts out into the Pentland Firth. The tip marks the northernmost point of mainland Scotland and it too offers fine views across to the Orkney Islands.

Oban

D 5

Region: Strathclyde. Population: 7500

Situation and characteristics   The busy town of Oban lies by a sheltered bay in the lee of the island of Kerrera (49 miles/78km south of Fort William; see entry). Since Victorian times the town has been one of Scotland's most popular resorts and it is also an important harbour for services to the West Highlands and the Hebrides (see entry). It also makes a good base for excursions into the Highland mountains and lochs. Ganavan Sands behind Dunollie Castle offers opportunities for bathing.

Sights

McCaig's Tower   McCaig's Tower makes a good vantage point for viewing the town. This replica of the Colosseum in Rome was built on Battery Hill at the end of the 19th c. by a wealthy banker named John Stewart McCaig. He claimed that the construction of the tower would provide work for the townsfolk but this "folly" was almost certainly intended as a memorial to himself and his family.

★The Promenade   Shops, hotels and restaurants line the Corran Esplanade which in summer bustles with activity. West Highland Yachting Week at the beginning of August and the Argyll Gathering in mid-September attract many visitors to the town, but other places of interest include the Caithness Glass Factory and Oban Experience, an audio-visual presentation on the town's Victorian past. In Stafford Street the Oban Whisky Distillery, established in 1794 produces a classic malt that enjoys a fine reputation (open: Mon.–Fri. 9.30am–5pm).

Oban Distillery

An unusual exhibition by the North Pier displays miniature furniture, toys, musical instruments and paintings all at a scale of 1:12.

A World in Miniature

The abandoned castle on the island of Kerrera was started c. 1582 for the MacDougall clan. It can be reached along a 1 mile/2km footpath from the jetty where the passenger ferry lands.

Kerrera
Gylen Castle

One of the boat trips from Oban takes in the small islands of Staffa (unusual basalt rock formation) and Iona ("Cradle of Christianity") with views en route of the beautiful east coast of Mull (see Inner Hebrides). This trip is one of the most popular island tours and is highly recommended.

★★Excursion to Staffa and Iona

★★From Oban to Inveraray

There are two routes from Oban to Inveraray from where the A83 continues eastward to Loch Lomond. The first itinerary follows the A85 to the north passing Loch Etive and the picturesque ruined site of Kilchurn Castle before heading south to Inveraray along the A819. The signposted Argyll Tourist Route on the other hand leaves Oban from the south (A816), passing Castle Kilmartin before turning to the left and running along the banks of Loch Fyne (A83) to Inveraray.

Travel tip

Dunstaffnage Castle (HS) 4 miles/6.4km north of Oban stands guard on a rock over the entrance to Loch Etive. The three round towers and the walls, in places 10ft/3m thick, date from the 15th c. when the castle belonged to the Campbell clan, while the residential tower was built in the 17th c. The cannon on the ramparts was salvaged from a Spanish galleon that sank in Tobermory Bay. A few yards further on, the ruins of a 13th c. chapel deserve special attention, as several early Scottish monarchs are said to be buried here alongside members of the Campbell family. At one time it was thought that Dunstaffnage was the capital of the Scottish kingdom of Dal Riata but that theory has now been discounted.

★Dunstaffnage Castle

Open: Apr.–Sept. Mon.-Sat. 9.30am–6pm, Sun. 2–6pm

The underwater world on view in the Sea Life Centre by Loch Creran offers something for everyone. Sharks, rays, squid, seals and other sea creatures can be seen in their natural habitat. Children will be thrilled by the magnificent playground (6 miles/9.6km north of Oban; open: in summer, daily, 9am–6pm or 7pm; in winter, weekends only).

Detour along the A828
★Oban Sea Life Centre

Kinlochlaich Gardens, situated about halfway between Oban and Fort William, are worth a visit for their primulas and rhododendrons (open: Apr. mid-Oct. Mon.–Sat. 9.30am–5.30pm, Sun. 10.30am–5.30pm; mid-Oct.–Mar. weekdays only).

Kinlochlaich House Gardens

Castle Stalker (25 miles/40km north of Oban) occupies a romantic setting on a small island in Loch Linnhe. Begun in the 14th c. as the home of the Stewarts of Appin, it was used by James IV as a hunting lodge. Denis R. Stewart Allward started work on restoring the castle in 1960 (guided tours Apr.–Aug. only by prior arrangement; tel. (01631) 740234).

★Castle Stalker

Meanwhile the A85 runs along the south bank of Loch Etive. The northern tip of the lake, only accessible from the road by boat (leaving in summer from Taynuilt Pier, Mon.–Fri. 10.30am, 2pm, Sat., Sun. 2pm), marks the start of the remote Glen Etive, where the magnificent golden eagle whose wing span can reach 8ft/2.5m may sometimes be seen. The narrow road through the valley joins the A82 near Kingshouse with Glencoe (see entry) to the left.

Loch Etive

The ruined Kilchurn Castle, 15th c. stronghold of the Campbells of Glenorchy, stands on a tiny peninsula at the northern end of Loch Awe. The original keep was strengthened in 1693 by the first Earl of Breadalbane, adding the massive surrounding wall. In the mid 18th c. Hanoverian troops were quartered here.

Ardchattan Priory Gardens

A priory founded c. 1230 by Vauliscaulian monks from the Burgundian Val des Choux is situated on the north bank of Loch Etive. Apart from the remains of the transept, Cromwell's troops left little else of the buildings (HS); however, the adjoining garden contains over 200 varieties of shrubs, including some fine bush roses (open: Apr.–Nov. daily).

Taynuilt
Inverawe
Smokehouse

Pickling and smoking are among the oldest ways of preserving food. The owners of the Inverawe Smokehouse use a secret recipe handed down from generation to generation. The fish is first pickled in brine (sometimes with herbs and sugar) and then smoked slowly over oak (guided tour and sales).

★Bonawe
Iron Furnace

A coal-fired ironworks that was in service between 1753 and 1876 has been faithfully restored with particular emphasis on the furnace and adjoining buildings. A few years before it closed the foundry made cannonballs that were used in the Battle of Trafalgar (1805; HS; open: Apr.–Sept. Mon.–Sat. 9.30am–6pm, Sun. 2–6pm).

Glen Nant
Forest Nature
Reserve,
Ardanaiseig
Gardens

To the south-east of Taynuilt (B845) a splendid nature trail has been laid out in the woods of Glen Nant Forest. A side road branches off at Kilchrenan to Ardanaiseig Gardens which boast superb rhododendrons, azaleas and old trees as well as a marvellous view across Loch Awe to Ben Cruachan (open: end Mar.–Oct. daily, 10am until dusk).

★★Loch Awe
★Pass of Brander

Cruachan Power
Station

The A85 follows the River Awe over the Pass of Brander where the mountain backdrop includes the majestic double peak of Ben Cruachan (3693ft/1126m). In the Visitor Centre at Cruachan dam it is possible to watch the turbines that lie at the end of a long tunnel. These generators convert the water that flows from the reservoir 1200ft/364.5m above into electricity (open: Easter–Oct. daily, 9am–4.30pm).

Lady Rowena

The restored Edwardian steamer "Lady Rowena" takes holidaymakers for cruises on Loch Awe, one of Scotland's largest and most attractive lakes. It leaves from the pier in the village of Lochawe and then heads south beneath wooded hillsides and past several islands including Priest's Isle, formerly a priests' colony, and Inishail, once the site of a Cistercian monastery.

★Kilchurn Castle

The ruins of Kilchurn Castle occupy a picturesque spot on a small peninsula at the northern end of Loch Awe. It was built by Colin Campbell of Glenorchy c. 1440. Originally the castle consisted of a tower and keep, but in 1693 the 1st Earl of Breadalbane reinforced the site with a curtain wall. In 1745 Hanoverian troops were billeted here (HS; open: Apr.–Sept. Mon.–Sat. 9.30am–6pm, Sun. 2–6pm; Oct.–Mar. Mon.–Sat. 9.30am–4pm, Sun. 2–4pm).

Inveraray

Inveraray (pop. 490) makes a good base for tours of the southern and western Highlands. Situated on the banks of Loch Fyne and surrounded by wooded hillsides, the town was the setting for several novels by Sir Walter Scott (a great admirer of Inveraray Castle), for stories by Robert Louis Stevenson and for works by the local poet Neil Munro.

★★Castle

The principal attraction in Inveraray is undoubtedly the castle and its fine parkland. The castle is the seat of the dukes of Argyll, the older branch of the Campbell clan, who moved here from Loch Awe in the first half of the 15th c. The "fairy-tale" castle with round corner towers and turreted conical roofs was built in the middle of the 18th c. from a design by the English architect Robert Morris. The medieval fortress was demolished by the 3rd Duke of Argyll but the foundations were kept intact and used for the new edifice. The Scottish designer Robert Mylne was responsible for the interior decor which was completed at the end of the 18th c. A disastrous fire badly damaged the castle in 1975 and to pay for the renovation work the

Campbells were obliged to sell their island of Iona (see The Hebrides). The "Fire Exhibition" serves as a reminder of the fire but, apart from that, the Neo-Gothic extravagance remains in all its splendour. Fine period furniture, Beauvais Gobelins and Aubusson tapestries, grisaille medallions and gilded stucco ornaments decorate the elegant lounges. Special displays include a large collection of weapons and an amazing range of fine porcelain, such as Derby, Meissen and Japanese. Family portraits are by Gainsborough, Kneller, Raeburn, Ramsay and Hoppner (open: Apr., May, June, Sept., Oct. Mon.–Sat. 10am–1pm, 2–5.30pm, Sun. 1–5.30pm; July, Aug. Mon.–Sat. 10am–5.30pm, Sun. 1–5.30pm).

A tour of Argyllshire's old and new jail is well worth the time. The old premises have been converted into a museum and the exhibits document in an unusual way the history of Scottish crime from the 16th to the 19th c. The old courthouse contains life-size models of well-known criminal figures during their trials, while displays in the tiny bare cells recount the crimes of the former prisoners (open: Apr.–Oct. daily, 9.30am–6pm, Nov.–Mar. daily, 10am–5pm). ★Jail

Only a few yards away, the Loch Fyne Whisky Shop which opened in 1993 can offer a very wide selection of Scotch whiskies. Loch Fyne Whisky Shop

The "Arctic Penguin" is moored by the old pier. This three-masted schooner, launched in Dublin in 1911, has been converted into a museum and its displays deal primarily with maritime travel on the west coast of Scotland (open: Apr.–Oct. 9.30am–6pm, Nov.–Mar. 10am–5pm). Maritime Heritage Museum

Ducks, swans, red deer, rare breeds of sheep and nature trails are among the attractions on offer in the nearby Argyll Wildlife Park (open: daily, from 9.30am). Argyll Wildlife Park

A visit to Glen Shira and the ruins of Rob Roy's birthplace (see Loch Lomond) makes a pleasant excursion. The River Shira, a popular haunt for trout fisherman, rises on Benn Bhuide (3106ft/947m). It opens out into Loch Dubh just before reaching Loch Fyne. **Glen Shira** Rob Roy's House

Only 3 miles/4.8km south of Oban the Argyll Tourist Route passes the Rare Breeds Park near Kilmore, where it is possible to observe many unusual varieties of sheep and cattle, as well as herds of red deer (open: Mar.–Sept. daily, 10am–5.30pm, in summer until 7.30pm). **Argyll Tourist Route** Rare Breeds Park

Many of the trees in the parkland surrounding Glenfeochan House (1875; 1 mile/1.6km to the south) are about 150 years old. Other colourful plant species to admire here include rhododendrons and peach and nectarine trees (open: Apr.–Oct. daily, 10am–6pm). Glenfeochan House

Gardening enthusiasts will enjoy the early 20th c. Arduaine Garden by Loch Melfort. (16 miles/25.6km to the south). It too has fine arrays of rhododendron and also a pretty herb garden (NTS; open: daily, 9.30am until dusk). Arduaine Gardens

Carnasserie Castle dates from the middle of the 16th c. but it was destroyed in 1685. It was once the seat of John Carswell, the first Protestant bishop of the islands. He translated the liturgy of John Knox into Gaelic and, when it was published in 1567, it became the first book to appear in this language. Carnasserie Castle

A line of unusual gravestones can be seen in the church graveyard at Kilmartin (pop. 150). The oldest cross dates from Pictish times, the most recent is 19th c. To the south of the tiny village near the A816 a number of standing stones have been preserved. The oldest, the Nether Largie South Cairn, dates from the early Bronze Age (c. 5000 B.C.). It was later extended on both sides with more cairns. The markings on the stone slabs in the glass-covered burial chamber are sacred symbols. **Kilmartin** ★ Sculptured Stones

In the 6th c. Dunadd Fort (HS), an Iron Age hill fort on the south bank of the River Add (4 miles/6.4km to the south), was the royal residence for the Dunadd Fort

Medieval grave slabs in Kilmartin cemetery

Scottish Dal Riata kingdom (500–850). It was here in 574 that St Columba crowned King Aidan and where according to legend the earliest rulers accepted the crown of Scotland on the "Stone of Destiny". Kenneth MacAlpin later united the Picts and the Scots and the Celtic Scone (see Perth) became their new capital. The famous stone was taken to Perth and later to London by Edward I but has recently been returned to Scotland. A rock on the hill bears what is known as an "Ogham inscription" or rune-like markings named after the Celtic god Ogmios. They are thought to be the oldest type of Gaelic symbol. Originating in Ireland in the 4th c. they were used until the 9th c.

Detour into Knapdale

★Castle Sween

A detour towards the southwest from Kilmartin to the Knapdale peninsula is worthwhile. Castle Sween (HS; 15 miles/24km) on the east coast is thought to be the oldest stone castle on the Scottish mainland. It was built in the middle of the 12th c. but destroyed in 1647 by Sir Alexander MacDonald.

St Columba's Cave

The narrow coast road passes St Columba's Cave. This rocky cavern just north of Ellary was probably used by Stone Age man. It is said the St Columba first set foot on Scottish soil here and a rock altar and cross symbols testify to the existence of an early Christian church.

Kilberry Sculptured Stones

A notable collection of late medieval gravestones are found 12 miles/19.2km to the south not far from the ruins of Kilberry Castle (15th c.; HS).

Lochgilphead
Kilmory Castle Gardens

The A816 continues south to the village of Lochgilphead, home of the Highland Porcelain Pottery. About 100 different species of rhododendron bloom in the gardens of Kilmory Castle (1770; open: daily).

Minard Castle

Minard Castle on the north bank of the picturesque Loch Fyne (14 miles/22.4km south of Inveraray) dates from the 16th c. Paintings

Munro Malcolm's kitchen, Auchindrain Old Village

associated with the Scottish and French royal families are displayed here (open: May–Oct. Mon.–Fri. 10am–4pm).

The last stop before Inveraray is the open-air museum of Auchindrain (6 miles/9.6km south-west). The buildings, traditional longhouses and peasants' cottages are displayed in their original condition and the museum's aim is to show how the rural population of the West Highlands lived during the late 19th c. Apart from the smallholders of Auchindrain who grew their cereal crops, potatoes and root vegetables on the flat land and then grazed their sheep and cattle on the hillsides, the village was also home to the cottars who as payment for their work received a small plot of land which they were allowed to cultivate. In the middle of the 19th c. the settlement had 65 inhabitants but the last tenant left the village in 1962. The farmers' longhouses consisted usually of a living room, a small side room, kitchen, toilet and barn or stables all under one roof, while the cottars eked out a very humble existence in a simple hut (open: June–Aug. daily; Apr., May, Sept. Sun.–Fri. 10am–5pm).

Auchindrain
★ Old Village

Orkney Islands

F/G 2/3

Region: Orkney Islands Area

The Orkney Islands off the north coast of Scotland are separated from the mainland by the Pentland Firth. The distance from John o'Groats at the north-eastern tip of the Scottish mainland (see North-West Highlands) to the most southerly point on the island of South Ronaldsay is 6½ miles/10.4km. The islands are home to about 19,000 people who are known as Orcadians. Of the 67 islands only eighteen are inhabited, although the principal island has a population of 14,000. Some 48 miles/76.8km separate

Situation and characteristics

north from south while the distance from east to west measures 35 miles/ 56km. Farming provides work for a good proportion of the population, and fishing, particularly for lobsters and prawns, is an important element in the local economy; however, of most significance today is the offshore oil industry. The island of Flotta on the east side of Scapa Flow Bay is a major loading station for oil tankers.

★★Topography

Fertile top soil on the Devonian Old Red Sandstone and the mild climate brought in by the Gulf Stream have created good conditions for farming. Long fields and green pastureland broken up by moors, grass and heathland characterise the islands. Ice Age glaciers left behind gently rolling hills with altitudes no higher than 1000ft/305m, although the island of Hoy with its extremely steep cliffs is an exception. Moorland vegetation includes sphagnum moss, cotton grass, chickweed wintergreen, sundew and many varieties of heathers. Sea grasses predominate by the coast, but a number of rare species such as the Scottish primrose do occur. The Orkneys are also, of course, an important resting and breeding ground for sea birds but kestrels and peregrine falcons, sparrowhawks and golden eagles (on Hoy) breed here, while the moors make good habitats for great skuas, hen harriers and short-eared owls. The wetlands are ideal territory for oystercatchers, golden plovers, curlews, widgeons and pintails. The rocks attract birdwatchers who train their binoculars on the shearwaters, Arctic skuas, long-tailed ducks, puffins, gannets, terns, greylag geese, Canada geese and snow geese. Close to the shore otters, grey seals and common seals are a frequent sight, while further out it is sometimes possible to catch a glimpse of a school of dolphins.

Holidays

The Orkneys are popular with walkers, nature lovers and birdwatchers, but anglers too are attracted by both the sea and the inland freshwater lakes. And yet there are also plenty of places of interest for the more traditional tourist. In prehistoric times early man appreciated the favourable climate and fertile soil and left a wealth of ancient sites, with probably more here than anywhere else in Britain. Many of these Stone Age and Bronze Age remains can only be reached on foot or by bicycle. Malt whisky is also produced on the Orkneys and the regional specialities such as lobster and smoked cheese ought not to be missed. Golfers will even find two eighteen-hole golf courses, one near Stromness and one at Grainbank near Kirkwall.

Communications
Ferries

Car ferries operate between Scrabster and Stromness (Mainland) and also between Aberdeen (see entry) and Stromness. Passenger ferries cross in the summer from John o'Groats to Burwick (South Ronaldsay; see Practical Information, Ferries). There are also day trips from Inverness to John o'Groats by bus, ferry and – before returning – a six-hour trip around the Orkneys. An inter-island ferry service operates on a regular basis and there is also a ferry to Lerwick (Shetlands; every Sunday; June–Aug. also Tuesday).

Flights

Direct British Airways flights connect the Orkneys (Kirkwall) with Aberdeen (see entry), Glasgow (see entry), Edinburgh (see entry) and Inverness (see entry). Loganair run services to Kirkwall from Glasgow, Edinburgh, Inverness, Wick and also to the other islands including the Shetlands.

History

When the Egyptians were building pyramids by the Nile, the first settlers on the Orkneys were also constructing their simple dwellings. These first inhabitants were driven out by Picts who themselves had been forced to flee from Nordic invaders. For centuries the Orkneys, along with the Shetlands (see entry), the Hebrides (see entry) and northern Scotland, belonged to Norway and many names serve as a reminder of that period. In fact, Nordic traces in the island's culture are not hard to find. Until the 17th c. the language of the Orcadians was "Norn", a dialect related to old Norwegian and the name "Orkney" derives from the Nordic word "orc" meaning "wild bear". The history of the Nordic rulers, the "Jarls", is outlined in the "Orkneyinga Saga". After the Battle of Largs in 1263 the Norwegians

Sand, sea and sky – a beach in Orkney

abandoned all their Scottish territories apart from the Orkney and Shetland Islands. In 1468 Christian I of Norway pledged the islands as surety for a dowry when his daughter Margaret (the Maid of Norway) married James III of Scotland. The debt was not paid so in 1472 Scotland annexed the islands. The Scots imposed their feudal system on the islanders, who were not familiar with the clan structure. Up until then the land had been administered and cultivated on a communal basis. Earl Patrick Stewart was executed in Edinburgh in 1615 for his tyrannical treatment of the islanders. Scapa Flow Bay was a major naval base for the British fleet during the First and Second World Wars.

Mainland

Kirkwall (old Norwegian "kirkjuvagr" = "church bay") lies by a broad bay and at the narrowest point on the island. Of the 14,000 Orcadians who live on Mainland, about half reside in the island's main town. Its narrow streets and grey houses with tiny windows and gables overlooking the street are reminiscent of Norwegian architecture.

Kirkwall

Since 1850 at Christmas and on New Year's Day a kind of football match has been held in Kirkwall. The Boys' and Men's Ba' Games involves a team of "Uppies" (churchmen/upper town) playing the "Downies" (king's vassals/lower town). The boys play in the morning and the men in the afternoon, but as many as 200 players can be involved. The Ba' Game reflects the conflicts within the divided town at the end of the 14th c. when Earl Henry St Clair controlled the castle (now no longer in existence) and the bishop the land around its base. The boundary was Kirk Green, now the starting point for a match that takes place on the streets and in which anyone can join in.

Boys' and Men's Ba' Games

The St Magnus Cathedral is by far the most impressive building in the town. Every year in June it is the venue for a music festival. The design of

★St Magnus

Kirkwall: island capital and fishing port

the cathedral is reminiscent of the cathedral in the Norwegian city of Trondheim. It was started in 1137 by Jarl Rognvald and was dedicated to his uncle Magnus Erlendsson who was murdered on Egilsay in 1116. The 250ft/75m long church with west front was completed at the end of the 15th c., but the oldest sections are the transept and the three niches in the chancel. Note that the huge Norman pillars are not spaced equally. Haakon the Norwegian king was buried in this church in 1263, but was later taken to Trondheim. During 1926 two pine coffins with skeletons were found in two of the pillars. These are thought to be the remains of Magnus and his nephew. St Magnus and Glasgow Cathedral (see entry) are the only two Scottish churches which survived the Reformation undamaged.

★Bishop's Palace

Diagonally opposite in Watergate stand the ruins of the Bishop's Palace which was started in the middle of the 12th c. by Bishop William the Elder to provide alternative accommodation for the cathedral's guests. It was here in 1263 that King Haakon died. The palace was restored in the late 15th c. and then again in the middle of the 16th c. by Bishop Robert Reid, the founder of Edinburgh University (see entry).

★Earl's Palace

On the other side of the road the Earl's Palace serves as one of the finest examples of 16th c. Scottish secular architecture. The light sandstone structure, now a ruin, was completed in 1607 by the tyrannical Earl Patrick Stewart. The mature trees in the garden, mostly maples, were planted c. 1840 (HS; open: Apr.–Sept. Mon.–Sat. 9.30am–6pm, Sun. 2–6pm).

Tankerness House Museum

Tankerness House is situated where Palace Road meets Broad Street, Kirkwall's main commercial thoroughfare with many small shops and welcoming pubs. The house originally consisted of two buildings which were converted for the first Protestant priest Gilbert Fulzie in 1574. It was later acquired by the Baikies of Tankerness, a merchant family. This fine town house now contains an exhibition on the history of the Orkneys (open: Mon.–Sat. 10.30am–12.30pm, 1.30–5pm; May–Sept, also Sun. 2–5pm).

Scotland's most northerly distillery stands on the edge of the town by the A961. It makes use of a traditional-style malting floor (see Baedeker Special, "Scotch Whisky") to produce a well-balanced, rather smoky twelve-year-old malt with a pleasant dryness (open: Easter–Oct. Mon.–Fri. 10am–4pm June–Aug. also Sat. guided tours every 30 minutes; Nov.–Easter, guided tours Mon.–Fri. 2.30pm).

★ Highland Park Distillery

A burial chamber to the north-west of the town by Wideford Hill provides evidence of a Stone Age settlement (c. 3000 B.C.). Rennibister Earth House (HS), nearly 5 miles/8km to the north-west of Kirkwall, dates from the Iron Age.

Wideford Hill Rennibister Earth House

A crusader knight built Orphir Church (dedicated to St Nicholas) in the first half of the 12th c. Situated by Scapa Flow Bay 8 miles/12.8km south-west of Kirkwall, it is Scotland's only medieval round church (HS).

Orphir Round Church

Nowhere provides a better insight into the Orkneys' prehistoric past than the Stone Age burial chamber at Maes Howe, situated in the centre of Mainland, on the road to Stromness (A965) about 9 miles/14.4km west of Kirkwall. Dating from 2500 B.C., it is almost certainly the best-preserved late Stone Age site of its kind anywhere in the British Isles. The interior of this grass-covered grave is vast, measuring 115ft/32m in diameter. The low and narrow entrance tunnel, almost 36ft/11m long, is built from long stone slabs up to 16ft/5m in length and it leads into a main chamber and three adjoining chambers; however, as some runic inscriptions indicate, the contents were plundered by the Vikings in the 12th c. "Haakon alone took the treasure from this mound" is just one of the many examples. Some researchers maintain that Nordic crusaders sought shelter here from a storm (HS).

★★ Maes Howe

Open:
Apr.–Sept.
Mon.–Sat.
9.30am–6pm,
Sun. 2–6pm;
Oct.–Mar.
Mon.–Sat.
9.30am–4pm,
Sun. 2–4pm

Orphir Church, the only medieval round church in Scotland

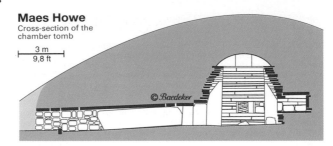

Maes Howe
Cross-section of the
chamber tomb

| 3 m |
| 9,8 ft |

© Baedeker

Standing Stones
of Stenness

Just before the junction of B9055 and the A965 the prehistoric Standing
Stones of Stenness come into view. Situated above the banks of Loch
Stenness, the stones originally formed a 100ft/30m circle but now only four
of the twelve stones remain.

★Ring of Brodgar

The 5000 year old Ring of Brodgar (HS), about 2 miles/3.2km higher up by
Loch Stenness, provides further evidence of the islands' earliest inhabitants. It remains a mystery as to what precise function these 27 (originally
60) stones performed. The monoliths, ranging in height from 6½ft/2m to
15ft/4.5m, are arranged in a perfect circle 340ft/103.7m in diameter. On the
northern side of the circle a stone bears the runic symbol for the Nordic
name "Björn". The stunning interplay of water, countryside, cloud and
stone pillars leaves a lasting impression.

★Unstan Cairn

Unstan Cairn (HS) is situated on a peninsula on the south side of Loch
Stenness. It is a burial chamber about 23ft/7m in total length although it is
divided into smaller sections. When the grave was excavated in 1884,

The Ring of Brodgar

The Earl's Palace, Kirkwall

archaeologists unearthed the largest piece of Stone Age pottery ever found in Scotland. It is now on display in the National Museum of Antiquities in Edinburgh (see entry).

Stromness (pop. 2800) is the second-biggest town on Mainland island and serves as the main ferry terminal for the archipelago (see Practical Information, Ferries). Although the narrow cobbled lanes and grey stone houses look older than those in Kirkwall, the town actually dates from more recent times. The growth of Stromness started at the end of the 17th c. when the Hudson Bay Company set up a base at the port and recruited sailors to crew the vessels that plied across the North Atlantic to northern Canada. During the 18th c. whaling fleets called in for supplies on their way to the coast of Greenland. Orkney islanders, always recognised for their seafaring skills, were among those who signed up to serve on such famous vessels as Scott's R.R.S. "Discovery" (see Dundee) and the legendary HMS "Bounty" of "Mutiny on the Bounty" fame.

★Stromness

Stromness boasts two interesting museums: the collection of modern art in the Pier Arts Centre was bequeathed to the town by the art-lover Mary Gardiner. Barbara Hepworth and other artists from the St Ives school are represented in the gallery (open: Tues.–Sat. 10.30am–12.30pm, 1.30–5pm; Stromness Museum demonstrates the influence of the Hudson Bay Company on the town and also details the wealth of bird-life on the island and the history of whaling. Sections of the German warships which were scuttled in Scapa Flow at the end of the First World War are also displayed here (open all the year round).

Pier Arts Centre, Museum

Stromness Museum

Skara Brae (10 miles/16.3km north of Stromness) is by far the most important prehistoric site on the Orkneys. It appears to have been inhabited without interruption between 3100 and 2500 B.C. The people farmed the land and bred animals from huts constructed of flat stones and slabs which were then covered with earth. The most remarkable thing about Skara Brae is that some of the Stone Age interior furnishings have survived such as hearths, bed boxes made from stone slabs (filled with straw), a similar stone structure rather like a cupboard and the occasional niche with a drainage channel, probably a toilet. Two buildings from the first phase remain, but the rest of the houses date from the second phase. These were bigger and, unlike the earlier dwellings, the bed box was not built into the wall but integrated into the living space. The houses at Skara Brae were

★★Skara Brae

Open:
Apr.–Sept.
Mon.–Sat.
9.30am–6pm,
Sun. 2–6pm;
Oct.–Mar.
Mon.–Sat.
9.30am–4pm,
Sun. 2–4pm

Skara Brae
Stone Age village

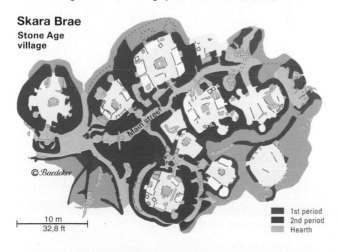

© Baedeker

10 m
32,8 ft

■ 1st period
■ 2nd period
■ Hearth

well preserved by a thick layer of sand until 1850 when a fierce storm exposed the ancient site. It is thought that the Stone Age community were wiped out by some natural catastrophe that laid waste their village. The skeleton of a boy and an old man have been found. The main finds are displayed in the National Museum of Antiquities in Edinburgh (see entry).

★Brough of Birsay

The island of Birsay on the north-west coast of Mainland (accessible on foot at low tide) was an important Viking settlement and as the erstwhile capital of Orkney it was the first place to have a church. The remains of the settlement here include typical Viking longhouses and an 11–13th c. Irish-Scottish church, while in the village of Birsay the remains of a 16th c. episcopal palace can still be seen.

Burgar Hill
Wind Turbine
Site

Following the coast road from Birsay round to the east (A966), it is hard not to miss the biggest experimental wind energy complex in Great Britain. The rotor on the tallest pylon measures 200ft/60m in diameter.

★Broch of Gurness

Open:
Apr.–Sept.
Mon.–Sat.
9.30am–6pm,
Sun. 2–6pm

A side road leads from Evie Village to Gurness Broch (HS). The tower served as a dwelling and as a fortification for the Picts in the first half of the 1st c. B.C. but continued to be used by Vikings until the 9th c. A.D. as the remains of Norse longhouses in the vicinity prove. These windowless brochs built from layers of stone had a cylindrical interior and an external wall tapering upwards. Galleries ran between the two and steps provided access to the upper floors.

★Corrigall
Farm Museum

About 12 miles/19.2km to the south near the tiny village of Brough (signposted on the A986) lies Corrigall Farm, a museum which documents rural life on the Orkneys during the 19th c. (open: May–Sept.).

Scapa Flow

History

Given its favourable strategic position, during the First World War the extensive Scapa Flow Bay was used as a base for the British navy. When the

5000 year-old Stone Age dwellings preserved at Skara Brae

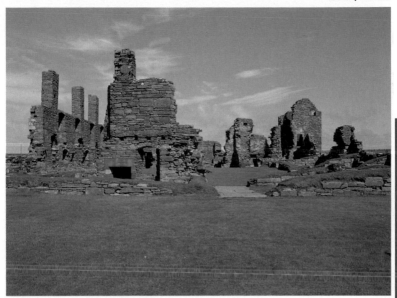

Birsay: ruins of the 16th c. episcopal palace

Germans surrendered, the remaining ships of the German navy, including 74 battleships, cruisers, etc. were interned in the western half of Scapa Flow Bay to await the final peace treaty. For seven months the crews waited on board their ships as they were not allowed to go ashore. On June 21st 1919 Admiral von Reuter gave the order to all the German captains to scuttle their vessels. The valves were opened and the men rowed ashore, whereupon the pride of the German Kaiser sank to the bottom of the bay – to the great displeasure of the Allied commanders. The action turned out to be a tragic mistake, as the admiral believed that the Germans had not signed the peace treaty. In fact the signing had only been postponed for two days but the news had not reached Scapa Flow. Most ships were raised and scrapped but seven German warships are still rusting on the sea bed.

In the Second World War the British Home Fleet was anchored in Scapa Flow. On October 14th 1939 the German U-boat U47 managed to enter the bay and sink the British battleship "Royal Oak". Over 830 of the 1200-strong crew lost their lives. A memorial plaque in St Magnus Cathedral and the Memorial Garden on Scapa Flow beach remember the victims. The British government blocked access to the bay by sinking decommissioned vessels between Mainland and the islands of Burray and South Ronaldsay. Italian prisoners-of-war later built Churchill's Barrier, a fixed cement barrage which now links these two islands to Mainland. The masts of the sunken vessels can still be seen projecting from the sea. Every year large numbers of divers descend on Scapa Flow to pick over the wrecks. For information on diving permits, consult the local tourist offices.

Sights on the other Orkney Islands

The island of Hoy shows a different side of the Orkney Islands. At 1564ft/477m Ward Hill, the tallest point on the archipelago, is also a part of one of the highest cliffs in Britain. The landscape could be described as

Hoy

Crofter's cottage, Corrigall Farm Museum

★St John's Head

★Old Man of Hoy

harsh and mountainous but the 1134ft/346m drop down to the sea at St John's Head on the north-west corner of the island is a stunning sight. This section of coastline is also noted for the sheer 450ft/137m-high stack known as the Old Man of Hoy a little further south. Fulmars, auks, shearwaters and gannets glide gracefully around the red sandstone column while the waves crash relentlessly against the base.

Dwarfie Stone

★North Hoy
RSPB Reserve

Surrounded by heathers in a lonely valley between Ward Hill and Knap of Trovieglen lies the Dwarfie Stone. This 5000-year-old burial chamber was carved from a huge rock by Stone Age man. The 9000 acres/3700ha of land around Ward Hill has been designated as a bird reserve (RSPB) and it makes an ideal spot for observing the great skuas and Arctic skuas that breed on the island.

**South
Ronaldsay**
Italian Chapel

The most southerly of the Orkney Islands is South Ronaldsay, which can be reached by crossing the Churchill Barriers. On the tiny island of Lambholm between Mainland and Burray stands an Italian Chapel that was built during the Second World War by Italian prisoners-of-war out of two Nissen huts. It is covered from floor to ceiling with brightly-coloured bricks and ornate stone panels.

Orkney Wireless
Museum

The Orkney Wireless Museum in the remote village of St Margaret's Hope (Church Street) displays radio transmitters and other telecommunication equipment used by the British navy (open: Apr.–Sept. daily, 10am–7pm).

Tomb of the
Eagles

At the south-eastern tip of the island lies the "Tomb of the Eagles" (also known as Isbister Tomb). The main burial chamber and three secondary chambers date from the 3rd millennium B.C. and were used as a graveyard for about 1500 years. The tomb's name derives from the large number of sea eagle bones that were found here. It can only be assumed that for the Isbisters the sea eagle was a sacred creature. When the graves were excavated, the bones of the various parts of the body had been sorted and stored together. More than 340 bodies were dismembered before being buried in a communal grave (open: daily, 10am–7pm/10pm).

The island of Rousay lies off the north coast of Mainland island. Here too there are a number of prehistoric burial sites such as Blackhammer Cairn (3rd millennium b.c.) and the 82ft/25m-long burial chamber at Midhowe Cairn, a huge "ship of the dead" stranded in the dunes. Midhowe Broch, dating from the Iron Age can be seen not far away. Parts of the walls at this enormous fort reach a height of 10ft/3m.

Rousay

Midhowe Cairn,
Midhowe Broch

Egilsay, to the west of Rousay, is where St Magnus was murdered. This Irish-style church with a round tower was built in the 12th c.

Egilsay
St Magnus Church

The crossing from Kirkwall to Westray will take about one and a half hours. Dominating the harbour at Pierowall is the ruined Notland Castle. Its massive walls are pierced with 60 embrasures. Gilbert Balfour ordered the construction of this Z-shaped castle in 1560, but it was destroyed by Covenanters in 1650.

Westray
Notland Castle

Noup Head, some 5 miles/8km in length and boasting a rocky north coast, is home to vast numbers of seabirds. The thousands of petrels, kittiwakes, guillemots and razorbills that gather here for the breeding season constitute one of the biggest bird colonies in Great Britain.

★ Noup Head

To see two of the oldest stone houses in Europe will require a trip to the tiny island of Papa Westray which lies just off the north east coast of Westray. Thought to be 5000 years old and, like Skara Brae, protected for centuries from the elements by a thick layer of sand, they were exposed after a fierce storm. Spoons, mallets and drills made from whalebones were found during the excavations (HS).

Papa Westray
★ Knap of Howar

As well as many other seabirds, a huge colony of Arctic terns breed here.

★ North Hill
Reserve

The sandy grassland and dunes on Sanday make excellent breeding grounds for sea birds, while Otters Wick Bay is noted for its seal colony. There are some fine bathing beaches on the island and amateur archaeologists ought not to miss the burial chamber at Quoyness which dates from 2900 b.c. (HS).

Sanday

★ Quoyness Cairn

Perth   F 5

Region: Tayside
Population: 42,000

When Sir Walter Scott (see Famous People) wrote his novel "The Fair Maid of Perth" he put this pretty town 22 miles/35km west of Dundee firmly on the map. Although relatively few historic buildings from this former Scottish capital have survived, the town can claim to have been the scene of a number of important events in the history of Scotland.

Situation

Sights

The parish church of St John which was built in the 15th c. and then restored in 1923/24 by Sir Robert Lorimer was the stage for the reformer John Knox (see Famous People) to launch his campaign against idolatry. His sermon culminated in a iconoclastic crusade in which the majority of art treasures in Scotland's churches were destroyed.

St John

Although Perth was the capital of Scotland until the 15th c., there are very few historic buildings to see. An exhibition in the medieval Round Tower,

**Historic
Buildings**

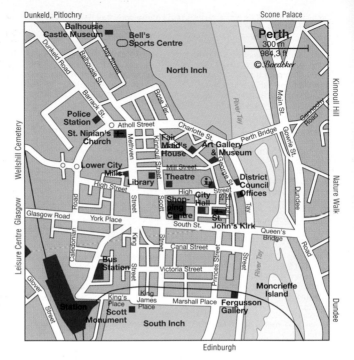

once used as a watertower, displays work by the Scottish artist J. D. Ferguson, while Perth's Art Gallery and Museum in George Street focuses on local history and also serves as a venue for temporary art exhibitions (open: Mon.–Sat. 10am–5pm). "Fair Maid's House" in Curfew Road which was acclaimed by Scott is now a handicraft shop. Lower City Mills is of interest, as an early 20th c. watermill has been faithfully restored and corn is still ground in the traditional style (open: Easter–Oct. Mon.–Sat. 10am–5pm, July–Sept, also Sun. noon–5pm).

★Balhousie
Castle Museum

Balhousie Castle by the North Inch documents over 250 years of British military history. The museum is devoted to the achievements of The Black Watch (Royal Highland) Regiment, Scotland's oldest Highland regiment (open: Easter–Sept. Mon.–Fri. 10am–4.30pm, Sun. 2–4.30pm; Oct.–Easter, Mon.–Fri. 10am–3pm).

Kinnoul Hill

A footpath leads up Kinnoul Hill (729ft/222m) which affords a fine view over the surrounding countryside.

Surroundings

Elcho Castle

This fortified mansion (3 miles/4.8km to the south-east) in Scottish baronial style (16th c.) was once the seat of the Wemyss family. Note the small corner towers and projecting round oriel windows.

HS; open: Apr.–Sept. Mon.–Sat. 9.30am–6pm, Sun. 9.30am–4pm; Oct.–Mar. Mon.–Sat. 9.30am–4pm, Sun. 2–4pm.

Scone Palace (2 miles/3.2km to the north) is situated near the old but now non-existent abbey of Scone where Scottish monarchs from Kenneth II to James IV were crowned. In the 9th c. Kenneth MacAlpin chose Scone as the royal residence and brought the Scottish coronation stone ("Stone of Scone") here, but in 1297 Edward I took it to Westminster Abbey in London. It has recently been returned to Scotland. The stone was once placed on Mote Hill, a spot where, according to legend, earth from all parts of the kingdom had been scattered.

The major part of the palace was built at the beginning of the 19th c. and it is now the seat of the earls of Mansfield, whose ancestors are shown in the portraits which line the Long Gallery. Porcelain from Meissen, Sèvres and Derby, fine Chippendale furniture, 17th and 18th c. ivory carvings and some extremely unusual papier mâché objets d'art (c. 1730) by the Parisian Martin brothers are the principal art treasures on view inside. The surrounding parkland boasts a number of rare trees.

Huntingtower Castle (2 miles/3.2km to the west), formerly known as Ruthven Castle, originally consisted of two single towers (15th c.) which were joined together in the 17th c. The most striking aspects of the interior decor are the wall and ceiling paintings in the Hall. According to legend, the daughter of the 1st Earl once jumped the 10ft/3m gap between the two towers to avoid being caught with her lover, hence the name "Maiden's Leap".

HS; open: Apr.–Sept. Mon.–Sat. 9.30am–6pm, Sun. 9.30am–4pm; Oct.–Mar. Mon.–Thur. Sat. 9.30am–4pm, Sun. 2–4pm

The A85 continues west passing close to the pretty village of Fowlis Wester, noted for an 8th c. market cross and the 13th c. St Bean Church. A9th c. Pictish stone can be seen in front of the church.

★★Scone Palace

Open:
Easter–mid-Oct.
Mon.–Sat.
9.30am–5pm,
Sun. 1.30–5pm;
July–Aug.
Sun. from 10am

**★Huntingtower
Castle**

Fowlis Wester
St Bean

Scone Palace: the Scottish kings were crowned near by

Crieff
Weaver's House
Visitor Centre

The Weaver's House in Burrell Street offers an insight into traditional Scottish weaving techniques and regional customs, while the Visitor Centre in Muthill Road has displays of local handicrafts (open: daily, 9am–5pm).

★Glenturret
Distillery

Situated to the west of Crieff by the A85 Glenturret claims to be Scotland's oldest distillery. It was founded in 1775, but the distilleries at Littlemille (Bowling, Dumbartonshire) and Strathisla (Keith, Banffshire) were also founded at around this time. Nevertheless, with only two stills producing malt whisky, it is one of the smallest distilleries in the country.
Open: Mar.–Dec. Mon.–Sat. 9.30am–4.30pm; Jan., Feb. Mon.–Fri. 11.30am–2.30pm; see Baedeker Special, "Scotch Whisky".

Innerpeffray
★Library

Innerpeffray (4 miles/6.4km south-east of Crieff) claims a place in Scotland's literary history. The public library, opened in 1691, is said to be the oldest in Scotland. The early volumes stored here are of theological and classical interest (open: Mon.–Wed., Fri., Sat. 10am–12.45pm, 2–4pm, Sun. 2–4pm).

Comrie
★Scottish
Tartans Museum

The history of tartans, plaids and kilts is covered in some detail at Comrie's Tartan Museum (Drummond Street). This collection belonging to the Scottish Tartans Society illustrates how the traditional patterns were made and how they are linked to the various clans (open: Apr.–Oct. Mon.–Sat. 10am–6pm, Sun. 11am–5pm). Information: STB, tel. (0044) 131 332 2433.

Drummond Castle
Gardens
Open:
May–Sept.
daily 2–6pm

The upper terrace provides the best view of these terraced gardens which were laid out in 1630 by John Drummond. After Cromwell's troops had burnt down the medieval castle (15th c.), it was gradually rebuilt. The castle was extended in the 19th c. and in early Victorian times alterations were also made to the lower sections of the parkland.

Pitlochry   F 5

Region: Tayside. Altitude: 420ft/128m. Population: 2500

Geographical
centre of
Scotland

Pitlochry in the Tummel valley is the geographical centre of Scotland. It is noted for its high quality woollen products and is also popular as a summer resort. Between May and October the "Theatre in the Hills" (modernised in 1981) is the venue for a successful drama festival and in September the Highland Games are held here. While enjoying a haggis or other traditional Scottish delicacy, kilted spectators watch the competitors tossing the caber, throwing the hammer and playing the bagpipes. The town itself can boast an eighteen-hole golf course, while further north in Blair Atholl is a nine-hole course.

Fish Ladder

A very popular attraction is the underwater observation room at Loch Faskally. Here it is possible to watch the thousands of salmon negotiating the ladder to reach their spawning grounds. The room was specially installed when a hydro-electric power station was built during the 1950s.

Blair Atholl
Distillery

Blair Atholl Distillery is the production centre for Bell and Sons' famous blended whisky and also for their excellent single malt (eight and twelve years old). The present distillery was built in 1949 but the origins of the firm go back to 1798 (open: Mon.–Sat. 9.30am–5pm; Easter–Oct. also Sun. noon–5pm; see Baedeker Special, "Scotch Whisky").

Surroundings

★Edradour
Distillery

The hamlet of Balnauld 3 miles/4.8km north-east of Pitlochry is the home of Scotland's smallest distillery. It dates from c. 1825 (open: Mar.–Oct. 9.30am–5pm; see Baedeker Special, "Scotch Whisky").

Bell & Son's Blair Athol distillery

On the way to Blair Castle it is easy to make a detour to Loch Tummel, a long lake with many bays. "Queen's View", named after Queen Victoria who once came to enjoy the magnificent panorama, should not be missed. The mountains surrounding Loch Tummel are made from almost pure barite, a mineral that is processed to provide radium for the chemical industry. The road west from Loch Tummel leads into desolate terrain.

Detour to ★ Loch Tummel and Loch Rannoch

Some 20 miles/32km to the west the black/brown, treeless cone of Schiehallion rises 3950ft/1200m into the sky. A climb to the summit will take about three hours.

★ Schiehallion

Loch Rannoch lies at the northern foot of Schiehallion. The sides of the lake were once inhabited by over 30 clans, including the MacDonalds, Mac-Gregors, Menzies, Robertsons and Stewarts (about 2500 people); now the lakeside supports barely 400 residents.

Loch Rannoch

Rannoch Moor, a brown-flecked, undulating plain dotted with small lakes stretches out to the west of Loch Rannoch and beyond Loch Laidon. It is an inhospitable region and yet it exerts a magical charm on those who venture forth. In this treeless countryside, Britain's largest moor, sphagnum moss and heathers grow among sundew, bilberries and cranberries, campion, cotton-grasses, low-growing willows and dwarf birches. The B846 finally ends 34 miles/54.4km west of Pitlochry near Rannoch Station, a tiny railway halt on the Glasgow–Fort William line.

Rannoch Moor

Return to the A9 and follow the road north through the Pass of Killiecrankie. In 1689 this breathtakingly beautiful gorge was the scene of a severe rout of the English army at the hands of the Highlanders under the generalship of the Viscount of Dundee.

★ Pass of Killiecrankie

The tiny mill (1613) in Blair Atholl (pop. 500) continues to grind corn in the traditional way. The flour is for sale but it can first be sampled as a biscuit

Blair Atholl
Meal and Flour Mill

293

in the tea-room (open: Apr.–Oct. Mon.–Sat. 10.30am–5.30pm, Sun. noon–5.30pm).

★★Blair Castle

Open:
Apr.–Oct.
10am–6pm

Blair Castle dominates the northern end of the village. It occupies an important, strategic spot on the Perth (see entry) to Inverness (see entry) road in the broad Garry valley. The castle has been the seat of the Duke of Atholl (Murray clan) since the 17th c. In 1845 Queen Victoria granted the owner the unique privilege of maintaining a private army, the "Atholl Highlanders" and on the last Sunday in May the soldiers stage a colourful

Blair Castle

SECOND FLOOR

11 4th Duke's Corridor
12 Library
13 Derby Dressing Room
14 Derby Room
15 Red Bedchamber
16 Drawing Room
17 Tullibardine Room
18, 19 Tapestry Room
20 Glenlyon Lobby
21–23 Banvie Room

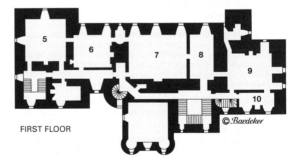

FIRST FLOOR

5 Small Drawing Room
6 Tea Salon
7 Dining Room
8 Ante-room
9 Blue Bedchamber
10 Blue Dressing Room

GROUND FLOOR

1 Stewart Room
2 Earl John's Room
3 Guard Room
4 Picture Staircase
24 Terrace Room
25 Armoury
26 Treasury
27 Old Scots Room
28 Natural History Museum
29 Ballroom
30 Porcelain Room
31 Costume Room

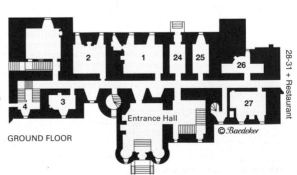

parade, while on other occasions one of the army's pipers stands in front of the castle and plays some popular Highland melodies.

A magnificent avenue of linden trees leads up to the gleaming white east front of the castle which was conquered only four times throughout its 700-year history. Famous guests include Mary Stuart (1564) and "Bonnie Prince Charlie", who stayed at the castle for one day with his Highland army in 1745. The oldest section of the castle is the two lower storeys of the main tower (started in 1269), known as the Cumming Tower after the builder. The upper floors were added in the 19th c. in Georgian style by the 2nd Duke of Atholl, but in 1869 David and John Bryce were commissioned by the 7th Duke to return the castle to its original baronial style.

The wood-panelled entrance hall is decorated with hunting trophies and a remarkable collection of arms which belonged to the Murrays. The Stewart Room contains portraits of Mary Stuart and her family and in Earl John's Room the helmet and armour of Viscount Dundee are displayed. Hanging on the Picture Staircase are family portraits covering three generations, including works by Ramsay, Lely and Raeburn; a life-size picture of the 1st Duke was painted by Thomas Murray, while the 1st Marquis of Atholl is immortalised on canvas in a Caesar-like pose by Jakob de Witt. Fine period furniture, chinoiserie and Sèvres porcelain can be seen in the two adjoining salons. Thomas Clayton was responsible for creating the splendid plasterwork in the Dining Room, although Thomas Bardell made the "Four Seasons" ceiling medallions. The landscapes on the panels are by Charles Stewart, while the silver stag on the dining table was a present from the tenants to the 7th Duke and his wife on the occasion of their silver wedding in 1888. The outstanding painting in the second floor corridor is David Allan's portrayal of the 4th Duke dressed in Highland costume and surrounded by his family. Also worth a mention are the furnishings in the Derby Dressing Room made almost entirely from broom wood, the painting of the 3rd Duke, his wife and seven children in the Drawing Room, the Jacobite portraits in the Tullibardine Room and the fine Brussels tapestries

Ornamental coat of arms, Blair Castle

(woven for Charles I) in the Tapestry Room. The showcases in the Treasury display jewellery belonging to the family and the natural history museum illustrates Highland wildlife. The Ballroom was completed in 1877 and above the stage hangs Raeburn's portrait of the famous fiddler Neil Gow. Look out for the comprehensive collection of porcelain which includes some delightful hand-painted pieces from Sèvres, Derby and Wedgwood. After a tour of the interior, the castle grounds are ideal for a stroll.

Glenshee
Skiing Centre

In the winter large numbers of skiing enthusiasts make for the Glenshee region (40 miles/64km to the north-east) and the slopes of the Cairngorms. Several ski-lifts give access to the ski runs and also the cross-country tracks.

Aberfeldy

A journey along the A924 and the A827 to Aberfeldy (pop. 1250; 15 miles/24km to the south-west) is worthwhile. This peaceful little village is situated by Urlar Burn near its confluence with the River Tay. The gorge here is as wild as it was 200 years ago when Robert Burns (see entry) climbed to the three waterfalls at Moness. By that time he was already very successful and, wherever he went, both ordinary people and the educated classes would listen attentively to what he had to say. These two contrasting worlds have found their way into his poems and "Come let us spend the lightsome days in the Birchs of Aberfeldy" was written, we are led to believe, by Burns as he sat on a rock above the birch forest. Nowadays, a nature trail leads visitors along the Urlar's stone staircase.

★General
Wade's Bridge

Black Watch
Memorial

The highlight of the village is the almost filigree design on the five-arched bridge over the Tay, which William Adam created for General Wade. Wade had devised comprehensive plans for opening up the Highlands and for making them much more accessible to English troops. In front of the bridge stands a memorial unveiled in 1877 in honour of the Black Watch Regiment which was first established in Aberfeldy. The statue on the memorial shows a kilted soldier standing on a cairn.

Aberfeldy
Distillery

The whisky distillery by the banks of the river was opened in 1898 by the sons of the famous blender John Dewar. The spirit has a slightly smoky-peaty flavour. Single malts have been in production here since 1991 (open: Mon.–Fri. 9.30am–4.30pm; see Baedeker Special, "Scotch Whisky").

Castle Menzies

Close on 2 miles/3km to the west stands the 16th c. Z-shaped Castle Menzies, which is owned by the Menzies Clan Society. The four huge corner towers dominate the building in which an exhibition documents the history of the Menzies clan (open: Apr.–mid-Oct. Mon.–Sat. 10.30am–5pm, Sun. 2–5pm).

★★Loch Tay

★Ben Lawers

The long, narrow Loch Tay is not just a haven for anglers and watersports enthusiasts but it is also one of Scotland's most beautiful lochs. Flanked on both sides either by bare or partly wooded hillsides, the full glory of the lake can be best appreciated from the summit of Ben Lawers (3981ft/1214m) on the north bank. Ben Lawers is the highest peak in Perthshire and the variety of its mountain flora will be of interest to botanists.

Dunkeld
★Cathedral

About 12 miles/19.2km to the south of Pitlochry lies the idyllic town of Dunkeld, which is noted for its cathedral, one of the oldest in Scotland. This church set in a delightful location in the green Tay valley was founded in 1107. Work started in earnest in 1318 but shortly after its completion in 1560 it was destroyed by the Reformers. The nave which remains roofless and the large north-west tower date from the 15th c., while the restored chancel continues to be used as the parish church. Pictish kings resided in Dunkeld and in the 6th c. St Columba established a settlement here to which Celtic monks later added an abbey. When in 844 Kenneth MacAlpin united the Picts and the Scots, he made Dunkeld and Scone (see Perth) his royal

residences. The pretty town with its attractive market place and picturesque little houses in Cathedral Street (faithfully restored by the National
Trust for Scotland; not open to the public) grew up in the late 17th c. after
the original settlement was destroyed by Covenanters in the Battle of
Dunkeld (1689).

★Little houses

One of the five Tyrolean larches planted in 1738 by the Duke of Atholl
survives in Hermitage Park (NTS), a wood with nature trails. At that time,
such exotic trees were much admired and they were planted widely in
Scotland until the turn of the century.

Hermitage Park

Thomas Telford's seven-arched Tay Bridge (1809) connects Dunkeld with
the resort of Birnam, which, with its smart houses with pointed gables, was
built to satisfy the Victorians' great enthusiasm for travel. Birnam Wood is
where Shakespeare's Macbeth met his death.

Birnam

St Andrews

G 5

Region: Fife
Population: 14,000

The small town of St Andrews, situated on the Fife peninsula (see entry)
about 12 miles/20km south-east of Dundee, overlooks a long sandy beach.
For many sports enthusiasts, St Andrews is the home of golf. The Royal and
Ancient Golf Club was founded here in 1754 and since 1897 its members
have been recognised internationally as golf's ruling body. Every two years
the famous "British Open" championship is held at one of St Andrews' five
eighteen-hole courses (there is one nine-hole course too). The little town
also boasts numerous ancient buildings and what is thought to be Scotland's oldest university. The many student bars around College Street and
Market Street contribute to the town's lively atmosphere.

★★Golfing centre
and university
town

The St Andrews Festival, a biennial (1995, 1997 . . .) cultural event featuring
music, drama, cabaret, films and art exhibitions, is held in the middle of
February. In April, at the end of the spring term, the students of San
Salvator College take part in the Kate Kennedy Procession, a colourful
costume parade through the streets around the university with a history
going back to 1848. The big Lammas Fair in August is one of the oldest such
fairs in Scotland, dating from medieval times.

Festival

Sights

The famous "Old Course" (par 72) runs alongside the coast. Originally
there were 22 holes, but in 1836 the number was reduced to eighteen ("nine
out" and "nine home"). With huge "double greens", putts of 100ft/30m or
more are sometimes required. Behind the first tee stands the majestic
clubhouse of the Royal and Ancient Golf Club – the European headquarters
of the sport's governing body.

★★Old Course

Golfing enthusiasts should not miss the new British Golf Museum (1990),
which documents the history of this home of golf from the Middle Ages to
the present day. As well as many historic exhibits, the exhibition shows the
development of the golf ball, the club, the rules and the techniques.
Detailed information is also given on some of the famous championships
and golfing celebrities, starting with Tom Morris (father and son), who in
the middle of the 19th c. both won the "Open" four times, Harry Vardon, six
times winner of the "Open" between 1894 and 1914, Lady Margaret Scott
who was Ladies Champion three times at the end of the 19th c., not
forgetting Peter Thompson and Nick Faldo, names from the recent past
who were both winners of the "British Open" on more than one occasion.

★★British
Golf Museum

Open:
Mar., Apr.
Thur.–Tues.
10am–5pm;
May–Oct. daily,
10am–5.30pm;
Nov.–Feb.
Thur.–Mon.
11am–3pm

Bogey, Birdie, Hole in One

According to the history books, golf was played on the east coast of Scotland as early as the Middle Ages. Both noblemen and commoners became preoccupied with a game that required just a club, a ball and a hole in the ground. The first mention of golf in historical documents – the word derives from the Gaelic word "goulf" or "gowf" meaning "hit" – was in 1457 when James II gave this order to his men: "Gowf and fitba to be utterly cryit doon and not usit", in other words his soldiers were to concentrate on the more important military skills such as archery instead of wasting their time playing golf and football. Evidence exists to show that James IV acquired a new set of golf clubs in 1504, that Mary Stuart was an enthusiastic golfer and that her son James VI, after he had acquired the English crown and moved to London, established the first golf course outside Scotland. The first record of any attempt to discuss technique was found in the diary of Thomas Kincaid, a medical student from Edinburgh. By the middle of the 18th c. the first golfing associations had been founded and the Gentlemen Golfers of Leith laid down some firm rules. The world's oldest golf club was set up in 1744 by "The Honourable Company of Edinburgh Golfers" some ten years earlier than the St Andrews club; however, "proper" golf was played for the first time at St Andrews. In 1834 William IV elevated the Society of St Andrews Golfers (founded in 1754) to the Royal and Ancient Golf Club and its members have been responsible for laying down the international rules since 1897. In conjunction with the United States Golf Association, the club publishes a revised edition of the rules every four years. The dream of every golfer is to play at least once on the Old Course at St Andrews, agreed by all golfers to be the world's top championship course. In Scotland alone there are over 430 golf courses in either private or public ownership. Unlike many other countries, in Scotland golf is not an elite pastime for the rich but it is a sport enjoyed by all sections of society. Apart from the exclusive clubs and magnificent golfing hotels such as those at Gleneagles or Turnberry, there are golf courses where the annual membership subscriptions are only moderate sums and a round can be played in return for the payment of a "green fee".

The object of the game – which some maintain started out as a pastime for Scottish shepherds who would strike a pebble into a rabbit burrow with a piece of driftwood – is to hit a small ball into a hole over a range of distances. The winner of the game is the player who completes a round in the least number of strokes.

A hole consists of three sections: the "teeing ground" from where the ball is first struck, the closely mown "fairway" and then the flawlessly smooth and very closely mown "green" where a flagstick marks the position of the hole (diameter 4.25in./10.79cm). When the ball (1.62 ounces/45.93g in weight and not less than 1.68in./42.67mm in diameter) is first struck from the tee, it may be placed on a small peg, also known as a tee, that is pushed into the ground. The fairways are surrounded by longer grass known as the "rough", by water or by shrubland. The ball could just as easily land here as on the man-made obstacles such as the sandy bunkers. If a ball is lost, golfers follow the rule that was agreed by the Royal Aberdeen Club in 1783: no longer than five minutes is to be spent looking for it! Until the end of the 19th c. most golf courses had 25 holes, but now a round is usually eighteen holes. On nine-hole courses a game consists of two circuits of the course.

A set of golf clubs will have up to fourteen different types of clubs. Heads may be made of wood or metal and the angles on the striking surface will vary. Wooden clubs ("woods" nos. 1 to 5) have heads weighted with lead and are used for driving shots, while the lighter, spoon-like "irons" (nos. 1 to 9) are for making shorter strokes. A "pitching wedge" is a special club with a flatter angle to the head and is used for hitting the ball high but only over a short distance on to the green, while a "sand-wedge" is for balls stuck in a bunker. A "putter" is used on the green to stroke the ball into the hole. The score-card gives the names to the different holes, the degree of difficulty and also the "par". The latter refers to the average number of strokes that each hole requires. Where the distance from tee to green is less than 750ft/228m then a par of three applies, up to 1425ft/434m par is four and beyond that the par is five. A top-class golfer should take between 63 and 74 strokes to complete each course. If a less experienced player is expected to complete the course in 84 strokes instead of 74, then he is said to have a handicap of 10. Each player is awarded a handicap and this number is arrived at by averaging out his scores over a year. If a player finishes a hole with the average number of strokes for that course, then he has completed a round at "par". If he completes a hole at one less than par, then he has scored a "birdie", two under par is an "eagle", three under par an "albatross". Every golfer's dream is, of course, a "hole in one" or an "ace", but novices and the average player are more likely to be satisfied with scoring a "bogey", one stroke above par. Anyone who scores an "ace" may end up having to buy a round of drinks at the club bar, otherwise known as the "nineteenth hole".

Guest players need to be clear about Scottish golfing etiquette. A round should be completed without any major interruptions at a steady pace – although weather conditions may intervene. As a good rule of thumb, a round of golf should last about 3 hours 30 minutes. Anyone who wishes to take their time should allow others to overtake them. Care should always be taken with the turf and divots replaced. Visiting players will value the assistance of a "caddy", not just to carry the clubs but also to offer advice on the idiosyncrasies of the course. Scottish golf clubs can be rather conservative with regard to dress, for example. In many places a jacket and tie must be worn and some clubs have balked at the thought of sexual equality, offering restricted playing times for women or until fairly recently excluding women from the male sanctuary of the bar.

Anyone with a serious interest in the history of the game and its place in the social history of Scotland should try to visit the meticulously kept museums at St Andrews and Gullane (East Lothian).

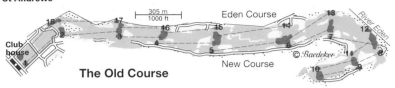

305 m
1000 ft

Eden Course

River Eden

Club house

The Old Course

New Course

© Baedeker

1 Burn	5 Hole o'Cross	8 Short	12 Heathery In
2 Dyke	Out	9 End	13 Hole o'Cross In
3 Cartgate Out	6 Heathery Out	10 Bobby Jones	14 Long
4 Ginger Beer	7 High Out	11 High In	15 Cartgate In

16 Corner of the
Dyke
17 Road
18 Tom Morris

★Sea Life
Centre

Only a short distance away, the Sea Life Centre gives a fascinating insight into the underwater world. Attractions include an aquarium, shark pool, seal enclosure and marine laboratory. The beach café with its sea view is a good place to conclude the visit.

★Cathedral

Open:
Apr.–Sept.
Mon.–Sat.
9.30am–6pm;
Oct.–Mar.
Mon.–Thur., Sat.
9.30am–4pm,
Sun. 2–4pm

St Andrews has played an important part in Scottish ecclesiastical history and this is evident from the wealth of churches and monuments in the town. According to legend St Regulus landed here in the 4th c. with the bones of St Andrew – although it now seems more likely that the reliquary actually arrived in the 8th c. (St Andrews' Cross in the Scottish Saltire, see page 22). Soon the small town was an episcopal see. About 1200, several churches were constructed in the town, including the huge cathedral and also the castle. By the 15th c. St Andrews was the centre of religious and spiritual power in Scotland and in 1472 it became the seat of the archbishop. Some 335ft/102m in length and 160ft/49m wide, the cathedral (built between 1160 and 1328) was once the largest church in Scotland. Robert I (see Famous People) attended the consecration and 200 years later James V and Mary of Guise married here establishing the Franco-Scottish "Auld Alliance". Destroyed in June 1559, the cathedral's stonework was plun-

The Royal and Ancient Golf Club at St Andrews

dered and now only parts of the late Romanesque east front, a section of the west front, the southern side aisle and a gatehouse remain (HS).

The tiny church of St Rule with its original chancel and square tower was built for Augustinian monks between 1127 and 1144 by master craftsmen from Yorkshire (HS).

St Rule

St Andrews University is both the smallest and oldest of Scotland's seats of learning. It was founded in 1411 by Bishop Henry Wardlaw (guided tours, twice daily, July and August). The Colleges of St Salvator (1450) and St Leonard (1511) which were combined in 1747 are devoted to the Arts and the Sciences, while St Mary's College, opened by Cardinal Beaton in 1538, serves as the theology faculty. The College Chapel in St Salvator contains the pulpit from Holy Trinity Church in the town where the reformer John Knox (see Famous People) first preached. St Leonard's Chapel houses some fine tombstones from the 16th and 17th c. and is certainly worth a visit.

★University Colleges

A rose bush that Mary Stuart (see Famous People) is supposed to have planted near St Mary's College still flowers and the house in South Street where she stayed is now St Leonard's College library.

A museum documenting local history is situated in former fishermen's houses on North Street (no. 12; open: Easter, mid-June-mid-Sept. and St Andrew's Day/30th Nov. daily, 2–4.30pm).

Preservation Trust Museum

The remains of the bishop's palace and stronghold (c. 1200) crown a rock that overlooks the sea. Cardinal Beaton lived here in great luxury until he was murdered by Protestants in 1546. Among the famous prisoners held captive here was John Knox, who was later condemned to work as a slave on a French galley. Interesting features inside the castle include the Bottle Dungeon and the underground escape passage. The Visitor Centre relates the full story of the castle and cathedral (HS). About 2 miles/3.2km to the south-east lies the bizarre rock formation known as the "Rock and Spindle".

★Castle
Open: Apr.–Sept.
Mon.–Sat.
9.30am–6pm,
Sun. 2–6pm;
Oct.–Mar.
Mon.–Sat.
9.30am–4pm,
Sun. 2–4pm

St Kilda   A 4

Region: Western Islands Area

The storm-battered St Kilda Islands have been under the stewardship of the National Trust for Scotland since 1957. They lie 110 miles/170km to the west of the Scottish mainland surrounded by the Atlantic Ocean. The last inhabitants of this inhospitable archipelago left their homes and barren soil on the main island of Hirta in 1930. Now the sea birds including huge colonies of fulmars, gannets and puffins have the islands to themselves. Unique to the islands are the St Kilda mouse and the St Kilda wren. In addition, some 14,000 wild Soay sheep graze here. The breathtaking cliffs near Conachair (Gabbro) are, at 1397ft/424m, the tallest cliffs in Britain.

★★Atlantic bird sanctuary

In 1986 UNESCO adopted St Kilda as Scotland's first World Heritage Site. Every year the National Trust for Scotland organises research and working visits for enthusiastic birdwatchers (for the NTS; tel. (0131) 226 5922; fax (01631) 570011.

Shetland Islands   H/J 1/2

Region: Shetland Island Area

Slightly more than 100 islands make up the Shetland (from the old Nordic "hjaltland") and they form the northern outposts of the British Isles. Surrounded by the swirling Atlantic Ocean and about 100 miles/160km from

Situation and climate

the north-eastern coast of Scotland, the Shetland Islands lie on about the same latitude as the Norwegian city of Bergen, the southern tip of Greenland, the Gulf of Alaska and southern Siberia. However, unlike some of these remote parts of the world, the Shetlands are not frozen wastes. Whipped by wind and rain they may be, but the Gulf Stream provides a relatively favourable climate, although the scope for land cultivation is not as great as on the Orkney Islands (see entry). Temperature fluctuations are not that great and a fresh, salty breeze seems to be ever present. At midsummer the sun stays above the horizon for nineteen hours and twilight ("simmer dim") persists between sunset and sunrise.

★★Topography

The islands, made predominantly of schist but also "old redstone" and granite, have breathtakingly beautiful coastal landscapes and bays (the so-called "Voes") that have cut deep into the land as a result of Ice Age glaciation. Compared to the Orkney Islands (see entry), the Shetlands present a more undulating picture. Heathers and broom flourish on the almost treeless hills of the larger islands, together with narcissi, primulas, marsh marigolds, red catchfly, orchids and wild thyme, whose colours contrast strikingly with the blue of the water, the green of the more fertile hollows and the brown of the open moorland. In many places peat is still cut for burning on domestic stoves. The Shetlands are popular with lovers of harsh, almost primeval nature. Walkers and mountain bikers will find plenty to challenge them and watersports enthusiasts can choose between over 350 lakes and the vast Atlantic Ocean which surrounds the islands. The lochs, well stocked with brown and rainbow trout, are close to paradise for fly fishermen, but there are also many opportunities for deep-sea fishing. For some golfers the chance of a round of golf at midnight on Britain's northernmost golf course is irresistible. Birdwatchers will be drawn to such islands as Fair Isle, Mousa, Noss and near Herma Ness to watch such sea birds as Arctic terns, shearwaters, razorbills, gannets, fulmars and the amusing puffins, known here as "Tammy Noirie". Out on

Hand knitted in Shetland . . .

. . . and Lerwick's equally warm welcome!

the moors live great skuas ("bonxies"), Arctic skuas, grouse, merlins and golden plovers, while on the lochs shovellers and rain geese are native species. Otters, seals and grey seals enjoy the protection of the sheltered bays and with a bit of luck on a short sea cruise it may be possible to catch a glimpse of dolphins, porpoises and even whales.

One kind of animal native to the Shetlands has become famous throughout the world: the rather unkempt looking Shetland pony which has inhabited the islands since at least Viking times. In the mid-19th c. these tough, short-legged animals were found to be ideal as beasts of burden in British coal mines and also as a work horse for Scottish crofters. Now these small ponies which attain a shoulder height of between 27in./70cm and 43in./110cm are favourites with children – but feeding the wild ponies is strictly forbidden. Riding and pony trekking on the other hand is a popular pursuit on the Shetlands.

Shetland ponies

Perhaps more than on the Orkneys, the influence of the islands' Nordic forefathers is keenly felt. The islanders are, after all, more orientated towards Norway and the Faroes than the Scottish mainland and their language exhibits a greater Nordic element than that of the Orcadians. Most place-names are of Nordic origin. Nothing more clearly reflects the islanders' Viking past than the midwinter festival Up Helly Aa ("the end of the holy days", from the Norwegian "helly"–"holy"), a fire festival of Norwegian origin held in Lerwick every year on the last Tuesday in January. A 32ft/10m long replica of a Viking longship adorned with shields and sails is paraded through the town led by the Chief Guiser (Guiser Jarl) and his 500-strong entourage, all magnificently costumed. At the harbour the ship is put to sea, but then the flaming torches carried by the marchers are thrown on to the vessel to set it alight. For about an hour the spectators watch the burning ship before adjourning to the bars where the celebrations continue until the early hours of the next day.

Nordic Inheritance

Up Helly Aa

Shetland ponies

303

Shetland Islands

Transport
Ferries

Car ferry services operate between mainland Scotland (Aberdeen) and Lerwick (once a day, Mon.–Fri.) and between Orkney (Stromness) and Lerwick (Sun. only, Jun.–Aug. Tues. also). Inter-island car ferries include Bressay–Lerwick/Mainland (daily, every 30 mins), Fair Isle–Grutness/Mainland (twice weekly), Fair Isle–Lerwick/Mainland (once a week), Foula–Walls/Mainland (twice weekly), Gutcher/Yell–Oddsta/Fetlar (four/five times daily), Gutcher/Yell–Belmont/Unst (daily, every 30 mins), Out Skerries–Lerwick/Mainland (twice weekly), Out Skerries–Vidlin/Mainland (Fri., Sat. three times daily), Symbister/Whalsay–Laxo/Mainland (daily, every two hours), Ulsta/Yell–Toft/Mainland (daily, every 30 mins). A passenger ferry operates three times a week between West Burrafirth/Mainland and Papa Stour. Summer schedule applies Apr.–Oct. During winter some ferries run less frequently.

Flights

British Airways fly direct to Sumburgh/Mainland from Kirkwall/Orkney, Aberdeen, Edinburgh, Glasgow and Inverness. Loganair also have direct flights to Sumburgh from Kirkwall/Orkney, Edinburgh and Glasgow, while Business Air serve Sumburgh from Aberdeen and Edinburgh and also fly to Dundee.

History

The history of the Shetland Islands is closely tied to that of the Orkneys (see entry) and some spectacular Stone Age sites have been uncovered proving that prehistoric man was able to sustain a living on these remote islands. Boats with dragon figureheads and full of Viking explorers in search of new territories landed here and subjugated the native Picts.

The Scandinavian settlers retained their control over the islands until the 15th c. and their influence is still clearly in evidence.

In the last 20 years, however, the two island groups have had to come to terms with change on a grand scale: the discovery of North Sea oil has had a dramatic effect on the Shetland Islanders' way of life (see Economy). More recently the loss of the oil tanker "Braer" and its cargo off the southern tip of Mainland was an example of how crude oil can wreak havoc on the environment (see below).

Economy

Some 22,000 Shetlanders inhabit thirteen of the islands, with more than half living on Mainland island. The main source of income for the native Shetlanders is farming, predominantly sheep-rearing for the highly-regarded Shetland wool. This is then used to produce jumpers and other warm woollen goods, often to new patterns, but always in accordance with the long-established style. Much of this work is done by homeworkers (follow the road-signs) but some spinning mills and wool factories have opened up on the islands and their products are marketed by the  Shetland Knitwear Trades Association, an organisation set up in 1983. Among the best-known patterns are those created by the knitters of Fair Isle, a remote Atlantic island with a huge bird population. Other popular souvenirs include the hand-made silver and gold jewellery based on Nordic symbols. The farmland surrounding the crofters' homes produces very

Fishing

meagre yields. Fishing and salmon farming, on the other hand, are much more profitable, although both have suffered from the decline in the herring stocks and also oil pollution from the offshore drilling rigs. The loss of the Liberian oil tanker "Braer" in 1993 on the south coast of Mainland turned out to be not quite as serious as was first thought but it showed the islanders how easily the oil industry could damage fish stocks, and thus

Oil industry

their livelihood. Oil is, of course, the third mainstay of the local economy.

When massive reserves of oil were discovered in the East Shetland Basin's Brent Field in 1972, the Shetland Islanders were able to look forward to years of prosperity. The unemployment figures on the islands are the lowest in Scotland, a country where unemployment is otherwise well above the UK average. The discovery of oil brought with it a large airport, new roads, Europe's largest oil terminal and thousands of oil workers from all over the world. The British government – unusually – allowed the island authorities a free hand in their negotiations with the oil companies. Now the initial boom has receded, a slightly more sober attitude has returned. Output has stabilised and many of the supply flights out to the oil rigs start from Aberdeen (see entry). Attempts have been made in recent years to improve facilities for tourism which is set to play a more important role in the islands' future.

Mainland

The largest island (54 miles/86.4km long) is Mainland. Its uneven coastline has so many fjords and inlets that nowhere on the narrow strip of land is further than 3 miles/4.8km from the sea. Lerwick (pop. 7600), the islands' administrative centre, lies on the east coast in a bay sheltered by the offshore island of Bressay and is Great Britain's northernmost town. The first settlers in Lerwick were Dutch fishermen who came during the 16th c. Herring fishing, which helped to establish the town's prosperity in the 18th and 19th c., remains an important industry alongside supplying the drilling rigs. Places of interest are few; the attraction of the town lies in its narrow alleys that wind up the slope from the main Commercial Road to the upper town.

★Lerwick

The Shetland Museum on Lower Hillhead documents the history and unique features of the islands (open: Mon., Wed., Fri. 10am–7pm, Tues., Thur., Sat. 10am–5pm).

Shetland Museum

Lerwick, the most northerly town in the British Isles

Shetland Islands

Fort Charlotte

Fort Charlotte, named after George III's wife, dominates the harbour area. These fortifications which were built in 1655 following John Mylne's design were burnt down by the Dutch in 1672 and then the English rebuilt them in 1781. At the turn of the century the fort became a prison, but it is now used to train cadets. A fine panoramic view of the town is possible from the clock tower above the town hall, which was built in 1882 from Bressay sandstone.

Shetland Fiddling

"The Lounge" pub on Saturdays is the best place to hear the local music, the "Shetland fiddling". Spring is the time for the Shetland Folk Festival and in October the Shetland Accordion and Fiddle Festival takes place.

Loch Clickhimin Broch

Just over a mile to the south-west of the town centre, Loch Clickhimin affords some fine views over the harbour and out to sea, while Clickhimin Broch (HS) is a Pictish round tower in remarkably good condition.

Scalloway
Castle

Museum

Scalloway on the west coast is the islands' former capital. The notorious Earl Patrick Stewart (see Orkney Islands) built a castle here c. 1600 as a small exhibition inside explains (HS). The Shetland Woollen Company displays its wares nearby. A small museum in Main Street recounts among other things the story of the "Shetland Bus", a boat that took Norwegian resistance fighters struggling against the German occupation of their country during the Second World War, back to their homeland (open: May–Oct. Tues., Wed., Fri. 2–5pm, Sat. 10am–1pm, 2–5pm, Sun. 2–5pm).

Tingwall
Agricultural Museum

An agricultural museum is housed in an 18th c. grainstore at Veensgarth near Tingwall a little further north (open: July, Aug. daily, 2–5pm).

St Ninian's Isle

The tiny St Ninian's Isle off the west coast is only accessible at low tide. A chapel was built on the island in the 7th c. to honour Scotland's national saint. In 1958 a hoard of Celtic silverware was unearthed nearby. It is thought that monks had hidden the valuables from Viking invaders. Only the ruins of a later chapel that dates from the 12th c. remain. The silver treasure is now on display in Edinburgh's National Museum for Antiquities (see Edinburgh).

★Shetland Croft House Museum

Near the hamlet of Dunrossness a road branches off to the east to Shetland Croft House Museum, a traditional crofter's house, where the rigours of everyday life for the islanders during the 19th c. are clearly shown (open: Mon., Wed., Fri. 10am–7pm, Tues., Thur., Sat. 10am–5pm).

★★Jarlshof

Open:
Apr.–Sept.
Mon.–Sat.
9.30am–6pm,
Sun. 2–6pm

Jarlshof (HS), situated opposite Sumburgh Airport, is probably the Shetland Island's principal prehistoric site. The complex covers a wide time-span. Round houses from the Bronze Age and Iron Age lie alongside Viking longhouses. The most recent buildings are a farmhouse dating from the 16th c. and a hall built by the infamous earls Robert and Patrick Stewart. A small museum details the course of the excavations. The name "Jarlshof" has no historic importance, but originates from the imagination of Sir Walter Scott (see Famous People) who visited the island in 1816 and immortalised it in his book "The Pirate".

★Sumburgh Head

Thousands of seabirds, including puffins and guillemots, have made their home at Sumburgh Head.

The "Braer" disaster

During a fierce storm in January 1993, the Liberian oil tanker "Braer" foundered on rocks to the west of Sumburgh near Garth Ness and 84,500 tonnes of crude oil poured into the sea. The stormy waters spread the oil over a wide area and, as a result, the coastline was spared from serious oil pollution. Now few traces of the disaster are visible, although thousands of sea birds were coated in oil and subsequently died. At the moment it is difficult to say whether fish stocks have been affected by the pollution and

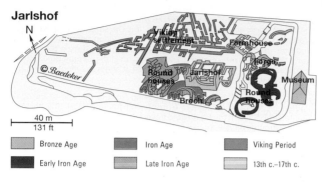

Jarlshof

N

© Baedeker

Viking settlement

Farmhouse

Round houses

Jarlshof

Broch

Broch

Round houses

Museum

40 m
131 ft

| | Bronze Age | | Iron Age | | Viking Period |
| | Early Iron Age | | Late Iron Age | | 13th c.–17th c. |

marine biologists will be studying the region in the next few years to see whether any permanent damage has occurred. The effect of the oil on marine life meant that many sea birds' lives were threatened by a shortage of food.

Northern Mainland is a place for communing with nature. It is difficult to explore the area by car as the roads often peter out and the coast has then to be reached on foot. The striking landmarks include the cliffs at Erne's Stack near Sandness, a truly breathtaking sight, while in the extreme north-west lies the fishing village of Stenness with its unusual rock formations nearby such as Dore Holm, the step-like porphyritic rock known as the Gate of Giants, the spectacular basalt formations at Esha Ness and the eroded lava cliffs of Hamna Voe. The highest point on the island is situated to the north-east: Ronas Hill (1486ft/452m) is a huge rock of red granite. The

★Northern
Mainland

Bronze and Iron Age houses at Jarlshof near Sumburgh

summit offers a magnificent view of the whole island. Finally, Lunna on the east coast north of Vidlin is worth a visit. It is the site of one of the oldest churches on the island and was also the embarkation point for the "Shetland Bus" used by the Norwegian resistance fighters during the Second World War. Before returning to Lerwick, stop off at the elegant Busta House near Brae. Built in 1714 and extended in 1984, it offers excellent cuisine and over 120 malt whiskies.

Sullom Voe

Sullom Voe is a different world. This deep fjord is the site of Europe's biggest oil terminal. Pipelines from the oil fields end at this harbour (opened in 1981) and the liquid gold flows into countless huge tanks. About 60% of Britain's oil is supplied from here.

Sights on the other Shetland Islands

Bressay

If the weather is fine, then a trip from Lerwick to Bressay (1 mile/1.6km) is worthwhile as the Ward of Bressay has some splendid viewpoints. Then take a boat trip through the Orkneyman's Cave at the southernmost tip of the island.

★★Noss

The uninhabited island of Noss can also be reached from Lerwick by boat (cruises include the seal colony on Green Holm to the north of Bressay). It is another island favoured by birdwatchers; some ornithologists even regard it as the finest spot in Britain for watching sea birds. In summer over 100,000 birds nest on The Noup (593ft/181m), a towering sandstone rock. Species worth looking out for here are puffins, guillemots, razorbills, fulmars, gannets, while great skuas ("bonxies") and Arctic skuas nest on the moors.

Mousa
★Mousa Broch

Mousa lies off the east coast opposite Sandwick. It is worth making the fifteen-minute crossing (May–Sept.) for the Iron Age Mousa Broch (HS),

Shetland puffin – "Tommy Noirie" to the islanders

probably the finest surviving example of its type in the whole of Scotland. The tower at Mousa rises to a height of 42ft/13m and measures 49ft/15m wide. In the central area was the hearth and also space for the cattle, while the three rooms around the outside were used for living and sleeping.

Pier House by the harbour on the north-eastern island of Whalsay was a 16th c. Hanseatic trading post where merchants found shelter and stored their goods.

Whalsay
Pier House

Yell (pop. 1000), and Lumbister Reserve in particular, is a favourite haunt for birdwatchers. Arctic skuas, great skuas and merlins nest on the moors, while the steep cliffs (400ft/122m) at Whalfirth make an ideal habitat for puffins and otters. Native fauna and flora and local history are documented in the Old Haa (1672) at Burravoe (open: Apr.–Sept. Tues., Wed., Fri.–Sun. 10am–4pm).

Yell
★Lumbister Reserve

★Old Haa

Ornithologists also appreciate Fetlar (pop. 100) where great skuas, merlins, curlews, red-necked phalaropes and stormy petrels are the main attractions. Seals also live along the shoreline.

Fetlar
★Fetlar Reserve

Unst, the most northerly of all the inhabited islands, supports a population of about 1000. On the east coast stands Muness Castle, Great Britain's most northerly castle that was built for Patrick Stewart by Laurence Bruce in 1589.

Unst
Muness Castle

The 74 acre/30ha nature reserve at Keen of Hamar is a must for amateur botanists. Wind, rain and frost have left a yellow-brown field of rubble behind. With a high metal content and scarcely any organic soil, all the plant-life occurs in miniature, including the Shetland chickweed (unique to the island and discovered in 1837), Nordic mountain rock cress and Norwegian sandwort.

★Keen of Hamar

The Atlantic Ocean crashes against gneiss rocks near Herma Ness at the northern tip of Unst. It is home to thousands of sea birds, including puffins and the rare black-browed albatross. The great skua colony on the island is the second-largest in Great Britain. The most northerly inhabited point in Great Britain is Muckle Flugga, where a lighthouse (1858) crowns the 200ft/61m rock. Just beyond here Out Stack marks the end of the British Isles.

★Herma Ness

Only the most enthusiastic birdwatcher will want to make the 19 mile/30km hazardous crossing to Foula on the west side of the Shetland archipelago. The reward is an opportunity to see Britain's largest great skua colony along with gannets, fulmars, razorbills and shags.

★Foula

Of more interest to ornithologists is Fair Isle, which lies 24 miles/39km south-west of the southern tip of Mainland in the middle of the Atlantic. It can be reached by ferry from Grutness (about 2hrs 30 mins) or by plane (25 mins by Loganair from Tingwall Airport). The name is derived from the Nordic word "fridarey" meaning "peaceful island". Designated in 1954 as a "National Scenic Area", the island is administered by the National Trust for Scotland. Only about 70 people live here and they have hundreds of thousands of birds to keep them company. About 340 different species have been observed, including fulmars, gannets, razorbills, stormy petrels, puffins, kittiwakes and great skuas predominate. In spring and autumn they are joined by countless migratory birds. Fair Isle Lodge and Bird Observatory was restored in 1989 and it offers overnight accommodation, plus the opportunity to catch up on the latest research.

Fair Isle has been inhabited for many years as the prehistoric earthwork that splits the island in half testifies. In the course of the centuries, many a ship's crew whose vessel came to grief on the rocks off the Shetland Islands found themselves washed ashore on Fair Isle. In 1588, for example, 300

★★Fair Isle

men from "El Gran Grifón", a flagship of the Spanish Armada, were lucky to reach safety here and in the 19th c. 465 German emigrants bound for the USA on board the "Lessing" were fortunate to end up on dry land here. According to legend, the famous Fair Isle pattern on Shetland jumpers was influenced by the Spanish sailors.

Stirling   F 5

Region: Central
Population: 24,000

Situation

Over the centuries Stirling has been a much disputed stronghold. It occupies a strategically important position in the Forth valley 28 miles/45km north-east of Glasgow (see entry). The earliest inhabitants were probably of Welsh descent and it is thought that the name Stirling is a corruption of the term "Place of Striving". No fewer than fifteen battlefields lie within close proximity of the castle.

Sights

★★Castle

Open:
Apr.–Sept.
daily,
9.30am–5.15pm;
Oct.–Mar. daily,
9.30am–4.15pm

The German writer Theodor Fontane who travelled extensively in Scotland during the 19th c. fell in love with Stirling and its castle. He spoke glowingly about the sun setting over the mountains and the Highland Regiment's pipe band playing on the castle forecourt. Visitors, he said, would "take home from Stirling the most beautiful picture that the Scottish landscape could provide". The town still leaves a deep and lasting impression on visitors. Much of Stirling Castle that is visible today, located in a commanding position above the town and crowning a 250ft/77m volcanic crag, dates from the 15th and 16th c. The history of the fortifications is closely linked with the Stewart dynasty. It has been historically proven that Alexander I died in 1124 in the castle. In 1296 the town was handed over to the English; however, a year later, after William Wallace won the Battle of Stirling Bridge, it was returned to the Scots, who held the castle as the last bastion of Scottish rule. In 1314 Robert the Bruce (see Famous People) decisively defeated the English at the Battle of Bannockburn (see entry) and under the Stuarts Stirling became an important royal seat. James II (1430), James III (1451) and James V (1512) were all born here. In 1543 Mary Stuart (see Famous People) was crowned as queen of Scotland in Stirling and she continued to live here before moving to France.

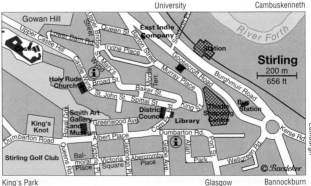

Stirling: King Street . . .   *. . . and historic Stirling Castle*

The castle can be reached via a steep lane lined by old houses. Located on the Esplanade is a memorial to Robert the Bruce and his victory at the Battle of Bannockburn (see entry). The defensive installations for the outer moat date from the time of Queen Anne. The entrance with its round towers (15th c.) opens on to the Lower Square which is overlooked by the Parliament Hall (1475–1503) and the Palace. This was designed by Andrew Ayton for James IV in 1496 and has a decorative façade showing allegorical figures. The "Stirling Heads" in the Royal Apartments deserve special attention. Some 35, originally 60, finely carved oak medallions display portraits of the Scottish rulers.

Situated on the north side of the Upper Square is the Royal Chapel (1594) where James VI's son Henry was baptised. The elegant early Renaissance building houses some fine 17th c. frescos and a Florentine frieze. The Garden (Nether Green) to the west of the chapel was laid out *c.* 1532 and the Argyll and Sutherland Highlanders' Regimental Museum is accommodated in the King's Old Buildings. The best views are from the north-western section of the fortification.

William Alexander of Menstrie, founder of the Scottish colony of Nova Scotia in North America, built this town house on Castle Wynd. About 1632 it was acquired by the Earl of Stirling, Governor of Nova Scotia, but some 24 years later the Renaissance house passed to the Earl of Argyll, whose name it now bears. The building is used as a youth hostel.

Argyll's Lodging

Buildings ranging from the 16th to the 19th c. line the bustling Broad Street in the old town. South-east of the castle, and separated from it by a dip, stands the Gothic Church of the Holy Rood. Its most impressive feature is the main nave with its Transitional-style huge oak ceiling. It dates from about 1270 but was altered in the 15th c. In 1542 at the age of eight months Mary Stuart (see Famous People) was crowned Queen of Scotland in the

Broad Street

Church of Holy Rood

church and, fifteen years later in 1567, her one-year-old son James VI received the crown here with the reformer John Knox (see Famous People) preaching the sermon.

Mar's Wark

The former town residence of the Earl of Mar at one end of Broad Street was built in Renaissance style in 1570 but was destroyed by the Jacobites in 1746. Further along Broad St lies Norrie's House (17th c.) followed by the Tolbooth, the former prison which was built between 1703 and 1706 and extended between 1806 and 1811.

Tolbooth

Stags Audio Walk

A two-hour "Walkman tour" takes the visitor to all the major places of historic interest in Stirling, inlcuding the monument to the freedom fighter and film hero William Wallace (Braveheart); Walkman hire: 24 Broad St.

King Street

King Street, now pedestrianised, and the Thistle Shopping Centre opposite the station offer the best choice of shops.

Old Bridge

The medieval stone bridge (c. 1400) over the Forth at the north end of the town should not be confused with the bridge about 100yd/100m further up river which gave its name to the battle of 1297.

Surroundings

Blair Drummond
Safari Park

It is possible to drive through the Blair Drummond Safari Park (4 miles/6.4km to the north-west) and observe the wild animals at close quarters. Children will probably most enjoy the sea lion performances, but boat trips and guided walks are also available (open: Apr.–early Oct. daily, 10am–5.30pm).

Doune
★ Castle

The castle in the small town of Doune (pop. 1200; 8 miles/12.8km to the north-west) was built at the end of the 14th c. by Robert Stewart, the 1st Duke of Albany and the Earl of Menteith and Fife. In 1570 the owner of the property Sir James Stewart was appointed Lord Doune and his son acquired through marriage the title of Earl of Moray. Since then Doune Castle with its 100ft/30m tower house, west tower and three-sided curtain wall has remained the seat of the earls of Moray. In 1883 the architect Andrew Kerr was commissioned by the 14th Earl to undertake comprehensive restoration work, with the provision that the character of the medieval castle be retained. In the Lord's Hall on the first floor, look out for a fine double fireplace and the Moray coat-of-arms, as well as the lancet windows and fireplaces in the apartments. An octagonal font in the chapel is of interest, while the Great Hall displays banners of all the families who have had links with Doune Castle. HS; open: Apr.–Sept. Mon.–Sat. 9.30am–6pm, Sun. 2–6pm; Oct.–Mar. Mon.–Sat. 9.30am–4pm, Sun. 2–4pm. The Earl of Moray has built up a fine collection of veteran and vintage cars and these are exhibited in the Motor Museum. Prized exhibits include Jaguars, Aston Martins, Bentleys, a 1930 two-seater MG, a 1951 Morgan Plus Four, a 1961 four-seater Austin Healey Mk 1, 1920s Sunbeam motor-cycles and the second-oldest Rolls Royce in the world. Open: Apr.–Oct. daily, 10am–5pm.

★ Motor Museum

Dunblane
Cathedral

The cathedral in the little town of Dunblane (pop. 7500; 6 miles/10km to the north) was consecrated by Bishop Clement in 1228, although the foundation stone had been laid in the previous century by David I.

The ground-plan of the church is remarkable in that the chancel has no side aisles or transept, unlike the main nave, which was fully restored by Sir Roland Anderson in 1893. The once freestanding church tower (12th c.) has been incorporated into the south side. In the interior, the highly-acclaimed, oval Ruskin window by John Ruskin and the 15th c. choir stalls merit a closer inspection.

★ Leighton
Library

The library that Robert Leighton (1611–62) established in Cathedral Square in 1687 is the oldest private library in Scotland. Faithful restoration work was undertaken in 1991 and it is now open to the public. The shelves are lined with some 4500 books written in more than 50 languages and dating from between 1500 and 1840. Open: May–Oct. Mon.–Fri. 10.30am–12.30pm, 2.30–4.30pm.

Situated in the delightful Dollar Glen (NTS) 1 mile/1.6km north of Dollar (pop. 2500), Castle Campbell was originally known as Castle Gloom. Built by the 1st Earl of Argyll at the end of the 15th c., it was burnt down by Cromwell's army in 1650. Nonetheless, the courtyard and Great Hall are worth inspecting. HS; open: Apr.-Sept. Mon.–Sat. 9.30am–6pm, Sun. 2–6pm; Oct.–Mar. Mon.–Sat. 9.30am–4pm, Sun. 2–4pm.

Dollar
Castle Campbell

Dominating the surrounding countryside and about 1½ miles/2.4km north-east of Stirling, the National Wallace Monument, was erected in 1869 in memory of the victors of the Battle of Stirling Bridge. Inside the square tower (220ft/64m), as well as the marble busts of famous Scots, there is an exhibition recounting the bitter struggle that took place between Sir William Wallace and the English invaders between 1296 and 1298. The film "Braveheart" (a name never attributed to Wallace in his lifetime), with Mel Gibson in the starring role, won two Oscars in 1996. Many people come to this well-known landmark simply to admire the splendid view. Open: Mar.–June, Oct. daily, 10am–5pm; July–Aug. daily, 9.30am–6pm.

★Wallace
Monument

In 1140 David I founded the Augustinian abbey at Cambuskenneth (1 mile/1.6km to the east) and the Scottish parliament met there a number of times in 1326. James III and his wife Margaret of Denmark were buried at Cambuskenneth in the 15th c. In 1604 the Earl of Mar decided to use the stones from the abbey for his town residence, so now only a tower and the church's west portal remain. HS; open: Apr.–Sept. Mon.–Sat. 9.30am–6pm, Sun. 2–6pm; Oct.–Mar. Mon.–Sat. 9.30am–4pm, Sun. 2–4pm.

Cambuskenneth
Abbey

See entry

Bannockburn

The stone pineapple in Dunmore Park near Airth, about 7 miles/11.2km south-east of Stirling, arouses considerable curiosity. This bizarre structure forms the dome of a building in the garden, which was completed in 1761 by Sir William Chambers (NTS; not open to the public).

Dunmore
★Pineapple

**Practical
Information
from A to Z**

Accommodation

Bed and Breakfast

Bed and Breakfast, or B & B for short, is inexpensive as well as being a perfect way of meeting Scottish folk in their own homes. In some of the remoter parts of Scotland such as the Highlands and Islands it can often also be the only form of accommodation available apart from campsites and holiday homes. B & B can simply be overnight accommodation in a farmhouse or someone's home or it can be in a guest house with a number of rooms which can cater for other meals as well. Whatever form B & B takes the rooms are usually pleasant and comfortable, with a hearty Scottish breakfast to look forward to in the morning.

Booking

With Bed and Breakfast there is usually no need to book in advance. Simply look for the B & B or Vacancy sign, knock on the door and ask. If you do want to book ahead this can be done through a travel agent, a central booking agency, or a Tourist Information Centre, using either their local booking services or their "Book-A-Bed-Ahead" scheme whereby, for a small fee, they can arrange accommodation in another locality.

If you want to contact somewhere directly yourself the Scottish Tourist Board (see Information) publishes a free "Scotland Accommodation" guide full of accommodation ideas, including some B & B addresses, and information on how to order their own annual "Scotland: Bed & Breakfast" where-to-stay guide covering over 1500 establishments. There is also the annual "Bed & Breakfast" guide published by the Automobile Association (see Motoring), as well as the accommodation guides produced by the Area Tourist Boards containing full listings of all types of accommodation in their area.

Holiday homes
Self-catering

Self-catering in holiday homes is becoming increasingly popular, and the Scottish Tourist Board's annual "Scotland: Self Catering" where-to-stay guide includes over 1200 cottages, apartments and chalets, many of them in scenic areas. Self-catering accommodation can be booked direct or through a travel agent. It pays to book early, and you will usually be expected to send a deposit. It is worth remembering that prices can be as much as 50% cheaper between October and March.

Farm holidays

In recent years many farms have started catering for visitors, usually on a Bed and Breakfast basis, but also providing half-board and packed lunches if required, and often with facilities for activities such as riding or fishing nearby. More detailed information is available in a free British Tourist Authority leaflet.

University campuses

Outside term-time many Scottish colleges and universities offer their campuses as a form of cheap accommodation, either with breakfast or on a self-catering basis. The local Tourist Information Centre will be able to supply the details.

Home exchange

In a home exchange overseas visitors can exchange their homes with a Scottish family. There is no rent to pay, just a fee to Home Interchange, the agency which acts as go-between, and whose address can be obtained from the British Tourist Authority (see Information).

Quality Assurance

The Scottish Tourist Board's quality assurance grading and classification scheme covers guest houses, B & Bs and self-catering holiday homes as well as hotels, with the grades ranging from De luxe to Approved (see Hotels), and the classification from 5 Crowns to Listed for guest houses and B & Bs, and from 5 Crowns to 1 Crown for self-catering holiday homes.

See also Camping and Caravanning, Hotels, Hotels in Country Houses & Castles, Youth Hostels

◀ *Heavyweights and heavy weights at the Highland Games*

Air Travel

British Airways (BA), the national airline, and many other international lines and domestic carriers provide air links to Scotland from other cities in the United Kingdom and the rest of the world, usually via London Heathrow and to a lesser degree London Gatwick, Birmingham and Manchester, but there are also direct flights into Glasgow from Boston, Calgary, Chicago, Dublin, New York, Toronto and Vancouver, plus services from Dublin to Edinburgh and Prestwick International. Other services include the BA Super Shuttle from London to Edinburgh and Glasgow where passengers need only arrive 10 minutes before departure (see also Getting to Scotland).

Scotland also has an excellent internal air network, much of it covered by British Airways Express (Loganair) in competition with a number of smaller domestic carriers. There are major airports at Aberdeen, Edinburgh and Glasgow, all of which have full bureau de change facilities, plus others at Inverness, Prestwick, Dundee, Wick, and in the Highlands and Islands.

Special flight packages include the British Airways European Air Pass for overseas visitors and the British Airways Express Highland Rover. For further details contact British Airways (see below). For information about the Freedom of Scotland Travelpass which allows discounts on British Airways Express flights within Scotland, see Rail Travel.

Airlines

One of the world's major international airlines, British Airways has flights to major cities throughout the world. Its Scottish offices include Edinburgh, Glasgow and Aberdeen:

British Airways

209 Union Street, Aberdeen AB1 2BA; tel. (0345) 222111   Aberdeen
30/32 Frederick Street, Edinburgh EH2 2JR; tel. (0345) 222111   Edinburgh
66 Gordon Street, Glasgow G1 3RS; tel. (0345) 222111   Glasgow

Several regional airlines have connecting flights to international destinations as well as within Scotland and the rest of the UK. Loganair, for example, connects with international flights via London as well as operating scheduled services to the Hebrides, Orkneys and Shetlands; Business Air flies from Aberdeen to Sumburgh and from Dundee, Inverness and Edinburgh via Manchester to the rest of Europe; Air UK and British Midland operate several flights a day from Edinburgh and Glasgow to London.

Other airlines

Tel. (0645) 737747	Aer Lingus
Tel. (0990) 247226	Air Canada
Tel. (0990) 074074	Air UK
Tel. (0345) 789789	American Airlines
Tel. (0345) 554554	British Midland
Tel. (0500) 340146 (within GB)	Business Air
Tel. (0345) 222111	Loganair

Bus and Coach Travel

The main UK companies offering express coach services to Scotland are National Express and Scottish Citylink Coaches, both of which provide direct services which run daily throughout the year to a variety of destinations and whose timetables are obtainable from all bus stations and coach terminals (see also Getting to Scotland). For further information, including the outlets for special tickets such as the Tourist Trail Pass, National Express Discount Coachcard and Scottish Citylink Smart Travellers' Discount Card (see below), contact any travel agent, British Tourist Authority, or the coach company offices. For information about the Freedom of Scotland Travelpass which allows discounts on many Scottish bus services, see Rail Travel.

Express coach services

National Express Regional Office Scotland
Leonard Street, Perth PH2 8HA tel. (0990) 808080

Scottish Citylink Coaches Ltd
Travel Centre, Buchanan Bus Station,
Killermont Street, Glasgow G2 3NP; tel. (0141) 332 7133

Postbus

Among the network of operators covering Scotland's smaller towns and rural areas there is the unique service provided by the Postbus, which, with its fleet of 140 postbuses, both delivers the mail and carries fare-paying passengers in areas beyond the reach of public transport. For times and services check with the local post office or tourist information centre or, for further details, contact:

Royal Mail Communications
West Port House, 102 West Port, Edinburgh EH3 9HS;
Tel. (0131) 228 7407

Postbus Controller
Royal Mail, 7 Strothers Lane, Inverness IV1 1AA;
Tel. (01463) 256273

Tourist Trail
Pass/National
Express Discount
Coachcard/Scottish
Citylink Smart
Travellers'
Discount Card

The Tourist Trail Pass allows unlimited travel on all services operated by National Express and Scottish Citylink coaches throughout Scotland, Wales and England for periods of 3, 5, 8 or 15 days, with a reduced rate for children under 16, young persons under 26 and Senior Citizens (over 60). The National Express Discount Coachcard, valid for 12 months and available to 16–25 year olds, mature students and over 50s, allows visitors up to 30% off normal adult fares on National Express and Scottish Citylink services throughout the UK (children aged 5–16 are charged the discount fares; under 5s travel free). The Scottish Citylink Smart Travellers' Discount Card, available in Scotland only, offers identical benefits to the National Express Discount Coachcard.

Camping and Caravanning

Camping and
caravan parks

Campers are well catered for throughout Scotland which has plenty of camping and caravan parks with good facilities. It also ranks as one of the last places in Europe where you can pitch your tent away from the recognised camping parks. However, always be sure to obtain the landowner's permission first. Scotland is a beautiful country, so please help to keep it that way by not leaving litter around.

Guides

In its annually updated "Scotland: Camping & Caravan Parks" the Scottish Tourist Board (see Information) lists over 200 parks, all of which are regularly inspected under the British Holiday Grading Scheme. The quality gradings range from Acceptable to Excellent (one to five ticks), with the Thistle Award being used to single out individual units as a sign of their high quality.

Car Rental

See Motoring

Castles and Historic Sites

Great British
Heritage Pass

The Great British Heritage Pass, valid for 7 or 15 days or a month, and obtainable from travel agents and the Scottish Tourist Board (see Informa-

Old-timer exhibition in front of Mellerstain House ▶

The principal castles, abbeys and prehistoric sites

* of particular interest
** outstanding

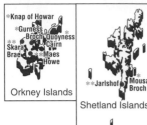

*Knap of Howar
*Gurness
Broch **Quoyness
** Cairn
*Skara *Maes
Brae *Howe

Orkney Islands

**Jarlshof *Mousa
Broch

Shetland Islands

Wick

*Black House
*Dun Carloway
Broch
**Callanish
Standing Stones

*Grey Cairn
of Cambster

**Dunrobin Castle

Ullapool

Outer Hebrides

Duffus Castle
*Spynie Palace
*Brodie Castle *Duff House
*Elgin *Huntly *Delgatie C.
Fort George *Cathedral Castle *Fyvie C.
**Cawdor Castle *Haddo
*Dunvegan Castle **Auchindoun House
*Urquhart Castle Castle *Leith Hall *Castle Fraser
Eilean Donan Castle *Kildrummy Castle *Drum C.
**Craigievar Castle Aberdeen
*Armadale Castle *Balmoral Castle **Crathes
Castle **Dunnottar
Castle

Inner Hebrides

*Castle Stalker
**Blair Castle *House of Dun
*Dunstaffnage Castle *Glamis Castle Arbroath A.
*Toresay Castle *Scone Palace Dundee
Iona *Kilchurn Castle *Huntingtower Castle *Earlshall Castle
Abbey **Inveraray Castle Perth *Hill of *St. Andrews Castle
*Falkland Palace Tarvit *Kellie Castle
*Stirling C. *Kinross H.
*Linlithgow P. **Dunfermline A. *Tantallon Castle
*Hill House *H. of the Binns *Inchcolm A.
*Castle Sween **Hopetoun H. *Stevenson House
*Kilberry Stones *Dumbarton Castle *Dalmeny H. *Lennoxlove H.
Paisley EDINBURGH *Rosslyn *Manderston H.
*Rothesay Castle Abbey Glasgow Chapel *Paxton House
*Chatelherault Castle *Mellerstain House
*Brodick Castle *Traquair House **Floors C.
Ayr *Thirlestane Castle *Dryburgh
**Kelso Abbey Abbey
*Culzean Castle *Bowhill House *Jedburgh
*Abbotsford House Abbey
**Melrose Abbey
**Drumlanrig Castle Hermitage
Castle
*Maxwellton House
*Threave
Gardens **Caerlaverock Castle
*Glenluce Abbey *Sweetheart Abbey
*Whithorn Priory *Dundrennan Abbey

tion) extends to more than 600 historic buildings and sites throughout the UK. In Scotland this will entitle you to free admission to over 130 castles, stately homes, museums, gardens and historic sites, some of them still in private hands, others owned or administered by the National Trust for Scotland (NTS), Historic Scotland (HS), or the Historic Houses Association (HHA). Many of these properties remain open throughout the year – though often with reduced opening hours from October to March.

The National Trust for Scotland (NTS) is an independent charitable body with the care of over a hundred sites ranging from historic buildings and gardens to battlefields, mountains and islands which it maintains at an annual cost of close on £12 million, much of this derived from almost 230,000 members' subscriptions. Information: National Trust for Scotland, 5 Charlotte Square, Edinburgh EH2 4DU; tel. (0131) 226 5922, fax 243 9501
National Trust for Scotland

Historic Scotland (HS) is a government body responsible under the Ministry of the Environment for historic properties such as castles, abbeys and pre-historic and industrial heritage sites. Information: Historic Scotland, Longmore House, Salisbury Place, Edinburgh EH9 1SH; tel. (0131) 668 8800, fax 668 8888.
Historic Scotland

The Castle Trail in Gordon District west of Aberdeen includes 6 castles and 3 historic houses and is described in a free leaflet available from Tourist Information Centres, etc.
Castle Trail

The Trust Pass, valid for 7 to 14 days, allows free entry to over 100 National Trust for Scotland properties. Information from the NTS (see above).
Trust Pass

Historic Scotland's Explorer Ticket, valid for one or two weeks, entitles holders to free admission to over 65 HS sites, including Edinburgh and Stirling Castles, the Border abbeys, Urquhart Castle on Loch Ness and Fort George at Inverness. Information from the Scottish Tourist Board (see Information) and Historic Scotland (see above).
Scottish Explorer Ticket

Chemists

See Health Care

Currency

The unit of currency for the United Kingdom is the pound sterling (£), made up of 100 pence (p). Bank notes are for £5, £10, £20 and £50; Scotland also issues banknotes for £1 and £100. Coins are 1p, 2p, 5p, 10p, 20p, 50p and £1.
Currency unit

Scotland has 5 major high street banks (Bank of Scotland, Royal Bank of Scotland, Clydesdale Bank, TSB Scotland and Girobank), three of which issue their own bank notes. All Scottish bank notes are legal tender in the rest of Britain, and Bank of England and Northern Ireland bank notes are legal tender north of the border.
Scottish bank notes

There are no controls on the export or import of sterling or of foreign currencies.
Currency controls

Foreign visitors will find it advisable to take sterling travellers' cheques or Eurocheques (which can be cashed up to a limit of £100) if coming from elsewhere in Europe. Remember to keep your receipt and record of travellers' cheques separately from the cheques themselves so that they can be replaced if necessary.
Travellers' cheques, etc

Credit cards are more widely used for payment in the UK than in many other parts of Europe and will be accepted by most larger shops, stores,
Credit cards

Scottish coins and banknotes

hotels and restaurants, although it is advisable to carry some £ sterling as well in case of difficulty. Switch cards, Eurocheque cards and credit cards can also be used for withdrawals at most banks and cashpoints.

Keep a note of the number to ring to put a stop immediately on any credit cards, cheque cards, etc. if they are lost or stolen.

Banks and exchange bureaux

The best exchange rates for foreign currency are generally those given by the banks, many of which can change money. Their opening hours are approximately 9/10am to 4/5pm during the week, with some closing later on Thursdays and a few open on Saturday mornings as well.

Money can also be changed in airports, the larger railway stations, travel agents and some of the big hotels (for residents). Exchange bureaux often charge a handling fee and commission.

Customs Regulations

Duty-free items on entry

Member states of the European Union (EU), and that includes Scotland as part of the United Kingdom, form a common internal market within which items for personal use are generally free of duty. There are, however, certain guidelines on maximum amounts and for the UK the upper limits for incoming travellers aged over 18 on items purchased elsewhere in the European Union are 800 cigarettes or 400 cigarillos or 200 cigars or 1 kilo tobacco, 10 litres spirits over 22% proof or 20 litres below 22% and 90 litres wine, plus an unlimited amount of perfume and toilet water and other goods and presents up to a total value of £420.

For items bought in duty-free shops or in non-EU countries the equivalent amounts are 200 cigarettes, or 100 cigarillos or 50 cigars or 250g tobacco, and 1 litre of spirits over 22% or 2 litres below 22% and 2 litres wine, plus 50g of perfume, 0.25 litre of toilet water and other goods and presents up to a value of £32.

The duty-free limits for Ireland, as a fellow member of the European Union, are approximately the same as for the United Kingdom. For other English-speaking countries the duty-free allowances are as follows: Australia 250 cigarettes or 50 cigars or 250g tobacco, 1 litre spirits or 1 litre wine; Canada 200 cigarettes and 50 cigars and 900g tobacco, 1.1 litres spirits or wine; New Zealand 200 cigarettes or 50 cigars or 250g tobacco, 1 litre spirits and 4.5 litres wine; South Africa 400 cigarettes and 50 cigars and 250g tobacco, 1 litre spirits and 2 litres wine; USA 200 cigarettes and 100 cigars and a reasonable quantity of tobacco, 1 litre spirits or 1 litre wine.

Re-entry to other countries

Diplomatic Representation

In the United Kingdom

High Commission
Australia House, Strand, London WC2B 4LA
Tel. (0171) 379 4334

Australia

High Commission
Mcdonald House, 38 Grosvenor Square, London W1X 0AB
Tel. (0171) 258 6356

Canada

Embassy
17 Grosvenor Place, London SW1X 7HR
Tel. (0171) 235 2171

Ireland

High Commission
New Zealand House, 80 Haymarket, London SW1Y 4TQ
Tel. (0991) 100100. Calls from overseas; (01344) 716100

New Zealand

High Commission
South Africa House
Trafalgar Square, London WC2N 5DP
Tel. (0171) 930 4488

South Africa

Embassy
24 Grosvenor Square, London W1A 1AE
Tel. (0171) 499 9000

USA

Disabled Access

The Scottish Council on Disability (see below) can supply general information for visitors with a disability. It publishes a disabled access guide to accommodation, attractions and leisure facilities and the Scottish Tourist Board (see Information) also produces a leaflet "Accessible Scotland".

Scottish Council on Disability

Scottish Council on Disability
Princes House, 5 Shandwick Place, Edinburgh EH2 4RG;
Tel. (0131) 229 8632, fax 229 5168

The National Trust for Scotland (see Castles and Historic Sites) has a free leaflet on access to its properties for disabled visitors.

National Trust for Scotland

Electricity

Voltage in the United Kingdom is 240V 50Hz AC. The sockets accept square-pin plugs and are different from most of those found abroad so overseas visitors will usually need an adaptor for any electrical appliances they bring with them.

Emergency Services

Call 999 — To call the emergency services – fire, police, ambulance, coastguard, mountain or cave rescue – press or dial 999 and tell the operator which emergency service you want. All 999 calls are free of charge.

Roadside emergency phones — Emergency roadside phones are located at intervals along all motorways and major trunk roads.

Breakdowns — See Motoring

Events

See Highland Games, Festivals and Folk Music in the Introduction

Ferries

Ferries from outside Scotland

From Europe — There are regular ferries to the North of England from Germany (Hamburg–Newcastle, every 4 days Apr.–Oct., Scandinavian Seaways, 23hrs), Belgium (Zeebrugge–Hull, daily, North Sea Ferries, 14hrs), the Netherlands (Amsterdam/Ijmuiden–Newcastle, every 2 days Apr.–Sept., less often Feb./Mar. and Oct.–Dec., Scandinavian Seaways, 14hrs; Rotterdam–Hull, daily, North Sea Ferries, 14hrs).

From Scandinavia — Norway (Bergen–Stavanger–Newcastle, 3 times a week in summer, twice a week in winter, Color Line, 24/26hrs; Bergen–Lerwick–Aberdeen, weekly June–Aug., P & O European Ferries, 12 hrs), Sweden (Gothenburg–Newcastle, weekly June–Aug., Scandinavian Seaways, 22hrs), and the Faroe Islands (Torshavn–Aberdeen, once or twice a week, Strandfaraskip Landsins, 23hrs).

From Northern Ireland — Larne–Cairnryan, frequent, P & O European Ferries, ferry 2hrs 15mins., Jetliner 1hr.
Belfast–Stranraer, frequent, Stena Line, ferry 3hrs, High-speed Sea Service (HSS) 1hr 30mins.

Ferries within Scotland

Firth of Clyde and Western Isles

As Scotland has about 790 islands and is surrounded on three sides by sea its ferries are an important means of transport. The majority of ferry services on the Firth of Clyde and the Western Isles are operated by Caledonian MacBrayne, sailing to 23 islands. The summer timetable operational for those listed below runs from late March to mid-October; the winter services are much less frequent. Unless otherwise stated these ferries take cars as well as passengers.

Island Hopscotch Island Rovers — Caledonian MacBrayne (see below, Ferry Operators) offer two flexible tickets for the Firth of Clyde and the Hebrides. The Island Hopscotch ticket, which is valid for one month from the date of the first journey, entitles you to economy fares for cars and accompanying passengers on one of 24 different Caledonian MacBrayne routes. The Island Rover ticket, valid for either 8 or 15 consecutive days, is for unlimited travel on almost all Caledonian MacBrayne's ferry services.

Ardrossan–Brodick (Arran), 3/6 daily, 55mins, Caledonian MacBrayne **Arran**
Claonaig–Lochranza (Arran), 8/10 daily, 30mins, Caledonian MacBrayne
Rothesay (Bute)–Brodick (Arran). 3 a week, summer only, 2hrs 5mins, Caledonian MacBrayne

Oban–Castlebay (Barra)/Lochboisdale (South Uist), 1/2 daily, 5hrs–6hrs **Barra and** 50mins, Caledonian MacBrayne **South Uist**
Ludag (South Uist)–Eoligarry (Barra), 4 a day summer, 2 a day winter, 35mins, passenger only, William Rusk

Otternish (North Uist)–Berneray, 8/10 daily except Sun., 5mins, Caledonian **Berneray** MacBrayne

Colintraive–Rhubodach (Bute), frequent daily, 5mins, Caledonian **Bute** MacBrayne
Wemyss Bay–Rothesay (Bute), frequent daily, 30mins, Caledonian MacBrayne

Oban–Tobermory (Mull)–Coll–Tiree. 5/6 weekly, 3hrs 5mins/4hrs 15mins, **Coll and Tiree** Caledonian MacBrayne

Kennacraig–Scalasaig (Colonsay), one a week, 3hrs 35mins, Caledonian **Colonsay** MacBrayne
Oban–Scalasaig (Colonsay), 3 weekly, 2hrs 10mins, Caledonian MacBrayne
Port Askaig (Islay)–Scalasaig (Colonsay), one a week, 1hr 10mins, Caledonian MacBrayne

Gourock–Dunoon (Cowal), hourly daily, 20mins, Caledonian MacBrayne **Cowal**
McInroys Point–Hunters Quay, ½ hourly daily, 20mins, Western Ferries Clyde

Tarbert (Loch Fyne)–Portavadie, hourly daily, 20mins, Caledonian **Cowal** MacBrayne **and Kintyre**

Largs–Cumbrae Slip, every 15mins June–mid Aug., ½ hourly rest of year, **Cumbrae** daily, 10mins, Caledonian MacBrayne

Ludag (South Uist)–Eriskay, 3/5 daily except Sun., 20mins, D J Rodgers **Eriskay**
Ludag (South Uist)–Eriksay, 2 a day, 10mins, passengers only, William Rusk

Tayinloan–Gigha, 6/10 daily, 20mins, Caledonian MacBrayne **Gigha**

Uig (Skye)–Tarbert (Harris), 2 daily except Sun., 1hr 45mins, Caledonian **Harris and** MacBrayne **North Uist**
Uig (Skye)–Lochmaddy (North Uist), 1/2 daily, 1hr 50mins, Caledonian MacBrayne
Otternish (North Uist)–Leverburgh (Harris), 3/5 daily, 1hr 10mins, Caledonian MacBrayne

Fionnphort (Mull)–Iona, frequent daily, 5mins, passenger only, Caledonian **Iona** MacBrayne

Kennacraig–Port Ellen/Port Askaig (Islay), 1/3 daily, 2hrs 10mins/2hrs, Cale- **Islay** donian MacBrayne
Oban–Port Askaig (Islay), one a week, 3hrs 55mins, Caledonian MacBrayne

Ferries

Jura	Port Askaig (Islay)–Feolin (Jura), frequent daily, 5mins, Western Ferries Argyll
Kilcreggan	Gourock–Kilcreggan–Helensburgh, 9/11 daily except Sun., 10mins/30–40mins, Caledonian MacBrayne
Lewis	Ullapool–Stornoway (Lewis), 3/4 daily except Sun., 2hrs 40mins, Caledonian MacBrayne
Lismore	Oban–Lismore, 2/4 daily except Sun., 50mins, Caledonian MacBrayne
Mull	Kilchoan–Tobermory (Mull), 5/8 daily, 35mins, Caledonian MacBrayne Lochaline–Fishnish (Mull), frequent daily, 15mins, Caledonian MacBrayne Oban–Craignure (Mull), 4/7 daily, 40mins, Caledonian MacBrayne See also Coll and Tiree
North Uist	See Harris
Raasay	Sconser–Raasay, 9/10 daily except Sun., 15mins, Caledonian MacBrayne
Scalpay	Kyles Scalpay–Scalpay, 10/12 daily except Sun., 10mins, Caledonian MacBrayne
Skye	Glenelg–Kylerhea (Skye), frequent daily, summer only, 5mins, Skye Connection Mallaig–Armadale (Skye), 6/7 daily, Sun. in summer only, 30mins, passengers only in winter, Caledonian MacBrayne
Small Isles	Mallaig–Eigg (1hr 30mins)–Muck (2hrs 15mins)–Rum (3hrs 30mins)–Canna (4hrs 45mins), once daily on weekdays, passengers only, Caledonian MacBrayne (on Sun. also a round trip Mallaig–Small Isles–Mallaig. Arisaig–Rhum 4 times a week; Arisaig–Eigg 6 6imes a week; Arisaig–Muck 3 times a week; all with a 2–5 hour stay on the island, passengers only, Murdo Grant (tel. (01687) 450224.
South Uist	See Barra

Orkney and Shetland

Orkney Islands	Aberdeen–Stromness (Orkney), 1/2 weekly, 8hrs (14hrs overnight), P & O Scottish Ferries
	Scrabster–Stromness (Orkney), 1/3 daily except Sun. in winter, 1hr 50mins, P & O Scottish Ferries
	John o'Groat's–Burwick (Orkney), 2/4 daily, May–Sept. only, 45mins, passengers only, John o'Groats Ferries
Shetland Islands	Aberdeen–Lerwick (Shetland), daily except weekends (subject to alteration Jan.–Mar.), 14hrs (20hrs overnight), P & O Scottish Ferries
Shetland/Orkney	Stromness (Orkney)–Lerwick (Shetland), 1/2 weekly, 8hrs, P & O Scottish Ferries
	Within the Orkney and Shetland Islands there also operates an inter-island ferry service.

Ferry Operators

Reservations	Reservations should be made as early as possible, especially for the summer months. Bookings can be made direct with the ferry operators or through travel agents and in some cases the motoring organisations. For details about vehicle size limits, etc. contact booking agents or the ferry companies.

The Ferry Terminal, Gourock PA19 1QP; Tel. (01475) 650100, fax 637607	Caledonian MacBrayne
The International Ferry Terminal, The Royal Quay, North Shields NE29 6EE; Tel. (0191) 296 1313	Color Line
Ferry Office, John o'Groats, Caithness KW1 4YR; Tel. (01955) 611353, fax 611301	John o'Groats Ferries
King George Dock, Hedon Road, Hull HU9 5QA; Tel. (01482) 377177, fax 706438	North Sea Ferries
P.O. Box 5, Jamieson's Quay, Aberdeen AB9 8DL Tel. (01224) 572615, fax 574411	P & O Scottish Ferries
The Royal Quay, North Shields NE29 6EA; Tel. (0191) 296 0101, fax 293 6222	Scandinavian Seaways
Seacat Terminal West Pier, Stranraer; Tel. (0990) 523523	Seacat
Sealink Travel Centre, Sea Terminal, Stranraer DG9 8EL; Tel. (01776) 802165	Stena Line
16 Woodside Crescent, Glasgow G3 7UT; Tel. (0141) 332 9766, fax 332 0267	Western Ferries (Clyde)

Food and Drink

Has the "Auld Alliance" with France really left its mark on Scotland's cui-   Scottish cooking
sine, or is Scottish food more likely to be plain and simple? Closer exam-
ination shows there is some truth in both these views, since fresh game,
lamb, beef, fish, vegetables, fruit and cereals, can produce the tastiest of
simple dishes as well as a whole range of culinary creations capable of
satisfying the most discerning gourmet.

Scotland abounds in truly fresh produce – wild salmon and native brown
trout, mussels, lobsters, and crabs from its lochs and its rivers, prime
Aberdeen Angus beef from the Lowlands, "Scotch lamb" from the sweet
grazing of the uplands, and among its game specialities grouse and venison
from hill and moorland. As for fresh fruit and vegetables, Scotland is
among Europe's leading soft-fruit growers and areas such as the Strathmore
valley north of Dundee have vast expanses of raspberries and strawberries, ready to be bought at the roadside or as "pick your own". Scottish

CROFTERS kitchen

Baedeker Special

Chieftan o' the Puddin-race!

TO A HAGGIS

Fair fa' your honest, sonsie face,
Great Chieftan o' the Puddin-
race!
Aboon them a' ye tak your place,
  Painch, tripe, or thairm:
Weel are ye wordy of a grace
  As lang's my arm.

The groaning trencher there ye
fill,
Your hurdies like a distant hill,
Your pin wad help to mend a mill
  In time o' need,
While thro' your pores the dews
  distil
  Like amber bead.

His knife see Rustic-labour dight,
An cut you up wi' ready slight,
Trenching your gushing entrails
  bright
  Like onie ditch;
And then, O what a glorious
  sight,
  Warm-reekin, rich!

Then, horn for horn they stretch
  an' strive,
Deil tak the hindmost, on they
  drive,
Till a' their weel-swalled kytes
  belyve
  Are bent like drums;
Then auld Guidman, maist like to
  rive,
  Bethankit hums.

[. . .]

Ye powers wha mak mankind
  your care,
And dish them out their bill
  o'fare
Auld Scotland wants nae
  skinking ware
  That jaups in luggies;
But, if ye qish her gratefu'
  prayer,
  Gie her a Haggis!

Robert Burns

cheesemaking, too, is undergoing a revival, with traditional cheeses such as Bonnet, Crowdie and Dunsyre Blue again coming into their own. And of course there is oatmeal, a staple ingredient in so much of the food and bakery products for which Scotland is rightly famous, including porridge oats for breakfast, and haggis, the national dish. Barley, on the other hand, is reserved almost exclusively for whisky.

Breakfast

The Scottish breakfast, usually even heartier than its English equivalent, consists of a bowl of porridge (the Scots take theirs with salt rather than sugar) or some other cereal, such as cornflakes or muesli, followed by eggs and bacon, sausages and spicy white or black pudding, sometimes with baked beans, kippers or haddock, and of course toast and marmalade, as well as tea or coffee with Aberdeen butteries, the Scottish version of croissants, and scones.

Lunch

Lunch at around 1 o'clock tends to be quite light, not surprisingly after such a big breakfast, and is often just a snack such as a cup of tea with a pasty, sandwich or bap. For something more substantial there is always a pub lunch, a three-course meal in a restaurant, or a fish supper – in Scotland a portion of fish and chips is called a fish supper even when eaten as lunch.

This ode appeared in two local journals in 1786, a few weeks after Robbie Burns arrived in Edinburgh. It was presumably written for a festive occasion at which the haggis, as "Chieftan o' the Puddin-race", would at that time have been the highlight of the meal, ranking as it did above the many other meat puddings, a fact due in no small degree to its lengthy recipe and great variety of ingredients. Nowadays, at Burn's Night suppers on January 25th when Scots celebrate the birth of their national poet, the steaming haggis is piped in and addressed with these words at Caledonian Societies all over the world.

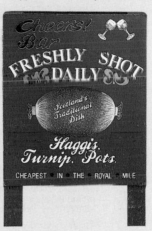

A cookbook from 1787 describes its making as follows: Thoroughly clean a sheep's stomach, then heat up the entrails and cook the liver until it crumbles. Dry some oatmeal before the fire, with care finely chop the entrails and a great piece of beef, cut up the half-liver, chop a few onions with ample kidney fat, stir in one or two handfuls of dry oatmeal and season with salt and mixed spices. Then take some of the stock in which the entrails have been cooked and prepare a hearty broth. Now stuff all the haggis meat into the sheep's stomach, add the broth and sew up the bag having forced out all air. Cooking time for a haggis: about 2 hours.

Besides afternoon tea between 4 and 5, when tea comes with cakes and bakery specialities such as scones, bannock bread and Scotch pancakes, there is also the Scottish institution of high tea, a meal served as a rule between 4.30 and 6pm consisting of a simple cooked main course accompanied by bread, cakes and usually tea or coffee. — High Tea

Restaurants and hotels are generally open for dinner from 6pm until midnight, although these times can vary, and in country places last orders will often not be taken after 9.30pm. Many hotels still observe all the formalities due to dinner as the main meal of the day, down to sounding the gong to summon diners for four or more courses. Scotland also offers a range of international eating places, especially in cities, which stay open longer, while its famous fish and chip shops often carry on serving until midnight and beyond. — Dinner

See Restaurants — Taste of Scotland

See entry — Restaurants

Traditional Dishes

Starters

Besides the inevitable fruit juice, starters in Scotland can include potted meats (potted haugh or potted heid), smoked salmon and smoked trout, and fresh seafood ranging from crayfish, crabs, shrimps and prawns, to cockles, scallops and oysters.

Soups

Traditional soups include Cullen Skink (smoked haddock and potato), Partan Bree (crab and rice), Hotch Potch (lamb and vegetables), Scotch Broth (vegetables with pearl barley), and Cock-a-leekie (boiled chicken with leeks) which, when plums are added, becomes Cock-a-leekie à la Talleyrand after the French statesman and gourmet who was so fond of it. Powsowdie (sheep's head with pot-barley and dried peas) is something of an acquired taste, while Mary Queen of Scots soup is a potato soup with sorrel, and Poacher's Soup, needless to say, has whatever game is in season.

Fish

First and foremost is that king of fish, Scotland's famous wild salmon, from the Spey, Dee, Tay, Tweed and Conon. This is served either grilled or poached, but the growth of salmon farming over the past 20 years means you need to check whether what is served is actually wild salmon or that at the very least it carries the Scottish Salmon Tartan Quality Mark.

Brown trout and pike are other similar fine fish to be had from local waters while the seas around Scotland make a major contribution to the menu with cod, haddock, hake and plaice. Shellfish such as mussels, clams, scallops and oyster are fresh and relatively cheap, as compared with crawfish and lobster which, like everywhere else, have their price.

Fish in Highland Sauce, a piquant combination of red wine and vinegar, anchovies, onions, horseradish and nutmeg, is a particular Scottish delicacy, along with smoked fish such as Arbroath Smokies (cod) and Finnan Haddock.

Meat

Scotland's "great Chieftan o' the Puddin-race", the haggis, gets its name from the French (hachis) for minced meat, and consists of sheep's offal, minced, well seasoned, mixed with oatmeal then boiled in a bag made from the animal's stomach. Served fresh with "neeps and tatties" it is a rare delicacy well worth trying.

Other choice Scottish meat dishes include prime Aberdeen Angus beef and various cuts of lamb such as lamb chops and roast lamb with red currant or mint sauce and also occasionally pork.

Game

The "Glorious Twelfth" of August marks the start of the grouse season when thousands of these game-birds are shot and can end up the same day in the pot. Other specialities include "Kilmeny Kail", Fife's wild rabbit cooked with kale; red grouse, another rare delicacy, roasted in butter and served with mushrooms; pheasant and partridge, and of course venison from the red deer of the Highlands.

Vegetables and side dishes

Kale, along with porridge, was for centuries part of the staple diet of the Highlander, and the hearty Shetlands winter dish of "Kail and Knockit Corn" (porridge oats) is just one of the many ways kale is still served throughout Scotland. Different versions of tatties (potatoes) and neeps (turnips) and various kinds of dumplings are amongst other favourite side dishes.

Sweets

Cranberries, raspberries and strawberries are a popular dessert but the Scots are renowned for having a sweet tooth and enjoy a great range of pies and tarts, not to mention cakes, pastries and biscuits such as scones, black buns, bannocks and shortbread.

Cheese

About 90% of the cheese produced in Scotland is still Cheddar in various degrees of maturity, but alongside the big cheese-makers like those of

Galloway, Lockerbie, Mull of Kintyre and the islands of Bute, Arran, Islay and Orkney, where the tastiest Cheddar hails from, a whole host of smaller individual cheesemakers have entered the market in recent years with a broad assortment of genuinely Scottish cheeses as well as adaptations of international varieties.

Probably the major specifically Scottish cheese is Dunlop, from Ayrshire, Arran and Islay, something close to Cheddar but not as firm. Brodick Blue, from ass's milk, is a product of Arran, while Scotland's creamier cheeses include Ross's Caboc, rolled in oatmeal and based on a rediscovered Highland recipe, Lochaber-smoked from Glenuig, and St Finan from Aberdeenshire. Dunsyre Blue is made from vegetarian rennet and unpasteurised cow's milk, Ettrick is a traditional blue cheese from the Borders, Crowdie a Highland cream cheese, Inverloch a goat's cheese from the island of Gigha, with a coating of red wax. Blue-veined Lanark Blue has much in common with Roquefort while, finally, St Andrews, one of the most popular products of the Howgate Dairy in Dundee, is a fullfat cheese with an edible golden rind.

Drink

One thing the Scots have in common with the English is their love of beer, and they too order it in pints or half-pints. Scottish brewing standards in general have actually improved considerably, with something of a revival of traditional brews, usually darker and sweeter than English beer. Ales are top-fermented beers so they have something of a fruity, often slightly sweet taste. Real ales have a secondary fermentation in the cask and are served from the pump. Dark and highly malted, Scotch Ale, also known as Heavy, is a particular favourite with the Scots. Quite a few small independent breweries also supply specially flavoured brews such as Heather Ales. The particularly strong ales trade under the name of Barley Wine, and because of their high alcohol content are only sold as "nips". Stouts – dark-brown, top-fermented, hoppy beers, not particularly high in alcohol but topped by a creamy foam – are better known as coming from Irish brewers such as Guiness, Murphy's and Beamish, but are also produced by Scottish brewers Tennent's and Gillespie's. Lager is gaining in popularity in Scotland as elsewhere, along with the whole host of canned and bottled beers nowadays found throughout the world and imported from North America and elsewhere in Europe.

Beer

The traditional aperitif for the Scots, like the English, is a glass of sherry, sweet, medium or dry, and usually of an excellent quality. After dinner often comes the port, also likely to be very good since the British take the lion's share and the best of Portugal's port production. The "Auld Alliance" has left its mark with the Scots' preference for the red wines of Bordeaux, or "claret" as they call it here, and the following Scottish verse reflects just how strong their preference is for claret over port:
  "Firm and erect the Caledonian stood, Old was his claret and his mutton good. 'Let him drink port!' the English statesman cried. He drank the poison, and his spirit died."

Sherry, port

See Baedeker Special, "Scotch Whisky".

Whisky

331

Gardens

The British have made gardening a fine art and their gardens are famous throughout the world. Scotland has its share of lovely formal gardens too, but, besides those found in the grounds of castles, palaces and other stately homes, many large and small lovingly tended private gardens are also open to the public and well worth a visit. An annually updated list of over 300 gardens – from royal parks to country cottages – which are open to visitors is available from:

Scotland's Gardens Scheme
31 Castle Terrace, Edinburgh EH1 2EL; tel. (0131) 229 1870, fax 229 0443

Getting to Scotland

By air

The quickest way to get to Scotland for visitors from outside the United Kingdom is by air, either by taking one of the direct flights from Ireland and North America into Edinburgh, Glasgow and Prestwick International, or by flying into London, Birmingham or Manchester and then on to Aberdeen, Edinburgh, Glasgow or Inverness, where there are connecting flights to the Hebrides, Orkney and Shetland (see Air Travel). For further information contact airlines or travel agents.

By bus

The main coach company offering scheduled coach services from most European cities to London is Eurolines. This is a division of National Express which along with Scottish Citylink Coaches is one of the main operators of scheduled express coach services between London and Scotland (see Bus and Coach Travel).

By car

Visitors from abroad travelling to Scotland all the way by car will usually have arrived in the United Kingdom from elsewhere in Europe either by ferry (see Ferries) or through the Eurotunnel (see below).
    The road journey north from London to Edinburgh and Glasgow can take just under 7 hours. To get to Edinburgh the quickest route is to follow the A41, M1, M6, A74 and A702, while to get to Glasgow after the A74 take the M74 and the A74. (see Motoring).

Eurotunnel

The Eurotunnel, opened in 1994, runs beneath the English Channel between Calais and Folkestone; terminals at either end link directly with the motorway – Exit 13 on the French side with the A16, Exit 11 on the English side with the M20. Le Shuttle provides a 24-hour shuttle service for passengers and vehicles, with trains departing every 15 to 20 minutes during the day and every 30 to 60 minutes at night. Each train can carry up to 120 cars and twelve buses and the journey takes 35 minutes. For further information tel. (0990) 353535 (see also Rail Travel).

By rail

For visitors travelling to Britain by rail from Europe the main departure points are Paris, Brussels and Amsterdam, with the possibility from Brussels and Paris of travelling by Eurostar through the Eurotunnel (for information on Inter-Capital Day Services contact European Passenger Services; tel. (01233) 617575). InterCity rail services from throughout England to and from Scottish destinations such as Aberdeen, Edinburgh, Glasgow and Inverness are provided by three operators, Cross Country, East Coast and West Coast. The quickest direct connections are London Kings Cross–Edinburgh Waverley (about 4 hours with Eurostar) and London Euston–Glasgow Central (about 5 hours). The "Flying Scotsman" completes the journey from London to Edinburgh in 5 hours, an overnight sleeper on the same route in about 8 hours. There are also through trains from London Kings Cross to Glasgow Central, Aberdeen and Inverness. Motorail services operate between London and Aberdeen, Fort William and Edinburgh. Further information on all these services including special fares and travel passes, is available from travel agents or British Rail (see Rail Travel).

Health Care

The United Kingdom has a National Health Insurance. This provides medical care free of charge for nationals of other European Union countries or other countries with which the United Kingdom has reciprocal health care agreements, but on an emergency basis only for all other visitors who should therefore ensure they have some form of health insurance to cover them during their stay (see Insurance). However, prescribed medicines must be paid for, and EU nationals should also bring with them an E111 form from their country of origin. For initial medical treatment go to the surgery of the local GP or "general practitioner" as family practice doctors are called in Britain. EU nationals should make it clear that they will subsequently want to make a claim on their own health funders. Anyone who is taken ill outside a GP's consulting hours should go to the nearest hospital accident and emergency department or, in an acute emergency, dial 999 for an ambulance.

National Health Service

Some dentists are part of the National Health Service, so the first dental treatment is free but subsequent treatment has to be paid for.

Dentists

Emergency services. See entry

Hotels

Overnight accommodation in Scotland spans a vast range from elegant Victorian town houses, modern hotel complexes, historic stately homes and castles, to comfortable guest houses and the more modest Bed & Breakfast (see Accommodation).

A considerable number of former stately homes have been refurbished as elegant and extremely comfortable hotels, with prices to match (see below, Hotels in Country Houses & Castles).

Country houses and castles

The old coaching inns scattered widely throughout Britain are where fresh relays of horses were kept and weary travellers could stay overnight. Many of these mostly small inns are therefore very old and characteristic of their time and place.
In Scotland they tend to be built of natural stone with stepped gables. If they are cottage style they have thatched roofs and ivy-clad walls,, while the Georgian and Victorian ones have impressive frontages with tall sash-windows and elegant doorways framed with pillars and porticoes. Inns are comfortably furnished without being unduly luxurious and are consequently relatively low-priced. Most have only a few rooms, and the food they serve, which can be very good, is mainly regional.

Inns

See Accommodation

Bed and Breakfast

It is wise to book in advance, particularly in the peak holiday season, either through a travel agent, a hotel chain or with the hotel direct. All Tourist Information Centres (TICs) can provide local accommodation lists and some of them will, free of charge or for a small fee, make the booking for visitors applying in person. Most TICs operate a Book-A-Bed-Ahead (BABA) service whereby for a small fee a temporary reservation can be made both locally and for the next destination.

Bookings and reservations

Each hotel listed is assigned to one of four categories – L (luxury hotel), I (high amenity hotel), II (good quality hotel), III (hotel with standard

Categories

amenities) – the category being given after the number of rooms. Hotels marked with the red asterisk are specially recommended.

Price guide per person (for double room with breakfast):
L	£50–£70
I	£40–£50
II	£30–£40
III	£20–£30

STB Quality
Assurance scheme

The Scottish Tourist Board's Quality Assurance grading and classification scheme covers guest houses, B & Bs and self-catering holiday homes (see Accommodation) as well as hotels. Grades are based on a wide-ranging assessment of quality and service aspects and range from de luxe (excellent), highly commended (very good), commended (good) to approved (acceptable). Classification shows the range of facilities on offer, from five crowns to listed, and both the grade and the classification appear on the distinctive blue plaques awarded by the Scottish Tourist Board.

Hotels (a selection)

Aberdeen

Area code: 01224

★ Ardoe House, Blairs, South Deeside Road, tel. 867355, fax 861283, 71r, L (3 miles/5km south-west of the city; towered granite Baronial-style house with splendid garden)

★ Marcliffe at Pitfodels, North Deeside Road, Pitfodels, tel. 861000, fax 868860, 42r, L (2½ miles/4km west of the city; elegant rooms, well stocked wine cellar and over 100 malt whiskies)

Caledonian Thistle, 10 Union Terrace, tel. 640233, fax 641627, 80r, I (rich in tradition, enjoying a lovely view over the Union Terrace Gardens)

Craighaar, Waterton Road, Bankhead, tel. 712275, fax 716362, 55r, I (1¼ miles/2km from the airport; mouth-watering selection of Scottish specialities from the kitchen)

Waterwheel, 203 North Deeside Road, Bieldside, tel. 861659, fax 861515, 21r, II (built around a grain mill, about 6 miles/10km from the city centre)

Manorville, 252 Great Western Road, tel. 594190, 3r, II (guest house offering immaculate accommodation)

Aberdour

Hawkcraig House, Hawkcraig Point, tel. (01383) 860335, 2r, I (old ferry house with view of Inchcolm's 12th c. abbey)

Aberfeldy

Guinach House, "By The Birks", Urlar Road, tel. (01887) 820251, fax 829607, 7r, L (friendly hotel with good food – try the lamb with herbs)

Ardentinny

★ Ardentinny, Loch Long, tel. (01369) 810209, fax 810241, 11r, II (300 years ago coaches called in here; delightful garden)

Arisaig

Area code: 01687

★ Arisaig House, Beasdale, tel. 450622, fax 450626, 14r, L (first class hotel set in enchanting gardens; fresh fish tops the menu)

Arisaig, tel. 450210, fax 450310, 13r, II (smartly appointed hotel with marvellous bay views)

Isle of Arran

Area code: 01770

Auchrannie Country House, Auchrannie Road, Brodick, tel. 302234, fax 302812, 28r, L (a bare 1¼ miles/2km north of the ferry landing; leisure centre with indoor swimming pool)

Kilmichael Country House, Glen Coy, tel. 302219, fax 302068, 6r, L (attractive house tucked away in a peaceful glen)

Auchterarder

Gleneagles Hotel, see Hotels in Country Houses and Castles

Ayr

Area code: 01292

Savoy Park, 16 Racecourse Road, tel. 266112, fax 611488, 15r, L (19th century sandstone building; public rooms with impressive panelled walls and ornate ceilings)

Elms Court, 21 Miller Road, tel. 264191, fax 610254, 20r, II (comfortable family-run hotel)

★ Darroch Learg, Braemar Road, tel. (013397) 55443, fax 55252, 13r, L (panoramic views)   **Ballater**
Tullich Lodge, Balgonie Country House, see Hotels in Country Houses and Castles

Area code: 01463   **Beauly**
Priory, The Square, tel. 782309, fax 782531, 22r, L (in a prime position in the village square; rooms offer every modern comfort)
Chrialdon, Station Road, tel. 782336, 9r, I (prettily furnished Victorian villa)

Tinto, Symington, tel. 308454, fax 308520, 29r, L (spacious public rooms   **Biggar**
and a choice of two restaurants)
Shieldhill Hotel, see Hotels in Country Houses and Castles

Boat, on A95, tel. (01479) 831258, 32r, L (long-established family run   **Boat of Garten**
Highland golfing and holiday hotel)

Braemar Lodge, Glenshee Road, tel./fax (013397) 41627, 7r, L (Victorian   **Braemar**
former hunting lodge, full of atmosphere)

Roman Camp Hotel, see Hotels in Country Houses and Castles   **Callander**

Seafield, Kilkerran Road, tel. (01586) 554385, fax 552741, 11r, L (on   **Campbeltown**
Campbeltown Loch; built by the founders of the Springbank Distillery)

★ Kirkton House, Darleith Road, tel. (01389) 841951, fax 841868, 6r, I   **Cardross**
(converted 19th c. farmhouse with lovely view of the Clyde; very friendly and extremely comfortable)

Douglas Arms, King Street, tel. (01556) 502231, fax 504000, 24r, L (former   **Castle Douglas**
coaching inn dating from 1779, in the centre of town)

Dunlaverock House, tel./fax (018907) 71450, 6r, L (cliff-top position; bed-   **Coldingham**
rooms with original Victorian fireplaces)

Coul House, tel. (01997) 421487, fax 421945, 20r, L (Victorian country   **Contin**
house in spacious grounds at the edge of the village)

see Wigtown   **Corsemalzie**

★ Craigellachie, Victoria Street, tel. (01340) 881204, fax 881253, 29r, L (el-   **Craigellachie**
egant Victorian hotel, tastefully furnished, with superb "Ben Aigan" restaurant and well stocked "Quaich" bar)

Esbank Motor, 29 Dalhousie Road, tel. (0131) 663 3234, 16r, L (modern   **Dalkeith**
hotel well equipped for business guests and tourists)

Dornoch Castle, Castle Street, tel. (01862) 810216, fax 810981, 17r, L   **Dornoch**
(comfortable rooms in historic building)

Station, 49 Lovers Walk, tel. (01387) 254316, fax 250388, 32r, L (tasteful   **Dumfries**
rooms, comfortable "Courtyard Else" bistro)

Stirling Arms, Stirling Road, tel. (01786) 822156, fax 825300, 7r, II (17th   **Dunblane**
century coaching inn, now a family-run hotel; panelled "Oak Room" restaurant)
Cromlix House, see Hotels in Country Houses and Castles

Area code: 01382   **Dundee**
Stakis Dundee Earl Grey, Earl Grey Place, tel. 229271, fax 200072, 104r, L (on the Firth of Tay, not far from Scott's Antarctic expedition ship, RRS *Discovery*)

The Enmore, Dunoon – charming country house

Invercarse, 371 Perth Road, tel. 669231, fax 644112, 32r, L (period house in its own grounds, tastefully converted into a modern hotel)

Dunfermline   Keavil House, Crossford, tel. (01383) 736258, fax 621600, 33r, I (an extended house, parts dating from the 16th century, in a rural setting just outside the city)

Dunkeld   ★ Kinnaird, Kinnaird Estate, tel. (01796) 482440, fax 482289, 9r, L (private house within large estate overlooking the Tay valley; sumptuous interior; bedrooms with gas fires and king-size beds)

Dunoon   ★ Enmore, Marine Parade, Kirn, tel. (01369) 702230, fax 702148, 10r, L (elegant Georgian country house made special by Angela and David Wilson's personal touch; extensive view over the Firth of Clyde)

Edinburgh   Area code: 0131

★ Balmoral, 1 Princes Street, tel. 556 2414, fax 557 8740, 189r, L (one of Europe's best hotels; panoramic views of Princes Street and the castle)

★ Caledonian, Princes Street, tel. 459 9988, fax 225 6632, 236r, L (elegant top quality hotel with deservedly renowned "La Pompadour" restaurant)

★ Carlton Highland, 1–29 North Bridge, tel. 556 7277, fax 556 2691, 197r, L (pure luxury from Queen Victoria's time)

★ George Inter-Continental, 19–21 George Street, tel. 225 1251, fax 226 5644, 195r, L (the best hotel in the New Town)

★ Marriott Dalmahoy, Kirknewton, tel. 333 1845, fax 333 1433, 43r, L (original Adam house with a modern extension; leisure club with poolside restaurant)

★ Sheraton Grand, 1 Festival Square, tel. 229 9131, fax 228 4510, 261r, L (handily situated for the Usher Hall, Traverse Theatre and International Conference Centre)

Copthorne Glasgow in elegant George Square

Edinburgh's Balmoral – No. 1 Princes Street

Channings, Edinburgh: five Edwardian town houses

★ Channings, South Learmonth Gardens, tel. 315 2226, fax 332 9631, 48r, L (five comfortable Edwardian town houses in the city's west end; faultless service; brasserie and excellent restaurant)

King James Thistle, St James Centre, 107 Leith Street, tel. 556 0111, fax 557 5333, 143r, L (modern building with bar, restaurant and brasserie)

★ Old Waverley, 43 Princes Street, tel. 556 4648, fax 557 6316, 66r, L (fine view of the castle)

★ Malmaison, 1 Tower Place, Leith, tel. 555 6868, fax 555 6999, 60r, II (large, comfortable rooms; lovely views across the Forth to the Fife peninsula)

Orwell Lodge, 29 Polwarth Terrace, tel. 229 1044, fax 228 9492, 10r, L (Victorian mansion in residential area convenient for transport to the city centre)

Rothesay, 8 Rothesay Place, tel. 225 4125, fax 220 4350, 46r, I (situated in the city's West End; a recently opened new wing has many modern facilities)

Stuart House, 12 East Claremont Street, tel. 557 9030, fax 557 0563, 7r, L (comfortable Georgian town house in the New Town)

★ Ellesmere House, 11 Glengyle Terrace, tel. 229 4823, fax 229 5285, 6r, I (well managed, centrally situated and good value)

Terrace, 37 Royal Terrace, tel. 556 3423, fax 556 2520, 14r, II (within easy reach of Princes Street)

Town House, 65 Gilmore Place, tel. 229 1985, 5r, II (stylish Victorian house)

Elgin

Area code: 01343

Mansefield House, Mayne Road, tel. 540883, fax 552491, 21r, L (Georgian town house with sauna)

★ Laichmoray, Station Road, tel. 540045, fax 540055, 35r, L (pretty and central)

Fort William

Area code: 01397

Mercury, Achintore Road, tel. 703117, fax 700550, 86r, L (panoramic view over Loch Linnhe)

★ Moorings, Banavie, tel. 772797, fax 772441, 21r, I (3 miles/5km outside Fort William on the Caledonian Canal; excellent food)

★ Myrtle Bank, Low Road, tel. (01445) 712004, fax 712214, 12r, II (panoramic view across to Skye) **Gairloch**

Area code: 0141 **Glasgow**
★ Copthorne Glasgow, George Square, tel. 332 6711, fax 332 4264, 141r, L (popular city-centre rendezvous)
★ Glasgow Hilton, 1 William Street, tel. 204 5555, fax 204 5004, 319r, L (modern luxury hotel with 4 restaurants and bars, including "Camerons" where chef Ferrier Richardson concocts superlative Scottish menus; health club)
★ Glasgow Moat House, Congress Road, tel. 306 9988, fax 221 2022, 284r, L (modern hotel next to the Scottish Exhibition Centre on the banks of the Clyde)
★ One Devonshire Gardens, 5 Devonshire Gardens, tel. 339 7878, fax 337 3980, 27r, L (superb Victorian town mansion with one of the best restaurants in Glasgow)
Quality Central, 99 Gordon Street, tel. 221 9680, fax 226 3948, 222r, I (centrally situated near the railway station)
Malmaison, 278 West George Square, tel. 221 6400, fax 221 6411, 73r, L (one of Glasgow's most stylish hotels)
Deauvilles, 62 St Andrews Drive, Pollockshields, tel. 427 1106, 6r, I (elegant Victorian private hotel in up-market suburb of Pollockshields)
Botanic, 1 Alfred Terrace, Great Western Road, tel./fax 339 6955, 17r, II (Victorian house close to the Botanic Gardens)

Balbirnie House, see Hotels in Country Houses and Castles **Glenrothes**

Area code: 01479 **Grantown-on-**
★ Garth, Castle Road, tel. 872836, fax 872116, 17r, L (old fashioned charm **Spey** and pretty garden)
★ Culdearn House, Woodlands Terrace, tel. 872106, fax 873641, 9r, II (Victorian mansion which Isobel and Alastair Little have furnished in the original style; very good plain cooking)
Pines, Woodside Avenue, tel./fax 872092, 9r, L (lovely Victorian villa)

Greywalls Hotel, see Hotels in Country Houses and Castles **Gullane**

Harris, Tarbert, tel. (01859) 502154, fax 502281, 25r, II (near the ferry pier; **Isle of Harris** friendly and comfortable)

Traquair Arms Hotel, Traquair Road, tel. (01896) 830229, fax 830260, 10r, **Innerleithen** I (attractive 19th c. inn)

Area code: 01463 **Inverness**
★ Culduthel Lodge, 14 Culduthel Road, tel./fax 240089, 12r, L (elegant Georgian country house on the River Ness, with pleasant garden)
Windsor, 22 Ness Bank, tel. 715535, fax 713262, 18r, L (riverside-position, nestling under the castle; all bedrooms are non-smoking)
★ Ballifeary, 10 Ballifeary Road, tel. 235572, fax 717583, 5r, III (charming Victorian villa; exceptionally choice menu)
Bunchrew House, Culloden House and Dunain Park Hotel, see Hotels in Country Houses and Castles

Willow Court, The Friars, tel. (01835) 863702, fax 864601, 4r, II (for a real **Jedburgh** gastronomic experience try the haggis with whisky sauce)

Post Office House, Cannisbay, tel. (01955) 611213, 3r, II (friendly guest **John o'Groats** house, 3 miles/5km west of John o'Groats)

Cross Keys, 36/37 The Square, tel. (01573) 223303, fax 225792, 24r, L (tra- **Kelso** ditional inn)
Sunlaws House Hotel, see Hotels in Country Houses and Castles

Hotels

Kildrummy Kildrummy Castle Hotel, see Hotels in Country Houses and Castles

Kinross ★ Muirs Inn, 49 Muirs, tel./fax (01577) 862270, 5r, L (the bedrooms are all named after famous whisky distilleries; choice of more than 100 single malts in the bar; imaginative cooking)

Kirkcudbright ★ Selkirk Arms, Old High Street, tel. (01557) 330402, fax 331639, 15r, L (Georgian town house where Robert Burns wrote "The Selkirk Grace"; very good food)

Lairg Overscaig, Loch Shin, tel. (01549) 431203, 9r, ll (welcoming hotel on the shore of Loch Shin; completely refurbished)

Leslie Leslie Castle, see Hotels in Country Houses and Castles

Isle of Lewis Area code for Stornoway: 01851
Cabarfeidh, Stornoway, tel. 702604, fax 705572, 46r, L (modern hotel on the edge of town)

Isle of North Uist Lochmaddy, village centre, tel. (01876) 500331, 15r, L (conveniently located beside the island's ferry terminal, a popular base for country sports)

Lochinver ★ Inver Lodge, tel. (01571) 844496, fax 844395, 20r, l (post-modern luxury hotel with view of the harbour; renowned for its cooking; on balmy summer evenings deer graze in front of the hotel)

Loch Lomond Cameron House, see Hotels in Country Houses and Castles

Lundin Links Old Manor, Leven Road, tel. (01333) 320368, fax 320911, 24r, l (converted mansion house; several golf courses close by)

Melrose Burt's, The Square, tel. (01896) 822285, fax 822870, 20r, L (1722 town house; elegant restaurant)

Moffat ★ Moffat House, High Street, tel. (01683) 220039, fax 221288, 20r, L (handsome 18th c. country house; outstanding service)

Isle of Mull ★ Western Isles, Tobermory, tel. (01688) 302012, fax 302297, 26,L (fabulous situation overlooking the bay; first-class rooms and excellent food)
Assapol House, Bunessan, tel. (01681) 700258, fax 700445, 5r, L (small country house hotel set by Loch Assapol)

Newton Stewart Kirroughtree House, see Hotels in Country Houses and Castles

Oban Area code: 01631
Caledonian, Station Square, tel. 563133, fax 562998, 70r, ll (modernised 19th c. building directly overlooking the harbour)
Dungallan House, Gallanach Road, tel. 563799, fax 566711, 13r, L (Victorian villa with view across to Mull)
★ Manor House, Gallanach Road, tel. 562087, fax 563053, 11r, L (Georgian house directly overlooking Oban Bay; excellent food)
Isle of Eriska Hotel, see Hotels in Country Houses and Castles

Orkney Islands On the main island, Mainland (area code: 01856)
Ayre, Ayre Road, Kirkwall, tel. 873001, fax 876289, 33r, l (refurbished seafront hotel)
★ Albert, Mounthoolie Lane, Kirkwall, tel. 876000, fax 875397, 19r, ll (traditional hotel in the town centre, with a lovely restaurant "The Stables")

Paisley ★ Myfarrclan Guest House, 146 Corsebar Road, tel./fax (0141) 884 8285, 3r, L (bungalow near Glasgow airport; non-smokers only)

The Tudor-style Old Manor, Lundin Links

Venlaw Castle, Edinburgh Road, tel. (01721) 720384, 12r, L (fine turreted mansion in wooded grounds above the town)   **Peebles**

Area code: 01738   **Perth**
★ Huntingtower, Crieff Road, Almondbank, tel. 583771, fax 583777, 27r, L (half-timbered house 5 minutes from the centre; oak panelled dining room and very beautiful garden)
Ardfern House, 15 Pitcullen Crescent, tel. 637031, fax 876289, 3r, II (rooms with fresh fruit and flowers)
Park Lane Guest House, 17 Marshall Place, tel. 637218, fax 643519, 6r, I (Georgian building near the golf course)
Ballathie House Hotel, see Hotels in Country Houses and Castles

Waterside Inn, Fraserburgh Road, tel. (01779) 471121, fax 470670, 109r, L (swimming pool, sauna and Turkish bath)   **Peterhead**

Area code: 01796   **Pitlochry**
Acarsaid, 8 Atholl Road, tel. 472389, fax 473952, 18r, L (tasteful Victorian-style furnishings and traditional cuisine)
Birchwood, 2 East Moulin Road, tel. 472477, fax 473951, 17r, L (friendly family hotel in Victorian villa)
Claymore, 162 Atholl Road, tel. 472888, fax 474037, 7r, L (surrounded by well-tended gardens)

★ Corsemalzie House, tel. (01988) 860254, fax 860213, 14r, L (halfway between Wigtown and Port William; typical 19th c. country house, excellent food)   **Port William**

Area code: 01334   **St Andrews**
Ardgowan, 2 Playfair Terrace, tel. 472970, 12r, L (near to town centre, offers fresh local seafood)
★ Old Course Hotel, tel. 474371, fax 477668, 125r, L (Mecca of the golf world beside the legendary Old Course)

341

Hotels

★ St Andrews Golf Hotel, 40 The Scores, tel. 472611, fax 472188, 23r, L (cliff-top situation with magnificent view of the links and St Andrews Bay)
★ Rufflets Country House, Strathkinness Low Road, tel. 472594, fax 478703, 23r, I (romantic country house; exquisite food)

Shetland Islands

On the main island, Mainland:
★ Busta House, Brae, tel. (01806) 522506, fax 522588, 20r, L (elegant country house, exquisite food)
Lerwick, 15 South Road, Lerwick, tel. (01595) 692166, fax 694419, 35r, L (within 10 minutes' walk of central amenities)
The Shetland, Holmsgarth Road, Lerwick, tel. (01595) 695515, fax 695828, 64r, L (hotel complex with spacious guest rooms)

Isle of Skye

Harlosh House, Harlosh, tel./fax (01470) 521367, 6r, L (4 miles/7km south of Dunvegan on the A863; small but good)
Rosedale, Beaumont Crescent, Portree, tel. (01478) 613131, fax 612531, 20r, L (very comfortable hotel in converted row of fishermen's cottages directly overlooking Portree harbour; full of winding corridors, nooks and crannies; imaginative cooking)

Stirling

Area code: 01786
Stirling Highland, Spittal Street, tel. 475444, fax 462929, 78r, L (luxury hotel occupying former high school)
Terraces, 4 Melville Terrace, tel. 472268, fax 450314, 18r, L (elevated position in a tree-lined terrace)
Castlecroft, Ballengeich Road, tel. 474933, 6r, II (modern hotel in the shadow of Stirling Castle; friendly atmosphere)

Strachur

Creggans Inn, tel. (01369) 860279, fax 860637, 19r I (tastefully furnished historic inn with fabulous view over Loch Fyne; fish dishes top the menu)

The waterfront Rosedale at Portree (Isle of Skye)

The Creggans Inn on Loch Fyne, an old coaching inn

★ North West Castle, Portrodie, tel. (01776) 704413, fax 702646, 70r, L **Stranraer**
(view of the harbour; curling rink, swimming pool, sauna and
whirlpool)

Pentland, Princes Street, tel. (01847) 893202, fax 892761, 53r, ll (newly re- **Thurso**
stored hotel in central position)

Ben Loyal, village centre, tel. (01847) 611216, 12r, L (splendid outlook **Tongue**
over the Kyle of Tongue)

Loch Torridon Hotel, see Hotels in Country Houses and Castles **Torridon**

★ Turnberry, tel. (01655) 331000, fax 331706, 132r, L (internationally **Turnberry**
famous golfing hotel with legendary Arran and Ailsa courses; stylish
bathing complex; superior restaurants)

Area code: 01854
★ Ceilidh Place, West Argyle Street, tel. 612103, fax 612886, 13r, l (re- **Ullapool**
laxed, informal atmosphere)
Ardvreck Guest House, Morefield Brae, tel. 612028, fax 61300010r, l
(tranquil location with fantastic view over Loch Broom)

Knockie Lodge, see Hotels in Country Houses and Castles **Whitebridge**

Mackay's, Union Street, tel. (01955) 602323, fax 605930, 26r, ll (long-es- **Wick**
tablished, family-run hotel)

Hotels in Country Houses & Castles

Anyone who wants to live, and dine, like a lord in the lap of luxury for a   Living like a Lord
few days will be in their element in one of Scotland's converted castles or

343

country houses. Even though money may be no object – a double room with breakfast can cost between £90 and £200 a night – the quality and service you get is generally extremely good value. The historic rooms in these top-class hotels are largely furnished with antiques, each place in its own style. Care is taken to provide a pleasantly intimate atmosphere, while drawing on cordon bleu cuisine and a well-stocked wine cellar, not to mention the parks and gardens all around where guests can wander at will and contemplate the scenery.

★★ Hotels (a selection)

Borders
Sunlaws House
Hotel

One of Scotland's prime sites, the elegant Sunlaws House Hotel in the heart of the Borders is owned by the Duke of Roxburghe who lives in nearby Floors Castle, itself well worth a visit. The comfortable rooms have open fireplaces and four-poster beds, guests can relax in the library or the spacious drawing room, while the restaurant features excellent game and fresh salmon from the Teviot which runs through the estate (Heiton, Kelso, Roxburghshire TD5 8JZ, tel. (01573) 450331, fax 450611, 3 miles/5km south-west of Kelso in Heiton, A698, 22r).

Cringletie House
Hotel

Cringletie House at Peebles was designed in 1861 by David Bryce and has a magnificent view of the Eddleston Valley and a table graced by Aileen Maguire's celebrated delicacies (Peebles, Borders EH45 8PL, tel. (01721) 730233, fax 730244, 13r).

**Dumfries and
Galloway**

Barjarg Tower

Built in the 16th c., Barjarg Tower stands in 40 acres/16ha of parkland some 17 miles/27km north-west of Dumfries, between Maxwelton House and Drumlanrig Castle. Its elegant guestrooms, with fine oak panelling, are luxuriously furnished. To sit by the crackling fire is to experience to the full the romantic atmosphere of a Scottish castle (Auldgirth, Dumfriesshire DG2 9TN, tel. (01848) 331545, fax 330918, 9r).

Sunlaws House: the best of Border hospitality

Kirroughtree House, just 1 mile/2km outside Newton Stewart, is also luxuriously furnished. Each of the spacious suites in this 1719 manor house has its own distinctive character, and in both dining rooms guests are treated to the best of Scotland's culinary arts (Minnigaff, Newton Stewart, Dumfries and Galloway DG8 6AN, tel. (01671) 402141, fax 402425, 17r).

Kirroughtree House

Knockinaam Lodge, (proprietors: Michael Bricker and Pauline Ashworth) is situated south of Portpatrick in the south-west corner of Dumfries and Galloway, an area where the unusually mild climate gives rise to enchanting gardenscapes. The relaxing tranquillity of the hotel, sheltered on three sides by steep cliffs, was evidently appreciated by Sir Winston Churchill who held his secret meeting with General Eisenhower here. The rooms are exceedingly comfortable, the service excellent and it would be hard to find better food – not to mention the wide vistas extending as far as the coast of Ireland (Portpatrick, Wigtownshire DG9 9AD, tel. (01776) 810471, fax 810435, 10 r).

Knockinaam Lodge

Golfing devotees visiting the celebrated Greywalls Hotel, half an hour's drive to the east of Edinburgh, will find themselves close to such legendary courses as Muirfield, famous for the British Open. The Edwardian house (1901) is the work of Sir Edwin Lutyens and Gertrude Jekyll was responsible for the wonderful garden (Gullane, Muirfield, East Lothian EH31 2EG, tel. (01620) 842144, fax 842241, 23r).

Around Edinburgh
Greywalls Hotel

About 16 miles/25.5km south-east of Edinburgh at the foot of the Lammermuir Hills, Johnstounburn House, amid its romantic gardens, has a mid–18th c. wood-panelled dining room (Humbie, East Lothian EH30 5PL, tel. (01875) 833696, fax 833626, 20r).

Johnstounburn House Hotel

Built about 1450, Dalhousie Castle, on the banks of the South Esk river 8 miles/13km south of Edinburgh, is another architectural gem. The drawing room and library have ornate stucco ceilings and fine wood panelling, while the dungeons make a fabulous setting for candlelit dinners (Bonnyrigg, Edinburgh EH19 3JB, tel. (01875) 820153, fax 821936, 25r).

Dalhousie Castle

The delighful Knockinaam Lodge near Portpatrick

Top hotel for top golfers: the Greywalls Hotel, Gullane

Borthwick Castle Hotel
The two-towered Borthwick Castle, 12 miles/19km south of Edinburgh, offers yet another breath of pure romanticism. Mary Queen of Scots and her husband the Earl of Bothwell once sought refuge in the massive tower house (1430). The castle was virtually in a state of siege when the young married couple donned disguise and made their escape. Today exquisite food – nouvelle cuisine, but in larger portions – is served in the great hall (Borthwick, Edinburgh EH23 4QY, tel. (01875) 820514, fax 821702, 10r).

Around Glasgow
Cameron House Hotel
The Cameron House Hotel stands on the shores of Loch Lomond to the north-west of Glasgow. It has three restaurants and a spacious leisure complex offering excellent sports facilities for the whole family: 9-hole golf course, pleasure pool, sauna, tennis and squash courts, windsurfing and extended walks through the well-kept park (Balloch, Dunbartonshire G83 8QZ, tel. (01389) 755565, fax 759522, 96r).

Montgreenan Mansion House Hotel
Half an hour's drive from Glasgow on the west coast at Kilwinning, Montgreenan Mansion House Hotel, built in 1817, wants for nothing with its elegant rooms, haute cuisine, tennis, croquet and 5-hole golf course (Montgreenan Estate, Kilwinning, Ayrshire KA13 7QZ, tel. (01294) 557733, fax 850397, 21r).

Ardfillayre Hotel
Ardfillayne House, built in 1835, is situated on the Firth of Clyde a mile south of Dunoon (reached by ferry from Gourock). Lovingly modernised in a thoroughly professional way, it is full of echoes of Victorian times. Wonderful wines, old port and malt whisky by candlelight add up to complete relaxation in style (Ardfillayne Hotel, West Bay, Dunoon, Argyll PA23 7QJ, tel. (01369) 702267, fax 702501, 7r).

Crinan Hotel
Crinan is an idyllic little spot at the northern end of the Crinan Canal, which links Loch Fyne to the West Coast proper. Anyone who loves fish will find a real gourmet paradise at the captivating Crinan Hotel (Crinan, by Lochgilphead, Argyll PA31 8SR, tel. (01546) 830261, fax 830292).

Shieldhill Hotel
Shieldhill manor house, at Biggar, south-east of Glasgow, dates back to the 12th c. Following extensive restoration, this luxury hotel now offers

spacious suites, lovingly furnished in Laura Ashley fabrics, and Brian Graham's excellent cooking. The old tower house is said to be haunted by the unfortunate Grey Lady (Quothquan, Biggar, Lanarkshire ML12 6NA, tel. (01899) 220035, fax 221092, 12r).

The Ballathie House Hotel, occupying a pleasant Victorian building about 20 minutes' drive north of Perth, has charmingly furnished guestrooms with four-poster beds; also a highly creative chef (Kinclaven, Perthshire, PH1 4QN, tel. (01250) 883268, fax 883396, 27r).

In the Heart of Scotland
Ballathie House Hotel

Simon and Alexandra Winton's celebrated Scottish specialities grace the table of this elegant hotel. Activity-seekers have the choice of a 9-hole golf course, fishing, hunting and the nearby Glenshee ski area (Spittal O'Glenshee, Blairgowrie, Perthshire PH10 7QG, tel. (01250) 885224, fax 885225, 18r).

Dalmunzie House Hotel

Gleneagles, owned by Guinness and built in the grand style early in the 20th c., has an international reputation. Besides exclusive 5-star accommodation, within its spacious (865 acre/350 ha) grounds it has 5 championship golf courses (the annual setting for the Scottish Open), one of them designed by Jack Nicklaus, the Captain Mark Philips' riding centre, a country club, brasserie, and select restaurants (Auchterarder, Perthshire PH3 1NF, tel. (01764) 662231, fax 662134, 234r).

Gleneagles Hotel

The suites in this 1874 country house near Dunblane have been furnished with hand picked treasures by David and Ailsa Assenti, carefully preserving the original character of this manor house, including the little chapel, an unforgettable setting for weddings. Dinner is rightly deemed a culinary experience of the highest order. Keen anglers will find three trout lakes on the 3000 acre/1200ha estate and salmon at Allan Water (Kinbuck, Perthshire FK15 9JT, tel. (01786) 822125, fax 825450, 14r).

Cromlix House Hotel

The Roman Camp Hotel's history began in 1625 when the dukes of Perth built a hunting lodge at Callander close by the Trossachs, but it owes its name to the camp of the Roman legions near by. Special features of the estate include a chapel and the lovely garden on the River Teith. Lounge, library and dining room have sumptuous panelling and ceiling frescos (Callander, Perthshire FK17 8BG, tel. (01877) 330003, fax 331533, 14r).

Roman Camp Hotel

This carefully restored 1777 country house has a magnificent long gallery and handsome library. Diners in its top restaurant look out over the park with its ancient yew hedges (Markinch by Glenrothes, Fife KY7 6NE, tel. (01592) 610066, fax 610529, 30r).

Balbirnie House Hotel

At their Kildrummy Castle Hotel on the Grampian Region Castle Trail opposite the ruins of the first castle (1245) Tom and Mary Hanna harmoniously combine tradition with modern comfort. The highly-praised Scottish cuisine is graced by excellent wine (Kildrummy by Alford, Aberdeenshire AB33 8RA, tel. (019755) 71288, fax 71345, 16r).

Grampian
Kildrummy Castle Hotel

Its aristocratic owners have transformed Leslie Castle, their home at Insch, into a showpiece following a ten-year restoration programme. Their guests are transported back over the centuries at the mere sight of its turrets, winding staircases and roaring open fires, but without foregoing any modern comforts. The food is also in the best Scottish tradition (Leslie, Aberdeenshire AB52 6NX, tel. (01464) 820869, fax 821076, 4r).

Leslie Castle Hotel

Muchalls Castle, north of Stonehaven, was built in the first half of the 17th c. by the first Baron of Leys. Restored to its former splendour by Glenda Nicol Cormack and Michael Acklom, the L-shaped castle stands on a ledge of rock with a fine sea view. Such elegant guestrooms are rarely to be found. The ground-floor lounge boasts a stucco ceiling (1624) ornamented with floral motifs and coats-of-arms (Muchalls, Stonehaven, Kincardineshire AB3 2RS, tel. (01569) 731170, fax 731480, 8r).

Muchalls Castle

For more than 25 years Neil Bannister and Hector Macdonald have made a stay at Tullich Lodge, a Late Victorian country house in the magnificent Dee valley, a quite unforgettable experience. Everything about the truly beautiful rooms reflects a love of detail. Meals – with an emphasis on healthy

Tullich Lodge Hotel

eating – are taken in the mahogany-panelled dining room (Ballater, Aberdeenshire AB35 5SB, tel. (013397) 55406, fax 55397, 10r).

Balgonie Country House Hotel
Another top name at Ballater is Balgonie House, built in 1899 on the golf course of the same name, with individually styled guestrooms named after the fishing waters of the Dee. The select menu includes fresh salmon, Angus beef and local game (Braemar Place, Ballater, Aberdeenshire AB35 5NQ, tel./fax (013397) 55482, 9r).

Raemoir House Hotel
Downstream at Banchory there is a splendid country house, set in magnificent parkland and beautiful gardens; Raemoir House dates from the 18th c. In the hotel the choice menus are complemented by a well-stocked wine cellar and a fine selection of single malt whiskies (Raemoir House, Banchory, Kincardineshire AB31 4ED, tel. (013302) 824884, fax 822171, 23r.)

Highlands
Isle of Eriska Hotel
Private islands have their own special attraction, and the little island of Eriska north of Oban is no exception. This country hotel, built in the baronial style in 1884 by a branch of the Stewarts of Appin, appears almost too good to be true. In 1973 the property was taken over by the Buchanan-Smith family, and made into a top luxury hotel – absolute comfort perfectly combined with excellent service and cordial hospitality. Activity-seekers are catered for in the new leisure complex with swimming pool opened in 1995 (Ledaig, Oban, Argyll PA37 1SD, tel. (01631) 720371, fax 720531, 16r).

Ardanaiseig Hotel
The Ardanaiseig Hotel at Taynuilt has an idyllic garden with a magnificent rhododendron display. This baronial-style manor house, built in 1834 for a member of the Campbell clan, has recently been taken over by the Gray family who have introduced many fine pieces of antique furniture (Kilchrenan, by Taynuilt, Argyll PA35 1HE, tel. (01866) 833333, fax 833222, 15r).

Knockie Lodge Hotel
In the Highlands above Loch Ness, with its inviting long walks, the head of the Fraser Clan built a hunting lodge in 1789, later extended to become Knockie Lodge. Lounge and dining room are graced with antiques hand-picked by Ian and Brenda Milward, experts at combining every possible convenience with Scottish conviviality (Whitebridge, Inverness-shire IV1 2UP, tel. (01456) 486276, fax 486389, 10r).

Dunain Park Hotel
Dunain Park, a Georgian country house just 1 mile/2km south of Inverness, offers tastefully furnished rooms, indoor swimming pool and sauna, plus a prize-winning restaurant with menus with a French flavour (Inverness IV3 6JN, tel. (01463) 230512, fax 224532, 12r).

Bunchrew House Hotel
West of Inverness on the Beauly Firth, Bunchrew House was built in 1621 by the Fraser Clan whose ancestral portraits grace the wood-panelled hotel bar. Guests can be chauffeur-driven to their picnics in the hotel's own Rolls Royce (Bunchrew, Inverness IV3 6TA, tel. (01463) 234917, fax 710620, 11r).

Culloden House Hotel
Before the famous battle in 1745 Bonnie Prince Charlie lodged at Culloden House, whose rooms, steeped in history, have been converted by the McKenzies into a first-class hotel with magnificent suites, sauna, solarium and excellent cuisine (Culloden, Inverness IV1 2NZ, tel. (01463) 790461, fax 792181, 23r).

Mansion House Hotel
A perfect example of Victorian architecture, Mansion House on the River Lossie is only a stone's throw from the centre of Elgin. The cuisine wins plaudits for its creativity, and guests can relax in swimming pool, sauna or jacuzzi (The Haugh, Elgin, Moray IV30 1AW, tel. (01343) 548811, fax 547916, 22r).

Loch Torridon Hotel
Originally built on Loch Torridon as a hunting lodge by the first Earl of Lovelace in the late 19th c., the hotel has spacious rooms all carefully restored and refurbished in true country house style by the Gregorys. Geraldine Gregory is also responsible for the culinary wonders on the menu (Torridon, near Achnasheen, Wester Ross IV22 2EY; tel. (01445) 791242, fax 791296; 21r).

Reservation centres
Further information on Scotland's hotels in country houses, castles and stately homes is available from:
The Heritage Circle, Meiklemosside, Fenwick, Ayrshire KA3 6AY, tel. (01560) 600769
Pride of Britain, PO Box 1535, Andover, Hampshire SP10 1XZ; tel. (01264) 324400, fax 324024.

Scotland's Heritage Hotels, Suite 2d Churchill Way, Bishopbriggs, Glasgow
  G64 2RH; tel. (0141) 772 6911, fax 772 6917
Scotts Castle Holidays, 11, Bruntsfield Crescent, Edinburgh EH10 4EZ, tel.
  (0131) 446 9717, fax 446 9718

Information

British Tourist Authority Overseas

The British Tourist Authority (BTA) is responsible for providing tourist information overseas and has offices in the following English-speaking
countries:

8th Floor, University Centre, Midland House, 210 Clarence Street,   Australia
Sydney, New South Wales 2000;
Tel. (02) 264 3300, fax 267 4442

Suite 450, 111 Avenue Road, Toronto, Ontario M5R 3J8;   Canada
Tel. (416) 925 6326, fax 961 2175

Suite 305, 3rd Floor, Dilworth Building, cnr. Queen/Customs Street,   New Zealand
Auckland 1; tel. (09) 303 1446, fax 377 6905

18/19 College Green, Dublin 2;   Republic of
Tel. (01) 670 8100, fax 670 8244   Ireland

Lancaster Gate, Hyde Park Lane, Hyde Park, Sandton 2196   South Africa
(personal callers);
P.O. Box 41896, Craighall 2024 (postal address);
Tel. (011) 325 0342, fax 325 0344

Suite 1510, 625 North Michigan Avenue, Chicago, IL 60611;   United States
Fax (312) 787 0464 (personal callers only);
7th Floor, 551 Fifth Avenue, New York, NY 10176-0799;
Tel. (212) 986 2200, fax 986 1188

Information in Great Britain

Central Information Department   **Scottish Tourist**
23, Ravelston Terrace, Edinburgh EH4 3EU;   **Board**
Tel. (0131) 332 2433, fax 315 4545
Mon.–Thur. 9am–5.30pm, Fri. to 5pm (written and telephone enquiries
only)

19 Cockspur Street, London SW1Y 5BL; Personal callers only
May–Sept. Mon.–Fri. 9am–6pm, Thur. to 6.30pm; mid Jun.–mid Sept. also
Sat. 10am– 5pm; Oct.–Apr. Mon.–Fri. 9.30am–5.30pm, Thur. to 6.30pm (in-
formation; travel and hotel reservations and tickets for the Edinburgh
Military Tattoo)

Edinburgh and Scotland Information Centre   **Edinburgh and**
3 Princes Street, Edinburgh EH2 2QP;   **Lothians Tourist**
Tel. (0131) 557 1700, fax 557 5118   **Board**
Mon.–Sat. 9am–6pm, Sun. 10am–6pm (handles enquiries relating to any
part of Scotland)

Scotland is well supplied with Tourist Information Centres (TICs). They   **Tourist**
generally open Mon.-Fri. 9am–4pm but stay open longer in summer; some   **Information**
are only open from Mar./Apr. to Sept./Oct. however.   **Centres (TICs)**

Scottish Area Tourist Boards

Edinburgh
Edinburgh and Lothians Tourist Board
see above

Glasgow
Greater Glasgow & Clyde Valley Tourist Board
39 St Vincent Place, Glasgow G1 2ER
Tel. (0141) 204 4480, fax 221 4772

The South of Scotland
Ayrshire & Arran Tourist Board
Burns House, Burns Statue Square, Ayr KA7 1UP;
Tel. (01292) 262555, fax 269555

Dumfries & Galloway Tourist Board
64 White Sands, Dumfries DG1 2RS;
Tel. (01387) 245550, fax (01387) 245551

Scottish Borders Tourist Board
Tourist Information Centre, Murray's Green, Jedburgh TD8 6BE;
Tel. (01835) 863435/863688, fax 864099

Central Scotland
Angus & City of Dundee Tourist Board
Market Place, Arbroath, Angus DD11 1HR
Tel. (01241) 877883, fax 878550

Argyll, the Isles, Loch Lomond, Stirling and Trossachs Tourist Board
41 Dumbarton Road, Stirling FK8 2QQ
Tel. (01786) 470945, fax 471301

Perthshire Tourist Board
Lower City Mills, West Mill Street, Perth PH1 5QP;
Tel. (01738) 627958, fax 630416

Kingdom of North Fife
St Andrews Tourist Information Centre
70 Market St., St Andrews, Fife KY16 9NU
Tel. (01334) 474606, fax 478422

Grampian Highlands and Aberdeen
Grampian Highlands and Aberdeen Tourist Board
101 Migvie House, North Silver St., Aberdeen AB1 1RJ;
Tel. (01224) 632727, fax 639836

Highlands of Scotland & Skye
Highlands of Scotland and Skye
Tourist Information Centre, North Kessock IV1 1XB
Tel. (01463) 731505, fax 731701

Western Isles
Western Isles Tourist Board
26 Cromwell Street, Stornoway, Isle of Lewis HS1 2DD;
Tel. (01851) 703088, fax 705244

Orkney and Shetland Islands
Orkney Tourist Board
6 Broad Street, Kirkwall, Orkney KW15 1NX;
Tel. (01856) 872856, fax 875056

Shetland Islands Tourism
Market Cross, Lerwick ZE1 0LU;
Tel. (01595) 693434, fax 695807

Luxury Travel

★M.V. "Hebridean Princess"
M.V. "Hebridean Princess" offers a wide choice of luxury cruises around the Highlands and Islands, with all the exclusiveness of country-house

Principal places of tourist interest

* of particular interest
** outstanding

For the principal castles, abbeys and prehistoric sites see p. 320

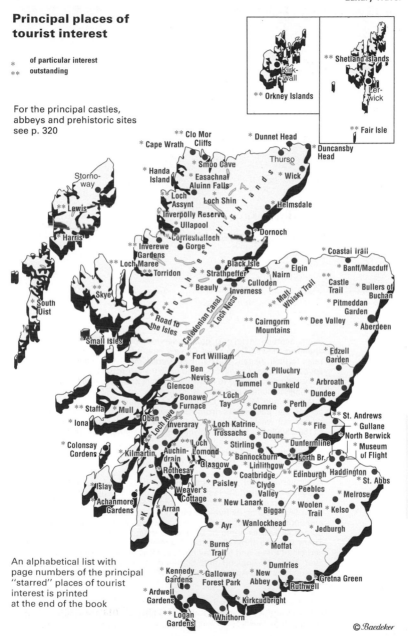

** Kirk-wall
** Orkney Islands

** Shetland Islands
Ler-wick
** Fair Isle

** Clo Mor Cliffs
* Cape Wrath
* Dunnet Head
* Duncansby Head
** Smoo Cave
Thurso
* Handa Island
* Easachnal Aluinn Falls
* Wick
Storno-way
* Loch Assynt
* Loch Shin
** Lewis
* Inverpolly Reservo
* Helmsdale
* Ullapool
* Harris
* Corrieshalloch
** Corrieshalloch Gorge
* Dornoch
** Inverewe Gardens
* Black Isle
* Coastal Trail
** Loch Maree
* Elgin
** Torridon
* Strathpeffer
* Nairn
* Banff/Macduff
* Beauly
* Culloden
* Castle Trail
* Bullers of Buchan
Skye
* Inverness
* Malt Whisky Trail
* Pitmeddan Garden
* South Uist
* Road to the Isles
* Caledonian Canal
Loch Ness
** Cairngorm Mountains
*** Dee Valley
* Aberdeen
** Small Isles
* Fort William
* Edzell Garden
** Ben Nevis
* Loch Tummel
* Pitlochry
* Arbroath
* Glencoe
* Dunkeld
* Dundee
** Staffa
* Bonawe Furnace
** Loch Tay
* Comrie
* Perth
** Mull
* Oban
* Loch Awe
** Loch Katrine Trossachs
** Fife
* St. Andrews
* Iona
* Inveraray
* Doune
* Gullane
* North Berwick
* Colonsay Gardens
** Loch Lomond
* Stirling
* Dunfermline
* Museum of Flight
* Kilmartin
* Auchin-drain
* Bannockburn
* Forth Br.
* Rothesay
* Glasgow
* Linlithgow
* Haddington
** Islay
* Paisley
* Coatbridge
* Edinburgh
* St. Abbs
* Weaver's Cottage
* Clyde Valley
* Peebles
* Melrose
** Achanmore Gardens
* New Lanark
* Woolen Trail
* Kelso
* Arran
* Biggar
* Ayr
* Wanlockhead
* Jedburgh
* Burns Trail
* Moffat
* Kennedy Gardens
* Dumfries
* Galloway Forest Park
* New Abbey
* Gretna Green
* Ardwell Gardens
* Ruthwell
** Logan Gardens
* Kirkcudbright
* Whithorn

North-west Highlands
Kintyre

An alphabetical list with page numbers of the principal "starred" places of tourist interest is printed at the end of the book

© Baedeker

351

Luxury cruising aboard the "Hebridean Princess"

living Scottish style, top quality service and comfort, and constantly changing views of the West Coast's fabulous scenery. Passengers can relax in their elegant cabins or by a crackling fire in the stylish lounge, savour the delicious meals served up in the grand dining room, and make daily excursions to get to know the lifestyle and culture of Scotland's fascinating Highlands and Islands. Cruises are of 6, 7, 8 and 14 days duration from mid March to October starting from Oban, with a collection service for passengers from Glasgow station and airport. Price per person per week, double cabin with full board, inclusive of excursions: £1150–£5600. For further information and reservations contact:

Hebridean Island Cruises Ltd., Unit 5, Acorn Park, Skipton, North Yorkshire BD23 2UE; tel. (01756) 701338, fax 701455

★The Royal Scotsman

A similar level of luxury can be found on land aboard the Royal Scotsman, a beautifully restored historic train. Equipped wth two dining cars, 5 sleeping cars and an observation car, the train can accommodate up to 36 guests on its five-day tour of the Scottish Highlands beginning and ending at Edinburgh. The tour includes visits to castles and stately homes as well as some of Scotland's most famous whisky distilleries. There are also three-day tours between London and Edinburgh. The combined three- and five-day tours are known as the seven-day "Grand Tour North of England and Scotland" and can be booked as such: season runs from April through to November. For information and bookings contact:

The Great Scottish & Western Railway Company Ltd,
46A Constitution Street, Edinburgh EH6 6RS Tel. (0131) 5551344/5551021.
Fax (0131) 5551345

Motoring

Breakdowns and Motoring Organisations

Dial 999 free of charge nationwide for police, fire brigade or ambulance.

Emergencies

Emergency phones are spaced at regular intervals along major trunk roads and motorways.

The Automobile Association (AA) and Royal Automobile Club (RAC) provide breakdown services for members of other affiliated motoring organisations.

Motoring organisations

Automobile Association (AA)
Fanum House, Melville Street, Edinburgh EH3 7PD
269 Argyll Street, Glasgow G2 8DW
These two addresses are for AA shops, they are for drop-in information only. For telephone enquiries 'phone 0990 500 600 (members only).

Royal Automobile Club (RAC)
RAC House, 200 Sinnieston Street, Glasgow G3 8NZ; tel. (0141) 221 5665

Royal Scottish Automobile Club (RSAC)
11 Blythswood Square, Glasgow G2 4AG; tel. (0141) 221 3850

Automobile Association (AA); tel. (0800) 887766 (freephone)
Royal Automobile Club (RAC); tel. (0800) 550550/828282 (freephone)

Breakdown assistance

Car Rental

The major car rental firms have offices or desks at airports and in all of Britain's major cities. There are also local rental companies who will often hire out their vehicles at cheaper rates than the better-known agencies.

Anyone wanting to rent a car must be over 21, or in some cases 23, be under 70, and have held a driving licence for at least 12 months.

Alamo; tel. (0345) 886688
Avis; tel. (0990) 900500
Budget; tel. (0800) 181181 (freephone)
Europcar; tel. (0113) 242 2233
Hertz; tel. (0181) 679 1799

Nationwide reservations

Road Traffic

All major roads are clearly signed and numbered: M, as in M6, indicates motorways (toll-free in Britain), A roads, as in A74, are single or dual carriageway, while B roads, as in B3004, are more minor roads and usually single carriageway. The UK road network in the South and the Midlands is well built up and maintained but although continually expanding tends to thin out north of a line from Liverpool in the north-west to Hull in the east. Minor roads in Scotland are often narrow and still single track, with passing places, in some of the remoter areas. Here courtesy requires that when two cars are approaching from opposite directions the first car to reach a passing place should pull in or stop opposite the passing place to allow safe passage. Extra care is also required on roads passing through unfenced grazing or moorland because of the free-roaming sheep which are also quite capable of choosing to snooze on the highway.
Scotland has ten National Tourist Routes – alternative routes through smaller towns and the countryide. Routes are signposted with a blue thistle

Roads

*Beware
Sheep*

National Tourist Routes

353

Motoring

symbol. Leaflets are available from Tourist Information Centres (see Information).

Drive on the left!

Drive on the left and overtake on the right. If unfamiliar with driving on the left take special care when starting out, particularly when moving away from service stations onto an empty road. If your car is left-hand drive, remember to mask the headlights so they dip to the left.

Traffic regulations

Traffic rules and regulations are published in the Highway Code. This is available at ports of entry, from bookshops and motoring organisations. Traffic signs are largely the same as in Europe.

Speed limits

The maximum speed limit on motorways and dual carriageways is 70mph/112kph (60mph/96kph with a trailer), on other roads outside built-up areas 60mph/96kph (50mph/80kph with a trailer) and in built-up areas 30mph/48kph. Towing vehicles may not use the outside lane of a three-lane motorway.

Right of way

Traffic on the main road generally has the right of way unless a "Stop" or "Give Way" sign indicates otherwise. At roundabouts give way to the traffic coming from the right already on the roundabout. Motorists must stop at road junctions with unbroken double white lines but may edge forward slowly if the white lines are broken.

Seat belts

Seat belts must be worn in rear seats as well as front seats. Children under 12 may only ride in the rear seats.

Distances by Motorways Kilometres (Roman) Miles (*Italic*)	Aberdeen	Carlisle	Dundee	Edinburgh	Fort William	Glasgow	Hull	Inverness	Kyle of Lochalsh	Mallaig	Manchester	Newcastle	Oban	Scrabster	Stanraer	Ullapool	London
Aberdeen	•	354	112	201	265	233	557	169	301	302	547	378	288	365	367	241	810
Carlisle	*221*	•	243	152	326	158	258	406	448	397	196	99	309	597	168	499	490
Dundee	*70*	*152*	•	93	193	131	466	210	283	258	434	267	189	400	273	302	730
Edinburgh	*125*	*95*	*58*	•	235	68	347	254	330	288	346	177	200	446	200	327	609
Fort William	*165*	*204*	*121*	*146*	•	167	570	106	122	70	507	407	78	296	296	145	800
Glasgow	*145*	*99*	*82*	*42*	*104*	•	409	267	290	240	346	238	150	458	135	312	693
Hull	*346*	*161*	*291*	*216*	*354*	*254*	•	602	702	654	154	195	566	819	404	675	270
Inverness	*105*	*254*	*131*	*158*	*66*	*166*	*374*	•	131	170	602	431	186	190	402	72	863
Kyle of Lochalsh	*188*	*280*	*177*	*206*	*76*	*181*	*439*	*82*	•	54	640	514	200	342	424	141	941
Mallaig	*189*	*248*	*161*	*180*	*44*	*150*	*409*	*106*	*34*	•	587	461	144	381	371	266	886
Manchester	*340*	*199*	*271*	*215*	*315*	*215*	*95*	*373*	*400*	*367*	•	213	499	792	354	673	298
Newcastle	*325*	*62*	*167*	*110*	*253*	*148*	*121*	*268*	*321*	*288*	*132*	•	273	621	213	254	441
Oban	*180*	*193*	*118*	*125*	*49*	*94*	*354*	*116*	*125*	*90*	*312*	*233*	•	376	285	266	798
Scrabster	*228*	*373*	*250*	*279*	*185*	*286*	*512*	*119*	*214*	*238*	*495*	*388*	*235*	•	598	200	1070
Stanraer	*228*	*105*	*171*	*124*	*184*	*84*	*251*	*250*	*265*	*232*	*220*	*132*	*178*	*374*	•	254	647
Ullapool	*150*	*312*	*189*	*203*	*90*	*194*	*419*	*45*	*88*	*166*	*418*	*220*	*166*	*125*	*158*	•	935
London	*503*	*306*	*456*	*378*	*597*	*397*	*168*	*536*	*588*	*554*	*185*	*274*	*499*	*669*	*402*	*571*	•

The blood alcohol limit is 0.8 per millilitre.

Double yellow lines mean no parking or waiting at any time and a single yellow line means night-time and Sunday parking only. Illegally parked vehicles may be wheel-clamped and only released after a long wait and the payment of a large fine.

Although petrol (gasoline) is nowadays sold almost everywhere in litres a few places still show the price in British gallons (1 Imperial Gallon = 4.546 litres). Grades obtainable are Super Fourstar (98 octane), Super (95 octane), leaded and unleaded. Diesel and LPG are also usually obtainable in most places. In the remoter parts of Scotland distances between filling stations are greater than in the south so remember this when planning a journey.

Tyre pressure is measured in pounds per square inch (see Weights and Measures).

Safety on the Road and Accident Procedure

In Britain vehicles only require third-party insurance, so visitors driving their own cars should take out comprehensive insurance to cover their stay (this can also include cover for vehicle recovery, transport home, etc.). They should in any case obtain a "Green Card" (international insurance certificate). If involved in an accident they should also inform their insurers as soon as possible.

However careful a driver you may be accidents can still happen. Whatever the provocation, do not lose your temper, stay calm, keep a clear head and be polite. Take the following steps:
    Make safe the scene of the accident (switch on warning lights, position warning triangle); apply first aid and keep warm anyone who has been injured; if necessary dial 999 to summon police and ambulance; get the names and addresses of other parties, and any witnesses, as well as vehicle makes and registration numbers, and names and numbers of insurers; make a sketch of the scene of the accident, or, better still, if you have a camera, take photographs; fill in an accident report if you have one and get the other party to sign it. Do not sign any acknowledgement of responsibility.

National Nature Conservation Areas

Famous as a country for the grandeur of its landscape, Scotland has no fewer than 4 major regional conservation areas – Loch Lomond, the Trossachs in Perthshire, the Cairngorms (peaking at 4084ft/1245m), and of course the region around Ben Nevis – and 40 National Scenic Areas, representing close on 2.5 million acres of nationally significant natural beauty. This is in addition to some 38,000 buildings with conservation status and over 5500 ancient monuments, testimony in stone to the culture of the past.

Since 1992 the agency responsible to the Minister for Scotland for administering the conservation of the Scottish countryside has been Scottish Natural Heritage who are responsible for 70 national nature reserves. Other conservation bodies concerned with natural areas such as mountains and islands include the National Trust for Scotland (see Castles and Historic Sites), while the Royal Society for the Protection of Birds and the Scottish Wildlife Trust are voluntary bodies with charitable status which ensure protection for wildlife habitats through their nature reserves.

Newspapers

Information	Scottish Natural Heritage
	12 Hope Terrace, Edinburgh EH9 2AS;
	Tel. (0131) 447 4784, fax 446 2277

Country code   Visitors to any nature conservation areas should behave appropriately and not upset the natural habitat. They should leave plants and animals undisturbed and not stray from the marked paths, trails or bridleways. Any litter should be taken home and dogs must be kept on a lead. There is a ban on taking plants, camping outside designated sites, carrying radios, etc., lighting fires and night-time hiking.

Newspapers

Broadsheets   Scotland's most famous daily paper is "The Scotsman", published in Edinburgh with a circulation of about 82,846 followed by "The Glasgow Herald" with a circulation of about 115,000. The popular evening dailies are Edinburgh's "Evening News" and Glasgow's "Evening Times", both with circulations of 120,000 and a colourful sports edition on Saturdays.

Tabloids   Dundee's "Sunday Post", with its populist, fiercely local style and content, holds a unique place in the tabloid press which has earned it an entry in the "Guinness Book of Records" for the density of its over a million circulation, probably comparable only with the Peking People's Daily, and which has made it virtually synonymous with a certain provincial Scottish mentality. "The Daily Record" sells about 750,000 copies, and the Scottish edition of Rupert Murdoch's "Sun" sells 400,000.

Local press and magazines   The major regional papers, with very much of a local focus on the news, are "The Aberdeen Press and Journal" and "The Dundee Courier and Advertiser". Scotland also has a whole series of magazines and journals. "Scottish Affairs", published by Lyndsay Paterson, has taken over from the sadly missed "Radical Scotland"; literary and arts magazines published in Edinburgh include "Cencrastus", "Chapman" and "Lines Review".

Opening Times

Banks   See Currency

Shops   The law governing shop opening hours have recently been relaxed; now shops, if they choose, may remain open round the clock. Shops generally open at about 9am and close around 5.30 to 6pm. Some close on Saturday afternoons and, in smaller communities, they often close for an afternoon during the week, although this early-closing day varies from place to place. In areas popular with visitors, on the other hand, many shops stay open until late in the evening, and in the cities Thursday is usually late-night shopping, when shops stay open until 7 or 8pm. Many shops in Scotland also open on Sundays, especially in cities and larger towns during the summer.

Post Offices   See Post

Pubs   With the reform of opening hours Scottish pubs are nowadays allowed to stay open Mon.–Sat. from 11am to 11pm but many landlords still keep to the traditional opening hours and close during the week between 2.30 and 5pm. Sunday opening is from 12.30 to 2.30 and from 6.30 to 11pm. Some pubs also have a special licence to stay open later, especially at weekends.

Post

Stamps   Postage stamps are sold in newsagents, service stations and outlets displaying the red sign "We sell postage stamps", as well as post offices. The current cost of a first class stamp is 26p, which is also the rate for letters up to 20g to other countries in the European Union. For letters and postcards to non-EU destinations the stamps must show the actual postage rate, not just 1st or 2nd (class).

Post offices generally open Mon.–Fri. 9am–5.30pm, Sat. 9am–12.30 or 1pm. Some sub post offices close at lunchtime.

Post office
opening hours

Public Holidays

January 1st (New Year's Day)
January 2nd
Good Friday
December 25th (Christmas Day)
December 26th (Boxing Day)
   If these legal public holidays fall on a Saturday or Sunday the following Monday becomes a public holiday as well.

Legal public
holidays

The highlight of the calendar of annual holidays and celebrations for the Scots is Hogmanay (December 31st), when traditionally they see in the New Year with a Black Bun, a typo of cake with plenty of seasoning and go "first footing", with a glass of whisky and a lump of coal, to be the first to cross the thresholds of friends and neighbours.

Hogmanay

English fixed date bank holidays such as Spring Bank Holiday and Summer Bank Holiday only apply in Scotland to banks and some other offices. Scottish towns and cities normally have a spring and summer holiday instead, on dates which vary from place to place but are always on a Monday.

Bank holidays

Scotland also has a number of its own traditional highdays and holidays:
January 25th: Burns Night (birthday of Robbie Burns)
October 31st: Halloween
November 30th: St Andrew's Day

Local highdays
and holidays

Rail Travel

InterCity rail services connect all the main cities in the United Kingdom, with the fastest run between London and Edinburgh taking just over 4 hours (see Getting to Scotland). Sleeper services must be booked, and seats should also be booked for longer journeys and journeys during peak travel periods.

InterCity
rail services

ScotRail is British Rail's operator in Scotland.

Information

Special tickets such as BritRail Flexipasses and Freedom of Scotland Travelpasses (see below) and information about services can be obtained from ScotRail and British Rail overseas offices:

Customer Relations, Room 508, Caledonian Chambers,
87 Union Street, Glasgow G1 3TA; tel. (0141) 335 4612

ScotRail

British Rail International,
123 Lower Baggot Street, Dublin 2; tel. 616238

Republic of
Ireland

British Rail International,
1500 Broadway, New York NY 10036

United States and
Canada

Restaurants

Information and tickets for Le Shuttle and Eurostar services	Information and tickets for Le Shuttle and Eurostar services via the EuroTunnel (see Getting to Scotland) can be obtained (by post) from British Rail. Holders of a BritRail Pass (see below) are entitled to reduced fares on the high speed Paris-London and Brussels-London Eurostar services.
BritRail Pass	A BritRail Pass allows unlimited travel (first or standard 2nd class) throughout the British Rail network in Scotland, Wales and England for periods of 4, 8, 15 or 22 days or one month. There are special prices for those aged 60 and over, or under 26. The pass is only available to those from outside Britain and must be bought before leaving home.
BritRail Flexipass	A BritRail Flexipass is valid for 4, 8 or 15 days in any one month.
Saver Return Ticket	Saver Return Tickets offer good value and allow the journey to be broken at any point along the normal route (e.g. London-Glasgow).
Freedom of Scotland Travelpass	The Freedom of Scotland Travelpass, valid for 8 or 15 consecutive days or any 8 days in a 15 day period, offers unlimited travel on the ScotRail network as well as those InterCity services to/from Berwick-Upon-Tweed and Carlisle. It is also valid on Glasgow's Underground System, all Strathclyde PTE ferries and Caledonian MacBrayne west coast ferry links apart from Raasay and Scalpay; on Kyles of Bute Cruises and the ferry from Mallaig to the Small Isles, holders are entitled to a discount of 33%. On P & O Orkney and Shetland sailings and Stena–Sealink's Stranraer–Larne service the discount is 20%. Travelpass holders are also entitled to 33% discount on many Scottish buses (Skyeways, Western Scottish, Henderson's, Morrison's Coaches, Oban and District Buses, West Highland Motor Services, Border Courier Services, Highland Scottish Omnibuses, Post Bus Services, D. Maclennan, Elizabeth Yule, Moffat & Williamson, Lowland Omnibuses, Gaelicbus, Midland Bluebird, Trossachs Trundler, Heather Hopper and Speyside Rambler, Harrier Scenic Bus Services, Tayside Trundler, West Coast Motors), also on various Loganair flights within Scotland and on Guide Friday Edinburgh city tours.
The Royal Scotsman	See Luxury Travel
Steam trains	Throughout the summer steam trains run on the exceptionally scenic line between Fort William and Mallaig. Information and reservations: ScotRail, Fort William Station Travel Centre, Fort William PH33 6DZ, tel. (01397) 703791.

Restaurants

Food and Drink	See entry
A Taste of Scotland	The best way of getting acquainted with the food typical of Scotland, both as traditional fare and creative new dishes which make the most of the country's fresh produce, is to be guided by the distinctive blue and white soup tureen logo of the "Taste of Scotland" scheme. This is promoted by the Scottish Tourist Board (see Information) and has an annual guide listing the restaurants, each of them regularly inspected, which meet their high standards in terms of service and welcome as well as traditional fare and Scottish haute cuisine. The guide is available from : Taste of Scotland, 33 Melville Street, Edinburgh EH3 7JF; tel. (0131) 220 1900, fax 220 6102.
Coffee shops, sandwich bars, tea rooms	Coffee shops, tea rooms and sandwich bars, most of which close in the evening, usually serve tea, coffee, cakes, pastries and sandwiches and simple lunchtime snacks. Sandwich bars have become very popular in recent years and sell sandwiches, baps and rolls with an imaginative range of fillings.

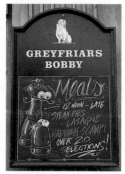

Pub signs: works of art in their own right

Fish and chips are the great British takeaway, typically eaten straight from the paper with a sprinkling of salt and vinegar. In Scotland the fish is usually haddock or whiting, and a portion of fish and chips is invariably called a fish supper, even if eaten at lunchtime. Fish and chip shops often stay open until midnight and beyond, and it is worth remembering that in Scotland's fishing ports this is certainly the cheapest way of enjoying absolutely fresh fish.

Fish and chip shops

As well as beer and other alcohol many pubs also serve food, ranging from simple snacks such as sandwiches and sausages to traditional dishes such as steak, lamb in various guises, venison, and steak and kidney pie. Many pubs also have rooms serving restaurant meals.

Pubs

Scottish bars offer comfort with tradition

Restaurants

To get served just go up to the bar, order your drink from the barmaid or barman and pay for it straightaway. There is no need to tip. Most traditional landlords still close between 2.30pm and 5 or 6pm (see Opening Times).

Cosmopolitan cuisine

Eating out in Scotland is an opportunity to sample a whole range of cosmopolitan cuisine, from elsewhere in Europe – especially France, thanks to the "Auld Alliance" – and from much further afield as the number of ethnic restaurants has grown. These include Turkish, Indian, Chinese, Mexican, and Middle Eastern to name but a few.

Restaurants (selection)

Opening times	Many local Scottish restaurants take last orders at 9.30pm, but foreign restaurants, and fish and chip shops, usually stay open much later.
Aberdeen	Ardoe House, South Deeside Road, tel. (01224) 867355, fax 861283
Anstruther	The Cellar, 24 East Green, tel. (01333) 310378
Archiestown	Archiestown Hotel, tel. (01340) 810218
Arisaig	Arisaig House, Beasdale, tel. (01687) 450622, fax 626
Ayr	Area code: 01292 Fairfield House Hotel, 12 Fairfield Road, tel. 267461 Fouters, 2A Academy Street, tel. 261391
Ballater	Area code: 013397 Balgonie Hotel, Braemar Place, tel. 55482 Darroch Learg Hotel, Braemar Road, tel. 55443 Green Inn, 9 Victoria Road, tel. 55701
Balloch	Cameron House Hotel, tel. (01389) 755565
Banchory	Area code: 01330 Banchory Lodge Hotel, tel. 822625 Raemoir House Hotel, tel. 824884
Braemar	Braemar Lodge Hotel, Glenshee Road, tel. (013397) 41627
Bridge of Marnoch	The Old Manse of Marnoch, tel. (01466) 780873
Craigellachie	Craigellachie Hotel, tel. (01340) 881204
Drybridge	The Old Monastery, Buckie, tel. (01542) 832660
Dufftown	A Taste of Speyside, 100 Balvenie Street, tel. (01340) 820860
Dulnain Bridge	Muckrach Lodge Hotel, tel. (01479) 851257
Dunblane	Cromlix House Hotel, Kinbuck, tel. (01786) 822125, fax 825450
Dundonnell	Dundonnell Hotel, tel. (01854) 633204, fax 633366
Dunfermline	Keavil House Hotel, Crossford, tel. (01383) 736258
Edinburgh	Area code: 0131 Atrium, 10 Cambridge Street, tel. 228 8882 Balmoral Hotel, Princes Street, tel. 556 2414 Caledonian Hotel, Princes Street, tel. 459 9988 Carlton Highland Hotel, North Bridge, tel. 556 7277

Channings, South Learmonth Gardens, tel. 315 2226
Dalmahoy Hotel, Kirknewton, tel. 333 1845
Ducks at Le Marché Noir, 2–4 Eyre Place, tel. 558 1608
George Inter-Continental, 19–21 George Street, tel. 225 1251
Iggs, 15 Jeffrey Street, tel. 557 8184
King James, 107 Leith Street, tel. 556 0111
L'Auberge, 56 St Mary's Street, tel. 556 5888
Martins, 70 Rose Street, tel. 225 3106
Norton House, Ingliston, tel. 333 1275
The Vintners Room, 87 Giles Street, Leith, tel. 554 6767
The Witchery by the Castle, Castle Hill, Royal Mile, tel. 225 5613

Area code: 01343   **Elgin**
Mansefield House Hotel, Mayne Road, tel. 540883
Mansion House Hotel, The Haugh, tel. 548811

Crannog, Town Pier, tel. (01397) 705589   **Fort William**

Wildings, Montgomerie Street, tel. (01465) 713481   **Girvan**

Area code: 0141   **Glasgow**
Buttery, 652 Argyle Street, tel. 221 8188
Crannog, 28 Cheapside Street, tel. 221 1727
Ewington Hotel, 132 Queens Drive, tel. 423 1152
Glasgow Moat House, Congress Road, tel. 306 9988
Hilton, 1 Williams Street, tel. 204 5555
Killermont Polo Club, 2002 Maryhill Road, tel. 946 5412
One Devonshire Gardens Hotel, 1 Devonshire Gardens, tel. 339 2001
Rogano, 11 Exchange Place, tel. 248 4055
Yes, 22 West Nile Street, tel. 221 8044

Area code: 01620   **Gullane**
Greywalls Hotel, Muirfield, tel. 842144
La Potinière, Main Street, tel. 843214

Area code: 01463   **Inverness**
Bunchrew House Hotel, tel. 234917
Dunain Park Hotel, tel. 230512

Sunlaws House Hotel, Heiton, tel. (01573) 450331   **Kelso**

Area code: 01540   **Kingussie**
The Cross, Tweed Mill Brae, tel. 661166
Osprey Hotel, Ruthven Road, tel. 661510. Booking is required in the
restaurant

Brisbane House, tel. (01475) 687200   **Largs**

Beechwood Hotel, Harthorpe Place, tel. (01683) 220210   **Moffat**

Area code: 01688   **Mull**
Druimard Hotel, Dervaig, tel. 400345
Killiechronan House, Killiechronan, tel. (01680) 300403

Manor House Hotel, Gallanach Road, tel. (01631) 62087   **Oban**

Allt-Nan-Ros Hotel, tel. (01855) 821210   **Onich**

Creel, Front Road, St Margaret's Hope, tel. (01856) 831311   **Orkney Islands**

Area code: 01738   **Perth**
Huntingtower Hotel, Almondbank, tel. 583771
Murrayshall Hotel, New Scone, tel. 551171
Newton House Hotel, Glencarse, tel. 860250
Number Thirty Three, 33 George Street, tel. 633771
Parklands Hotel, St Leonards Bank, tel. 622451

Shopping and Souvenirs

Pitlochry	Area code: 01796 Knockendarroch House Hotel, Higher Oakfield, tel. 473473 Pine Trees Hotel, Strathview Terrace, tel. 472121
St Andrews	Area code: 01334 Parkland Hotel, Kinburn Castle, tel. 473620 Rufflets Hotel, Strathkinness Low Road, tel. 472594 St Andrews Golf Hotel, 40 The Scores, tel. 472611 St Andrews Old Course Hotel, Old Station Road, tel. 474371
St Finllans	Area code: 01764 Achray House, Crieff, tel. 685231 Four Seasons, Crieff, tel. 685333
Isle of Skye	Three Chimneys, Colbost, tel. (01470) 511258
Stanley	The Tayside Hotel, Mill Street, tel. (01738) 828249
Stirling	Stirling Highland Hotel, Spittal Street, tel. (01786) 475444
Troon	Area code: 01292 Highgrove House, Old Loans Road, tel. 312511 Lochgreen House, Monktenhill Road, Sothwood, tel. 313343
Ullapool	Altnaharrie Inn, tel. (01854) 633230

Shopping and Souvenirs

Woollen textiles and sheepskins

Among Scotland's most famous products are its distinctive tweeds, tartans and woollens. Tweed is probably the most famous of British textiles, especially when made up in a sporty tweed suit, complete with leather elbow patches; Scottish tweed, the best known being Harris tweed, tends to be more finely patterned. Other Scottish textile specialities include hard-wearing thick Shetland wool jerseys, kilts in the different tartans, plaid shirts, rugs and blankets, paisley shawls and scarves, and fine cashmere cardigans and twinsets, not forgetting sheepskin rugs and jackets.

Jewellery, glass, pottery, china

Other special souvenirs of Scotland include gold and silver jewellery, often inspired by ancient Celtic devices or patterns, glassware such as Caithness Glass and Edinburgh Crystal, and the locally manufactured pottery and china.

Food, drink and tobacco

Tea drinkers can find many different blends of their favourite brew, along with the Scottish shortbread, scones, oatcakes, etc. to go with it. Anyone with a sweet tooth can opt for old-fashioned fudge, or some jam or marmalade, usually also the product of a traditional recipe. Whisky drinkers will find Scotland their idea of heaven, especially when it comes to sampling the excellent single malts (see Baedeker Special, "Scotch Whisky"), but just remember that the Scots' "elixir of life" is highly taxed as well as high proof. For pipe smokers there are some wonderful tobaccos and everything else they need for a good smoke.

Anyone interested in antiques will find a wide selection to choose from, including fine furniture and the famous sterling silver. CDs are another good buy, and budding musicians can take a fiddle or bagpipes home.

Antiques and other souvenirs

Value Added Tax (VAT; currently 17½%) is levied on all services and most goods apart from children's clothing and foodstuffs.

Value Added Tax

Visitors from non-EU countries can reclaim the VAT on goods bought in most shops to be taken out of the country by using the Foreign Exchange Tax Free Shopping scheme. This is done by obtaining a Tax Free Shopping Voucher (on production of passport) from the shop in question. This completed form should then be presented to the British customs on departure, along with the item in question. Visitors from non-EU countries can also avail themselves of the services of Europe Tax Free Shopping (ETS) which operates a simplified procedure for VAT refunds on purchases over £50. Shops in the ETS scheme can supply a Tax Free Shopping Cheque showing the amount of the refund which is then stamped by customs so that it can be cashed at ETS outlets at airports and other departure points.

VAT refunds

Sport

The British love of sport is well known, but what is probably less well-known is that Scotland has a number of sports it can call its own. Visitors will have plenty of chances to join in sporting activities, and the opportunity of watching some of the typically Scottish traditional games and sporting events is one not to be missed.

Spectator Sport and Traditional Games

Listings of sports events can be found in the What's On columns of the daily press. Another source of information is the Scottish Sports Council, Caledonia House, South Gyle, Edinburgh EH12 9DQ; tel. (0131) 339 9000.

Information

One of Britain's great national sports, cricket, the ultimate bat and ball game, is played in summer at every level from series against national teams from other Commonwealth countries down to local teams on the village green for whom this particular game, with its complicated rules and scoring system, is as much a social occasion, complete with tea and sandwiches, as a sporting event. In Scotland cricket is at its most popular along the east coast.

Cricket

Curling, one of Scotland's own traditional games, originated in the Highlands and is played on ice, mainly nowadays at purpose-built rinks. It consists of propelling curling stones, polished lumps of granite weighing over 44lb/20kg, at a target (tee) over a distance of 139ft/42m.

Curling

Most pubs have their own dartboard since darts is the kind of popular game anyone can play, but it has been made even more popular by television coverage of professional championship darts. The winner is the first to score 301 or 501, but the skill lies in throwing the darts into the right sections of the board, combining doubles, trebles and bullseyes, to get to the target score first.

Darts

Britain is the birthplace of football – or soccer as it is also called – and this is reflected in the United Kingdom's unique position among the world's

Football

footballing nations, since it fields four national teams, one each from England, Scotland, Wales and Northern Ireland, in the World Cup and European football championships.

Scotland has its own football league featuring traditional clubs such as Dundee United and Hibernian (the "Hibs") from Edinburgh, but football north of the border tends to be dominated by Glasgow's two rival clubs, Celtic and Rangers. Their bitter rivalry has a long history behind it, dating back to the 19th c. when red, white and blue Rangers at Ibrox Park was Glasgow's Protestant team, and green and white Celtic at Celtic Park was the team of the city's Irish Catholics. Local Derbies between the two are still quite tense affairs but the fanaticism has abated somewhat since 1989 when, despite loud protests from the fans, Rangers took on its first Catholic player, Mo Johnstone.

The top league games usually kick off on Saturdays at 3pm or Wednesday at 7.30 or 7.45pm, although increasingly these dates and times are being changed to suit the needs of television.

Greyhound racing Greyhound racing, where greyhounds race after an artificial hare, is said to be "horse racing for the common man", but a race meeting at, say, Edinburgh's Powderhall is something everyone will find worth a visit.

Highland Games See Introduction

Horse racing Scottish racegoers particularly enjoy steeplechasing, controversial though this may be in some quarters because of the jumps the horses have to contend with. Their top national racecourses include Hamilton, Musselburgh, Kelso and Ayr.

Polo Polo, in which Britain is one of the leading nations along with Argentina, is another sport involving horses and, like show jumping and horse racing, is also a favourite with Britain's royal family, chief among them Prince Charles.

Rugby Rugby, another team ball game invented in England, is much more popular here than elsewhere in Europe apart from France, and during the season (September–May) the international games, especially England against Scotland, can attract as large a crowd, if not larger, than many top football matches. Scottish teams from the Borders such as Melrose and Hawick are generally well on a par with the top teams from Wales and elsewhere in the United Kingdom.

Shinty Shinty is a type of hockey which in Scotland has two leagues – North and South – competing for the Comanachd Cup; its centre is Inverness.

Snooker Snooker is a more complicated version of billiards. Although popular as a game played by the general public, snooker also has its professionals who have achieved star status thanks to frequent television coverage.

Activity sports

Anyone who enjoys taking part in activity sports can find public facilities for their use just about everywhere, and a wide variety of sports centres also offer both accommodation and tuition. Information about activity holidays is available from travel agents, the Scottish Tourist Board (see Information) and the Scottish Sports Council (see above).

Angling Its rivers, lakes, lochs and coastal waters make Scotland an angler's paradise, whether it be for game fishing, coarse fishing or deep sea fishing. Tackle can usually be hired locally. The Scottish Tourist Board (see Information) can provide information on hotels with good angling waters as well as guides such as "Scotland for Fishing" and "Scotland for Sea

Angling" which give full details of permits, fishing clubs, boat and tackle hire, etc.

Game fishing for salmon and trout requires a permit. This can be obtained from fishing tackle centres and shops, some hotels and the offices of the local fishery board or district. Many trout and salmon waters are privately owned. In Scotland the trout-fishing season goes from mid-March to early October although the dates of the close season can vary between late August and late February. The season for salmon fishing starts in January and lasts till October.

Game fishing

No permit is required for coarse fishing. The main fish caught are pike, bream, tench, rudd, roach, perch, carp and eel, and most of Scotland's coarse fishing is in its central waterways, with the season from mid-June to mid-March.

Coarse fishing

The Scottish rivers the Tay, Spey, Dee and Tweed are internationally famous for their trout and salmon. The big sea trout are to be found in the lochs of the north-west.

Fishing waters

The top deep sea fishing grounds are in the waters warmed by the Gulf Stream off the west coast. The season lasts all year round and catches include shark, ray, cod, pollack, hake, bass, grey mullet and sea bream.

Deep sea fishing

Bicycles can be hired in many places, and can be carried on trains relatively cheaply. The best places for a cycling tour (fewer hills and even some travelling on the flat) are Aberdeenshire, the Borders, Dumfries and Galloway, the region around the Moray Firth and a few islands such as the Orkneys. The Long Distance Cycle Way, from Glasgow via Loch Lomond to the western end of Loch Tay, is another good route. Further information, including "Cycling in Scotland", is available from any Tourist Information Centre (see Information).

Cycling

Golf was born in Scotland which, with over 430, has more golf courses per head of the population than anywhere else in the world (see Baedeker Special, "Bogey, Birdie, Hole in One"). Most of them will also take visiting holidaymakers on payment of the usual fee. For the Scots golf is a people's sport, which is why the fees are within most of the people's means. The highlight of the golfing year is the British Open, played on alternate years in England and Scotland, but every sixth year at St Andrews. Alongside this most venerable of Scottish clubs (the Royal and Ancient, 1754) and its illustrious peers such as Muirfield's Honourable Company, 1744, Royal Dornoch, 1877, Royal Troon, 1878, there are a number of famous golfing hotels with their own courses, including the five-star Gleneagles, home of the Scottish Open (see Hotels, Country Houses & Castles), and Turnberry (see Hotels). The Scottish Tourist Board (see Information) can also supply "Scotland, Home of Golf", a guide detailing over 400 courses and clubs.

Golf

The hunting and shooting of game requires a gun licence. There are different seasons for game, starting with roebuck (Apr. 30th-Oct. 31st), grouse ("glorious twelfth" Aug.–Dec. 10th), red deer (July 1st–Oct. 20th), wildfowl (Sep. 1st–Jan. 31st), capercaillie (Oct. 1st–Jan. 31st) and pheasant (Oct. 1st–Feb. 1st). In its brochure "Shooting and Stalking in Scotland" the Scottish Tourist Board (see Information) gives information about hotels and other relevant details. Hunting with horse and hounds is particularly popular in the Borders, with probably the Buccleuch the most famous of the hunts. The British Association for Shooting & Conservation (BASC) Trochry, Dunkeld, Tayside PH8 0DY. Tel. (01350) 723226 can give information on agencies which can organise hunting & shooting expeditions & also give advice about facilities, seasons & hire. Also look for monthly journals, magazines such as The Shooting Times & Shooting Gazette.

Hunting and shooting

Sport

Riding

Apart from riding schools, where horses can be hired, some travel firms also offer package riding holidays ranging from several days of pony trekking to courses in jumping, dressage and cross-country. The Scottish Tourist Board publishes "Trekking and Riding", and further information can be obtained from: The Secretary, Trekking and Riding Society of Scotland, Boreland, Fearnan, by Aberfeldy, Perthshire PH15 2PG, tel. (01887) 830274, fax 830606.

Tennis

Scotland can offer visitors plenty of tennis courts and tennis halls. Falkland Palace, a Stuart hunting lodge on the Fife peninsula, had its own tennis court as early as 1539. Information is available from travel agents and tourist offices.

Walking and Mountaineering

Many of Scotland's loveliest landscapes are far from the beaten track and only accessible on foot. There are some particularly fine long-distance paths in the National Scenic Areas and along the Heritage Coasts. For climbing and mountaineering the best areas are around Ben Nevis and some of the other "Munros" (see Baedeker Special, "How to become a Munroist"). Even on short hill-walks you need to have the proper equipment and make allowances for the changeable weather. On the mountains you must have good footwear, maps, rainwear, a warm pullover and suffcent provisions, while rubber boots are essential for walking over the moors. When hill-walking leave word of your intended destination with the place you are staying. It is also advisable to carry a torch for signalling your position in an emergency. A number of operators have tours with accommodation and separate facilities for forwarding luggage. Information about hill-walking and suggested routes is included in "Scotland: Walking", obtainable from the Scottish Tourist Board (see Information).

Southern Upland Way

The Southern Upland Way from Portpatrick in Galloway to Cockburnspath in the Borders is a 212 mile/339km walk from coast to coast. Some sections require a fair amount of walking experience but others are suitable for inexperienced walkers or family outings. You need to allow between 10 and 20 days for the whole walk. Information is available from, amongst others, the Scottish Borders and Dumfries and Galloway Tourist Boards (see Information).

West Highland Way

For experienced walkers the extremely scenic but very challenging West Highland Way from Mingavie near Glasgow to Fort William (95 miles/153km) is recommended.

Speyside Way

The Speyside Way, which is easier but no less scenic follows the Spey Valley from Tomintoul to Spey Bay for 42 miles/68km through this prime malt whisky country, taking in most of Scotland's distilleries.

Water sports

Scotland has plenty of water sports to offer, from canoeing on its rivers and sailing and windsurfing off the coasts, to boating holidays and even swimming and surfing in the warm Gulf Stream waters of the West Coast. Details are available in a guide "Watersports" from the Scottish Tourist Board (see Information), the Scottish Sports Council (see above), the Royal Yachting Association Scotland (Caledonia House, South Gyle, Edinburgh EH12 9DQ; tel. (0131) 317 7388) and the Scottish Windsurfing Federation (c/o Royal Yachting Association Scotland, address above).

Travel agents can also supply information about chartering boats and yachts on the Caledonian Canal and the west coast, activity holidays at watersports centres, wreck-diving, etc.

Winter sports

Scotland has its own winter sports centres, complete with ski-lifts, ski-hire, etc. at Aviemore in the Spey Valley and Glenshee, Britain's two major skiing areas, plus the Cairngorms and Glencoe detailed in "Ski Scotland" avail-

How to become a "Munroist"

It has something to do with mountains and mountaineering, so they say. And what would Scotland be without its mountains? In terms of height they may not bear comparison with the Alps or the Himalayas but they are very impressive nonetheless, and all the more so when they have peaks higher than 3000ft/914m. Which brings us to the "Munros", the name given to those over 3000ft. There are 277 of them, of which 8 are over 4000ft/1219m. But why Munros? They get their name from a certain 19th c. Sir Hugh Munro whose family estate was in the Highlands, hence his fascination for mountains. In his day it was thought that about 30 Scottish peaks were over 3000ft. When the Scottish Mountaineering Club was founded in 1889 and the figure 300 appeared in its journal Sir Hugh, a passionate climber, wanted to be sure of the fact. Equipped with a primitive altitude meter he set out to conduct his own survey. Lo and behold his list, published in 1891, contained descriptions of 538 peaks, of which he finally concluded 283 separate mountain peaks exceeded that magic figure. Although various surveys subsequently reduced this to 279 they have since borne the name of Munros in honour of Sir Hugh.

Since mountaineering soon progressed to become a favourite pursuit of the British, the "collection" of Munros has evolved in recent decades into a popular sport. Anyone who has all 279 peaks under their belt is entitled to call themselves a Munroist. The first in their line was not as you might think Sir Hugh himself – he was defeated by the aptly named Inaccessible Pinnacle on the Isle of Skye, a challenge even to hardened professionals, and his untimely death in 1919 came before he could conquer Carn Clioch-mhulinn in the Cairngorms. The first Munroist was in fact the Reverend A. E. Robertson in 1901. By the First World War there had been eight Munroists but by 1971 their number had grown to 100, since when the boom in "Munro bagging" has seen the membership of this exclusive club top the thousand mark. Not surprisingly this has led to new challenges. In 1974 Hamish Brown climbed all the Munros in one go, taking 112 days to cover almost 1555 miles/2500km by bike, boat and on foot in order to do so. In 1978 Charlie Ramsay conquered 24 Munros in 24 hours, while in 1991 John Broxap actually managed 28 within the same time, although omitting Ben Nevis. At 4411ft/1344m this ranks not only as the highest Munro but also as Britain's highest mountain. Then Mark Elsegood achieved the remarkable feat of all the Munros in 66 days.

But records aside – ascending a Munro is as much part of visiting the Highlands as the dram of Highland Malt that follows – even those not aspiring to become Munroists will experience an unforgettable side of Scotland: unspoilt ranges of hills, the constant beauty and grandeur of the mountains, views over craggy, dramatic landscapes, dark forests and deep lochs, their clear waters mirroring the breathtaking scenery of their setting. Many of the Munros are relatively simple hillwalking, but always find out beforehand what the paths are like, how steep they are and above all what kind of weather is in store – the mountain mist can hold some nasty surprises. The Scottish Mountaineering Trust's "Guide to the Munros" has become a Highlands best-seller. And if you do manage to bag all 279 Munros be sure to inform the Scottish Mountaineering Club's Recorder: Bill Brooker, 25 Deeview Road South, Cults, Aberdeenshire, Grampian AB1 9NA.

able from the Scottish Tourist Board (see Information). In the absence of snow there are plenty of dry ski slopes to practise on. Further information: Aberdeen and Grampian Tourist Board and the Highlands of Scotland Tourist Board (see Information).

Taxis

Taxis can be hired from ranks such as those outside stations and airports, and can be hailed on the street if the TAXI or FOR HIRE sign on the roof is lit up to show they are not carrying passengers.

Telecommunications

Public telephones

Britain's privatised national telephone company British Telecom (BT) has largely completed the process of replacing the once familiar old red telephone boxes with modern glass-encased kiosks. BT's push-button phones take 10p, 20p, 50p and £1 coins. Kiosks with the green "Cardphone" sign can be used only with a phonecard, available in denominations of 20, 50, 100 and 200 units (costing from £2 to £20) from post offices, newsagents and shops displaying the green BT Phonecard sign. The blue public telephone kiosks belonging to Mercury Communications, another private company, are all card operated and require either a Mercury phonecard or one of the major credit cards (Visa, Mastercard, Diners, American Express).

Long-distance calls

Long-distance calls are cheaper between 6pm and 8am and at weekends. The minimum amount for an international call from a public payphone is £1.

International direct dialling codes

The international dialling code for the United Kingdom (including Scotland) is 44.

From Scotland to:

Australia: 00 61
New Zealand: 00 64
Republic of Ireland: 00 353
South Africa: 00 27
United States and Canada: 00 1

Omit the first 0 of the area code (does not apply to the United States or Canada)

Operators

For help in making a call in the UK call the operator free on 100.
For help in making a call outside the UK call the international operator free on 155.

Emergency

For police, fire or ambulance dial 999.

Directory enquiries

For help in finding a UK number or dialling code call directory enquiries on 192.
For help in finding an international number or dialling code call international directory enquiries on 153.

Home country direct

Some visitors to the UK can make a reverse charge (collect) call or telephone credit card call home via an operator in their own country by calling 152.

Telegrams

For telegrams/telemessages call BT Telemessage on 0800 190 190.

Still in use: old-style telephone kiosk . . .   *. . . and Victorian letter-box*

Time

From the end of October to the end of March the United Kingdom observes Greenwich Mean Time (5 hours ahead of New York, for example). For the rest of the year the clocks are put forward an hour to British Summer Time.

Tipping

In hotels and restaurants where service is not included it is usual to tip 10–15% of the bill. The same applies to taxi drivers.

Travel Documents

All foreign visitors to the United Kingdom must have a valid passport unless they are citizens of the Republic of Ireland with which there are no passport controls. In the case of nationals from some Commonwealth countries a visa is required as well, so it is advisable to check before departure with the British Consulate or the British Tourist Authority (see Information).

Passports

Motorists driving their own car should bring their vehicle registration document and a "Green Card", an international insurance certificate obtainable from their normal vehicle insurers. Cars registered abroad must carry the approved oval sticker for their country of origin. Any visitor intending to drive should bring their national driving licence. For a stay of longer than one year a British driving licence is necessary.

Vehicle papers

Pets   The strict 6-month quarantine regulation makes it most inadvisable to bring any pets such as cats and dogs into Britain. For further information contact:

Ministry of Agriculture, Fisheries and Food, Government Buildings, Toby Jug Site, Hook Rise South, Tolworth, Surbiton, Surrey KT6 7NF; tel. (0181) 330 4411

Weights and Measures

Linear measure	1 inch (in.) = 2.54cm	1cm = 0.39 in.
	1 foot (ft) = 30.48cm	10cm = 0.33ft
	1 yard (yd) = 91.44cm	1m = 1.09yd
	1 mile = 1.61km	1km = 0.62 miles
Surface area	1 square inch = 6.45cm^2	1cm^2 = 0.155sq.in.
	1 square foot = 9.288dm^2	1dm^2 = 0.108sq.ft
	1 square yard = 0.836m^2	1m^2 = 1.196sq.yd
	1 square mile = 2.589km^2	1km^2 = 0.386sq.mile
	1 acre = 0.405 ha	1ha= 2.471 acres
Liquid measure	1 pint (pt) = 0.568 litre (l)	1 litre = 1.76 pt
	1 gallon (gal) = 4.546 litres	10 litres = 2.20 gallons

Imperial (i.e. British) liquid measures are different from those of the same name used in the United States.

Weight	1 ounce (oz) = 38.35 grams(g)	100 g = 3.527 oz
	1 pound (lb) = 453.59 g	1 kilogram (kg) = 2.205 lb
	1 stone = 6.35 kg	10 kg = 1.57 stone

Clothing sizes	Women	Men
	UK 32 34 36 38 40	UK 36 38 40 42 44 46
	EUR 36 38 40 42 44	EUR 46 48 50 52 54 56

Shoe sizes   UK 3 4 5 6 7 8 9 10 11
EUR 36 37 38 39 40/41 42 43 44 45

When to Go

Scotland's legendary hospitality is forthcoming all year round but life is more leisurely outside the peak holiday season. The weather is often quite good, especially in May/June and September, all the attractions are open but the sights are not so crowded, there is less traffic, people have more time to spare and prices are lower.

Springtime is awash with colour when the gorse turns the hillsides into a sea of yellow, summer is full of spectacular open air events and festivals, chief among the Edinburgh Festival and Highland Games in all the traditional places, while outings into the Highlands in the quieter late autumn days are enlivened by the warm tints of moor and woodland.

Between late October and early April Scotland can offer a host of attractions in which the weather plays no part, such as visits to museums, galleries, whisky distilleries and even some gardens thanks to the mild climes of the Gulf Stream.
In crisp mid-winter the snow-clad peaks of Scotland's mountains become a playground for skiers, while winter is also the season when theatre, opera and ballet come into their own once more.

Youth Hostels

Scotland has an extensive network of youth hostels throughout the mainland and islands, ranging from cottages to castles. It makes good sense to book in advance and to check when they are open since many close for long periods in the winter. Full details are available from the Scottish Tourist Board (see Information) or the Scottish Youth Hostels Association, 7 Glebe Crescent, Stirling FK8 2JA; tel. (01786) 451181, fax 891333.

Index

Index

The Principal Sights at a Glance

Important castles, abbeys and prehistoric sites see p. 320

A map showing the most important places of tourist interest can be found on p. 351

Note: The above list gives the best centres in Scotland with interesting places in the area. Other sights of special interest are marked with one or two Baedeker stars in the A to Z section.

218 illustrations, 16 ground-plans, 9 special plans, 8 town plans, 8 general maps, 6 draw-ings, 1 large map

German text: Dr Madeleine Reincke (Scotland A to Z; Baedeker Specials; Nature, Culture, History, part; Practical Information, part) with contributions from Eberhard Bort (Culloden; Glencoe; Highland Games, Festivals and Folk Music; Practical Information, part), Helga Cabos (Famous People; Practical Information, part); Rainer Eisenschmid (Tartan, Plaid and Kilt), Dr Hansjörg Meyer (History; Language and Literature), Dr Reinhard Paesler (Geography, Climate, Flora and Fauna, Political Structure and Population, Economy, Transport), Ulrike E. Weiss (Art History)

Editorial Work: Baedeker-Redaktion (Dr Madeleine Reincke)

Cartography: Ingenieurbüro für Kartographie Harms, Erlenbach bei Kandel; Mairs Geographischer Verlag GmbH & Co., Ostfildern (large map)

General direction: Dr Peter H. Baumgarten, Baedeker Stuttgart

Source of illustrations: Baedeker-Archiv, Cabos/Reincke, Harding, IFA Bilderteam, Jarrold Publishing, Lade Fotoagentur, Müller, Schapowalow/Heaton, Schuster Bildagentur, Ullstein-Bilderdienst, ZEFA

Front cover: Pictor International, London. Back cover: AA Photo Library

English language edition:
Translation: Wendy Bell, Brenda Ferris, Paul Fletcher
Editorial Work: Margaret Court, Crispin Warren
Revised text: David Cocking

3rd English edition 1999

© Baedeker Stuttgart
German edition 1998

© 1999 The Automobile Association
English language edition worldwide

Published in the United States by Fodor's Travel Publications, Inc. 201 East 50th Street, New York, NY 10022.

Distributed in the United Kingdom by the Publishing Division of the Automobile Association, Fanum House, Basingstoke, Hampshire RG21 2EA

Licensed user: Mairs Geographischer Verlag GmbH & Co., Ostfildern-Kemnat bei Stuttgart

The name *Baedeker* is a registered trademark

A CIP catalogue record of this book is available from the British Library

Printed in Italy by G. Canale & C.S.p.A – Borgaro T.se –Turin

ISBN 0 7495 1994 0

Notes

Notes

Notes